SWAMI SAHAJANAND AND THE PEASANTS OF JHARKHAND: A VIEW FROM 1941

SWAMI SAHAJANAND AND THE PEASANTS OF JHARKHAND: A VIEW FROM 1941

An edited translation of *Jharkhand ke Kisan*
with the original Hindi text and
an Introduction, Endnotes, and Glossary by

WALTER HAUSER

MANOHAR
2005

First published 1995
First paperback edition 2005

ISBN 81-7304-599-2

Published by
Ajay Kumar Jain for
Manohar Publishers & Distributors
4753/23 Ansari Road, Daryaganj
New Delhi 110 002

Distributed in South Asia by
Foundation Books
4381/4, Ansari Road
Daryaganj, New Delhi 110 002
and its branches at Mumbai, Hyderabad,
Bangalore, Chennai, Kolkata

Printed at
Lordson Publishers Pvt. Ltd.
Delhi 110 007

We have snatched the fields from the jaw of the tiger and the fang of the snake, we have ploughed and sown, Singbonga sends the rain and the sunshine! What has the Diku done that we should pay him anything? The burial stones are our title deeds.

--- A Munda view of the fields and forests of Jharkhand.
From the *Encyclopaedia Mundarica*, Vol. II, p. 515.

Salutations to you, Mother Jaher Era.
On the occasion of the *Asadia* festival we offer to you
young fowls and freshly husked rice.
Kindly accept it.
We pray to you:
Bring us rain-bearing clouds
and make our fields fit for cultivation.
With rain-waters wash away
the insects and germs that cause disease.
Let not snakes and scorpions harm us
as we work in the fields weeding out grass. . .
Be kind to us that we may live in peace and happiness
and that our desires and expectations may be fulfilled.

--- A Santal invocation during the Replowing festival.
From Sitakant Mahapatra,
Bakhen: Ritual Invocation Songs, 1979.

Contents

Dedicated to the memory of Swami Sahajanand
and his commitment to a life of justice and decency
for the peasants of Jharkhand.

Preface to the Paperback Edition

There has been an increasingly wide interest in recent years in the environment and indigenous peoples, and in no place has the idea and the literature it has produced been richer and more significant than India. I think of the important work of Amita Baviskar, Ramachandra Guha, and Mahesh Rangarajan among many others. To this larger conversation about environmental politics and tribal societies has now been added the seminal series of essays by Stuart Corbridge, Sarah Jewitt and Sanjay Kumar published under the title *Jharkhand: Environment, Development, Ethnicity* (New Delhi: Oxford University Press, 2004).

The publication of these essays by Corbridge and his colleagues comes at a particularly crucial juncture in the history of Jharkhand, which, as we all know, became the 28th state of the Indian Union in November 2000. The citizen voters of the new state have made fundamental political choices in the parliamentary elections of 2004 and the state assembly elections of February 2005. By the same token, the parties that assume responsibility for governance following the 2005 elections will be making equally fundamental development choices, designed to take the state into the immediate decades of its new future. An ideal image of that future was released in 2003; that is the *Vision 2010* document, which promised universal literacy by 2010 and made equally dramatic promises for dealing with poverty, roads, irrigation and the restoration of degraded forests, and to benefit in the process all citizens of Jharkhand, including among these the poorest of the poor.

These goals were reinforced in November 2004 when the Department of Information Technology released its draft infotech policy, promising as it did, vigorous growth of that sector of the economy as well. Among other things, the idea is to connect Ranchi, the state capital, to all gram panchayats by 2006 and to computerize all major departments in five years. Beyond this the hope is to achieve 10 per cent computer literacy within 10 years and 30 per cent within 20 years. These are indeed noble goals, but failing a deeper and more realistic sense of the political and institutional landscape in which these development ideals are to be carried out, a point made by Corbridge, Jewitt, and

Kumar, one is inclined to share their skepticism at the claims of *Vision 2010* and so too of the proposed infotech project. Corbridge's point and mine are affirmed by the October 2004 report of the Sampuran Gram Vikas Kendra that no more than 21.29 per cent of children in the age group 6-14 are presently attending school in the state. To underline the point, these numbers beg for determined and persistent attention to the core infrastructure requirements of Jharkhand, thereby to create the necessary enabling environment for change. Otherwise, the thoughtful goals of *Vision 2010* and other policy projections will remain no more than grand exhortations. In the circumstances, the state is confronted with a rare opportunity to move in positive and creative directions.

As with any human experience, it is important to keep in mind that Jharkhand is now as it always has been, a deeply complex social and cultural place. Understanding is not achieved by easy and obvious explanations. For example, it is important to remember that Jharkhand is rather more than the tribal movement whose name it has adopted. It has a rich potential for development in many directions, so long as the relationships between those development opportunities and the ethnicity and environment that define its social and natural space, are seen as symbiotic in the fullest sense of the term. These cannot be exclusionary relationships; they inevitably bear dramatically one on the other. At the practical level this has to do with how the remarkable resources of land, water, forest and minerals are managed for the greater good of all citizen of Jharkhand, and how this is done at ground level where Jharkhandis live their lives, and what kinds of political culture exist, or can be devised, to make these possibilities a social reality. *Vision 2010* effectively represents the official image its authors have for the state, while the essays of Corbridge and his colleagues introduce into the scholarly literature some of the most sensitive reflections on the development possibilities embedded in the political culture of Jharkhand, and indeed, in the wider community of change. While scholarship and state policy seldom intersect, the work of Corbridge, Jewitt, and Kumar comes closer to providing us with a "social science that matters", to use another Corbridge term, than anything that has been written about Jharkhand heretofore.

An earlier and equally powerful vision of Jharkhand as those of 2003 and 2004, was that imagined by Sahajanand Saraswati in 1941, when, not coincidentally, he was a political prisoner in the Hazaribagh Central Jail. That fact is important; because it helps define the man and the document he produced. Whereas the authors of *Vision 2010* are politicians and presumably bureaucrats, and Corbridge and colleagues are engaged academic scholars, Sahajanand was the quintessential political activist. It was that activism which accounted for his being in the Hazaribagh Central Jail, in this case as a result of his direct involvement in the Anti-Compromise agitation of April 1940. He obviously learned much during that imprisonment about the districts of Santhal Parganas and Chotanagpur, which then comprised the region that Sahajanand was among the first to identify as Jharkhand. He learned from his fellow prisoners, many of whom belonged to Jharkhand, and he learned from the literature that was provided him, surprisingly, I suppose one could say, by his jailors. Sahajanand knew what he wanted to read based on his vast experience in Bihar, and his more limited, albeit not inconsequential experience in the Jharkhand districts in the decade of the 1930s. Among the many productive results of Sahajanand's jail time in Hazaribagh was the tract *Jharkhand ke Kisan*, published for the first time in 1995 in the unedited Hindi original, and in my edited English translation as *Swami Sahajanand and the Peasants of Jharkhand: A View From 1941*. It is that title which now appears in this 2005 paperback edition.

Writing a fresh preface for the paperback edition of a book that was first published ten years ago, and that reproduced a political tract that was written in 1941, would on the surface appear to pose serious problems. Happily, in the case of *Jharkhand ke Kisan*, that is not the case. Re-reading Sahajanand ten years later, or as in my case more than 45 years after my first encounter with this tract in 1958 and 1959, the ideas are as fresh and lively as they were the first time around. The language and the meanings it conveys are as powerful now as they were then, which says much about the commitment and level of understanding Sahajanand brought to his activism. I have suggested that Sahajanand was the quintessential political activist. Put another way, this is to say that his life was his activism. It was an activism that had to do with the social, economic, and ultimately with the cultural freedom of the Indian peasant, just as it had to do with the political freedom of the nation.

So if the point of a fresh preface is to show how the ideas of the original publication are relevant to the contemporary present, then Sahajanand has made my task an easy one. He produced a broad activist literature, and explicitly so in the case of the *Jharkhand ke Kisan* tract, that reflects an awareness, an understanding, and a sensibility that is remarkable for the richness and depth of its insights. It is a sensibility and understanding that is as relevant in 2005 as it was in 1941 when it was written. Indeed, one might speculate that Sahajanand himself, or perhaps his successors at the Shri Sitaram Ashram at Bihta in Patna district, might have thought his *Jharkhand ke Kisan* tract rather too advanced in its ideas or too explicit in its descriptions of the "open loot" to which the adivasi peasants of the region and their resources, were subject. But that is an issue quite beyond the limited purposes of this preface. What we know today is that Sahajanand had a powerful sense of the lives of tribal peasants in the Jharkhand districts of the 1930s, and that his formulations are as painfully on target today as they were in 1941 when their author put ink to paper.

These points have been made rather more effectively than I could begin to do by three reviewers of the 1995 edition of *Jharkhand ke Kisan*, who between them certainly represent some of the most penetrating scholarship and reflection of anyone concerned with the idea of Jharkhand in its historical and contemporary manifestations. I am more than pleased to rely on their specialized insights to make my point. I turn first to Arvind Das, whose committed and dynamic voice we lost far too soon by his untimely death in August 2000. It is helpful also to note that Arvind Das, historian, journalist, and thoughtful critic of Bihar, which he knew and loved as the place of his birth, was certainly more aware of Sahajanand the peasant activist than most professional observers of India in the twentieth century. This background provided Arvind a wonderful perspective in examining the *Jharkhand ke Kisan* tract, which he did at length in the July 1995 issue of *Biblio:* under the heading "A man before his times," referring to Sahajanand, whom he described as "a unique communicator," with "historical insights [that] are so powerful as to stand out even today."

A critical point made by Das and reinforced by the historian Kumar Suresh Singh and the human geographer Stuart Corbridge is that Sahajanand was centrally concerned with "the condition of the ordinary people", that is, the peasants of Jharkhand who were actively defining their lives as tribal peasants on the land and in the forests of Jharkhand when Sahajanand was writing. Again, all three reviewers note that Sahajanand was making this point in the 1930s and 1940s long before other activists or academic observers, who were concerned more with the cultural idea of "tribe", and the political potential inherent in that concept. Das notes the folly of the debate over "whether tribals can be peasants" by observing that the debate was going on "even as agriculture [was being] carried out, surplus extracted and agrarian resistance taking place in both dramatic and everyday forms".

These are themes which Kumar Suresh Singh, the pre-eminent historian of Chotanagpur and the former Director General of the Anthropological Survey of India pursued in his review, with a somewhat more specific historical gloss, when he noted "that Swamiji wrote about peasants and agrarian issues at a time when the tribal leaders of political movements who demanded autonomy had put the land and forest question on the back burner. In fact, as tribal political aspirations were articulated by the Adibasi Mahasabha and later by the Jharkhand Party, agrarian issues receded into the background. The situation is not very different even today, in spite of the rapid erosion of tribal rights in land – and its alienation on a large scale – and in forest." Suresh Singh then concludes with the broader issue of connectedness with which I began these brief observations, namely that the "publication of the *Jharkhand ke Kisan* tract is a timely reminder that land and forest questions concerning tribal people, which are now part of an international agenda on environment and indigenous people can no longer be ignored". (*Indian Economic and Social History Review* 34:1, January-March 1997)

Finally, Stuart Corbridge reinforces these points from his more contemporary development perspective, namely the issue of open exploitation and the manner in which it was politicized in the early years and in the present, and the matter of tribals being peasants. Referring to the manner in which tribal India has been romanticized, Corbridge writes, "It is remarkable, therefore, to find in *Jharkhand ke Kisan* an account of the underdevelopment of the Jharkhand which speaks of the open looting of the region's resources and adivasis by Dikus (outsiders). This is the language deployed to such telling effect by the Jharkhand Party in the 1950s, when it was demanding a separate Jharkhand State in the federal Republic of India. In subtly different ways, it is also the language of the Jharkhand Mukti Morcha today. More than that, Sahajanand provides an often persuasive empirical account of the processes which reproduce the Jharkand as an internal colony." On the peasant issue, Corbridge concludes that throughout the *Jharkhand* tract, "Sahajanand resists the temptation to stereotype Jharkhandis as adivasis alone; he insists, rightly, that most adivasis in Jharkhand were, by 1940, earning their living as peasants or mineworkers or even as agricultural labourers. Shifting cultivation and pure jungle dwellers were the exception, not the rule. All of this gives Sahajanand's work a distinctly modern feel." (*Pacific Affairs* 69:2, Summer 1996)

I would suggest that it is this modern feel about Sahajanand's writing, about his being able to reach into the contemporary present from his experience sixty and seventy years ago, that gives his work the prescient sensibility to which I have referred both in this preface and throughout the earlier 1995 edition of *Jharkhand ke Kisan.* And it is obviously this complex sensibility that has most impressed Arvind Das, Suresh Singh, and Stuart Corbridge about Sahajanand the activist critic of life and society in Jharkhand.

Other than this brief preface prepared specifically for the paperback edition of this title, and incidental corrections made in the Devanagari text, the edited translation, and other parts of the 1995 edition, this edition reproduces without change the 1995 publication. I repeat what I noted in that original edition, namely that this is not a history of Jharkhand or of the Jharkhand movement, but rather a reflection of the Jharkhand experience as witnessed and understood by Sahajanand Saraswati from his place as a political prisoner in the Hazaribagh Central Jail. It is precisely because the ideas and images conveyed here are those of Sahajanand that we have included as a central component of this bi-lingual publication the unedited Devanagari original of Sajahanand himself. There are obviously many reasons for including both the original Hindi text of this tract together with the edited English translation, reasons which most readers and reviewers have understood. But the main issue, to repeat, is that Sahajanand's ideas can only be fully and honestly conveyed in the language in which he wrote and not in a translation that is inevitably remote in space, time, and experience from that of Sahajanand in 1941.

Among the specific qualities of the Hindi text that a bi-lingual edition permits, is to convey the richness of language Sahajanand uses in describing the life experiences of the peasants of Jharkhand. I have attempted to convey some of the dynamic and vivid qualities of Sahajanand's descriptions in the translation itself and in an extended glossary of more than 350 terms taken from the Hindi text and presented here in transliterated form. A notable feature of the glossary and indeed of the *Jharkhand ke Kisan* tract as a whole is the story of exploitation it reveals. Sahajanand wrote of it as "open loot", and almost 150 of the terms I have abstracted from Sahajanand's *Jharkhand* text, refer in one way or another to ways in which the peasants of Jharkhand were looted. This is part of the sad history of Jharkhand which Sahajanand's tract reminds us. It also reminds us that Sahajanand's descriptions had imbedded within them the hope for a better life for all the citizens of Jharkhand.

Further background on the *Jharkhand ke Kisan* tract and Sahajanand's social and political activism leading up to his imprisonment in 1940 can be found in the editor's preface and introduction to the 1995 edition. The most systematic summary of Sahajanand's reflections on Jharkhand and its people can be found in his brief introduction and the thirteen chapter headings of this small tract. I have written a short introductory note to each chapter, and more extended explanatory endnotes, which are meant to provide the historical and ideological context for the argument Sahajanand makes in each of his short chapters. The endnotes also include bibliographic references meant to sustain Sahajanand's argument, given that he was writing while in jail and did not have the advantages of a library or archive at his disposal. It is a tribute to Sahajanand's historical sensibilities that he could be so thorough as he was in his representation of life and society in Jharkhand and its historical antecedents. I should also point out, however, that the bibliographic references are exactly that; they are meant to clarify and sustain Sahajanand's text. This tract is not a history of Jharkhand or of the Jharkhand movement, and accordingly the references are not meant to provide a bibliography of that history or movement.

There are, however, several new titles that have seen the light of day since 1995, and because of their quality and the importance of their scholarship to the issues raised in Sahajanand's tract, I take the liberty of listing them in this brief preface. I have referred a number of times to the recent work of Stuart Corbridge, Sarah Jewitt, and Sanjay Kumar touching on the intersection of environment, development, and ethnicity in the Jharkhand. Without assuming more than an editor should 63 years after Sahajanand wrote the *Jharkhand ke Kisan* tract, I sense that he would almost certainly have been sympathetic to the issues Corbridge and his associates have raised in this new book of essays. It is the kind of thick description Sahajanand would have understood and absorbed, which is precisely why he could write *Jharkhand ke Kisan* while sitting in a remote jail cell in Hazaribagh in the late months of 1941. Apart from his remarkable career of lived experience in rural India he had read widely and deeply, and the *Jharkhand* tract is testimony to that personal and intellectual background.

One of the co-authors of the Corbridge title has provided another example of the kind of thick ethnographic description I mention above. This is Sarah Jewitt's book, *Environment, Knowledge and Gender: Local Development in India's Jharkhand* (Aldershot, UK: Ashgate, 2002). This title is a full-scale treatment of issues raised by Jewitt in a number of essays in the 2004 Corbridge volume. It is an important addition to the literature.

The most recent and one of the very good anthologies of scholarship touching on the Jharkhand movement is that edited by Ram Dayal Munda and S. Bosu Mullick, two prominent scholar-activists long involved in the movement. This is their *The Jharkhand Movement: Indigenous Peoples' Struggle for Autonomy in India* (Copenhagen: International Work Group for Indigenous Affairs, 2003).

While Sahajanand was concerned specifically with the peasants of Jharkhand, he does touch very briefly in this context on the Tatas and Jamshedpur in one of his final chapters. His experience in that arena was perhaps more limited than elsewhere in Jharkhand, especially so in his treatment of the role of Manik Homi, a key leader of the Tata Iron and Steel workers. This is an issue raised in a personal conversation with Dilip Simeon for which I thank him. A fuller and more sensitive treatment of the role of Manik Homi can be found in Dilip Simeon, *The Politics of Labour Under Late Colonilaism: Workers, Unions and the State in Chota Nagpur, 1928-1939* (New Delhi: Manohar, 1995); and Vinay Bahl, *The Making of the Indian Working Class: A Case of the Tata Iron and Steel Company, 1800-1946* (New Delhi: Sage Publications, 1995).

All of the acknowledgements that were made in the 1995 edition of *Jharkhand ke Kisan* are as relevant now as they were then, and I repeat here everything that I expressed then by way of appreciation. But I have incurred new debts in preparation of this paperback edition and in familiarizing myself anew with the fascinating experience of Jharkhand and its people. No one has been more helpful in sharing what he knows about this remarkable place than Stuart Corbridge and I thank him especially for his many kindnesses in our common inquiry. So too Manoj Srivastava, Kailash Chandra Jha, Philip McEldowney, and Florence Hauser. I thank all these friends and colleagues each of whom will quickly recognize how I have relied on their help in this modest effort. But at the same time, the standard disclaimer applies; whatever interpretation appears in these preliminary pages is entirely my responsibility. I must also thank Ramesh Jain and Ajay Jain of

Manohar Publishers for their continued support of the Sahajanand project, and especially in this case for agreeing to the bi-lingual publication of *Jharkhand ke Kisan*. This is the only reasonable way this tract could have seen the light of day and Messrs. Ramesh and Ajay Jain immediately recognized the importance of what we were doing, and for that I thank them.

Finally, my original dedication of the *Jharkhand ke Kisan* tract to the memory of Swami Sahajanand and his commitment to a life of justice and decency for the peasants of Jharkhand is worth repeating because it is as important in 2005 as it was in 1995. The most important players in the Jharkhand experience remain the 27 million people of that new state of the Indian Union. But beyond my earlier appreciation, I should like to add a new dedication for this paperback edition of *Jharkhand ke Kisan* that happily complements the 1995 dedication. No one among our academic friends and colleagues has been more committed to the welfare of Jharkhand and its people, or to understanding their history and their lived experience than has Dr. Kumar Suresh Singh. It pleases me to dedicate this paperback edition of *Jharkhand ke Kisan* to Kumar Suresh Singh.

Charlottesville, Virginia Walter Hauser
November 2004

Preface to the First Edition

The idea for this book began some years ago in my early efforts to understand the nature of peasant activism in Gangetic north India. For me the problem as a post graduate student in the late 1950s and early 1960s was that historical scholarship was legitimately and almost uniformly consumed by the Freedom Movement and its major players whose names were Gandhi, Nehru and others far too numerous even to begin listing here. The idea that peasants might be prominent actors not only in that wider history of political freedom, but major players in their own history of freedom was still too remote at the time to be taken seriously in India or elsewhere. But research students are sometimes sufficiently naive to persist in efforts that might be viewed by the profession more generally as quaint.

And so the *Jharkhand ke Kisan* text presented here in an edited translation and in the unedited original Hindi of its author, was preserved in a rough photocopy version with one other of Swami Sahajanand's several unpublished political tracts. But it was the 1970s before a new generation of scholarship was prepared to view the world of human experience more holistically, and not until the 1980s that its work took published form. Only then did publishers begin to consider reissuing some of the vast corpus of Sahajanand's writing, virtually all of which had initially been published in Hindi during his life time, or soon after his death in 1950.

In the meantime there was a spate of symposia and published memorials in 1989, the centenary year of Sahajanand's birth, which in turn gave rise to efforts to reissue individual volumes and ultimately the full body of Sahajanand's published and unpublished work touching primarily on his career as social reformer and as India's leading peasant activist of the 1930s. It was in that climate that it seemed appropriate to put into print an edited English translation of Sahajanand's *Khet Mazdoor*, which was issued earlier this year under the title *Sahajanand on Agricultural Labour and the Rural Poor* (New Delhi: Manohar Publishers, 1994), and as in the present case, included the full, unedited Devanagri Hindi original. While the effort in that volume and in the present instance has been less to be concerned with canons of postmodernism, nevertheless the combination of an edited translation with the Hindi original permits the reader to arrive at what he or she may judge to be the "truth value" of this text and the discourse in which it is engaged. The additional value of this tract, as anyone even vaguely familiar with the issues it raises will quickly recognize, is both the divergence and in Sahajanand's representation, the convergence of what James C. Scott refers to as the public transcript and the hidden transcript. In his *Hidden Transcripts* (Yale, 1990), Scott draws much evidence from cases not dissimilar to the one Sahajanand presents here, "on the premise that the relationship of discourse to power would be most sharply etched where the divergence between what I call the public transcript and the hidden transcript was the greatest" (p. x). A closer examination of these suggestive ideas is not possible in a volume whose primary object is first and foremost to make this remarkable document accessible in the market place of ideas where historians and other social scientists ply their trade. The hope also is that with a wider public availability of this text both in Hindi and in English, the importance of Sahajanand's role as a thinker and doer in the political life of India in this century will be more fully recognized and that his massive published record will be sought out more diligently than has heretofore been the case. But it is nevertheless important in considering Sahajanand's representation of the peasants of Jharkhand to appreciate his sensitivity and sensibility to the conflicts and contradictions within and between the established and dominant structures of power and the peasants in the fields and forests of Jharkhand where this story is played out.

I discuss the mechanics of translation across cultures and time in an introductory note to the Editor's Glossary following the Hindi text. It is also at that point where I comment briefly on whatever conventions of transliteration I follow both in the translation itself and in the glossary. The effort has been to adhere as closely as possible to Sahajanand's style and meanings, while at the same time achieving a reasonably readable English text. I have maintained some of Sahajanand's metaphorical usages and cut others, and tightened the text in other ways especially by eliminating some of the repetitions Sahajanand used to reinforce his point. Obviously, it is precisely to make this as complete a text as possible that the edited translation and the unedited Hindi original are included here. I comment at many places in the Editor's Endnotes about Sahajanand's powerful use of language in communicating his ideas to his peasant audience. The same point is made briefly in my introductory remarks to Part II of this volume, and in the introduction to the glossary.

The Editor's Endnotes are meant to provide the intellectual and political context within which Sahajanand was discussing the agrarian economy of Jharkhand and the cultural matrix which defined its unique character. The Endnotes are also the place where I attempt to provide as complete a set of bibliographic references for Sahajanand's various sources and to mention other relevant titles. But this is neither a history of Jharkhand or Chotanagpur, nor a comment on the Jharkhand movement, historically or in 1994. And accordingly it must be made clear at the outset that I have not attempted to present here even a fraction of the enormous body of literature which this place and its politics have generated over many years. Titles are cited in many Endnotes and those for chapters I and IV include more extended references.

Writing acknowledgements for a project that has been in a dormant state for decades, except as I have occasionally tapped into this tract in my own writing, is next to impossible. But some few names need to be mentioned, keeping in mind the point I have just made, namely that this is not intended to be dense scholarship either of the history or politics of Jharkhand. It is literally a reflection on the perceptions and representations of Swami Sahajanand of what he saw and thought and believed about the peasants of Jharkhand. It must be further noted that my perspective is in some sense very similar to that of Sahajanand, namely that of Gangetic Bihar, which was the primary arena of his activism as it has been of my scholarship. I comment frequently in the Endnotes about the relatively more limited role Sahajanand played in the life of Jharkhand and will not reexamine that issue here. And by the same token, while I have been in the Chotanagpur districts and Santal Parganas more than once over thirty five years of visiting India and Bihar, I make no claim to being a specialist in the history or culture of Jharkhand. I have cited many of the scholars who are, in the Endnotes, and am obviously familiar with the work of many more, but to repeat, the idea here is not to provide a complete reference guide, but rather to illuminate Sahajanand's images of this fascinating agrarian and cultural history through the window of his unpublished *Jharkhand ke Kisan* tract.

My greatest debt in that effort is by definition to Swami Sahajanand himself and to the people of Jharkhand who were the subjects of his inquiry. This was for me obviously the starting point. I am also indebted to everyone at the Swami's Shri Sitaram Ashram at Bihta in west Patna district for the warm hospitality, the many kindnesses, and the generous cooperation I was shown from my first visit there in the late 1950s and on each of many succeeding visits. I must also acknowledge the thoughtful cooperation and assistance of Sahajanand's family in Ghazipur in eastern Uttar Pradesh, especially his nephew Ram Chandra Sharma, and in this same circle, my appreciation to the late Keshav Prasad Sharma who welcomed me in 1993 to the Swami Sahajanand Degree College in Ghazipur which he was so instrumental in founding.

Among the specialists in the field on whom I have relied heavily, their contributions to my efforts will be immediately visible in the Endnotes. My friend of many years and the distinguished historian of Chotanagpur, Dr. K.S. Singh has been absolutely invaluable especially as I was completing this manuscript in the summer of 1994. I have also relied heavily on the Scheduled Tribes volume of his monumental People of India project, which was literally his creation as Director General of the Anthropological Survey of India. Dr. Sachchidananda of Patna responded to my unannounced visit in June 1994 with the same kind welcome and candid reactions to the social and cultural world of Jharkhand and Chotanagpur he has always shown me over the years. And in Delhi, Dr. Sitakant Mahapatra, Secretary of the Government of India and himself an eminent scholar of Adivasi literature, kindly provided me rare copies of some of his publications, from one of which I have cited a Santal invocation in the frontispiece of this volume. I appreciate Dr. Mahapatra's generous cooperation. I have cited Dr. Prabhu Mohapatra's important scholarship on the agrarian economy of Chotanagpur frequently in these pages and I am grateful for his providing me copies of both his published and unpublished work.

Because this is not a book about the Jharkhand movement I have not sought out many of the major players in the politics of Bihar and Jharkhand who are directly involved and who would certainly have informed my understanding of what is happening in that political arena at the moment. But I must mention the name of Dr. Ram Dayal Munda who is both scholar and activist, and with whom I share an old-boy connection with the University of Chicago. Our friendship goes back some years and I continue to appreciate the sensitivity of Munda's thoughtful reactions of and from within the Adivasi culture of Jharkhand. So too my thanks to N.E. Horo who is certainly the elder statesman of the movement and whose vast knowledge and kindness in sharing it I have mentioned in one of my Endnotes.

There are of course many others who made this book possible. While my Hindi has improved significantly over the years, I have nevertheless relied on the collaboration of Dr. Jadunandan Prasad in doing an initial rough, literal translation when I first encountered this document, and more recently at the stage of refining that original translation into a fluid text, K.C. Jha has been absolutely invaluable. I comment on our association later in this Preface. Dr. S.K. Goyal, Director of the Institute for Studies in Industrial Development in New Delhi again welcomed me to the Institute and its superb computer and electronic mail facilities. And without the warm and ingenious cooperation and support of Bhupesh Garg at the ISID, this project could not have been completed in the limited time at my disposal. It was also Mr. Garg who helped create the map of Bihar in 1941 which appears in this volume. Others at the Institute whom I should like to thank are K.S. Chalapati Rao, Sudhir Aggarwal, and Umesh Singh who were always helpful when help was most needed. At the other end of the email connection in Charlottesville, was Dr. Philip McEldowney, the South Asia Bibliographer at the University of Virginia, who again was immediately responsive to my many bibliographic queries, and who will see much evidence of his labour in many Endnote citations. I should also like to thank Gail Moore and Judy Birckhead of the Arts and Sciences Computer Facility at Virginia. They too were always there when the most difficult problems arose.

Dr. Om Prakash, Professor of Economic History at the Delhi School of Economics literally volunteered to give the entire manuscript an editorial reading, and he too will recognize many of his thoughtful suggestions. Vikas Murarka, Makhan Lal Saha, Ajay Jain, D.N. Sahay, and Ajit Jha were all important in responding promptly to my sometimes urgent requests. Of course these kinds of projects would never get off the ground without necessary funding and while many agencies have supported my work over the years, here I would like to acknowledge the support, both personal and institutional of Dr. Pradeep Mehendiratta of the American Institute of Indian Studies. And for making possible the ten weeks required to bring this volume to press this summer the University of Virginia responded in the way I had hoped. I should especially like to thank Raymond J. Nelson, Dean of the Faculty, Gene D. Block, Associate Provost for Research, and Paul R. Gross, Director of the Centre for Advanced Studies at Virginia, as well as my colleagues in the Department of History and the Centre for South Asian Studies.

The two people who have been most directly involved in the work I have done in India, including this edited translation of *Jharkhand ke Kisan* are my friend and associate K.C. Jha of Ranti village in Madhubani district and now living in Delhi, and Rosemary Hauser, to whom I am related by marriage. Mr. Jha and I have collaborated in many ways in our personal and professional lives, and this immediate project benefitted most directly not only by his subtle understanding of Hindi, but of its social and cultural meanings in the agrarian world of the peasants of Bihar. I could not have done it without him and the best thing I can do by way of appreciation is to say that I owe him a maund of mangoes of his choice, which would presumably be Chausa or Maldah, or both. In fact, to him and his family I say thank you, many times over.

This is as much Rosemary Hauser's project as it is mine, so there is little I can put on the printed page that would express a lifetime of appreciation. She has worked on this project as she has on all the others, as though it were her own. But to make it easier for myself, I will report that apart from everything else, she has proofed this manuscript and has indexed it, and for that I can thank her more easily.

To each of these friends and colleagues, so generously prepared to share both their time and their understanding of Indian society and culture, I am deeply grateful. The responsibility for what appears on these pages and its interpretation is inevitably, of course, mine alone.

New Delhi Walter Hauser
August 15, 1994

Introduction

It is 7:30 AM on August 15, 1994 and Prime Minister Narasimha Rao is taking the salute at the Red Fort in Delhi. The Indian Tricolor is unfurled as the national anthem is played and the nation celebrates its Independence Day, forty seven years after the fact. The Prime Minister is firm in his walk and in his delivery invoking in the first minutes of his hour long speech the name of Mahatma Gandhi, the Father of the Nation and assuring the people of India that much has been achieved in forty seven years, that much more needs to be achieved, and conceding that some among India's states are not maintaining the required pace of development. It is a sedate and by comparison with Indian political rallies, a small crowd, but at the same time the streets of Delhi are strangely quiet, and one needn't listen closely to hear the Prime Minister on the television sets which are now commonplace in middle class flats throughout the city and in much of the country.

It is in short, a time for affirming the nation's identity, for remembering its past, and assuring and asserting its future as a free democratic polity, with the Indian National Congress as both the party of government and of history. Whatever cynics may say about the hollowness of the day, as reflected for example in a front page story in *The Times of India* (August 15, 1994), it is nevertheless a time of celebration and definition, and the role of the Indian National Congress, or the Congress (I), to be technically correct, in these proceedings cannot be overlooked or undervalued. Whatever the strength of the opposition, it is a Congress Party Prime Minister who took the salute on this day, and who spoke for the nation.

This introductory aside is a comment on the historic role and persistence of the Congress Party, and the fact that it has overshadowed other parties and other leaders almost from its inception in 1885, and certainly from the 1920s and 30s to the present. I make this longish point to help account for the fact that while there is some awareness of other party figures historically, by comparison with those who were in and with the Congress, they are still largely hidden from public view. For example, the collected works of Govind Ballabh Pant are currently in press under the editorship of B.R. Nanda, a senior historian of India. Pant was a contemporary of Sahajanand's, and a prominent Congress leader in U.P. And I have already indicated that whatever is being done to define Sahajanand's political role or to publish his speeches and writing, is being done privately and by comparison, with very little fanfare.

The question is often asked, why was Sahajanand not more successful in his mission to mobilize the peasants of Bihar, or Jharkhand, or any other place, to the level of achieving more of the justice and change which he sought in his vigorous career. There is certainly room for speculating about what might have been, or what policy course or personal decisions and political affiliations Sahajanand might have made to bring greater success to his efforts. But his achievements were many, certainly in Gangetic Bihar, and we now know that he was more active in Jharkhand than we had heretofore been aware. The point I make is not a new one, but the suggestion is that for a man who was perceived from the mid to late thirties by the dominant Congress Party as a serious threat, it is just as logical to presume that Sahajanand was defeated by the political weight and dominance of the Congress as that he somehow failed in his mission by what he did or didn't do. This is not the place to examine his career either before or after he wrote the *Jharkhand ke Kisan* tract, but rather to learn from it and from Sahajanand what his views were at a critical transition time in the nation's history and in his career. The fact that many of the issues he raised in 1941 are still before us, reveals the importance of this tract as a document of historic importance even more directly.

In mid-April 1940 Sahajanand was arrested and imprisoned at the Hazaribagh Central Jail in Bihar. He had served as chairman of the Reception Committee of the Anti-Compromise Conference at Ramgarh in March, where in association with Subhas Chandra Bose and others he called for immediate direct action against the British. It was a call he repeated shortly at the Palasa session of the All India Kisan Sabha of which he was General Secretary, and again in early April during the agitations of the National Anti-Compromise Week. Almost immediately thereafter he was arrested and jailed as a political prisoner at Hazaribagh. He was released in March 1942, a year before the end of his three year term.

If this was a time of political and intellectual transition for

Sahajanand as a social and political activist, these were also two of the most productive years in Sahajanand's career in terms of the prodigious amount of writing he completed in those twenty-three months. The history of his jailing and release is another story, but apart from the numerous pamphlets, political tracts, and Kisan Sabha speeches, most of which were published either in Hindi or English, and all of which were reported on by the intelligence arm of the colonial state, most of Sahajanand's political writing and personal reflections were produced during the time he was in jail. He had had an earlier career of social activism in the teens and 1920s, which also resulted in a substantial record of publication, but that too is another story.

With rare exception the vast corpus of Sahajanand's writing, whether social and political advocacy or personal reflection on his remarkable career, was published almost immediately it was written, especially in the advocacy phase of that career in the teens, twenties, and thirties when he was most active. Others of his writings were published after his release from prison, and yet others after his death in 1950. The *Jharkhand ke Kisan* tract, somewhat longer than many of the pamphlets he had published as a Kisan Sabha activist before his imprisonment and after, was among those few manuscripts that were not published either during his lifetime or after, although literally within recent weeks there is evidence of other unpublished material by his hand. To speculate why these manuscripts were not published would be no more than conjecture at this point. What we do know is that as a historical text *Jharkhand ke Kisan* provides us access to the thought and mind of one of the more remarkable thinkers and doers of his time. Certainly, few would dispute that as a peasant leader he was among the two or three most eminent activists of his time. The *Jharkhand ke Kisan* text opens a window into that activism at a crucial stage of Sahajanand's career in 1941 and in a dimension for which he was little known, namely to have moved beyond Gangetic Bihar into Jharkhand and its Adivasi or tribal population in ways that however limited they might have been, are here revealed to have been not insubstantial. I leave it to the text itself to make that point.

The public and academic image of Sahajanand, insofar as it has emerged in the last decade or two, has largely been that of a caste politician reflecting the early stages of his career, and then in the 1930s active as the leading figure in the Bihar Provincial Kisan Sabha, and in the later thirties the All-India Kisan Sabha. During that phase it is presumed that he was essentially representing the interests of well-to-do, or at best middle peasants. There is enough truth in these images to carry much weight, depending on who is making the argument. But critically these are perceptions which dramatically undervalue the mind and activism of an exceedingly complex man, whose most common characteristic was one of being intellectually, and hence socially and politically constantly on the move in the direction of change, not simply for the sake of change but in the interest of justice and equity wherever injustice and exploitation, whatever its form, might be found. The change he sought was transformational as I have suggested and this is evident from his entire career and certainly from the *Khet Mazdoor* and the *Jharkhand ke Kisan* essays, both of which he wrote in 1941 while in the Hazaribagh Jail.

Sahajanand was born in the Ghazipur district of eastern U.P. in 1889, took vows of renunciation in 1907 to become a Dandi Sannyasi of the Dasnami order. By the early twenties Sahajanand's interests shifted from the politics of caste and status reform to the Gandhian politics of the Freedom Movement, and then in the late twenties and early thirties to what we may refer to as the politics of peasant activism. His admiration for Gandhi shifted in the middle and late thirties to sharp opposition over the issue of peasant rights within the context of the struggle for political freedom from the British. It is in fact correctly assumed, as I indicate above, that Sahajanand in the 1930s was involved in an activism of peasant tenants, many of whom had tenancy rights in whose defence the Kisan Sabha and Sahajanand were engaged. What is however not fully understood is that among those peasants were not only upper caste Rajput, Bhumihar, and Kayasth tenants, but also tenants from middle agricultural castes, Yadavs, Kurmis, and Koeris among others, and indeed from lower middle castes and Untouchable castes as well. In fact, into the late thirties, Sahajanand was systematically moving in the direction of an activism representing the marginal poor whether peasants or landless agricultural labourers or some permutation of the two, regardless of caste and it is presumably in the reflective years he spent in the Hazaribagh Jail that this same sensitivity to the conditions of the Adivasi kisans of Jharkhand was sharpened.

Without attempting to characterize the thirteen chapters of *Jharkhand*

Ke Kisan we may say that this is a reflective yet first hand account of what Sahajanand again and again refers to as "open loot." The perpetrators are the Dikus, the outsiders who have come to exploit the land, the people, and the resources of this place, rich in all of these ways. The attitudes of the Adivasi tribals to this invasion, so to speak, is conveyed throughout this volume, and summarized in the first quote in the frontispiece of this book. The manner and means of this exploitation, the responses of the local population, and Sahajanand's anticipation of what might have been achieved given the strength of the people and what he describes as modern methods of mobilization, these are the issues at the core of this book. He concedes at the outset that his understanding and involvement were not what they might have been or should have been, but the text before us reveals not only a man of integrity and candor, but someone who knew much and learned more about the lives of the peasants of Jharkhand. The chapter titles themselves provide a summary of the text which Sahajanand produced in late November and early December 1941.

Rather than provide a concluding observation in this introductory note, I refer the reader to Editorial Endnote 4 of Chapter XIII which is meant to provide a brief assessment of the book and the man. Here I simply want to make passing reference to the concerns some activists and scholars have to the idea of characterizing people who are Adivasis, or the original inhabitants of this place as peasants. This was a non-issue for Sahajanand and recent scholarship would certainly confirm Sahajanand's understanding. That someone who cuts his cultivable land from the jungle, and whose life has been historically defined by the jungle and its products cannot be equated with a peasant of Gangetic Bihar, of that there is no question. And Sahajanand certainly makes no such suggestion. Indeed, he defines in dramatically specific and graphic terms what the life experiences of the Adivasi peasants are. It is useful to point out here that while he uses many terms to define the people of Jharkhand who are the focus of his inquiry, Adivasi peasants is one of them. There are of course many peasants in Jharkhand who are not Adivasis, a fact which is examined in detail in the Editorial Endnotes of this book. But the life of the jungle has historically also become a life of settled agriculture which the work of Prabhu Mohapatra confirms in detail, and which is referred to for the Scheduled Tribes population of India as a whole in the most recent work of K.S. Singh.

Two final notes will conclude this introduction. First to explain that in my experience the terms tribe and tribal for the Adivasis, or original inhabitants of Jharkhand, are viewed by the Adivasis themselves as categorizing them in someone else's terms. Many of the Adivasis who reflect on these issues do not use the term tribal. Accordingly, I have used the term Adivasi and reverted to tribal only when it was contextually relevant. The extended Editor's Glossary following the Hindi text of this manuscript examines many of these terms in detail.

I have indicated in these preliminary remarks that I would not provide detailed bibliographic references beyond those appearing in the Editor's Endnotes following each of the chapters of this tract. I will conclude by citing only by name several authors whose work has been useful in my own reflection on the Jharkhand phenomenon as defined by Sahajanand. The first of these is Stuart Corbridge whose essays cut across a range of issues touching on the economic, social, and political, and offer a useful point of departure for anyone unfamiliar with Jharkhand. Recent books edited or written by S. Narayan, Govind Kelkar and Dev Nathan, Sajal Basu, Geeti Sen, and Anirudh Prasad and Sachchidananda are all more specialized and valuable studies. But as I have indicated more than once, there is an enormous literature on the subject. There are in the Tribal Studies of India Series now 148 titles, the most recent being that of Prasad and Sachchidananda. The electronic data base catalogue of any major university library, including that at the University of Virginia will reveal literally thousands of titles, and this does not begin to access the journal literature which is equally vast. Some of these references of course appear at relevant points in the Editorial Endnotes of this volume. And the numbers and level of inquiry continue to mount. As these lines are being written, I have learned of the forthcoming book by Dilip Simeon on workers, unions, and the state in Chotanagpur, 1928-1939 to be published by Manohar in 1995.

To end on a note about the activism of non-government organizations in the region, it is useful to report that one of the central anxieties of Sahajanand and the peasants of Jharkhand was that of access to the forest and its products. That was true in 1941 and is apparently still true in 1994. The fact that the Government of Bihar is now in preliminary negotiation with the World Bank on a major Bihar

Forests Project, whose intent will be to follow the local will of the people directly involved, thereby to avoid the decisions and influences of the officially sponsored forest committees, suggests that the issues which concerned Sahjanand in 1941 are still issues of the moment in 1994.

BIHAR

SHOWING DISTRICT BOUNDARIES IN 1941
WITH CHANGES OF 1954 AND 1956

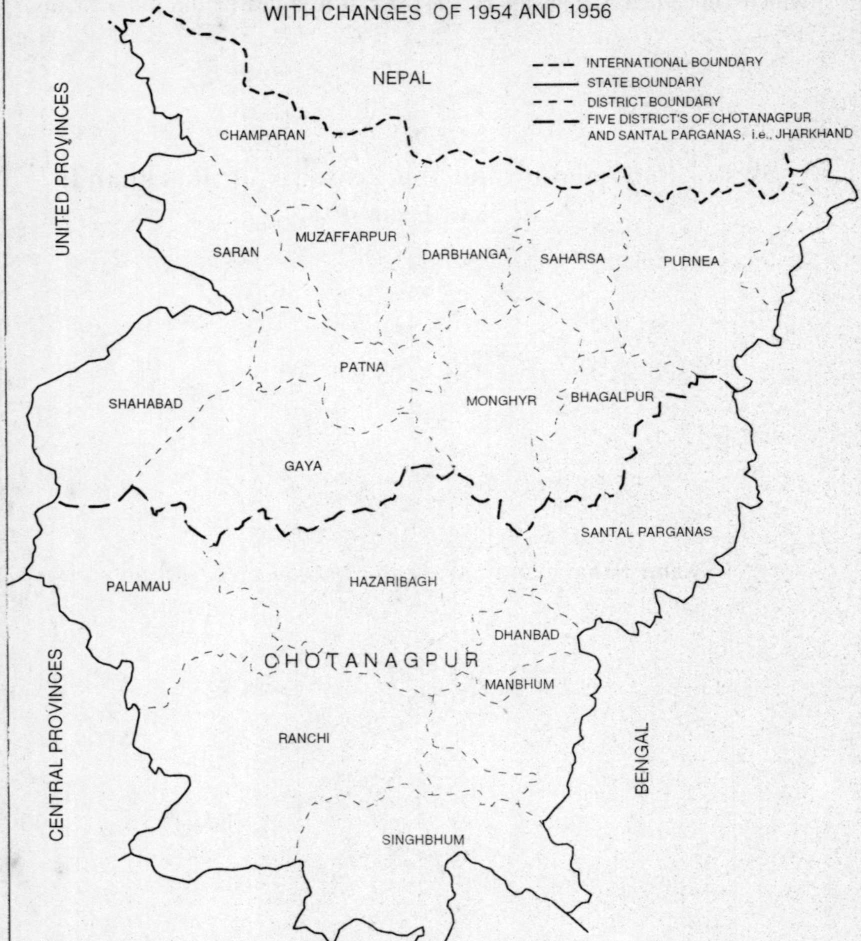

BASED ON CENSUS OF INDIA, VOL. IV, Pt.IX, 1961.
CENSUS ATLAS OF BIHAR (PATNA, 1967), MAP NO. 3, P.8.

NOTE: SEE EDITOR'S ENDNOTES 2 AND 3 OF THE INTRODUCTION FOR DETAILS ON 1954 AND 1956 BOUNDARY CHANGES.

Part I

Swami Sahajanand and the Peasants of Jharkhand: A View From 1941

An Edited Translation of
Swami Sahajanand Saraswati, *Jharkhand ke Kisan*

Editor's Endnotes follow each chapter.

Sahajanand's Introduction: A Justification For This Project

[In the brief introduction to this political tract of 1941, Sahajanand sets the framework for the argument he elaborates in the thirteen short chapters to follow. The peasants of Jharkhand have historically been victimized by outsiders and by laws they do not and cannot understand. If any relief or movement in that direction is to be achieved, it is important first to inform ourselves of the real conditions in which the people of Jharkhand live. Sahajanand's effort is to do precisely that, both for himself, he candidly explains, and for the wider public. Ed.]

The province of Bihar is most often referred to as Bihar and Chotanagpur although sometimes it is simply called Bihar. Then when Orissa was added [in 1912] it became Bihar and Orissa, and with the separation of Orissa [in 1936] it again became appropriate to use the full name Bihar and Chotanagpur rather than simply Bihar. Even when Orissa was a part of the province, it was common to use the abbreviated term Bihar for the province as a whole. But whatever terms may be used, the importance of Chotanagpur to Bihar is enormous, and whether we fully appreciate it or not, that fact remains.[1]

Of the sixteen districts of this province, only five, namely Saran, Champaran, Darbhanga, Muzaffarpur and Purnea have no hills and mountains.[2] Of the remaining eleven districts all are more or less interspersed with mountainous terrain. No doubt, unlike Gaya, Monghyr, Patna, Shahabad, and Bhagalpur which have some modest hilly tracts, the five districts of Chotanagpur, that is Palamau, Ranchi,

Hazaribagh, Manbhum and Singhbhum, plus the Santal Parganas are predominantly mountainous.[3] These six districts are in fact covered by mountains and jungles, while only small tracts of Gaya and the other districts are mountainous and forested. And of the districts with minimum mountain and forest cover, Patna clearly has the least. Thus it is the predominance of forests which led the people of this mountainous plateau to refer to Palamau and the other five districts as Jharkhand, that is the land of jungles and forests.[4] Then during the Buddhist period *maths*, or monasteries and other dwelling places were constructed for the Buddhist mendicants (*bhikshuon*) and these study and living cells came to be called *vihara* by the followers of that sect (*sampraday*). It is for this reason that the districts of Gangetic Bihar where these *vihara* were located came to be called Vihar, or Bihar. As a matter of fact, in this large province, it was entirely appropriate to term those districts covered with jungle as Jharkhand and to call the other part of the province Viharkhand, or Vihar. However, why the entire province came to be called Vihar, or Bihar, I cannot say.

Thus the province of Bihar or Vihar is essentially divided into two parts and it must be noted that serious efforts have been made in recent years for ameliorating the condition of the peasants of Biharkhand.[5] But this has not happened in the case of Jharkhand and the Bihar Provincial Kisan Sabha has also not given as much attention to Jharkhand as it has to Biharkhand.[6] As a result outsiders are very often unaware of the real problems of the kisans of this area. In fact even now we do not have an authentic and detailed knowledge of the conditions there. The original inhabitants who are also called *Adivasis* are, generally speaking, a very quiet and simple people quite apart from the question of their education or their ability to read and write. And it is also true that most non-Adivasis cannot understand their languages. Their culture and customs are obviously different, and hence perceived by outsiders not simply as unfamiliar, but as remote and strange (*nirale*).

This province is not especially large. The sixteen districts comprising Bihar and Chotanagpur have a population of approximately three and one half crores (36,340,000).[7] But surprisingly the condition of the kisans is governed by three different sets of tenancy legislation. The Bihar Tenancy Act applies only in the ten districts of Viharkhand while two sets of legislations are current in Jharkhand.

The first of these is the Chotanagpur Tenancy Act applicable only in the five districts of Chotanagpur. But the conditions which obtain in the Santal Parganas are unique and there a third type of legislation, namely the Santal Pargana Manual is applicable to that district alone. This manual is largely based on the regulations of 1872 and 1886. Because of this multiplicity of regulations agrarian relations in Jharkhand are especially complex.

Unfortunately, the leadership of the original inhabitants of Jharkhand is in the hands of others, i.e., outsider non-Adivasis. And Christian missionaries have been active in the area for the last many years as well. They have propagated Christianity widely and have accordingly assumed positions of leadership among the kisans as well. Furthermore, at various times, educated, moneylending *banias*, or traders from the northern part of the province have gradually settled in Jharkhand. Either they or the Bengalis constitute the bulk of the educated class practising law either as *vakils*, or *mukhtars*. People from all over India and other countries have also settled in the region, engaged in trade in mica, coal, and iron, as well as *lac* and timber. Accordingly it is almost inevitable for such people to try to assume the leadership of the poor. For example, all the influential leaders of an important organization like the Indian National Congress in Jharkhand come from among these outsiders.[8]

No doubt an Adivasi movement has been formed and its leadership is said to be in the hands of the Adivasis. There are also Adivasis who have started an organization in the name of the Kisan Sabha. But its leadership is in the hands of those who are opportunists and no more than lukewarm to the real issues. They are little concerned for the welfare of the peasants but are rather concerned to exploit them for their own purposes. The great weakness of the Adivasi movement is that it is being run purely on the lines of a middle class affair.[9] Had it been running on the basis of the real class interests of the kisans, its power would have been immense, so much so that it would certainly have affected a dramatic change in the condition of the people of Jharkhand.[10]

These are some of the reasons it has become difficult to determine the realities of this increasingly complex situation. It is with a concern for the real welfare of the peasants that I wish to identify the actual conditions in Jharkhand. The greatest difficulty we and our workers face in this task is our ignorance of these conditions. We are not familiar with the salient features of the Chotanagpur tenancy legislation, nor its shortcomings. How then can we launch any movement for reforming the agrarian system in Jharkhand?[11] From an outsider's point of view the agrarian laws of Jharkhand appear exceedingly complex. During the Congress Ministry some of these laws were reformed on the pattern of the Bihar Tenancy Act.[12] But the question arises as to how many members of the Bihar Assembly, or of the Congress leadership in fact, understood the complexities of this legislation at the time it was being framed.

Unless we know the real conditions of the people and are fully aware of their most urgent needs and are also familiar with how the functioning of government and the courts affects the welfare of the poor, how can we do anything to benefit them? Neither government officials nor others understand the language of the Adivasis. Vakils and mukhtars from the outside have only a superficial knowledge of the language, inevitably to the detriment of the Adivasis. And what do the Adivasis themselves know about the intricacies of the English law which might enable them to prepare an appropriate legal defence when they are entangled in the courts? On the one hand they are quite unaware of the law, and on the other they are subjected to its most severe penalties. Through my many encounters with the Adivasis in the jail and outside, I have learned how they are literally entrapped by the law.[13] No doubt they have more than sufficient proof in their defence. Yet their failure to submit this evidence at the correct time or in accordance with established procedure traps them in the grips of the law! They are essentially in the dark about the official rules and regulations which govern their lives. Who has tried to teach them these things? All legislation is written in English, and what to speak of the common people, even among their elected representatives in the Assembly, hardly one or two have any acquaintance with the English language. Even a limited knowledge of Hindi helps little at this level.[14]

In these circumstances whatever I write will be done for the knowledge of everyone. I do not mean to criticize or defend any group (*dal*), party (*parti*), or sect (*sampraday*) in undertaking this task. If we truly wish to serve the people of Jharkhand, particularly its peasants, we must gain access to that "no man's land," (*andheri gufa*) in order fully to understand it. Otherwise we ourselves will be misled and in that event anything we might do will be superficial at best. The degree to which we succeed in this venture, of course, remains to be seen.

Central Jail, Hazaribagh
Friday, 7 November 1941

Swami Sahajanand Saraswati

Editor's Endnotes to Sahajanand's Introduction

1 Bihar and Orissa was created as a province at the time of the repartition of Bengal in 1912, and each became a separate province on April 1, 1936.

2 In June 1944 the Supaul and Madhepura subdivisions of Bhagalpur district were constituted as the Saharsa subdistrict and in April 1954 Saharsa was created as a separate district. Until the more recent administrative and political divisions and redivisions of the districts, Bihar was comprised of these seventeen districts, with one modification noted immediately following. Please see accompanying map showing the Bihar districts in 1941 indicating also the changes of 1954 and 1956, and outlining the five Chotanagpur districts and Santal Parganas which together constitute the region historically defined as Jharkhand. At the present writing, with the creation of Lakhisarai district on July 3, 1994,and Sheikhpura district on July 31, 1994, there are 53 districts in Bihar. See "CM Inaugurates New District," in *The Hindustan Times*, Patna Edition, July 5, 1994, and the July 6, 1994 issue memorializing the event photographically. See "Bihar gets its 53rd district", in *The Telegraph*, August 1, 1994.

3 Dhanbad became a subdistrict of Manbhum in 1927 and was constituted as a full fledged district on November 1, 1956. Chas and Chandankiyari police stations of the Purulia Sadar subdivision of the old Manbhum district were added to Dhanbad when Purulia Sadar was transferred to the state of West Bengal in 1956 in implementation of the recommendations of the States Reorganization Commission. Seventeen thanas or police stations of the former Manbhum district were transferred to West Bengal at that time. Simultaneously, three thanas and part of a fourth situated in the southwest corner of Manbhum adjoining Singhbhum were transferred to that district. Chandil, Nimdih, and Ichagarh were added to the Seraikela subdivision and Patamda to the Dhalbhum subdivision. What were thanas in 1956, by the time of the 1961 Census had come to be called anchals. A border realignment with West Bengal involving six thanas of Purnea district in the northeast part of Bihar also took place in 1956. See Ranchor Prasad, *District Census Handbook, Purulia* (Patna: Secretariat Press, 1956); and Ranchor Prasad, *District Census Handbook, Singhbhum* (Patna: Secretariat Press, 1956), including especially the population map insert of the district showing the original boundary. The best representation of the changes in Manbhum, Dhanbad, and Singhbhum districts can be

found in the anchal map of Bihar in Census of India 1961, Vol. IV, Bihar, Pt. III (ii), *Household Economic Tables* (Patna: Superintendent of Census Operations, [1964]). See also Census of Bihar 1961, *District Census Handbook 16, Dhanbad* (Patna: Superintendent Census Operations, 1966), p. viii; Census of India 1961, Vol. IV, Bihar, Pt. IX, *Census Atlas of Bihar* (Patna: Superintendent of Census Operations, 1967), esp. Map 3, p. 8; and Census 1961, Bihar, *District Census Handbook 17, Singhbhum* (Patna: Superintendent of Census Operations, 1967), p. xvi. The Superintendent of Census Operations in 1961 was S.D. Prasad. See also P.C. Roy Chaudhury, *Bihar District Gazetteers, Dhanbad* (Patna: Secretariat Press, 1964), Ch. I. See the accompanying map in this edited translation for visual details of these border changes. Please note that the Dalbhum subdivision of Singhbhum district is also spelled Dhalbhum in the official literature.

4 Sahajanand uses the Devanagri *jangal* almost exclusively in these chapters, with an occasional exception when he refers to protected and reserved forests. In this edited translation we will vary our usage to include both terms, namely jungle and forest as seems most appropriate in terms of style and context.

5 Note that Sahajanand's explanation of the etymology of the name of the province as Bihar from the term vihar, refers both to the history of the term and the phonetic similarities between the two sounds. But after these initial common usages, Sahajanand shifts to a fairly consistent use of Vihar in the remainder of this manuscript. This comes to him as second nature given the fact that he does the same for Bengal, that is Vengal, and other similar usages. When he writes in English, however, he does use Bihar, Bengal, etc. In an effort at consistency and using the familiar English Bihar, this is the spelling we will use most often in this translation.

6 Sahajanand is entirely candid on this issue and returns to the theme again and again in this tract. Indeed, the failure of the Bihar Provincial Kisan Sabha to have been more active in Jharkhand is for Sahajanand a key intellectual justification for undertaking the revealing examination of conditions in Jharkhand which this tract represents. His imprisonment in the Hazaribagh Central Jail provided him the intensely reflective time necessary for the effort. It must also be noted that while Sahajanand and the Kisan Sabha had relatively limited contact in Jharkhand during the heyday of the peasant movement in Gangetic Bihar in the middle and late 1930s, there were a number of notable exceptions. In the latter half of Chapter VI of this tract Sahajanand refers with much emotion to his tour of Palamau district in December 1939, and to his specific encounter with the Adivasi kisans of Mahuadand thana in the southern part of the district. He had also

presided over the Singhbhum District Kisan Conference at Ghatshila, July 3 and 4, 1939. One might conjecture that these efforts in late 1939 may in fact have been the beginning of Sahajanand's growing sensitivity to Jharkhand as a place of grievous agrarian trauma, urgently in need of change, and hence of activist peasant mobilization. Certainly, as a political document, *Jharkhand ke Kisan* suggests that this is the direction in which Sahajanand's thinking was moving. Apart from other peasant meetings and activisms in which he was involved and to which he refers throughout this tract, it is not a coincidence perhaps that he was jailed in Hazaribagh itself only weeks after the Anti-Compromise Conference in which he was a central player, and which was held at Ramgarh in the southern part of Hazaribagh in March 1940. It is not as though Jharkhand was for Sahajanand a remote and unfamiliar place.

7 A crore in the Indian numeric system is equal to 10,000,000. Sahajanand's estimate of approximately three and one half crores is in fact more accurate than the actual numbers he provides. The decennial series in the 1991 Census gives the 1941 Bihar population as 35,170,840, although it must be noted that because of wartime conditions the 1941 Census was a limited, incomplete, and thus probably not an entirely accurate enumeration. I include following the decennial series from 1931 to 1991 for Bihar. The numbers in column three indicate the per cent of decadal variation.

1931	31,347,108	+11.45
1941	35,170,840	+12.20
1951	38,782,271	+10.27
1961	46,447,457	+19.76
1971	56,353,369	+21.33
1981	69,914,734	+24.06
1991	86,374,465	+23.54

See Census of India, 1991, Series-1, Paper-2 of 1992, *Final Population Totals: Brief Analysis of Primary Census Abstract* (New Delhi: Registrar General and Census Commissioner, 1992), esp. Table 2, p. 88 and Table 2.1, p. 98. See also Census of India, 1931, Vol. VII, *Bihar and Orissa, Part II, Tables* (Patna: Superintendent Government Printing, 1932), Table I, p. 2, which shows the 1931 Bihar population as 32,371,434, which is the figure Sahajanand in fact shows for 1931 in his more extended discussion of the demographic profile of Jharkhand in Chapter II. Based on the evidence of this tract and confirming with the relevant 1941 Census volumes, we know that the 1941 figures were indeed available to Sahajanand when he was writing Jharkhand ke Kisan in November of that year. It is certainly the kind of detail he would search out. Actually, the figures which are at variance from the original 1931 and 41 figures are those provided by the 1991 Census given above. The reasons for those adjustments are not a matter of immediate concern to us at this point. See Census of India 1941, Vol. I, *India, Pt. I, Tables* (Delhi: Manager of Publications, 1943), p. 124.

8 This was an issue in 1941 and remains so in 1994. For an extended comment, see my Editor's Endnote 18 of Chapter II, where I examine the relative balance of Adivasi and non-Adivasi population in the region. This is one of the central issues in the scholarship which deals with Jharkhand and Chotanagpur as well as in the public press and the political arena. At a time when there are fewer foreign missionaries in the area and when the leadership of the various Christian denominations is almost wholly Indian, it can of course be expected that the participation of that leadership in the politics of the day will by definition be more direct in representing the interests of its constituents and the region.

Sahajanand's use of the term vakil and mukhtar refers to advocates, pleaders, and lawyers, and in the case of mukhtars to legal professionals at the most local level. In contemporary India this latter term is no longer in use. Everyone practising the law is now an advocate.

9 This is almost certainly a veiled criticism to the early activities of Jaipal Singh, a key figure in the Adivasi Mahasabha formed in 1938. The Mahasabha emerged out of the Unnati Samaj in that year, unsuccessfully contested the 1946 general elections, and was reconstituted in 1950 as the Jharkhand Party thus to represent the political interests of the entire Chotanagpur region, tribal and non-tribal. It contested the 1952 general elections and won 32 of the 325 seats in the Bihar Legislative Assembly, thereby becoming the major opposition party. The sources for this history are many. I have relied here primarily on the essay by Ram Dayal Munda and Biseshwar Prasad Keshari, "Recent Developments in the Jharkhand Movement," *India International Centre Quarterly* 9:3 (Monsoon 1992), pp. 71-89, and a long interview with N.E. Horo, currently an M.L.A. of the Jharkhand Party and formerly representing that party in Parliament, that is the Lok Sabha. I am especially grateful to Mr. Horo for sharing so candidly with me his experiences in the party and the movement over many years. We spoke at Ranchi, June 22, 1994. More vague in memory is a brief encounter I had with Jaipal Singh when he spoke at the University of Chicago in the early 1950s; my best recollection is that it was in 1953 or 54. The importance of the meeting for me as a young post-graduate student was not only that Jaipal Singh was the first prominent public figure of India

I had met, but that the concept of Jharkhand crossed my intellectual horizon for the first time on that occasion. It is worth noting here that while Sahajanand is being critical of this being essentially "a middle class affair," later in this tract he justifies Jaipal Singh's movement in rather more favorable terms. See Editor's Endnote 11 of Chapter III.

10 Sahajanand uses the term varg svarthon here specifically to refer to the class interests of the Adivasi kisans defined in social and economic terms. He does so regularly in this tract where he is, however, more consistently concerned with the Adivasi cultural and physical environment and its exploitation by non-Adivasi outsiders. This is not to suggest that Sahajanand does not condemn agrarian exploitation in clear class terms here, but rather to note the relative emphasis and definition of the issue, especially considering that barely three months before undertaking the Jharkhand ke Kisan manuscript he had completed the *Khet Mazdoor* tract, in which the relative priorities of emphasis were essentially reversed. There the focus was significantly on issues of class exploitation of the agricultural labourers couched in Marxist terms as he understood them. That argument was then sustained, as it were, by the cultural element of injustice, whereas in the present instance, as I have suggested, the emphasis is somewhat different. See my edited translation of Khet Mazdoor, issued as *Sahajanand on Agricultural Labour and the Rural Poor* (New Delhi: Manohar Publications, 1994).

11 This is the candor to which I referred in Endnote 6 above. Sahajanand was openly honest in admitting that there was much he did not know about the lives and conditions of the peasants of Jharkhand.

12 The ministry led by the Indian National Congress was in office in Bihar, as in other provinces of British India and under terms of the Governmnent of India Act of 1935 from 1937 to October 1939, when, with the onset of World War II, these ministries resigned in protest against the Viceroy's not having consulted the Indian National Congress on the issue of drawing India into the war. The Assembly Sahajanand refers to is the Bihar Legislative Assembly, or lower house in a bicameral legislature system. In Hindi it is the Vidhan Sabha and the upper house is the Legislative Council or Vidhan Parishad. These are almost literal meanings and translations. A member of the Legislative Assembly is an MLA, and of the Council an MLC.

13 Sahajanand makes the point frequently in this manuscript that he did not know Jharkhand as well as he should, on the other hand there are many references to tours and meetings in the Jharkhand districts and to encounters of the kind he mentions here. To repeat my reaction to this history which is evident in much of this tract, while the Swami did not know Jharkhand the way he new Gangetic Bihar, it was not

unfamiliar ground. The other point he makes here which emerges again and again in his experience and that of many other political activists of the time is that jail were key places for political, social, and ideological interaction. He and we will come back to this issue in later chapters. Of course this is not a new idea, but to have it revealed as it is here in a first person account makes it that much more impressive as a political fact of that time.

14 Again, the issue of social, cultural, and linguistic entrapment is one to which Sahajanand returns again and again. The system and its non-Adivasi managers were not only not benefiting the population they were charged to serve, they were in fact working at cross purposes with it and going beyond that to exploit the people and their cultural and historic home in the process. This is one of the central themes of this book. See Editor's Endnote 5 of Chapter 1 for comments on an example and related issue based on the experience of the Santal Parganas Inquiry Committee of 1938.

Chapter I

Jharkhand: The Geography and Culture of Place

[In this initial chapter Sahajanand defines Jharkhand in terms of its spatial location and its physical configuration. He is equally concerned with the tensions this geography creates between the indigenous Adivasi population on the one hand and the outsiders, whether Bihari, other Indians, or foreigners, who have come to Jharkhand to exploit its people and its great wealth, whether that of the fields and forests, or the rich mineral resources of this mountain plateau. His personal involvement in mobilizing resistance to this exploitation, he concedes candidly, has been less than adequate. Ed.]

<24.11.41> The southern part of the province of Bihar and Chotanagpur is known as Jharkhand.[1] It is an old name. In the Sanskrit texts the word *vankhand* or *vanshand* is often mentioned in the sense of jungli or mountainous tracts. Even now, in local usage, the word "jhar" refers to trees, scrub, and underbrush. Thus, as already indicated, Santal Parganas and the five districts of Chotanagpur constitute the main jungle tracts of this province. There are also contiguous parts of Bihar, Bengal, Orissa, the Central Provinces and the United Provinces of similar terrain which makes Jharkhand at the same time more extensive and more inaccessible. This includes the jungle and mountain tracts of Sasaram subdivision in the district of Shahabad and a larger area of the southern part of Gaya and a major segment of the southern parts of Monghyr and Bhagalpur. The western part of Singhbhum in Jharkhand extends to the Gangpur state in Orissa while its southern part reaches the native states of Mayurbhanj, Bonai,

and Keonjhar, also in Orissa. In this same sense Palamau and Ranchi districts in Chotanagpur are bordered by districts and princely states in U.P., the Central Provinces, and Orissa of similar terrain including Mirzapur, Sarguja, Jashpur, and Gangpur. The eastern part of Singhbhum and Manbhum extends up to the borders of Bengal as does the southeast portion of the Santal Parganas.

It is this jungle and mountain geography which accounts for the Jharkhand being regarded as a unique and different world of its own. Just as the creatures of the deep and fathomless sea feel themselves safe and secure, so too the people of Jharkhand have regarded themselves equally secure. For them nature itself was the protector. Who would dare to penetrate the dense and inhospitable jungle to oppress the Adivasis? In order to protect her progeny the goddess of nature had provided a large population of wild beasts to work as powerful sentries of this formidable natural fortress. Those daring to venture into this domain would be warned from afar by the roar of the lion to go no further into this forbidden land.

Yet, despite all of these protections, have the people of Jharkhand been able to save themselves? Have their enemies not been able to penetrate into their inaccessible fortress? Have they not ravaged and plundered them ruthlessly and are they still not doing so? My effort in *Jharkhand ke Kisan* is meant to provide no more than a description of this organized loot. Just as human ingenuity has devised vast nets to entrap the fishes and creatures of the sea, so too clever persons and usurers have devised hundreds of methods for entrapping the people of Jharkhand and extracting their flesh and blood. Such persons have laid out a complex network of trapping devices to ensnare the Adivasis, so that if they pierce through one, two or three nets, they are bound to be enmeshed in the fourth. They are in fact like fish out of water, gasping for life till they finally succumb. And it is also true that the further south one proceeds in Jharkhand, the greater this exploitation. It is this very region which abounds in the immeasurable wealth of coal, mica, iron, and many other mineral riches

Before dealing with these issues it is necessary to understand the physical configuration of the southern, eastern, and western segments of the Jharkhand region. I have already referred to the native states in Orissa. These states surround the entire southern ring and a large part of the western fringe of Jharkhand as well. A small part of the western ridge is also surrounded by the native state of Sarguja in the

Central Provinces. Saraikela, Karaikela and Kharsawan, three princely states of Orissa penetrate into the centre of Singhbhum.[2] It appears that they have literally been carved out of this district. Saraikela is sandwiched between Dalbhum (or Dhalbhum), the eastern subdivision of the Singhbhum district and the Sadar or Chaibasa subdivision in the western part of the district. The tiny state of Kharsawan lies to the west of Saraikela. Thus even after separating the district into two parts (there are only two subdivisions in Singhbhum district) the northern part of Chaibasa was further truncated by carving out the small state of Karaikela.

The boundary of Bengal starts from the southeastern fringe of Dalbhum and the district of Midnapur lies adjacent to it in this direction. The whole of Bankura and a part of Burdwan lie to the east of Manbhum. Parts of Burdwan, Birbhum, Murshidabad and Malda are to the east and south of the Santal Parganas. Thus the whole eastern fringe of Chotanagpur is surrounded by these several districts of Bengal. It is for this reason that those border regions of Chotanagpur have become very much like Bengal and are either inhabited by Bengalis or others speaking the Bengali language. It is an area more similar to Bengal than it is to Bihar. The Adivasis of this region speak a mixed tongue and its strangeness to our ears is due to its being a by-product of the union between Bengali and their own language. This new dialect is described as Khortha *boli.*

Sarguja and the native states of Orissa bordering Chotanagpur are governed by autocratic rulers who seem to live by feudal standards of the middle ages. These *rajas*, while maintaining all modern facilities for themselves, force their subjects to live no better than animals. Shri Sarangdhar Das, minister of the state council of Orissa, produced the report of an enquiry committee on the native states, which reveals a remarkable picture of a world where taxes or government permission is required for performing marriages, cremating the dead or holding panchayats, sabhas, and other meetings. Even betel leaves are subject to a sales tax. The firing tragedy which occurred only three or four years ago in some of the states of Orissa and a similar tragedy in Gangpur state neighboring Singhbhum are still fresh in our memory. It is only natural that Jharkhand which is surrounded by these native states, should be influenced by these conditions and circumstances.

In the same way, those parts of Jharkhand bordering immediately on Bengal face another kind of problem. There is a constant sense of uncertainty over whether these border regions should remain in Bihar or become a part of Bengal. Anxieties of this kind are commonly voiced in towns like Jamshedpur, Ranchi, and Purulia, and now this Bengali-Bihari issue has raised its ugly head throughout Bihar. And the negative consequences of these animosities are borne primarily by the people of Jharkhand. Because of this dispute and the uncertainties it generates, real development projects do not get implemented. The circumstance is similar to what is found in jointly owned fields, which often go uncultivated because those involved cannot agree on their shared responsibilities. In the case of the Bihar Bengal question, the third claimants in the dispute, so to speak, have been the middle class organizers of the Adivasi movement. Seeing two rivals quarrelling among themselves, they saw an opportunity to take advantage of the situation. It is this "triangular fight," in which Jharkhand is essentially caught in the middle to its great disadvantage[3].

<25.11.41> Santal Parganas district is surrounded by so-called civilized peoples on all sides. Apart from the districts of Bengal already mentioned, Santal Parganas is also surrounded by the Bhagalpur and Monghyr districts of Bihar. The parts of these two districts which border Santal Parganas and Hazaribagh also have a good number of Adivasi population. This infiltration of populations inevitably results in a heavy influence on the Adivasi people. There is a similar pattern in other parts of Jharkhand touching the districts of Gaya, Patna, and Shahabad, which also have a jungle and mountainous terrain and are inhabited by a semi-civilized Adivasi population. This continuous movement of an educated and non-Adivasi population deeper into the interior of the Jharkhand districts has led to the exploitation of these simple people in every conceivable way. They have literally been robbed and deprived of their lands and incomes and driven into complete ruin. A more detailed treatment of the methods of their exploitation will be taken up later in this manuscript.

This much is clear that these exploiters in the form of moneylenders and userers are ruining the people of Jharkhand. Had the Adivasis not come into contact with these so-called civilized groups, they would not be in the miserable plight in which they now find themselves, or at worst the process would have been slower and its intensity less severe. Their ruin would not have been so swift or on such a mass scale. Earlier it was held that only in the Santal Parganas had there been this kind of penetration of civilized persons for exploiting its Adivasi population. This is also the view of government, which is why a special set of administrative regulations were adopted for governing this district. It is possible that this process occurred here on such a vast scale because Santal Parganas is a principal centre of Hindu pilgrimage.[4] These exploiters, though they came in the guise of true devotees, were in fact here to deceive the Santal people. In the process they were doing no less than engaging in fraud on God himself. But now, to a greater or lesser degree, the same state of affairs is found uniformly in all the district of Jharkhand. Everywhere the ownership of land is being taken over by non-Adivasi outsiders. The description on page four of the report of the Santal Parganas Inquiry Committee, submitted during the time of the first Congress Ministry, holds true for all the districts of Jharkhand. It runs thus:

> The system was designed and created to meet the needs of an area which contains a large proportion of somewhat primitive aboriginals and semi-aboriginals intermingled in varying proportions with a more advanced population. The problems arising out of this mixture of population are intensified by the fact that, unlike the other large aboriginal tracts in the province, the district is almost surrounded by areas inhabited by more advanced people[s] and suffering from an excessive pressure of population on the soil. This has throughout the last century produced a steady tendency for the surrounding population to encroach upon the land of the aboriginals and to exploit that population. [The necessity of protecting the aboriginals against this continued pressure led to the creation of the special system of administration which still survives.][5]

To assert that these conditions are applicable to the Santal Parganas alone would not be accurate. For example, there are in Hazaribagh and Manbhum a large number of non-Adivasis who migrated and settled there in order to exploit the original inhabitants. This process continues to the present day. Much of the land of the Adivasis has been expropriated in this way. And if one narrates the story of the seizure of the Parasnath Hills [in Hazaribagh] and the nearby lands and forests, it will bring tears of blood to the eyes of anyone with a sense of human kindness in their heart. Just as Baidyanath Dham is a place of pilgrimage for the Hindus, so Parasnath is sacred to the Jains. But those who abstain from taking life and who claim to abstain from injury to any living creature (*jeev himsa*), who practise kindness to all life forms (*jeev daya*), the tortures which these very same wealthy Jains have inflicted on the Santals and other Adivasis in this tract are beyond description. They have managed to purchase the mountain and its springs and the nearby jungles, and have gotten these registered in their own names in the official record of rights. What do the poor and exploited Adivasis understand about the government's survey and settlement procedures? But it is on the strength of this legal procedure that the Santals have been deprived of their water, grass, leaves, timber, firewood, flowers, fruits, and everything else.[6] Their misery is such that no one seems to be concerned over their plight. Even during the days of the Congress Ministry, there was no one who lent an ear to their entreaties! So we see that Santal Parganas is not unique in the degree of its exploitation of the Adivasis. The practice extends widely in Chotanagpur, including Hazaribagh, and I will also consider the loot of the Tatas in Singhbhum district in a later chapter of this manuscript.

This much is certain that because of the constant tension over the Bengali-Bihari issue, and the predominantly mountainous features of the region, the task of bringing real awakening (*jagriti*) among the Adivasis, the kisans of Jharkhand, and the people generally, has not been adequately undertaken. If I have been unable to do this in the hilly tracts of the southern parts of Gaya, Patna, Monghyr, and Bhagalpur, which are relatively more backward than the plains areas of those districts, how can I presume to bring a real awakening to the Adivasi kisans by moving even deeper into the more remote Jharkhand districts? My personal experience has been that I did not travel much into these southern tracts. Although their number is few and far between, there are places which I have not visited even once. While I have toured all over Jharkhand, yet I have not been personally able to do any important work among the Adivasis. My efforts in this direction have clearly been inadequate. These have been no more than beginnings and nothing else can be claimed.[7]

As already stated, the Jharkhand tract is one of deep jungle and mountains. However, in the sense that the mountains are not continuous, one can find plains terrain in some parts of Palamau, Hazaribagh, and Manbhum. But even in those places there will be an occasional outcropping of small hills. The topography of Santal Parganas is more or less the same. But there is no denying that the fertile fields of Bihar proper are not to be found in Jharkhand. Here there are rivers and rivulets everywhere and these not only break the ground and cause unevenness in the surface but wash away the vegetation and thus render the land lifeless. Hence the fields are generally much less productive in Jharkhand. And Palamau is the most barren. There only narrow strips of land between the mountains ridges are at all productive.[8] From the point of view of fertility these mountainous tracts are especially inhospitable whether in Jharkhand or elsewhere, and unlike China this terrain is not well-suited to paddy cultivation.[9] Consequently the peasants of this region are very poor and live on the verge of hunger much of the time.

Chotanagpur is relatively cooler than the rest of Bihar, inasmuch as the whole tract is a plateau area, similar to the outer shell of a tortoise. Parts of Hazaribagh and Ranchi are at a very high altitude and accordingly pleasantly cool. Hence governors and other government officials spend their summers in Ranchi and at Netarhat. Netarhat lies at the border of Mahuadand thana and Ranchi in the far south of Palamau and is also very cool, in fact the coldest place in Bihar.[10] This cool and inviting climate and the backward condition of the place have been yet another reason to attract exploiters, who have come on a thousand and one pretexts to fleece the simple people of Jharkhand.

But the dryness, barrenness and sterility of the soil of Jharkhand is more than compensated for by its priceless underground wealth. Beneath its soils lie vast deposits of coal without which factories, railways, and the entire administrative establishment would come to a standstill. This coal is also known as "black gold" and this description is entirely accurate. The scarcity of this invaluable material can render ineffective the entire commercial work of the world. The foundation of present-day capitalism rests on materials like coal, petroleum, iron, and rubber. Mica is also one of these critical materials. It will be no exaggeration to describe this region as the life blood of the entire province.[11] This mineral wealth is found in abundance in the Santal Parganas, Manbhum, Hazaribagh and some parts of Ranchi. The coal mines of Katras and Jharia are of course, famous the world over.[12]

The area abounds in large deposits of iron ore as well. The famous iron works of the Tatas who control dozens of such workshops in this region are after all situated in Jharkhand. Jamshedpur is the administrative headquarters of Dalbhum subdivision in the district of Singhbhum. Over and above the manufacture of steel, other goods are also produced there. Copper and brass goods are manufactured in and around Jamshedpur and Ghatshila of that subdivision. The Tata Iron Works here is the largest in India. There is no factory of this scale in any other place in the country.

Jharkhand also abounds in vast deposits of mica. The mica mines are found primarily in the northern parts of the Hazaribagh district. The entire surface of this region is literally full of mica. Kodarma has the largest deposits and the Giridih subdivision of Hazaribagh is also famous for its mica. From here it is exported to all parts of India and the world. I have come across mica mines and workshops every place I have moved in this area. Americans and other foreign nationals hold many of these mines on lease. Giridih of course is also famous for its coal.

Thus far I have spoken mostly about the underground wealth of Jharkhand. The dense jungle of *sal* trees growing in the region and many other kinds of trees are no less valuable for their timber. The bamboo which is grown widely here is a rich resource for paper manufacture. Another valuable product of the jungle is *lac* produced chiefly on three kinds of trees, that is the *palas*, *kusum* and *ber* which are found especially in the districts of Manbhum, Palamau, Ranchi, and Santal Parganas.[13] Lac is a major product of the area, but it is also a source of great harassment to the peasants. Historically, the zamindars have forcibly taken possession of lac producing trees. The fields belong to the kisans but the Palas trees, on which lac worms are fed, are regarded as belonging to the zamindars! This is not simply a verbal arrangement; it is a right legitimized in the survey *khatian* [i.e., the official record of rights in the land]! This peculiar arrangement may appear unintelligible to others, but it is written in black and white to the detriment of the kisans. Consequently, even officials of the administration accept this arrangement as fact. They attach no importance to ordinary common sense in the face of the documentary evidence to the contrary and deliver their judgements accordingly! God alone can save the kisans! Who else is there to bother about them in these circumstances?

<26.11.41> Thus we find that the land of Jharkhand is producing wealth without limit. Its vast deposits of mica, coal, iron, lac, valuable timber, and many varieties of gem stones have enabled large numbers of Indians and foreigners literally to become multi-millionaires. Almost all the mines are owned by outsiders.[14] The Tatas of Bombay earned or in a sense looted vast wealth from Jharkhand. But the original inhabitants of this place have remained as poor as before. People say that Lord Shiva himself is a Jharkhandi inasmuch as he lives in a jungle abode. And Shiva is also proverbially poor yet showers fortune upon fortune on his worshippers thereby increasing their wealth many times over. The same is true for the people of Jharkhand. They too remain poor but have helped others to become rich beyond measure.

Editor's Endnotes to Chapter I

1 Notations indicating the day, month, and year appearing in the margins of Sahajanand's original copybook manuscript of *Jharkhand ke Kisan* are retained in this translated edition at the same point in the text. Sahajanand dated the introduction November 7, 1941 and began Chapter I seventeen days later on November 24. The last date entry is December 5, 1941, which means Sahajanand completed the 158 pages of handwritten text (exclusive of the six page introduction) in the two copybooks of this manuscript in twelve days, or approximately fourteen pages a day. His initial pace was rather slower but from November 28, the pace quickened dramatically. No marginal dates appear for November 29, and December 4, but the number of pages written at the time, suggest that Sahajanand had simply failed to make date notations on those days. The manuscript copy was passed by the prison superintendent on December 7, 1941, although there is no indication whether this means the copy books left the prison at that time. Note that the original and unedited Hindi text of *Jharkhand ke Kisan* appears as Part II of this volume. Sahajanand's date notations are of course retained in the Devanagri text as well.

Sahjanand was in the Hazaribagh Central Jail at the time he was writing *Jharkhand ke Kisan.* He was imprisoned for a three year term in April 1940, following his involvement in organizing, with Subhas Chandra Bose, the All India Anti-Compromise Conference at Ramgarh in March of that year, his role as General Secretary of the Fifth Session of the All India Kisan Sabha at Palasa, and in mobilizing the National Anti-Compromise Week in early April 1940. In each instance he took a strident anti-war position, which would change only following the entry of the Soviet Union into the war in June 1941, and the Kisan Sabha policy statements supporting the Communist Party of India's "People's War" stand on the war issue. Those statements were issued by the All India Kisan Committee in October 1941, and by the Central Kisan Council in February 1942. Sahajanand was released from prison in March 1942, a year before the expiry of his three year sentence. For a brief account of this history see the last chapter of my forthcoming book, *Sahajanand and the Kisan Sabha: The Politics of Peasant Activism in Twentieth Century India.*

2 The 1931 Census of India shows Saraikela and Kharsawan as feudatory states of Chotanagpur rather than Orissa as Sahajanand suggests here,

and the 1931 Census makes no mention of Karaikela. The 1921 Census of India map of the area does show two separated segments of Saraikela in Singhbhum district, the larger one comprising the thanas of Saraikela and Gobindpur, the smaller segment to the west and beyond Kharsawan is in fact thana Karaikela of Saraikela state. This minor piece of administrative and political history was apparently the reason for Sahajanand's misunderstanding of this geography. There is of course also the question of what sources Sahajanand had at his disposal in the Hazaribagh Central Jail while he was writing. While some books were certainly available it is also presumably the case that Sahajanand was working largely from memory and experience in the region, which we have already indicated by his own description, was relatively limited. What is impressive, however, is that his descriptive geography of this very complex network of political and administrative units, is essentially accurate. And whether a feudatory state came under Orissa or Chotanagpur was perhaps more of an official concern than it was for people on the ground. See Census of India, 1931, Vol. VII, *Bihar and Orissa, Part II, Tables* (Patna: Superintendent Government Printing, 1932), Table I, p. 2; and Census of India, 1921, Vol. VII, *Bihar and Orissa, Part I, Report* (Patna: Superintendent Government Printing, 1923), foldout map; also Khan Sahib Shaikh Abdul Hakim, *Final Report on the Survey and Settlement Operation in the Saraikella State, District Singhbhum, 1925-1928* (Patna: Superintendent Government Printing, 1953), foldout map and Ch. I, p. 1; and N.C. Bosu, *Final Report on the Revisional Settlement of the Kharasawan Feudatory State, Chotanagpur, 1925-1927* (Patna: Superintendent Government Printing, 1953).

While the politics of the Jharkhand movement in 1994 is quite beyond the scope of this edited translation of Sahajanand's 1941 *Jharkhand ke Kisan* tract, nevertheless the point he makes about the similarities in geography and Adivasi culture of the immediately contiguous princely states and districts bears directly on the various proposals being mooted in 1994 for a Jharkhand state. The number of districts to be included in such a state depend entirely on the groups, parties, and leaders making the proposal at any given time. The figure appearing most often in the public press suggests that a potential Jharkhand state would include a total of twenty six districts, sixteen from Bihar and a total of ten from West Bengal, Orissa, and Madhya Pradesh. But to repeat, this is a fluid figure influenced by all the variables of contemporary politics which I have mentioned.

3 The details by which this issue were resolved are given in my Editor's Endnote 3 of the Introduction. The settlement involved the transfer of

a substantial portion of the old Manbhum district to West Bengal thereby implementing recommendations of the States Reorganization Commission of 1956. There was also a smaller tranfer of the south-western most parts of Manbhum to Singhbhum district at this time.

4 Sahajanand is referring here specifically to the Shiva temple at Deoghar, or Baidyanath Dham which is in fact a major pilgrimage site, especially for Hindu devotees of Bihar. It is also the case that Deoghar, because of its elevation has served as a holiday retreat for many visitors from Bengal.

5 I have added in brackets the concluding sentence of the paragraph which Sahajanand quotes here. See *Report of the Santal Parganas Inquiry Committee* (Patna: Superintendent Government Printing, 1938). The chairman of the committee was R.E. Russell, I.C.S., a prominent British administrator in Bihar. Its Indian members were Devendra Nath Samanta, Krishna Ballabh Sahay, Binodanand Jha, Abdul Bari, and Charan Murmu, all of whom were Members of the Legislative Assembly, and Maheshwar Prasad Jha, Pleader of Deoghar, and Rai Bahadur Shyam Narayan Singh, Member and Secretary. I list the Indian members here to note that it includes the name of one Santal participant in the committee's proceedings. It is a matter of representation and qualification Sahajanand refers to on many occasions in this manuscript as reflecting on the nature of politics and education in Jharkhand. The committee was constituted by resolution of the Bihar Legislative Assembly, September 2, 1937, "to inquire into the present administration of the Santal Parganas and report necessary changes to be made therein. (p. 1). As indicated in Endnote 12 of the Introduction, the first Congress Ministry in Bihar held office for a period just exceeding two years between mid-1937 and October 1939.

Note the variation in the spelling of Santal and Santhal in the name of the largest Adivasi group in Bihar. Sahajanand uses these spellings interchangeably though most often Santhal. I will follow the convention among most leading scholars in the field in using Santal. It is also the case that the Inquiry Committee's report of 1938 uses Santal as does the Peoples of India Project in 1994. See K.S. Singh, *The Scheduled Tribes*, People of India, National Series, Vol. III, Anthropological Survey of India (Delhi: Oxford University Press, 1994), pp. 1041-1051. I am also grateful to Dr. Sitakant Mahapatra, Secretary to the Government of India, Department of Culture, and himself an eminent scholar of Santal culture for clarifying this point in a recent conversation, New Delhi, July 15, 1994. As an example of Mahapatra's published usage see for example his "Bakhens: A Note on the Invocations of the Santals." in his edited volume, *The Realm of the Sacred:*

Verbal Symbolism and Ritual Structures (Calcutta: Oxford University Press, 1992), pp. 31-55.

6 Sahajanand refers specifically to Santals when speaking of Parasnath and there is of course a widely distributed Santal population outside of Santal Parganas including that in Hazaribagh. But Sahajanand's inference here is clearly to the general Adivasi population as well. There is a wide literature on the Adivasi diaspora and specifically on Santal migration. See for example Christopher V. Hill, "Philosophy and Reality in Riparian South Asia: British Famine Policy and Migration in Colonial North India," *Modern Asian Studies* 25 (May 1991), esp. pp. 273-279; and his "Santhal Bataidars in Purnia District: Ecological Evolution of a Sharecropping System," *EPW* (August 22, 1987), pp. 1450-54; and also Anand Chakravarti, "The Unfinished Struggle of Santhal Bataidars in Purnea District, 1938-42," *EPW* 21:42-43 (October 18-25, 1986), pp. 1847-65, and 1897-1909. For a more extended treatment of this issue see Hill, *River of Sorrow: Environment and Social Control in Riparian North India, 1770-1994* (Ann Arbor: Association for Asian Studies Monograph Series, forthcoming), based on Hill's 1987 University of Virginia dissertation, "History in Motion: the Social Ecology of Purnia District, 1770-1960." A final note to make clear that when Sahajanand was writing, Parasnath was in Hazaribagh. That part of Hazaribagh has now become the district of Giridih.

7 Sahajanand candidly defines here the limits of his activism among the peasants of Bihar and Jharkhand. There is a note of regret in these pages that the social and physical remoteness of the place and its tribal population in a sense prevented him from engaging in the kind of mobilization which he achieved so significantly in Gangetic Bihar. His experience in Jharkhand was limited and so too his full awareness of painful conditions of exploitation which he reveals so graphically in these pages. His reflections in the Hazaribagh Central Jail suggest an anxiety at an opportunity missed in serving the objects of justice and equity in Jharkhand as he had done elsewhere in his long career. It was an opportunity that would not present itself again or be seized in the years of activism that remained to Sahajanand before his death in 1950. This is a larger issue than there is space for in these brief remarks, though I have touched on the question of what did or did not happen after 1941 in the Editor's Intróduction to this edited translation. See also Editor's Endnote 6 to Sahajanand's Introduction of this tract.

8 Palamau has a long history of drought and near-famine conditions, most recently in 1993. Apart from the matter of topography and soil fertility to which Sahajanand refers here, there is the climatologically more

complex issue of Palamau's location in a monsoon rain shadow, resulting in rain shortfall even during years of a good monsoon elsewhere in the vicinity. The response to the drought conditions of the middle sixties in Bihar generally and Palamau specifically is recounted in K. Suresh Singh, *The Indian Famine, 1967: A Study in Crisis and Change* (New Delhi: People's Publishing House, 1975). The chief minister of Bihar at the time, Krishna Ballabh Sahay, paid daily air visits to Palamau to oversee the administration of famine relief efforts. I am indebted to Dr. K.S. Singh for his comments on this history in a conversation in New Delhi, June 26, 1994. Dr. Singh was Deputy Commissioner of Palamau at the time and in that capacity directly responsible for mobilizing famine relief. The Palamau famine can be dated from late 1965 to early 1968, with the most severe conditions in 1967.

9 Sahajanand makes no further reference to China either at this point or elsewhere in this tract and accordingly the precise point of his comparison is not entirely clear. The comparison with the fertile fields of Gangetic Bihar are rather more obvious, although more than fifty years after the fact one might want to qualify Sahajanand's observation on fertility generally in Jharkhand and the receptivity of the area to paddy cultivation. Changes in land use patterns, seed varieties, and techniques of cultivation will presumably have made some difference in agricultural production generally and including paddy more specifically. Certainly a casual drive and train trip through parts of Jharkhand in the early weeks of the monsoon season in June 1994, suggest widespread cultivation of paddy in the valleys and terraces of the region, barring of course the mountainous terrain to which Sahajanand rightly refers as imposing severe limitations on paddy cultivation by comparison with the fertile plains of Gangetic Bihar. As the People of India project makes clear, there is a more widely settled agriculture among the tribal populations of India in the 1990s than heretofore. The photographs on the dust jacket of this book suggest something of the prevalence of paddy as crop and food in the region. For patterns of cultivation and specifically with reference to rice, see K.S. Singh, People of India, National Series, Vol. III, *The Scheduled Tribes*, Anthropological Survey of India (Delhi: Oxford University Press, 1994), esp. pp. 6 and 10.

10 Netarhat lies at an elevation of 1140 metres above sea level. The minimum winter temperature can get as cold as zero degrees centigrade, that is, freezing.

11 Sahajanand's descriptive insight in 1941 that the natural wealth of Jharkhand is critical to the economy of the province as a whole obviously bears a significant relationship to the prospects for a separate

Jharkhand state and the various political responses to that demand in 1994, whether from the perspective of Patna or New Delhi.

12 Jharia is in the Dhanbad district which was before 1956 a part of the old Manbhum district. See Editor's Endnote 3 to Sahajanand's Introduction for details. Dhanbad and the Bokaro coalfields of the neighboring district of Hazaribagh, now Giridih, are major depositories.

13 There are of course many varieties of productive trees in the Jharkhand jungle, among them the Sal [Shorea Robusta], Palas [Butea Frondosa, Butea Mono Sperma], Kusum [Schleichera Trijuga, Schleichera Olcosa], Ber [Zizyphus Jujuba], and Mahua [Bassia Latifolia, Madhuka Latifolia]. The Sal is locally alse referred to as the sakhoo, or sakhua which are terms Sahajanand uses in this tract frequently. See also Glossary references under Sal, Lac, and Mahua.

14 It should be noted that the coal mines were nationalized by Prime Minister Indira Gandhi in 1971. It should further be noted that that act in itself has not ended the exploitation of the local population of Jharkhand. For a brief discussion of this issue see Victor Das, *Jharkhand: Castle Over The Graves* (New Delhi: Inter-India Publications, 1991), esp. pp. 192-93; and Arun Sinha "Struggle Against Bureaucratic Capitalism," and Nirmal Sengupta, "Background of Jharkhand," both in Nirmal Sengupta, ed., *Fourth World Dynamics: Jharkhand* (Delhi: Authors Guild Publications, 1982). Essays by Das, Sinha, and Sengupta, among other authors appear with some regularity on Jharkhand issues in the pages of the *Economic and Political Weekly* as well. See for example the five part series by Nirmal Sengupta, "Reappraising Tribal Movements," *EPW* 23:19-23 (May 7-June 4, 1988).

Chapter II

The People of Jharkhand and Their Languages

[In a sense this second chapter is a continuation of the first where Sahajanand defined the qualities and constraints geography placed on the people of Jharkhand. Here he makes comparisons with the other districts of Bihar to establish a scale of poverty based on population density, and of course, Jharkhand comes out near the bottom. It is an exploited place in every sense of the word, yet it is a source of enormous wealth and opportunity, and unless responsive changes are made, quite apart from attaching blame to the British, moves for a separate Jharkhand are likely to gain strength. In the latter part of the chapter Sahajanand refers to the richness of the languages and cultures of the Adivasis, to their distribution in the region and to the potential power an effectively organized movement could provide these heretofore voiceless people. Ed.]

In geographical terms, Jharkhand is essentially equal to the area of Viharkhand.[1] The total area of Bihar including Chotanagpur is 70,181 square miles of which Bihar proper measures 37,560 square miles and Jharkhand 32,621 square miles.[2] There is hardly a difference of 5,000 square miles between their respective areas. It is difficult to say why the Santal Parganas Inquiry Committee mentions in its report that the area inhabited by the Adivasis is little more than one-third of the total area of the province. To say so is inaccurate at best inasmuch as both regions are almost equal in land area.

As to population, the total numerical strength of the whole province in 1931 was 32,371,000 and by 1941 it had risen to 36,340,000.[3] One might assume that because the land area is almost identical the populations might also be the same, but in fact this is not the case. The total population of the six Jharkhand districts including the Santal Parganas is only 9,750,000, that is, less than one crore [10,000,000]. It is clear that the total population of this region is a little more than one-fourth of the total population of the whole province. And these figures include the Adivasis as well as non-Adivasis in the area! It is thus evident that the struggle for existence here is extremely difficult which is why the population has remained sparse. Where the soil is fertile, the population is always bound to be dense and the reverse is equally true.

The density of the four districts of Muzaffarpur, Darbhanga, Saran, and Patna is over 750 per square mile. If we now compare the area of these districts with their population, the relationship between density and fertility will become more clear. The area of Muzaffarpur is 3,444 square miles and its population is 3,244,651; that of Darbhanga is 3,451 square miles and the population is 3,457,070; that of Saran is 2,613 square miles and the population is 2,860,537 and that of Patna is 2,079 square miles and the population is 2,162,008. Of these districts, Darbhanga and Muzaffarpur have the most fertile soil. The Bagmati and Kamla rivers, however, do much damage to the soil in Darbhanga. This factor is absent in Muzaffarpur and hence the population of Muzaffarpur is more dense than that of Darbhanga, as is evident from the above statistics.[4] Saran District with its *mat* and *doras* soil is relatively less fertile than these two.[5] The soil of Patna is perhaps a little better [than that of Saran] and it produces a good paddy and dal [pulses] crop, which benefits from a developed canal system. However, it must be noted that the combined population of Patna and Danapur towns is somewhere between two and one-half to three lakhs. If this figure is excluded from the total population of the district, then it becomes clear that the productive capability of Patna would be less than that of Saran. This view is confirmed when we consider that the soil of north Bihar across the Ganges is generally held to be more fertile than that of south Bihar. Moreover the canal system in Patna is limited to only one of its four subdivisisons, that is Danapur, and covers only parts of that subdivision.

These points will be demonstrated in the same way in our analysis of the districts of Jharkhand. The total population of the Santal Parganas is 2,234,497 and the area 5,512 square miles; that of Manbhum is 2,032,146 and the area 4,204 square miles; that of Hazaribagh is 1,751,339 and the area 7,059 square miles; that of Ranchi is 1,675,413 and the area 7,099 square miles; that of Singhbhum is 1,144,717 and the area is 3,879 square miles and that of Palamau is 912,734 and the area is 4,868 square miles. But except for a few strips of paddy land, Palamau is essentially a barren plateau and the fertility of its soil is very poor. The Survey and Settlement Report confirms this assessment. Accordingly, the density of its population per square mile is the lowest in Jharkhand, that is between 100 to 200 per square mile [the actual density using Sahajannd's figures is 187.5].[6] Of the remaining districts, Ranchi [236], Hazaribagh [248.1], and Singhbhum [295.1] have an approximately equal capability of food grain production, and a population density varying between 200 and 350. The remaining two districts of Manbhum [483.38] and Santal Parganas [405.3] have a population density varying between 351 to 500 per square mile, making them somewhat higher in density than the other districts.[7] This is as reported by the Santal Parganas Inquiry Committee, which also comments on the production of rice and rabi crops and the various soil types in the district.

Of course, the district of Shahabad in Bihar proper is one whose density of population is comparable to that of Manbhum and Santal Parganas.[8] Without the presence of the Ganges, its fertility would have been less than these districts. It would have been, in many respects, similar to that of Palamau. But on account of its diara lands [land on the banks of the Ganges] and the irrigation facilities provided by a network of canals which are spread over its three subdivisions except Bhabhua, its productivity is relatively much better. As in Santal Parganas, its population density is between 351 and 500 per square mile. Its total area is 4,372 square miles and the population is 2,328,581.

Purnea is similar to Shahabad inasmuch as its density of population per square mile is also between 351 to 500. Purnea is no doubt a fertile area. But the ravages of the Kosi River is so sweepingly devastating that it has significantly affected the density of population. Thus Shahabad, on the south of the Ganges and in the western most part of the province, has essentially the same density of population as that of Purnea, the eastern most district of this province on the northern side of the Ganges. The total population of Purnea is 2,390,105 but with 5,175 square miles, its area is somewhat larger than that of Shahabad.

Let us now consider the other four districts of Bihar, that is Monghyr, Bhagalpur, Champaran and Gaya. They are in many respects very similar. The density of population per square mile in these areas varies between 501 to 750. The population of Bhagalpur is 2,408,879 and the area is 4,226 square miles. The total population of Monghyr is 2,564,544 and the area is 4,089 square miles. The population of Champaran is 2,397,569 and the area is 3,422 square miles and that of Gaya is 2,775,361 and the area is 4,689 square miles.

In making these demographic comparisons, it becomes clear that Jharkhand is at the bottom of any scale of poverty among all the districts of Bihar, and Palamau is the poorest of all. It is followed by Hazaribagh, Ranchi, and Singhbhum. Only two districts, Manbhum and Santal Parganas rank favourably with the two worst-placed districts of Biharkhand, namely Purnea and Shahabad. Accordingly, it is fair to say that when compared with Chotanagpur, Bihar is prosperous in all respects.[9]

There is no doubt, however, that the real centre of Bihar's wealth is Chotanagpur. If it were to be separated from Bihar it would be a death blow to the province. Of course it is already the case that the wealth of Jharkhand is largely exploited by outsiders. Even today a very insignificant proportion of this wealth is shared by the Biharis. But a time will come when this exploitation by outsiders will have to end, when the Tatas and others will not be able to exploit its wealth and drain it out to Bombay, Punjab, Gujarat or even outside the country.[10] Either they will have to surrender a significant portion of their income to Bihar or wind up their trade. Unless this is done the poverty of Bihar cannot be ended. And even now there is a powerful movement to separate Jharkhand from Bihar and if that were to happen, as I have already said, it would mean the death of the province. And it would also be a consequence of the neglect which Bihar has so long shown in discharging her responsibilities towards the people of Jharkhand. There is still time to avoid this result, but we will have to move positively and expeditiously in the effort.[11]

Thus far we have been concerned with the population of Jharkhand in numerical terms; now we will turn our attention to the actual condition of the people. Although the population of the region is roughly one-third that of Bihar proper, yet its inhabitants are in a sense voiceless. They lack the power to speak out about their sufferings and grievances nor are they familiar with present day means of agitating for their just rights. Otherwise, despite their smaller numbers, they could have threatened the entire province with their protestations of discontent. As a matter of fact they are so backward, so enveloped in darkness that they do not know of the new kinds of mass meetings, rallies, and demonstrations, nor how to mobilize them. Hence, whatever meetings or demonstrations they do manage to hold, fail to convey the true nature of their pain and suffering. The voices of the downtrodden and oppressed kisans are in fact not being heard. Their cries of agony and anguish are not audible in the present political environment. It is only the agitation of the middle class which we now see, and their concern for jobs, for electing their representatives to local boards and to the [Bihar Legislative] Assembly, and making public representations of their loyalty to government![12]

Had there been some political awakening among the original inhabitants of Jharkhand, a feeling of class consciousness as well as a sense of their just rights, had they possessed the ability of representing these rights and demands with conviction and without fear, the present state of affairs would not have existed. Though the condition of the kisans in Gangetic Bihar as well as other provinces is more or less similar, still, they have made some strides in mobilizing their interests. But here in Jharkhand the people are still lying in the depths of backwardness. It seems as if there has been an intentional attempt by certain groups to leave them in this state of affairs. Otherwise why have they not been educated till now? Whereas all round efforts have been made for educating the progressive castes [pragatisheel jatiyon], the cause of the Adivasis has suffered on account of total neglect.[13] I shall deal with this issue in detail at a later stage. Here I will only quote from page 44 of the Santal Parganas Inquiry Committee Report:

> There has been no development of aboriginal schools in recent years; in fact the position is now worse than it was 15 years ago. There is not a single school for the 60,000 Paharias in the

Damin Hills. In fifteen years the number of Santal children attending school has risen only from 12,020 to 13,448. The number of Santal primary schools has actually decreased from 465 to 403. This was largely due to the financial straits of the District Committee during the period of economic depression which affected all classes of schools. But the salient fact emerges that while between 1922 and 1937 the total number of schools have been reduced by 73, 62 of these were Santal schools. In fact, the most of the education retrenchment of the District Committee has been at the cost of the Santals.[14] <27.11.41>

It would be a weak excuse to say that the British government and its committees are responsible for these conditions. After all the British administration will not last forever. Sooner or later whichever government will be formed to run the administration of this province will be composed of and controlled by Biharis, the inhabitants of this province.[15] It is they who will have to bear the consequences of the conditions described in the Santal Parganas Report. Is it that someone else must bear the responsibilities for keeping a part of our collective body diseased, weak or paralytic? The one great consequence of having so long neglected our backward brethren (*pichre bhaiyon*) of this region is the persistent attempt on the one hand of uniting Chotanagpur with Bengal, and on the other hand of constituting it into a separate province. Wherefrom do the protagonists of these proposals get the issues (*masala*) which enable them to wage these agitations? In the background of our having neglected them so long, these simple people are being persuaded to believe that as long as they are a part of Bihar no one will take care of them. Is it not agreed that despite its being the source of much of Bihar's wealth and having the same area as that of Bihar proper, not even one Adivasis was included in the first Congress Ministry? Have not the Biharis all along been opposing the transfer of the headquarters of the Bihar government to Ranchi? Is this alone not sufficient reason for blame? Is it not a fact that a parliamentary secretary during the Congress Ministry, who belongs to Chotanagpur, had opposed the holding of the Legislative Assembly session at Ranchi?[16]

However, I was referring to the backwardness of the people of

Jharkhand. Its one most solid proof is the existence here in lakhs of upper castes of the Brahmans, Kshatriyas, Bania Mahajans, Kayasths, and others. Still, among a population of one crore the number of these outsiders is very insignificant.[17] They are like a drop in the ocean. I am not concerned, however, with who is Adivasis or who is non-Adivasis. We are only concerned with this much that those who are backward and are not able to raise their voices themselves, as the Biharis or the Bengalis do, constitute not less than eighty percent of the population of this region.[18] We are in fact concerned mainly with the true kisans of Chotanagpur. The upper sections of the population have actually migrated here from the outside to loot. Had they lived in harmony with the local population and earned their livelihood as such, I would have no criticism. In that case, they would have become a fully integrated part of the local population. Then the question of exploitation would not have arisen. For example, it is said that the Oraons migrated from Rohtasgarh to this place at some point in the past. And it is an accepted fact that the Paharias lived in the Santal Parganas from before and that the Santals appeared for the first time in 1810.[19] But it is never suggested that they came here as exploiters. Whenever and under whatever conditions they migrated they came with the sole purpose of earning their livelihood and gradually mingled with the original inhabitants.

The Sakas, Huns, and others migrated to India as well, as did the Muslims and the English. All except the English mingled with people and settled here; they came to live and to earn their livelihood. But the Britishers came here only to exploit the people and the country. Hence they never mixed with the people. This is exactly the condition of these civilized, educated and so-called high caste people (*unchi kahi janewali jatiyon*), who came to Jharkhand and settled down here purely as exploiters. Perhaps unlike the Britishers they have no connection with the outside world as such, yet their exploitation continues unabated. Certainly they are all connected with the world outside Jharkhand through marriage relationships. But there are others who have identified themselves with the Adivasis. Instead of being exploiters, they have remained backward like them. The *gwalas* [Yadavs or Ahirs], *kurmis*, and other such castes fall into this category. They came here to raise cows and buffaloes or to cultivate the fields and in course of time settled permanently. The Kurmis of this place are unlike the Kurmis of Bihar, but I am not here concerned with this issue and attach no importance to it. Whether they belonged to this place or came from the outside, in every circumstance they have mingled with the Adivasis. It is on this basis that the total population of the backward people of Jharkhand consitutes between eighty to ninety percent of the population of the region.[20]

In this connection the government have developed a new strategy designed, at least on the surface, to satisfy both the groups engaged in agitating for the cause of the Adivasis.[21] In the process government have served their purposes while at the same time posing problems for everyone else. They have added certain sections to the existing Tenancy Act in order that men of other castes may neither mortgage the lands of the backward castes [tribes] of this region for a temporary period nor buy them outright. This regulation is found in Sections 48, 208, 240 and 242 of the Chotanagpur Tenancy Act. A list of these tribes has been prepared by government. The Bihar Tenancy Act also includes such sections and there is a list of a number of castes there as well. Both the Adivasis [here meaning Scheduled Tribes] and the *pichri jatiyon* [Backward Castes, but here meaning Scheduled Castes] are included in this list.[22] The list for the Adivasis include the following: 1) Asur, 2) Banjara, 3) Bathuri, 4) Bentkar, 5) Binjhia, 6) Birhor, 7) Biyajiya, 8) Chero, 9) Chik Baraik, 10) Godaba, 11) Ghatwar, 12) Gond, 13) Gorait, 14) Ho, 15) Juang, 16) Karmali, 17) Kharia, 18) Kharwar, 19) Khetauri, 20) Khond, 21) Kisan, 22) Koli, 23) Kora, 24) Korwa, 25) Mahli, 26) Mal Pahariya, 27) Munda, 28) Oraon, 29) Parhiya, 30) Santal, 31) Sauriya Pahariya, 32) Sabar or Savar, and 33) Tharu.[23]

The table of the Scheduled Castes (*pichri jatiyon*) includes the following: 1) Chamar, 2) Chaupal, 3) Dhobi, 4) Dusadh, 5) Dom, 6) Halalkhor, 7) Hari, 8) Kanjar, 9) Kurariyar, 10) Lalbegi, 11) Mochi, 12) Musahar, 13) Nat, 14) Pasi, 15) Bauri, 16) Bhokta, 17) Bhuiyan, 18) Bhumij, 19) Ghasi, 20) Pan, 21) Rajwar, 22) Turi.[24]

There is no mention here of the Koeris, Gwalas, Kurmis, etc. Probably some of the educated among these castes might have felt a sense of pride in not being included in the list of the *pichri jatiyon* [Backward Castes and here meaning Scheduled Castes]. They might have felt ashamed at being enumerated along with the Pasis, Chamars, and other similar castes. But this is a mistake. What is the benefit in concealing the truth? For example, when one considers the relative degree of education and literacy among these groups, the results are very revealing. Yet when the question of special seats in the Legislative Assembly or on the local boards arises, or concessions to appointments in the services are considered, these castes at once demand special facilities on account of their being members of the backward castes too. There is no scope for this kind of mentality.[25]

When we think about the population of the region we must also consider the question of languages and dialects. It is true that the Bengalis and the Biharis who have settled here speak their own Bengali and Hindi. It is also true that people from different districts of Bihar have come and settled here and speak their own dialects of Magahi and Bhojpuri and write in the Kaithi script. Even the survey *khatian* is written only in Kaithi. It is thus clear that Bihar has put its mark on Jharkhand, although no one has this right. How can the indigenous people who constitute the majority of the population have any knowledge of the Kaithi script?[26] But who cares for the voiceless poor? It is only the educated few who are taken care of inasmuch as they know how to agitate and represent their interests. When the poor are reminded of this fact, they certainly feel its pain. They cannot understand what is happening or why, and can only stand by in helpless agony. For example, it is on the basis of these *khatians* in the Kaithi script that they have been deprived of all their rights in the jungle! These *khatians* are regarded as more authentic than the Vedas, the Bible and the Koran as far as the question of rights over lands are concerned! What an unmitigated travesty this is!

In fact the Adivasis have their own languages and dialects. The Santal, the Oraon and the Munda have their own languages as do the Ho. If one knows the Santali and Mundari languages, then even without knowing the languages of the Oraon and the Ho, one can manage. Similarly can one manage knowing Oraon or Ho. It is said that these two languages are more or less similar to the other two. The truth, however, is that these four languages, the Santali, Mundari, the Oraon and the Ho, have their own independent existence. For example, when peasants speaking these languages begin to talk among themselves in their colloquial tongue, then they will not understand, or be understood by a kisan speaking a different language. Hindi or Bengali speakers may by guesswork follow a bit of such a conversation. But it is quite a different thing to know a language intimately. When ordinary persons cannot understand one another's languages, it must be accepted that their languages are in fact different.

Although both the Munda and the Oraon are addressed by the common word Kol, yet these are two different tribes (*jatiyon*) and have no points of similarity. So too the Santals are different from these two and the Ho are again separate from these three. Their languages are different as are their manners and customs, so much so that they are mostly found living in separate regions. The Paharia, like the Santals are also different with their own language. They are mostly found in the Damin-i-koh or the Damin area of the Santal Parganas. This area, technically called the Khas Mahal is directly controlled by the government. The common border of the four subdivisions, that is Godda, Rajmahal, Pakaur and Dumka and the lands surrounded by them are commonly known as the Damin or the Khas Mahal tract. It lies at the foot of the hills and is surrounded by them. In Persian the word *koh* means mountain and *daman* means lap, womb, stretching at the foot of, or in Hindi *terai*. Hence Damin or Damin-i-koh literally means at the foot of or in the lap of the mountains.

The Santals have their homeland in the Santal Parganas. They are also found in the north eastern part of Hazaribagh as well as in parts of Manbhum which are contiguous to that district. Generally speaking nearly the whole of Hazaribagh is interspersed with a Santal population. The whole of the foot of the Parasnath Hills is inhabited by the Santals. The Santals also stretch into parts of Dhanbad as well. And from parts of southern Hazaribagh the Santals merge into Ranchi, a large part of which they also inhabit. The western and middle portions of Ranchi are mostly inhabited by the Oraons, and the Mundas are largely found in the southerwestern parts of that district. This area stretches into parts of Singhbhum and is a contiguous whole with it. Then, parts of Singhbhum and especialy the Dalbhum subdivision are inhabited by villages of Hos. As I have already mentioned, the Paharias are largely settled in the Damin area. The border between Palamau and Ranchi is mostly occupied by the Oraons who are to be found in both the districts as are a number of other tribes (*log*). A particular tribal group (*log*) called the "Kisan" are to be found in the area where the Mahuadand thana of the Palamau district and the Lohardaga thana of the Ranchi district meet. I have myself talked to the people of this area. But only Adivasis are found in the western, southern, eastern, southeast, southwest, and some parts of northeast and northwest portions of the Palamau district. Kurmis are found in several parts of Manbhum on the border with Hazaribagh and a good number in Hazaribagh itself. Finally, while I have indicated the concentrations of Adivasi populations throughout Jharkhand, it is also true that all groups are found scattered throughout the region living in peaceful interaction.

The most important fact about the Adivasis of Jharkhand is that though they are backward, yet they are not so depressed as are the backward people of Bihar proper or of other areas. There the backward classes [meaning Untouchable castes] are most often found to be khet mazdoors [agricultural labourers], or just like khet mazdoors, excepting in those areas where they are in a majority and own their own fields. The Mundas, Oraons etc. are kisans (*pakke kisans*) in the real sense of the term, indeed they have been so for generations. They love their land as much as they love their jungle. They cannot live without these two central elements of their lives.[27] The varieties of agricultural lands which they own and cultivate is proof of this deep attachment. A detailed description of their agriculture will be provided later in this manuscript.

As I have indicated, a particular tribe (*jati*) known as the "Kisan" is found in Jharkhand. I have encountered this "Kisan" name only in one other place, in Farrukhabad in the United Provinces. The word "Krishani" prevalent in the Santal Parganas is used in the same sense. The term is also used to describe a type of *bhaoli* or *batai* cultivation practised there. This fact is also mentioned in the Santal Parganas Inquiry Committee Report.[28] It is for these reasons and because the Adivasis are true kisans that I have titled this book *Jharkhand ke Kisan*, i.e., *The Kisans of Jharkhand* rather than *Jharkhand ke Niwasi*, i.e., *The Inhabitants of Jharkhand.* No one other than these Adivasi kisans are the original inhabitants of this place. The Kurmis and the Gwalas are also true (*pakke*) kisans. The Adivasis are a vital and active people. They are not weak, depressed, and crushed like the Harijans [Untouchables] of Gangetic Bihar.[29] Hence if they are organized on the basis of their class interest (*varghit*) they can become a powerful force (*apurva shakti*) whom no one can crush. They have only recently been deprived of their freedom (*azadi*). Hence a feeling of great strength still flows in their blood.[30]

Editor's Endnotes to Chapter II

1 See Sahajanand's Introduction and Editor's Endnote 5 of the Introduction for a consideration of the terms Viharkhand and Biharkhand.

2 The differences between Sahajanand's area figures for all of Bihar and those of the 1931 Census are incidental and we will accordingly not concern ourselves here with modifications and qualifications. For details see Census of India, 1931, Vol. VII, *Bihar and Orissa, Part II, Tables* (Patna: Superintendent Government Printing, 1932), Table I, p. 2. Boundary changes resulting from the recommendations of the States Reorganization Commission of 1956, as they affected Bihar are discussed in Editor's Endnote 3 of the Sahajanand's Introduction.

3 For the decadal population figures and variation between 1931 and 1991, see Editor's Endnote 7 of Sahajanand's Introduction. Sahajanand's 1931 figure is accurately based on the 1931 Census which varies from the 1931 figure shown in the 1991 series by one million. It turns out that Sahajanand's 1941 figure is also correct. He had rounded it off from the official 1941 Census total of 36,340,151. Like the 1991 figures for 1931, this figure also varies upward by approximately one million from that given in the 1991 series.

4 Sahajanand's calculations here are not entirely accurate and his area figures are apparently also somewhat skewed. If we use his figures we have per square mile densities as follows: Muzaffarpur, 942; Darbhanga, 1001.7; Patna, 1040; and Saran, 1094.7. The actual densities for these four districts are respectively, 1075, 1034, 991, and 1072. So in fact Muzaffarpur does have a somewhat higher density than Darbhanga although Sahajanand's figures show the reverse. In the two districts where his density figures are lower, namely Muzaffarpur and Darbhanga, Sahajanand apparently used area figures greater than is the case, and for Patna and Saran he apparently used lesser area figures. Finally, whichever set of figures we use, it should be noted that population densities in the Gangetic districts being discussed here are substantially above the 750 benchmark Sahajanand employs. See Endnote 7 below for a full list of population densities for the Bihar districts based on Sahajanand's data.

5 Doras is a kind of mixed soil, consisting of soils known as matiar and balua, that is, clay and sand. Again, using Sahajanand's figures, Saran would have the highest density, therefore by his logic be potentially the most fertile. In any event both by his calculations and the actual densities, Saran has a greater density than that of Patna, whether

one includes the Patna urban complex in the calculations or not. It should also be noted that the densities for Saran, Darbhanga, and Muzaffarpur were almost identical in 1941. See Editor's Endnote immediately above.

6 We need to keep in mind that Sahajanand is writing in late 1941 and that the figures he is using are 1941 Census figures. In the remainder of this discussion of population densities and soil fertility in Jharkhand, we will include the densities in brackets at the appropriate point in the text, using Sahajanand's area and population figures in making this calculation. While the 1941 Census was a limited one, nevertheless it needs to be said that Sahajanand's population figures for the province and the Jharkhand districts are entirely accurate. His variations on area for the Jharkhand districts are minimal.

7 Sahajanand was apparently using given benchmark figures rather than making calculations based on the area and population figures he was using, hence the rather substantial variation in some cases in the actual densities and the benchmark group in which he places them. For purposes of comparison, I will list following the densities by district as Sahajanand gives them, placing them in the benchmark categories he provides. For all the districts excepting the first four, Sahajanand's data reveal density figures very close to the actual densities. Accordingly, I will indicate the actual densities only for the first four districts. See also Endnote 4 above for a more detailed comment on these four districts.

	(Over 750 per square mile)	
District	Given Density	Actual
Muzaffarpur	942	1075
Darbhanga	1001.7	1034
Saran	1094.7	1072
Patna	1040	991
	(Between 351-500)	
Santhal Parganas	405.3	
Manbhum	483.34	
	(Between 200-350)	
Hazaribagh	248.1	
Ranchi	236	
Singhbhum	295.1	
	(Between 100-200)	
Palamau	187.5	
	(Between 351-500)	
Shahabad	532.6	

Purnea	461.8
	(Between 501-750)
Monghyr	627.18
Bhagalpur	570
Champaran	700.63
Gaya	591.88

8 Actually, as is apparent in the listing of densities immediately above, Shahabad's density is substantially higher than that of Manbhum and especially that of Santal Parganas. Similarly, the variation between Shahabad and Purnea is rather more considerable than Sahajanand allows in the paragraph following, where he suggests that they are essentially identical.

9 Sahajanand's comparisons between population density or man-land ratios, agricultural productivity, and levels of poverty are of course revealing but need to be qualified and elaborated as he himself begins to do. For example, he tells us that productivity is affected not only by soil types, but by the availability of water whether that of rivers, rains, or irrigation, and that it can also be seriously damaged by rivers, most notoriously in Bihar the Kosi of Purnea. Among other factors which need to be considered are inputs of seed types and the use of fertilizers and pesticides, quite apart from the need for modest investment capital. At a larger macro level of meaning, cropping patterns from one place to another must be taken into account, as does the history of changing land use patterns region-wide and within given areas like Jharkhand. The most recent scholarship on the Kosi and what it has meant historically for Purnea and its people is the work of Christopher V. Hill, *River of Sorrow: Environment and Social Control in Riparian North India, 1770-1994* (Ann Arbor: Association for Asian Studies Monograph Series, Forthcoming). See Editor's Endnote 6, Chapter I for related references.

The literature on the relationship between agricultural production and population is vast, and I will cite only one or two references which make specific connections with Bihar. The most important title, essentially contemporaneous with Sahajanand's writing and raising some of the same regionally comparative questions within Bihar, is Birendra N. Ganguly, *Trends of Agriculture and Population in the Ganges Valley: A Study in Agricultural Economics* (London: Methuen & Co., 1938). The best recent work on changing land use patterns historically in Bihar is that of James R. Hagen. See for example J.F. Richards, James R. Hagen and Edward S. Haynes, "Changing Land Use in Bihar, Punjab and Haryana, 1850-1970," in *Modern Asian Studies,* 19:3 (1985), especially pp. 705-711, and Tables 2 and 3, and Appendix I. Hagen defines three related historical phenomena, first, the process through which agriculture reached the optimal natural limit or "margin" of cultivation, in other words, the point in time when population relative to arable land was essentially equalized. Near margins were reached as early as the late 19th century, and in most districts of Chotanagpur the limit of cultivable arable was reached by 1950. For the six districts of Jharkhand this fact had two critical and identifiable results, namely an expansion of arable land between 1870 and 1970 of 30.6 percent and a consequent decline of forest and woodland cover of 40 percent. The process by which this deforestation happened involved not only the expanding of arable land but timber and firewood extraction, among other causes, and is part of the experience of the peasants of Jharkhand with which Sahajanand is concerned in this tract. The Richards, Hagen, and Haynes essay provides additional titles for those readers who wish to pursue this complex issue beyond this brief introductory note. It might also be noted here that the official literature of the time was certainly aware of the fact and consequences of deforestation, if in somewhat subdued tones. See for example, Report of the Santal Parganas Inquiry Committee (Patna: Superintendent Government Printing, 1938), pp. 35-36.

Apart from the few references I have provided on the relationships between deforestation and arable space, there is a wide literature both on the ecological and social meanings of deforestation. Madhav Gadgil and Ramchandra Guha, *This Fissured Land: An Ecological History of India* (Delhi: Oxford University Press, 1993), is a valuable introduction; and Guha's, *The Unquiet Woods: Ecological Change and Peasant Resistance in the Himalaya* (Delhi: Oxford University Press, 1991), is a more specialized but equally valuable title. For a brief consideration of the forest in the current discussion of Adivasi identity and rights, see S. Basu Mullick, et al., *Indigenous Identity: Crisis and Reawakening* (Delhi: Navdin Prakashan Kendra, 1993), especially the brief section on "The Adivasi and Forest," pp. 46-58. The work of Prabhu Mohapatra cited throughout these Endnotes especially his "Aspects of Agrarian Economy of Chotanagpur, 1880-1950," PhD thesis, JNU, 1990, is specifically relevant here.

A final and related point which Sahajanand also touches on is the question of who controls the resources of agricultural production and how are those resources and the product itself distributed to the population at large, in this case the kisans of Jharkhand. An incidental but pointed vignette from the contemporary present tells an important part of the story. It is reported that in the 1990s the largest number of tractors in Bihar is found in those districts now comprising the former Purnea district, which Sahajanand ranked among the least well-off districts in the province. Tractors in this case may be an index of production, but they are even more certainly an index of the large number of landlords with holdings sufficiently large to justify tractor ownership in their farming operations. Those holdings are presumably in many cases beyond the ceiling limits imposed by law for those landholders. In this agrarian environment, this then reveals much about the mechanisms of control in social and economic terms in this place. It is an issue to which Sahajanand devoted most of his career of peasant activism in Gangetic Bihar and which is at the core of much of his argument in the present text.

10 Based on current press reports and much of the published literature on Jharkhand, New Delhi and indeed Patna would perhaps now be added to that list both for economic and political reasons. See for example, Janak Singh, "Bill On Jharkhand May Again Create Problems," *The Times of India*, New Delhi edition, July 14, 1994, p. 5, quoting both Mr. Gyan Ranjan, the leading Congress Party spokesman on Jharkhand and Mr. Shibu Soren, M.P. and president of the Jharkhand Mukti Morcha (Soren) on the issue in these terms. See also Editor's Endnote 14 of Chapter I.

11 That Sahajanand should be observing on this issue in these terms in 1941 is a remarkable comment on his sensitivity to the emotional and political weight which the Jharkhand idea was already generating more than five decades ago. It is also a comment on the persistence of the idea, and one might suggest, on the remoteness of its realization despite the determination of literally generations of tribal and non-tribal activists in the effort since, all in effect elaborating the argument about the condition of the kisans of Jharkhand and their exploitation which Sahajanand adduces in this tract.

12 This paragraph and the next are among Sahajanand's most pointed in describing the tension between the condition of the kisans of Jharkhand, their exploitation and voicelessness on the one hand and the great potential for positive change should their rights and demands be represented in serious, "new kinds" of political mobilization. This is Sahajanand the deeply committed peasant activist speaking, reflecting on the possibilities for achieving a measure of justice in Jharkhand based on his experience of twelve years of such efforts in Gangetic Bihar itself. See also Editor's Endnote 6 of the Introduction, and Endnote 7 of Chapter I, for related observations on Sahajanand's background and his perceptions of his role in the history and possibilities he sees for Jharkhand as an arena for agrarian change.

A parenthetic aside from the perspective of 1994 and the 20/20 hindsight it provides on what has transpired in the five decade since Sahajanand wrote these lines, might be of related interest to the Swami's

1941 call for "new kinds" of political mobilization. Apart from the early history of the Jharkhand Party to which I have referred in my Endnote 9 to Sahajanand's Introduction, there has of course been a proliferation of political groups, movements, and parties mobilized to achieve one object or another for Jharkhand and its people. The rallies, bandhs, dharnas, blockades, and other agitations which are a daily part of all Indian politics and parties, are no less so for the various Jharkhand parties, movements, and activists in 1994. Sahajanand's observation on this new politics of mobilization would presumably be one of considerable interest in what is happening and perhaps some degree of qualified cynicism in the way it was happening.

13 While the political and social lexicon has changed over the 53 years since Sahajanand's writing, his term pragatisheel jatiyon refers to upper castes, most of whom are outsiders whether Bihari, Bengali, or from other parts of India. The 1994 usage here would be "forward" castes. But it is useful to remember that for Sahajanand this is a broad category almost always followed by an etc., which includes, if he does not specifically mention them Punjabis, Jains, Pathans, Muslims, Banias, and others, most often outsiders.

14 See also Editor's Endnote 5 of Chapter I on the Santal Parganas Inquiry Committee Report, and the constitution of the Committee. Of interest here, in that segment of the Report from which Sahajanand quotes but does not use here, the Committee candidly explains that it is the "Dikku schools [which] always get the preference," in educational funding, to the neglect of the "interests of the aboriginal population in this matter." (44) The Dikkus [also Diku] are the non-tribal outsiders who dominate Jharkhand and whom Sahajanand refers to again and again in this tract, in precisely the terms I have mentioned in the preceding Endnote. The dominant and exploiting Dikkus are to be distinguished from the non-tribal Sadans who are also outsiders, but who have integrated into the local social and cultural environment. See Report of the Santal Parganas Inquiry Committee (Patna: Superintendent Government Printing, 1938), p. 44.

15 However obvious it may seem in 1994, Sahajanand's observation that even in British India the British are not responsible for everything, and that they will in any event be leaving sooner than later, and that there will be a new Indian leadership in positions of power and responsibility, these observations tell us much about the man and his insights both for his time and for the nature of India's future as a free society.

16 The specific reference here is to Krishna Ballabh Sahay, parliamentary secretary during the first Congress Ministry, and subsequently Bihar's fourth Chief Minister from October 1963 to March 1967. Sahay was

from Hazaribagh. Again in this paragraph Sahajanand touches some of the raw political nerves that are at issue in the relationship between the advocates of autonomy or statehood for Jharkhand and the Government of Bihar, and indeed the Centre. See especially Endnotes 10, 11, 12, 18, and 20 of this Chapter II, and any of the daily press reports, scholarly monographs, and political tracts on the Jharkhand issue over the last many decades. Sahajanand's observation is in that sense pointedly relevant to the current debate although its central importance obviously is that of a historical document of its time. That relevance simply reinforces its importance as a text from 1941, 53 years removed from the perspective of hindsight we have in 1994.

17 As indicated previously, one crore is 10,000,000. A lakh is 100,000, and accordingly 10 lakhs equals 1,000,000 and 100 lakhs equals one crore. I have referred in Endnote 13 immediately above to whom Sahajanand is referring when he ends his sentence either with etc., as he does often, or with the words, and others.

18 Sahajanand's reference to the "not less than eighty percent of the population," who are the voiceless Adivasi and backward peasants, is a percentage number constantly in flux with the Adivasi proportion in decline against the population as a whole, thereby in fact reinforcing some of Sahajanand's central logic in this tract. The one qualification to keep in mind is that Sahajanand includes in his percentage figure non-tribal backward castes. See Editor's Endnote 20, following. In a 1990 report, Ram Dayal Munda examines the tribal non-tribal issue in the following terms:

"The influx of an outside population has led the 60/40 tribal/non-tribal population ratio in 1951 to become 40/60 in 1981, just the reverse in 30 years. The irony of the situation is that while the external population is coming in, people from the Chotanagpur area are forced to leave in search of menial jobs in far away places like Punjab, Assam, and elsewhere. There are provisions for 80 percent reservation for tribal and local people in training and jobs but the fact is that nearly 90 percent of the training facilities and jobs (in general education, engineering and medicine) are filled by an external population." See Ram Dayal Munda, *The Jharkhand Movement: Retrospect and Prospect, A Report Submitted to Home Minister Buta Singh* (Ranchi: Jharkhand Coordination Committee, 1990), p. 10.

The point here is clear, namely that if Sahajanand's 1941 estimate was correct, the ratio of the tribal and backward population to the total population has been substantially reduced however one makes the calculation. We should also keep in mind that Munda's figure was for 1981 and it is now 1994. The issue is still a major bone of contention as revealed in the reactions to the Centre's proposal for an Autonomous Council in Jharkhand, but which would apply only to those 116 blocks with a heavy tribal concentration rather than to the 200 blocks comprising the Jharkhand districts of the Chotanagpur plateau, a solution meant to respond to the needs and demands of the region as a whole. See Janak Singh, "Bill on Jharkhand May Again Create Problems," *The Times of India*, New Delhi Edition, July 14, 1994, p. 5. While it is outside the scope of these Endnotes and this 1941 political tract, it might be noted parenthetically that the Centre is presently processing a Bill for formal Presidential Orders under Article 201 of the Constitution on this issue. This procedure follows on the failure of the Centre to gain acceptance by the State Government of Bihar to proposed modifications of the Jharkhand Area Development Council Bill of 1991. The present bill which would provide for another Jharkhand Autonomous Council may or may not be introduced in the current monsoon session of the Parliament, and if it is, of course, like all other bills, subject to amendment. As I have indicated before, the public press in Delhi, Patna, and many other major dailies covers this story regularly and in detail. For example, a thorough treatment can be found on the front page of *The Pioneer*, July 22, 1994, under the title "Jharkhand by August 15, Says Soren Faction." This is a reference to the Jharkhand Mukti Morcha (S), but the demand for a separate state has the support of virtually every major political party in the country, and certainly all the regional parties in Bihar. The point is nicely made by noting that the Starred Question on the subject in the Lok Sabha session of July 28, 1994, was raised jointly by Bihar MPs from the JMM(S) and the Bharatiya Janata Party, and the Unstarred Question on the Jharkhand Autonomous Council in the Rajya Sabha or Upper House was raised on August 3, 1994 by a Communist Party of India MP.

The Janak Singh report further notes that the non-tribal population of the Jharkhand belt "constitute more than 60 percent of the region's population," thus reinforcing Munda's 1981 figure and suggesting that the trend of a growing non-tribal population in the region continues. The most dramatic figure is the suggestion made by Ranjit Hoskote that through a continuing process of "mass evictions," and land alienation, the tribal population of Chotanagpur has "now been reduced to a mere 30 percent." See "If You Are Poor, You Are Out," *The Sunday Times of India Review*, July 17, 1994. It is perhaps relevant to note in view of the general perceptions of tribal and non-tribal populations in Bihar that as early as 1961, the Census of that year noted that whereas "93.7 percent of the tribals [of Bihar] are to be found in

[Chotanagpur and Santal Parganas], they constitute just one-third of the plateau's population." Census of India, 1961, Vol. IV, Bihar, Part V-A, *Special Tables for Scheduled Castes and Scheduled Tribes* (Patna: Superintendent of Census Operations, 1965). Based on the 1981 Census the 30 percent figure is the one now generally accepted and used in official discussions. This figure is also confirmed by Dr. Sachchidananda, a scholar intimately familiar with the region, who in fact places the Adivasi percentatage of the Jharkhand population at between 26 to 30 percent. (In a conversation at Patna, June 25, 1994.)

If these figures are accepted as representing an approximation of the proportion of Adivasi population in Jharkhand, it is then perhaps relevant to note that the Sadan population of non-Adivasis, long resident in the region and in many respects significantly integrated into the tribal environment, are generally presumed to constitute approximately 50 percent of the population of the region. For example the Kurmi Mahatos are an important element of this Sadan population. The balance of the population is then comprised of those who have migrated into Jharkhand historically and more recently from other parts of Bihar and India and whom Sahajanand in 1941 refers to as outsiders and exploiters, pejoratively defined as Dikus. See also Editor's Endnote 8 of Sahajanand's Introduction, Note 14 of Chapter I, and Notes 10, 11, 16, and 23 of this Chapter II; and Endnote 9 of Chapter III.

19 The most recent reference on tribal India confirms the Oraon story and puts the date of Santal migration into the present Santal Parganas as starting "after the famine of AD 1770," which is not significantly at variance with Sahajanand's 1810 date. See K.S. Singh, *The Scheduled Tribes*, People of India, National Series, Vol. III, Anthropological Survey of India (Delhi: Oxford University Press, 1994), pp. 948-957, and 1041-1051. Please note that I also use the spelling of Paharia preferred in the People of India project rather than Pahariya as used by Sahajanand and others. See Singh, *The Scheduled Tribes*, pp.714-718.

20 In referring to Gwalas and Kurmis as among those non-Adivasis who are however integrated into the local society, Sahajanand is making the distinction between Sadans on the one hand and Dikus, or non-Adivasi outsiders who have come to exploit the land and the people of Jharkhand. While Sahajanand uses the term Diku, he distinguishes between Dikus and Sadans descriptively without in fact actually using the term Sadan. These distinctions continue to be important in the contemporary debate. See for example the critical reactions of both Mr. Shibu Soren, M.P. of the Jharkhand Mukti Morcha (Soren) and Mr. Gyan Ranjan, M.L.C. of the Indian National Congress to the pro-

posed Autonomous Council Bill presently being mooted by the Centre, to the effect that the "Centre will be playing with fire if it tried to divide the tribals and non-tribals by creating separate administrative set-ups for them." Mr. Gyan Ranjan is reported to have asked ". . . why [is] the government determined to create a divisive wall between communities who have been living together for generations? Both tribals and non-tribals have suffered from the stepmotherly treatment of the Patna-based government. Then why ignore the Sadans (the non-tribals)?" Details on the issue and the debate can be found in Janak Singh, "Bill on Jharkhand May Again Create Problems," *The Times of India*, New Delhi Edition, July 14, 1994. See also Editor's Endnote 18, this Chapter, above. Ram Dayal Munda makes a similar point when he writes that "In Chotanagpur the biggest sufferers of the reservation policy . . . have been the local non-tribals (i.e., the Sadans and the Kurmis). Most of these posts [Grade III and Grade IV positions] go to the outsider non-tribals, fake certificates are issued to the outsider non-tribals as in most cases it is the outsider non-tribal who sits in the chair of authority that issues these fake certificates. There have been cases where higher caste candidates have changed their names to fit the job description meant for the weaker sections." See Munda, *The Jharkhand Movement: Retrospect and Prospect* (Ranchi: Jharkhand Co-ordination Committee, 1990), p. 11. See also Editor's Endnote 18, immediately above on this issue.

Please note that whereas Dikku and Diku are both common English spellings for the disparaging reference to non-Adivasi, exploiting outsiders, I will most often use the term Diku which my professional informants tell me is the proper English spelling. Sahajanand most often uses Dikku, so some of those spellings may appear in this edited translation as well.

21 Sahajanand's reference here is presumably to the demands and movements of the forward castes and other outsiders on the one hand and to those expressed by the Adivasis and other backward groups, or to the demands for political and social change made on their behalf.

22 Depending on the context, Sahajanand here uses the term backward castes to mean either Scheduled Tribes or Scheduled Castes, i.e., Adivasis or Untouchables, respectively. He does not use the term tribe in this manuscript but jati, or most often Adivasi, Adi Janata, Moolvasi, Mool Nivasi, Adivasiyon, Adi Nivasiyon, Asli Nivasi, referring to the original inhabitants of Jharkhand. In reading Sahajanand's 1941 tract we perhaps also need to remind ourselves that the terms Scheduled Castes and Scheduled Tribes are essentially a post 1947 terminology, and that the term Backward Classes, or Other Backward Classes is a

function of the more recent definitions of the Mandal Commission and its reflections in the politics of the 1990s. For a further discussion of the politics and terminology of these categories see my essay, "Violence, Agrarian Radicalism and Electoral Politics: Reflections on the Indian People's Front," in *The Journal of Peasant Studies* 21:1 (October 1993), Note 5, p. 117; Marc Galanter, "The Abolition of Disabilities—Untouchability and the Law," in J. Michael Mahar, ed., *The Untouchables in Contemporary India* (Tucson: University of Arizona Press, 1972), pp. 243, 298; and R.S. Khare, *The Untouchable as Himself: Ideology, Identity, and Pragmatism Among the Lucknow Chamars* (Cambridge: Cambridge University Press, 1984), pp. 83-84, 154. See also Endnotes 13 and 25 of this Chapter for related observations.

23 Sahajanand includes 34 groups in his list of Scheduled Tribes. The 1961 Census of India identifies 30 Scheduled Tribes in its list, and K.S. Singh identifies 26 Scheduled Tribes in Bihar of the 461 listed for all of India. There is heavy overlap in these lists and the difference in numbers is accounted for at least in part by variations in spelling and by Sahajanand including Adivasi groups identified by the People of India Project as situated in neighboring states. The Census volume also has an unclassified category which will inevitably account for some variation in numbers as well.

The population of Scheduled Tribes in Bihar for 1931 was 3,145,082; 1961, 4,204,770; and 1991, 6,617,000. In 1961 that population constituted 9.05 percent of the population of the state, and was concentrated almost wholly (93.7 percent) in Chotanagpur and Santal Parganas; in 1991 the tribal population constituted 7.66 percent of the population of Bihar which was 86,374,000. The all-India figures are a Scheduled Tribe population of 67,758,000, or 8.08 percent of the total 1991 population of 838,584,000, excluding Jammu and Kashmir where there was no census in 1991 (The 1981 figure for Jammu and Kashmir when the last census was conducted in the state, was 5,987,389. The estimated projection for 1991 is 7,723,732, which would thus give us a 1991 all-India figure of 846,307,732). Accordingly, the Adivasi population of Bihar constituted 9.76 percent of the Adivasi population for all of India. See K.S. Singh, People of India, National Series Vol. III, *The Scheduled Tribes*, Anthropological Survey of India (Delhi, Oxford University Press, 1994), pp. 1212-1228; Census of India, 1961, Vol. IV, Bihar, Part V-A, *Special Tables For Scheduled Castes and Scheduled Tribes* (Patna: Superintendent of Census Operations, 1965), pp. x, xiii; and Census of India, 1991, Series I, India, Paper-1 of 1993, *Union Primary Census Abstract For Scheduled Castes and Scheduled Tribes* (New Delhi: Registrar General and Census Commissioner, 1993),

Table 1, p. 11. Refer also to Endnote 13 of this Chapter.

24 Sahajanand shows 22 Untouchable Castes, what he refers to as Backward Castes, in his list. The 1961 Census lists 23 Scheduled Castes apart from an unclassified category of Harijans. The population of Scheduled Castes in Bihar for 1931 was 4,504,593; for 1961, 6,536,875; and for 1991, 12,572,000 out of a Bihar population of 86,374,000, or 14.55 percent. The all-India figure is 138,223,000 of an Indian population of 838,584,000 (see Endnote 23 preceding for figures on Jammu and Kashmir), or 16.48 percent. See Census of India, 1961, Vol. IV, Bihar, Part V-A, *Special Tables For Scheduled Castes and Scheduled Tribes* (Patna Superintendent of Census Operations, 1965), pp ix, xii; and Census of India, 1991, Series-1, India, Pater-1 of 1993, *Union Primary Census Abstract For Scheduled Castes and Scheduled Tribes* (New Delhi: Registrar General and Census Commissioner, 1993), Table I, p. 11. See also Galanter, Hauser, and Khare references in Endnote 22 above on the issue of the terms Scheduled Caste, Harijan, and Untouchable as they have developed historically and are presently used.

25 Sahajanand would refer to this mentality as "false pride," as he has in other contexts and elsewhere in his writing. Sahajanand anticipates here the whole Mandal Commission and reservations issue for Other Backward Classes (OBCs) and which is central to the public discourse in the 1990s involving all political parties. See also Editor's Endote 22 of this Chapter.

26 As indicated in several preceding endnotes, what may have been a majority Adivasi population at one time in Jharkhand, is no longer so.

27 The other central element of this agrarian environment is of course water, which with agricultural land and access to the jungle were in 1941, as they remain today the critical requirements and demands of the kisans of Jharkhand. Given the fact that the jungle and its products provide the primary economic base of the region, some Adivasi activists take exception to the use of the term kisan, or peasant. Sahajanand is obviously not prepared to accept this distinction, and refers here to the Adivasis as pakke kisans, that is true peasants in the full sense of the term. He does this without denying the central role of the forest and its products in the lives of the Adivasi kisans, as a reading of this tract will reveal in graphic and compelling terms. The central role of the forest as distinct from the lesser importance of settled agriculture in the region is a point emphasized by Dr. Ram Dayal Munda in a conversation in New Delhi, July 17, 1994.

28 See Chapter XII of the Santal Parganas Inquiry Committee Report, especially pp. 50-51, on bhacli, batai, and krishani as forms of subletting, in the latter case "often indistinguishable from serfdom (p.51).

Elsewhere in Bihar, bhaoli refers to rent payment in kind and batai to sharecropping.

29 Sahajanand discusses the economic and cultural exploitation of the Untouchables, many of whom are agricultural labourers in his 1941 tract, Khet Mazdoor. See my edited translation, together with the Hindi text in *Sahajanand on Agricultural Labour and the Rural Poor* (New Delhi: Manohar Publishers, 1994.)

30 Sahajanand concludes this chapter with a restatement of the conceptual tension between the Adivasis as backward and exploited but with an inner strength that makes them a potential force of great power, if only they were to be organized.

Chapter III

The Matter of Education

[In this chapter Sahajanand comes to specific cases of exploitation of the kisans of Jharkhand. The subject here is education and Sahajanand is unremitting in his criticism of the imbalance in educational resources, development, and facilities as between the districts of Bihar and Jharkhand on the one hand and between the outsiders and the Adivasis of Jharkhand, on the other. No one is spared, neither the British, the Congress, nor the Tatas, but the most damning criticism is directed to the failure of anyone to provide an education of any kind to the Adivasis in their own languages on the one hand, while developing a network of Hindi medium and Bengali schools, essentially on demand, for everyone else. This, says Sahajanand is "an absolute fraud.' The Swami reserves praise only for the Christian missions and their efforts in educating the people. Ed.]

I have referred briefly to the issue of education in the previous chapter. Here I will go into greater detail. It is necessary to do so in order to throw full light on the material condition of the people. Moreover, in the interests of comparison it is also necessary to consider the state of education in Bihar proper and its several districts along side that of Jharkhand. I shall begin by presenting the statistics published by the first Congress Ministry in 1938 and shall finish by drawing conclusions on the basis of these figures.

<28.11.41> The first and foremost thing to be mentioned in this connection is that in Bihar proper there are 173 high English schools,

630 middle schools, 2,502 upper primary schools and 13,219 lower primary schools.[1] In Jharkhand there are in all forty high English schools, 167 middle schools, 690 upper and 4,344 lower primary schools. The number of middle schools in the former is essentially the same as the number of upper primary schools in the latter. It has to be kept in mind that as compared to Bihar, the population of Jharkhand is between one-half and one-third that of the rest of the province.[2] But except the number of lower primary schools here which is one-third of the former, the number of high, middle and upper primary schools in Jharkhand is only one-fourth as compared to Biharkhand. The number of high schools here is even less than one-fourth the number in Bihar! In the former case there are 173 and Jharkhand the number is only forty! The case is so clear that no further comment is needed.

If a district-wise assesssment of these facts is made, the case becomes still more interesting. Champaran is the only district in Bihar which bears any comparison with Ranchi, Manbhum and the Santal Parganas, the three districts with the strongest educational facilities in this region. Next comes the case of Purnea, which in some ways is better than that of Champaran. But even these two unfortunate districts of Bihar are far better off than the most advanced districts of Jharkhand. It is by any consideration a remarkable circumstance. In the district of Ranchi there are ten high schools, 44 middle schools, 146 upper primary and 1,094 lower primary schools; in Manbhum their number is 11, 41, 161, and 981 respectively; and in the Santal Parganas their number is 10, 31, 168, and 947 respectively. The strange thing is that where the number of lower primary schools has increased, there has been a proportionate decrease in the number of schools of other categories. And where the number of lower primary schools has not gone up there has been a proportionate increase in the number of schools of other categories. This fact becomes obvious when we compare the figures of the other two districts with that of Ranchi. But when we compare their areas and population, new facts emerge. As the population of Ranchi is less than the population of the other two districts, it seems that the former is more progressive than the other two. Its total area is more than that of the others, but its population is certainly less. I shall discuss this issue further, later on.

However, let us again examine the case of the two Bihar districts. In Champaran there are ten high schools, 49 middle schools, 220 upper and 866 lower primary schools. It has also to be remembered that in Champaran primary education is provided free of any charge.[3] In Purnea the number of schools is 9, 43, 173, and 1,136 respectively. Although the population of the two districts is nearly equal, that is, a bit over 23 lakhs in each case, there is a marked difference in their total area. And on this score the condition of Purnea is much worse than that of Champaran inasmuch as the former is 1½ times larger in area than the latter. Even then, except for lower primary schools, the number of other categories of schools is less than that of Champaran. No doubt the number of lower primary schools is somewhat larger. It might be noted that of these two backward districts especially prided themselves on being followers of Gandhiji. Was there then no concern for educating the people in those districts? If by merely turning the spinning wheel one can be called a devotee of Gandhism (*Gandhi Bhakti*) then God help us.[4]

Now I must turn to the educational condition of the remaining Bihar districts. Darbhanga occupies the foremost place in this respect. Thereafter comes the district of Gaya and other districts. So far as the number of lower primary and other schools is concerned, the position is as follows. If we take into consideration the area and population and then compare the number of schools on that basis, Patna will occupy the foremost place in that respect. The area and population of this and other districts have been provided in Chapter II. There are 26 high schools, 59 middle schools, 249 upper and 1,400 lower primary schools in this district. In Gaya their number is 15, 41, 162, and 1,701 respectively, in Shahabad their number is 17, 58, 249, and 1,129 respectively; in Monghyr their number is 17, 77, 244, and 1,437 respectively; in Bhagalpur their number is 18, 53, 270, and 1,210 respectively; in Saran their number is 25, 88, 238, and 1,125 respectively; in Muzaffarpur their number is 19, 77, 306, and 1,470 respectively, and in Darbhanga their number is 17, 85, 388, and 1,745 respectively.

We must now examine this issue further and on other criteria. Perhaps the most important consideration so far as education is concerned is the presence of several mission centres including the German, English, Roman Catholic, and one or two others in the Jharkhand tract. They are running a large number of schools in the area. For example, the German mission is running nearly 200 schools, the English mission is running about 150 schools and the Roman Catholics and others have nearly 100 schools in this region. Thus the credit of running between 400 and 500 schools goes to these Christian missionaries. Hazaribagh, Ranchi and the Santal Parganas have the largest number of such schools. The only college in Hazaribagh is run by the missionaries. It is the large number of mission schools which makes Ranchi the foremost district in this respect in the area. Whereas the Tatas and other capitalists are draining away at least 8 to 10 crores of rupees annually from Jamshedpur and other centres of this region and say much about their philanthropic activities, they have not established a single college in the area. One might ask, what kind of Hindustanis are they? The Christian padres, missions, and churches of different religious orders and denominations have done much better in this regard. Indeed, they were educational pioneers here at a time when no Hindu pandits or Muslim maulvis could even dare to come to Jharkhand. About a hundred years ago, that is in the year 1845 they came and started their work.[5] Consequently, these padres, pastors, and missions are far better than the Tatas and others, inasmuch as they do not earn a single paisa here, but spend lakhs of rupees every year on educational advancement and the running of hospitals, etc. It is true that their chief object is to convert people to Christianity in ever larger numbers and thus to strengthen the pillars of imperialism and foreign capitalism.[6] But why do the Tatas and their friends not strengthen the foothold of indigenous capitalism in the spirit of sheer imitation? No doubt, these priests and other missionaries try to convert the local people to Christianity. But along with this they educate them as human beings! We have driven the Adivasis to live a life worse than that of animals and persist in this course. Yes, we have no quarrel with the Christians and the missionaries on this score. If we have any grievance against them, it is on a different matter, which we will refer to subsequently. If the Hindus or others are concerned over the role of the missionaries, then why don't they compete with them by their deeds and by their own philanthropic activities? Only by shouting religion, religion, we will achieve nothing. That day is past.[7]

So maximum credit for whatever educational advancement has been achieved in Jharkhand, should go to the different missions. It is neither due to the Biharis or the government of Bihar. Was it not the duty of government to establish colleges, at least at Jamshedpur, Hazaribagh and Ranchi? For the last twenty years or more, the education secretary of Bihar has been an Indian. What has been done to educate the voiceless peasants of Jharkhand during this time? What serious attempts have even been made in this direction? What was the amount this department recommended that government should expend on education? A large majority of the Council members were Biharis as well. Did they ever care to consider this issue? Did they even take a thoughtful and sympathetic view of the issue? To assume office only for the sake of taking an oath has no meaning whatsoever.

Another factor to be considered in the matter of education is the degree to which the backward Adivasis have benefitted from the schools already in existence in the area. How many Adivasi boys are studying in these schools, leave alone the education of girls? If an estimate is made of the outsiders or the progressive sections of the population and the class of exploiters who live in the main towns and large villages of Jharkhand, it will be seen that these in fact are the people who receive the maximum benefit from the educational institutions already running here. Only a miniscule number of Adivasis or other backward people are found in the schools of Jharkhand. If we were to exclude the Christians from this number, the imbalance would be even more dramatic. We cannot in any event claim any credit for educating the Christians. It is the missionaries who educate them. I have made calculations based on every thana in Jharkhand and have concluded that the largest number of schools are situated either in important towns or market places. The great neglect that has been shown in educating the Adivasis and the other true kisans of this region is thus abundantly clear. It is also clear from the Santal Parganas Inquiry Committee Report that the education of the backward peoples of Jharkhand has been sacrificed in order to provide full educational facilities to the rest of the population.[8]

The third remarkable fact which clearly proves how sincere we have been in educating the real kisans, the voiceless masses of the people, is in knowing that up to now not one school has been started for teaching the Santali, Oraon, Mundari or Ho languages! Hindi speakers must have Hindi medium schools in Calcutta or Bombay, otherwise they would raise a storm of protest on this issue. The Muslims will not rest quietly so long as they do not have schools for teaching Urdu and will invoke religion when necessary to achieve their goals. Don't even ask about the Bengalis. They have provisions for teaching in Bengali everywhere. In those districts of Jharkhand where they are in fairly good numbers, they have arrangements for the teaching and study of Bengali. The Manbhum district Board has made arrangements for the teaching of Bengali. In Dhanbad and other adjoining areas, a movement is afoot for the propagation of Hindi. Similarly, in the district of Hazaribagh in Ramgarh, Gola, Petarbar, and other areas, Bengali has been introduced as the common medium of instruction. When the District Board of Hazaribagh wanted to replace it with Hindi, a great hue and cry was raised in opposition. No doubt it is correct and proper to teach the young in their mother tongue. Those who do not do so not only commit a grave injustice, on the contrary, apparently they do not want that boys speaking languages different from theirs should succeed! After all the idea behind the movement for replacing English with Hindi as the medium of instruction while retaining English teaching as well, has that very motive as its driving force.

So when the progressive and civilized amongst us show our impatience to educate our children in the medium of their mother tongue, as is evident from the recent agitations raised by the protagonists of Bengali and Hindi, then why should these poor Adivasis have no apparent provision for educating their children? And why if there is any such provision, is it only through the medium of Hindi or Bengali and not in their own languages? On the one hand the Adivasis are already deprived and backward with the result that their children are little able to take advantage of any opportunities which might be available. Secondly, what a great injustice it is to teach them through a language with which they have had no contact from birth! Such an education is like prescribing poison for them. In the process their minds are dulled rather than improved, inasmuch as they have to labour doubly hard. First they must engage their minds to learn and then to do so in a language which is not their own. Accordingly they remain only half educated. It is an education which serves little purpose. It has no immediate practical use nor does it prepare them to go in for higher studies which might prepare them for a constructive career later in life. Thus they neither benefit immediately nor in the more distant future.

In Soviet Russia, there are some very small republics quite adjacent to the frontier of India. These are tribes (*jatiyan*) like the Tajik, and other familiar names. They did not have any script or written books of their own, but it is to the credit of the Soviet government that it has evolved new alphabets for them and new books have been written in their local languages. And these books are taught in their schools and colleges. They are governed with the help of their own language and all their activities are carried on accordingly. The Soviet government realized that the Tajiks and others would neither prosper nor succeed in other ways unless their own mother tongue was developed. Hence this was one of the first tasks which the government there undertook. After all, it is in a real sense a government of the people run by the kisans and the workers. One wonders why the government here is not doing the same thing?[9]

But here where we are in fact strangers we treat the people of Jharkhand as aliens.[10] They are not like us, so why should we care for them. Rather we are bent upon civilizing them forcibly in our own image, moulding them in one way or another into some ideal form of our perception. Thus, what concern do we have for the medium of their instruction? Their own language is uncivilized and we have to make them civilized. Hence they must read the civilized languages such as Hindi, Bengali or English! This is simply an expression of our hopelessly venal attitude toward the peasants of Jharkhand. And it is on this strength that we Biharis are out to oppose the Adivasi movement led by Jaipal Singh and want to keep Chotanagpur attached as a tail of Bihar![11] Had facilities for the teaching of Bengali and Hindi not been demanded and provided throughout Jharkhand, certainly there would not be nearly so many schools in these districts as we find today! In that case neither the Biharis nor the Bengalis would have shown any interest in local education in this place! These schools exist only because they teach in the Bengali, Hindi, and English medium. Hence, without the least hesitation we can say that no effort has been made to educate the real peasants, the Adivasi population of this region. And whatever has been done is an absolute fraud.

In the Damin-i-koh alone there are 60,000 Paharias. But there is not one single school for their children! This is not simply our report. This is the government version published by its Inquiry Committee. And the tragedy is that the Damin-i-koh is a Khas Mahal area of the government. It is not owned by any private zamindar! And look at its plight! There can be no better example of finding poverty in the land of plenty. By way of statistical illustration the report goes so far as to mention that one percent of the entire Khas Mahal revenue, in addition to rupees eighteen thousand are annually spent on education! But for whom? For those who can themselves afford to prosecute their studies? The report itself describes this as an area "which is 85 percent aboriginal, which is very primitive and which is wedded to its own tribal traditions (page 64)." It is a remarkable observation at best. There are other interesting facts in the report with specific reference to the Santals but which are applicable more or less, to the whole of Chotanagpur and the Santal Parganas. It runs as follows; I quote from page 44 of the report:

> The first essential for the aboriginals is more education. Until they have advanced in this respect they cannot hope to compete with their Dikku neighbours or improve their own conditions. The percentage of literacy recorded in the district at the last census of 1931 is very low indeed, being only 2.9 against a provincial average of 5.2. The figures for aboriginals are even lower. While the percentage of literacy among Dikkus is 4.72 it was only 0.40 among the aboriginals. The wastage is also abnormal. For, although the educational returns show that an average of over 13,800 Santal children have attended school annually during the last 15 years, the Census figures show that there were in 1931 only 3,490 literate Santals. ["There has been no development of aboriginal schools in recent years; in fact the position is now worse that it was 15 years ago."][12]

As has been mentioned before, the district of Santal Parganas does not lag behind any other district of the Jharkhand region so far as its "literacy" is concerned. In this respect it can compare favourably with any of its counterparts. If it is slightly behind Ranchi or Manbhum, it is certainly more advanced than Singhbhum, Hazaribagh and

Palamau. Hence taking everything into account, it is on average somewhat more advanced than the rest of the area or certainly equal to any other district. It is thus revealing to note that among the Adivasis of Santal Parganas, only one in 250 adults is "literate," while in Chotanagpur the figure is one in 300! For Bihar, on the other hand, the literacy rate is 5.25 percent, or [nearly] fifteen times that of Jharkhand! This is the real position of education in Jharkhand.

The truth about the one fourth [*sic*] figure given before must now be tested.[13] I had pointed out then that if we were to exclude the advanced non-Adivasi section of the population from among the Adivasi kisans, the Adivasi population would then be shown to be very backward indeed. The reason for this is now obvious. I have just shown how Bihar is fifteen times more advanced in terms of literacy than Jharkhand. But this calculation is based on a 5.2 average for Bihar as a whole, including Jharkhand. But if we compare the ten districts of Bihar with the remaining six districts of Jharkhand, and still more if we exclude the progressive castes of this area and include them with those of the ten Bihar districts and compare this aggregate with only the Adivasis and other backward castes, then the distinction between the two regions will be markedly visible. In fact, literacy among the Adivasis is 1/25th that of the rest of the population! This is the harsh truth.

As I have already explained, the tragedy lies in the fact that there is no provision for teaching the Adivasis through their own mother tongue. Though their children may attend schools, they are not able to learn. Their minds must bear the weight of mountains as they struggle with an unfamiliar language. Instead of creating an interest in education and an excitement for learning new things, they are rather compelled to learn new and alien languages. This fact has been mentioned in the Santal Parganas Inquiry Committee Report by the term "wastage" or wasteful expenditure. It is not only a waste of money but also the dissipation of the physical and mental capital of the Adivasis and the labour of everyone. The whole effort is alarmingly harmful. Its evil consequences are borne most directly by the young Adivasis. It is a pity that we have not realised this hard truth. The authors of the Santal Parganas report which included among them some responsible Congressmen, could not appreciate this truth. The consequences are obvious.

Editor's Endnotes to Chapter III

1 At the time Sahajanand was writing lower primary schools covered grades 1 to 3; upper primary, grades 4 to 7; middle schools, grades 8 and 9; and high English schools, grades 10 and 11. That distribution of grade categories varied regionally and of course has changed in many ways over the years since.

2 Based on the population figures provided by Sahajanand in Chapter II, the 1941 Jharkhand population of 9,750,000 was 36.6 percent of the 26,590,000 which comprised the population of the rest of the province, together constituting the total Bihar population of 36,371,000.

3 Sahajanand makes this observation quite randomly in the following paragraph of the original manuscript with no further explanation of whether the Champaran case was unique in the matter of providing primary education free of cost. In this edited translation I have taken the liberty of placing Sahajanand's comment at the point in the text where he is discussing Champaran.

4 Sahajanand had of course long since fallen out with Gandhi, in fact in 1934 at the time of the Bihar earthquake. Although until then he was a committed admirer of the Mahatma, he subsequently seldom lost an opportunity to chide those he considered false prophets of Gandhian values.

5 The literature on this subject is very substantial indeed. I cite only two recent titles, as examples, one by a contemporary of Sahajanand's, Father P. Ponette, S.J, and the second providing a series of biographical sketches of 19th century Jesuit pioneers, many in the field of education with which Sahajanand is here concerned. See P. Ponette, S.J., *The Dawn of the Ranchi Mission, 1869-1885* (Ranchi: Catholic Press, 1992); and Peter Tete, S.J., *To Chotanagpur With Love and Service: Pioneers in the Ranchi Jesuit Province* (Ranchi: Ranchi Jesuit Society, 1991).

6 There is a poignant irony here in Sahajanand's praise for the Christian missionary effort in education and in his conflating the larger mission effort of conversion with the political objects of imperialism and foreign capitalism. That conversion was the core element of the missionary venture is obviously a given, and that among the missionaries there were those more than sympathetic with the imperial project and its related political and economic goals, that too would cause no reasonable observer much surprise. But to make the categorical assertion that

the missions were somehow witting tools of imperialism and capitalism, and to do so without qualification, suggests a shading in Sahajanand's thinking reflecting, at least in part, the influences of his Communist Party of India associates at the time.

The ironies here are in Sahajanand's personal background, the timing of his observation, and most pointedly in the deep commitment of many of the missionaries themselves to Adivasi culture and society, most notably of course Father John Hoffmann, the German Jesuit scholar, ethnologist, linguist, and priest, whose remarkable *Encyclopaedia Mundarica* in fact has much of the same critical edge, literally on every page of its sixteen volumes, which Sahajanand himself directs at the invasive exploitation of the kisans of Jharkhand in the 1941 tract published in the present volume. See for example, the Frontispiece of this edited translation as well as frequent Endnote references. There is no evidence that Sahajanand either knew about Hoffmann or the *Mundarica*, thirteen volumes of which were published between 1930 and 1941/43. Hoffmann himself came to Chotanagpur in 1893, was externed by British military authorities in 1915 during World War I and returned to his home in Dortmund in Germany where he continued to work on the *Mundarica*, which was essentially completed at the time of his death in 1928 at the age of 71 (interestingly, he was born in 1857). The tortuous history of the writing and publication of the *Encyclopaedia Mundarica* by Hoffmann and his successor collaborators is recounted briefly in Volume 16 of the 1990 reprint edition by Father P. Ponette, S.J. who was himself involved, and at the age of 84 remains active in Chotanagpur at the present writing. See the reprint edition, John Hoffmann and Arthur Van Emelen, *Encyclopaedia Mundarica*, In 16 Volumes (New Delhi: Gian Publishing House, 1990); and also P. Ponette, ed., *The Munda World: Hoffmann Commemoration Volume* (Ranchi: Catholic Press, 1978). See also Editor's Endnotes 5 and 9 of Chapter VI on the conceptual links in the thinking of Hoffmann and Sahajanand.

As Father Ponette explains in his note on the publication history of the *Mundarica*, Dr. K.S. Singh, then Commissioner of South Chotanagpur, was instrumental in overcoming major administrative and type-setting hurdles at the Bihar Government Press with the happy result that Volume T of the *Mundarica* was completed in November 1978, and Volume U in March 1979, and issued in those years in what was presumably an extremely limited edition. While it is not directly germane to the point of this note, the steps from the publication of the final volumes of the *Mundarica* in 1979, to assembling a complete set of this remarkable document thereby making a reprint edition possible, is nevertheless a matter of some interest. In 1980, apparently with the encouragement of Professor Norman Zide of the University of Chicago, Mr. Gene Smith, then the Director of the United States Library of Congress office in New Delhi took the initiative to bring together a full sixteen volume set of the *Mundarica.* The responsibility for doing so was put in the hands of Mr. K.C. Jha, then also on the Library of Congress staff, and over the next two years and more Mr. Jha was able to assemble, in several formats the full sixteen volumes. Thirteen of the volumes originally published in the 1930s and 40s were still available for purchase at the Bihar Government Press in Gulzarbagh, and a copy of the illustrations volume was located by Mr. Jha at the Patna University Library. This left the elusive T and U volumes unaccounted for. The last remaining press copy of the U volume was provided by the Bihar Government Press at Ranchi and the T volume was made available by Father Ponette from the Archbishops's library in Ranchi. A full sixteen volume microfiche set was produced by the U.S. Library of Congress in 1982. Mr. Jha then made multiple xerox copies of the three "missing" volumes which were distributed to concerned scholars in India. He retained one complete original set, including the three xeroxed volumes, in hard copy, and it was that set which he provided to the Gian Publishing House late in 1989 at the instance of Mr. Satkari Mukhopadhyay, resulting in the 1990 Gian reprint edition of this invaluable document.

In referring above to Sahajanand's observations on the links between Christian missions and imperialism, I mentioned the matter of the timing of his assessment, which came at almost exactly the very moment the All India Kisan Committee (October 1941) and the Central Kisan Council (February 1942) was issuing statements supporting the Communist Party of India's, People's War stand following the German invasion of the Soviet Union in June 1941. That position, however legitimate its political and ideological justification may have been, did place the CPI, the Kisan Sabha, and in this case Sahajanand, in a position which might be viewed as sympathetic if not supportive of British imperial interests in India. Certainly Sahajanand's statements immediately following would permit such an interpretation. All of this is of course, another story but this history conveys something of the irony to which I refer at the head of this Note. Sahajanand, incidentally, was released from the Hazaribagh Central Jail in March 1942, a year before the expiry of his three year sentence.

Less relevant perhaps to the irony of Sahajanand's critique of the missionary imperialism link, is the fact that he himself as Navrang Rai, was a brilliant product of the German Mission English High School at

Ghazipur in the years immediately before he entered the Dasnami order in 1907 as Swami Sahajanand Saraswati. He was aged eighteen in that year. One might infer on the basis of this evidence that missions and missionaries came to India not only in many denominational and sectarian configurations but in many shades of cultural and social sensitivity, not all of them defined by the colours and meanings of the Union Jack of the Raj.

7 Sahajanand's observations here on issues of education generally, that for Adivasi children specifically and including girls, are no less remarkable for their candor about what is happening and who is responsible than they are for the time he was expressing these thoughts. The same thing of course may be said for the candor and honesty with which this Shaivite, Dasnami, Ḍandi sannyasi comments on the role of religion and its abuses on the one hand, or positively in the furtherance of the education of a deprived Adivasi people by the Christian missions, on the other. In either case, Sahajanand's concern is for justice and decency in the human experience, wherever or whenever it may occur. The present *Jharkhand ke Kisan* tract is a powerful reflection of that concern in the life and mind of Sahajanand. I examine this phenomenon in a somewhat broader context in my essay "Swami Sahajanand and the Politics of Social Reform, 1907-1950," in the *Indian Historical Review* 18:1-2 (July 1991-January 1992). A Hindi version of this essay appears in the new journal *Itihas* 3 (1994), published by the Indian Council for Historical Research.

8 See especially the painfully revealing description of the state of Adivasi education in Santal Parganas on page 44 of the Committee's Report, part of which Sahajanand quotes later in this chapter. See SPICR, (Patna, 1938), p. 44.

9 This is one of the few references Sahajanand makes to the Soviet experience in this tract as opposed to the *Khet Mazdoor* manuscript completed literally a matter of months before the present Jharkhand text was begun. *Khet Mazdoor* is replete with ideological references and numerous examples and citations from the Soviet experience. In the present case Sahajanand was in a sense consumed with the gravity of the Jharkhand phenomenon in its own terms; apparently it required little comparative justification. See also Editor's Endnote 10 of the Introduction for further comment on the emphasis in the present tract.

10 Sahajanand's term here for the general perception outsiders have of the Adivasis of Jharkhand is *doosre hi*, in effect, emphatically others, which I have translated as alien. He also uses the Hindi *begane* to describe the ironic twist of those who are in fact literally outsiders viewing and treating the original inhabitants, the Adivasis as "the other."

Sahajanand's conceptual sensitivity to these realities and their meanings as he defines them in this paragraph, chapter, and book might be viewed by some in 1994 as impressive anthropology or critical theory. That the insights came from Sahajanand's fertile mind and intellect as it surveyed the social, cultural, and political experience of 34 years, is something of which we need to remind ourselves in assessing Sahajanand's role in defining the qualities of life and society in 20th century India. I take the year 1907 when Sahajanand took the vows of renunciation, i.e., sannyas, as the effective beginning of his intellectual and public career. The date was 34 years before his imprisonment and the writing of *Jharkhand ke Kisan*.

11 Whereas in the Introduction of this tract, Sahajanand made a veiled criticism of Jaipal Singh and the Adivasi movement as a "middle class affair," he now offers a justification for the movement based on the cultural exploitation he develops in this chapter on education or the lack of it among the Adivasis. See Editor's Endnote 9 of the Introduction.

12 I have added the sentence immediately following Sahajanand's quote from the Santal Parganas Report essentially to emphasize the point he is making here and throughout this tract, namely that Jharkhand is a place which has historically suffered exploitation, in all respects. See SPICR, (Patna, 1938), p. 44.

13 My assumption here is that Sahajanand is referring to the 0.40 figure in the quotation from the Santal Parganas Inquiry Committee Report which he cites directly above, rather than one fourth as he indicates here. The 0.40 percentage figure would be slightly over 1/13th the 5.25 literacy percentage for Bihar as a whole, whereas he argues in this paragraph that a more accurate calculation would show that the rate of Adivasi literacy is in fact 1/25th that of the province as a whole if one excludes the Adivasis from that provincial calculation.

Chapter IV

The Peasant and the Zamindar

[Sahajanand in this chapter turns to some of the core issues of the Adivasi peasant experience in Jharkhand. He provides a brief historical introduction explaining the presence of outside jagirdars, zamindars, traders, merchants, and moneylenders, all of whom engaged in the exploitation of the people, what Sahajanand refers to here as "open loot." This inevitably resulted in a continuing series of peasant rebellions, uprisings, and movements which Sahajanand characterizes as providing clear evidence of a class consciousness among the Adivasis. In the case of the Tana Bhagat movement of the early twentieth century it also demonstrated how by their will and action the kisans of Jharkhand in fact reinforced the wider movement for political freedom. Sahajanand provides a brief description of the various zamindari tenures in Jharkhand and comments also on the issue of jungle control and exploitation, to which he will return in far greater detail. Ed.]

In order to understand the actual condition of the kisans and the Tenancy Act which governs their relationships, it is necessary first to examine briefly the system of land tenure in Jharkhand. A poor education certainly makes the problems of the peasants more difficult. But if they have the courage to fight for their rights and are prepared to lay down their lives in this effort, then the awareness which education can provide will make their task that much more achievable. And even if the element of courage is missing, education can nevertheless ultimately carry them towards their goal. Hence education is absolutely essential; it is at the basis of all progress. And I have already spoken of the bravery of the kisans of Jharkhand and their love of the land, so the question of courage does in fact not arise.

It is said that the Nagvanshi kings of this region were the original rulers of Jharkhand and belonged to the families of the Adivasis.[1] According to the traditional panchayati system the people chose the Nagvanshis to be their headmen (*sardars*) and chiefs (*mukhiyas*), and in the course of time they became their masters. This has been the history of feudalism in all countries and here it became the foundation of the zamindari system. Until the Mughal period the relationship with the Nagvanshis was an accepted, functioning system of rulership. But then the practice of visiting the Delhi Durbar proved harmful. So long as the Nagvanshis lived in the jungles of Jharkhand they did not fall prey to the pomp and grandeur of court life and its evil influences. But frequent visits to the durbar tempted them to acquire cavalry, elephants and other paraphernalia of the court. It further led them to indulge in luxurious and licentious living. This in turn produced retainers to carry this equipment and maintain the cavalry and elephants. Bands of Sikhs, Pathans and other traders began to infiltrate the area from the western provinces, bringing with them this paraphernalia of the courts and other articles and in the process began to loot the local population. When payment in cash was not available for these goods, village after village was farmed out to these traders on contract as payment in revenue. In this way a group of zamindars from the outside were introduced into the region. Some had come into the area on other accounts, either as allies or participants in local wars. After the year 1765 A.D. some came either in the garb of flatterers of the Mughal potentates of the area or in the service of their British masters. More recently many have settled here as traders and merchants while still others who had come earlier now brought their kith and kin from the outside. Many erected castles and fortresses to live in the safety of the dense and impenetrable jungle.

It was the exploitation and pressures of these outsiders which ultimately led to the awakening of the peasants of Jharkhand. No less than these, the Marwari merchants and other moneylenders also took advantage of the peasants. Their hard-earned money thus went into the coffers of these zamindars, Marwaris and moneylenders, literally drawing into question the very honour and prestige of the Adivasi kisans. The new British regulations helped these exploiters to squeeze the very life blood out of these simple peasant folk, depriving them of their land and in effect reducing them to the condition of slaves. They were frequently sent to prison. All of this ultimately drove the kisans of Chotanagpur to rise in rebellion (*bagavaten*) times without number. Especially memorable in this series of uprisings were those of 1820 and 1831-32. It was such oppressions and atrocities which led to the insurrection of 1855, beginning from June 30 and culminating on July 7, with an attack by 30,000 Santals on a police squad in Birbhum. They inflicted heavy damage on the area. The disturbances began again in 1889-90 and led to the Birsa movement (*andolan*) of 1895 in the district of Ranchi which spread like wildfire. Last but not the least was the Tana Bhagat movement which started at the time of the Great European War of 1914 and continued with great intensity till the Non-cooperation movement of 1921. This was clearly a kisan movement. A powerful group of Tana Bhagats openly refused to pay rent (*lagan*) to their zamindars, courted imprisonment, and with the auction of their lands, they were ruined.[2]

When our well known and famous leaders were guiding the course of the nation's political struggle consequent on the promulgation of the Rowlatt Act, martial law in the Punjab, and coupled with it the Khilafat agitation, the simple but brave kisans of Jharkhand were waging a powerful peasant struggle (*zabardast larai*) at the very same time. It was absolutely remarkable to see them refusing to pay any kind of rent or other taxes. In fact it was they who by their deeds, gave a real shape to our wider political struggle.[3] This massive demonstration of their demands was done both in the absence of any education, which they did not have, or of dramatic words. What after all could they say? Such sophisticated speeches and agitations were no doubt being carried on by our leaders throughout the country. Vocal protest was for those leaders, while demonstration by deed and action fell to the kisans of Jharkhand. As a matter of fact the Tana Bhagat movement of refusing to pay any land rent would not have come to a dead stop had Gandhiji not visited Ranchi in September-October of 1921 and personally persuaded them to withdraw their demands. Subsequently Congress volunteers went about urging that the Tana Bhagats must now pay land rent to the zamindar! This is an example both of our wider politics as well as the true form of the kisan struggle of Jharkhand.[4] These ordinary and simple peasants have great faith in religion and the wisdom preached by the sadhus and mahatmas. It was for this reason that they were called Bhagats, or devotees. They at once accepted Gandhiji's plea and withdrew their anti-tax and anti-rent movement, inasmuch as they ultimately regarded him as a real mahatma.

These simple people are aroused to action only when they are driven to the point of desperation. Otherwise they bear all oppressions like any dumb animal. Here I quote the words of E.T. Dalton, describing how during 1820 and 1831-32 the kisans were oppressed and how they reacted. Dalton was Commissioner of Chotanagpur at the time he was writing.

> The oppressions of these men (Jagirdars) were however borne with courage, but a far worse class of men had obtained a footing in the country about the year 1820, when the late Maharaja Jagarnath Sahi Deo obtained his ancestral gadi [literally here, throne] on the death of his father in July of that year. These men were Musalmans, Sikhs and some others who came to the country as horse-dealers and shawl and brocade merchants, fetched enormous offers for their goods from the Nagvanshi Chiefs and obtained farms of villages instead of cash, of which latter the Chiefs were always in want. The foreign farmers having but temporary interest in the villages squeezed as much as possible from their raiyats [tenants] in the shape of rents, abwabs and salami. But this was not all. They proved their yoke to be galling indeed and rendered true the very name thikadar in Chotanagpur in farms.
>
> 'The Pathans have taken our hoormat and the Sikhs our sisters, our lives are of no value, and being of one caste let us stand fast to each other and commence to plunder, murder and loot,' thus said they.[5]

There is no need to provide analysis for what the Adivasis did under the desperate circumstances which they faced. It was ultimately they themselves who bore the full consequences of their actions. My concern here is only to show that the peasants of Jharkhand engaged in life threatening struggles, literally when they had no other options.

They then started to plunder and murder and were ultimately ruined in the process. And this is where they have found themselves. The remark cited here in their own words, in the E.T. Dalton quote, that they belong to the same caste or class, is of great significance. It confirms a sense of "class consciousness" (*varg chetna*) among the Jharkhand peasants since long. It may be that this consciousness is of an earlier cultural kind and must be recast in modern terms, but their organization is a formidable one and that is why lakhs of Adivasis can be mobilized into action at a moment's notice. This is their real strength. But its application now requires proper leadership and this they presently lack. It is perhaps our responsibility to provide such leadership.[6]

It will be useful here to quote a few lines from the *Annals of Rural Bengal* by W.W. Hunter on the Santal Insurrection of 1855, to indicate the nature of the loot and oppression visited on the poor Adivasis. Hunter writes [on p.230] as follows:

> They cheated the poor Santal in every transaction. The forester brought his jars of clarified butter for sale, the Hindus measured in vessels for salt, oil, cloth and gun-powder. The Hindu used heavy weights in ascertaining the quantity of grain, light ones in weighing out the articles given in return. If the Santal remonstrated he was told that salt, being an excisable commodity had a set of weights and measures peculiar to itself. The fortunes made by traffic in produce were augmented by usury.
>
> The Hindu dealer gave them a few shillings worth of rice and seized the land as soon as they had cleared it and sown the crop. Another family, in a fit of hospitality, feasted away their whole harvest, and then opened an account at the grain dealer's, who advanced enough to keep them above starvation during the rest of the year. From the moment the peasant touched the borrowed rice, he and his children were the serfs of the corn merchant. No matter what economy the family practised, no matter what effort they made to extricate themselves, stint as they might, toil as they might, the Hindu claimed the whole crop, and carried on a balance to be paid out of the next harvest.
>
> Year after year the Santal sweated for his oppressor. If the victim threatened to run off into the jungle, the usurer instituted

> a suit in the courts, taking care that the Santal should know nothing of it till the decree had been obtained and execution taken out. Without the slightest warning, the poor husbandman's buffaloes, cows and little homestead were sold, not omitting the bronze household vessels which formed the sole heirloom of the family. Even the cheap iron ornaments, outward tokens of female respectability among the Santals, were torn from the wife's wrists.

The Santal Insurrection of mid-1855 already referred to was a direct consequence of this history. The last Survey and Settlement Report clearly indicates that the Santals rose in rebellion literally to shield themselves against usurers and other oppressors. Just as 30,000 Santals had assembled in 1855 to undertake this task, similarly, in 1831 the Adivasis of Chotanagpur had done much the same thing. It is clearly written that "they unnaturally became excited by the weakening of the authority and thought the occasion opportune for squaring with the oppressive moneylenders and others. Several bands of Santals collected for marauding purposes".[7]

Here there is a reference to the weakening of governmental authority. It is also reported that the Santals of the Santal Parganas wanted to present a petition to the Governor-General in Calcutta pointing out that oppressions were being committed upon them and that the courts were in fact party to these oppressions. When it became clear that the British laws and their courts were siding with the exploiting moneylenders, it became inevitable for the peasants to express their wrath upon the government, and government authority in turn saw that this situation required more delicate handling than had ever before been the case. Government finally found it necessary to take into account the manners and customs of the people they were governing. The effort was to provide for such rules and regulations as might meet the needs of the people of Jharkhand. On the one hand there was a government sitting at the peak of civilization, on the other a peasant population literally on the edge of darkness and exploitation! How were these two opposites to meet? Though the government could, times without number, pronounce that it would govern in accordance with the social values of the Adivasis, yet the purpose for which they had come to India was fundamentally based on exploitation. However, in accordance with the provisions of the Chotanagpur Tenures Act of 1869, the Chotanagpur Landlord-Tenant Procedure Act of 1879, the Chotanagpur Commutation Act of 1897 and the Chotanagpur Tenancy Acts of 1903, 1905, and 1908, etc., the administration of this area did begin to run on a pattern designed to limit the extent of this kind of exploitation. In the same way, the Santal Parganas began to be administrated in accordance with the provisions of the special rules and regulations of 1855, 1859, 1872, 1888, etc. Since then the Santal Parganas was declared to be a "non-regulation" area and Chotanagpur was proclaimed to be a "backward" tract, a practice which continues in some form or other, even today. The sufferings and sacrifices of the peasantry had achieved at least these minimum changes and opened the way for future progress.

Side by side with a knowledge of the frequent peasant uprisings and turmoil (*bechaini aur uttejna*), it is necessary to familiarize ourselves with the system of land tenure in Jharkhand. The various types of agricultural lands of the Adivasis will be specifically identified inasmuch as these peasant holdings are a cardinal feature of this region. I shall also throw light on the zamindari system or the practice of landownership in this place. The real struggle of the peasantry is against this zamindari system. Hence in order to understand the system and the regulations connected with it, we must know who are the main zamindars and what are their characteristics.

In all the six districts of Jharkhand three categories of zamindars are to be found, as is also true in Bihar. But the distinguishing feature of this region is that the government itself is the biggest zamindar. We have already dealt with the case of Damin-i-Koh and the Santal Parganas. Lying in a wooded mountainous tract and extending to one-fourth the area of the entire district, that is to say, 1,500 square miles, it is directly owned by the government and is called the Khas Mahal or government estate. It is the most backward area and inhabited by 60,000 Paharias. There is no arrangement by the Khas Mahal authority to educate even one child in this estate. Yet this government has the temerity to press other zamindars to provide for the educational needs of peasants on their estates, when in its capacity as a Khas Mahal proprietor, it has done absolutely nothing! There are other hardships here as well, which will be dealt with later.

A large area of Dalbhum subdivision in the district of Singhbhum known as Kolhan is also a Khas Mahal area. The administrative headquarters of that subdivision is Jamshedpur or Tatanagar. Kolhan is at least as backward as the Damin-i-Koh. The same Advasis constitute the peasant population and they too have no voice. But they have achieved a kind of self-government by waging a stormy agitation against British authority. Appreciating the force of the movement the government has made necessary adjustments. There are other Khas Mahal areas of varying sizes in this region. In accordance with the provisions of the Encumbered Estates Act, management of private zamindaris are taken over by the government and looked after by the Court of Wards, another government department.

The government performs a third function here, namely that it owns and manages many of the dense forests of Chotanagpur. Other zamindars also own and control forest areas which are designated as "reserved," but the "reserved forests" (*surakshit jangal*) owned by the government are nevertheless vast.[8] All these reserved forests are sources of great hardships to the local population. It is an issue I will examine in more detail later. As a matter of fact, these dense jungles are a rich source of water with their rivers and streams, yet the kisans living nearby and their animals literally die in the summer for want of water. To dig wells in these mountainous tracts is beyond their means, yet if the kisan goes into the reserved jungle with his animals, he is subject to legal action. Neither the government nor the zamindars are concerned with meeting this need. Yet for the peasant it is an everyday matter of life and death, and his only recourse is to shed tears of blood.

Now let us come to the private zamindars. They are of two kinds, one is known as the *ghatwar* and the other is the ordinary zamindar. The ordinary zamindar is similar to his counterpart found in the rest of Bihar. So far as their relationship with the kisans is concerned, there is no fundamental difference between the two regions of the province. Of course the Chotanagpur zamindars do have special rights granted to them by the government in the collection of outstanding debts. When large arrears accrue, it is the zamindar's responsibility to determine the real amount of arrears and he is then appointed by government to realize those debts, pay off the arrears and assume management of the land in question. There are some other minor points of difference but these variations have no great meaning to the kisans.

But the *ghatwars* or *ghatwal* are a peculiar type of zamindar. They have been granted this zamindari right for performing certain duties or services. Hence in English this is called a "service tenure" or "jagir granted for performing certain duties."[9] As in earlier days a zamindar or cultivator would grant some land to the village watchman, barber, or priest in the form of a rent free jagir; similarly this jagir is of that type. The only difference is that now the government itself grants this right. Hence this jagir can also be seized like the jagirs of an earlier day, if the ghatwal fails to fulfill his assigned duties. In fact the Deputy Commissioner will move against the ghatwal for the slightest infraction and deprive him of his ghatwali tenure.[10] In Jharkhand there is also a jati called the *Ghatwar*. It is just possible that the people of that caste (jati) used to perform the functions of the ghatwari tenure holders, which were subsequently transferred to the present day ghatwars. In addition to the Ghatwar jati, there is also in Jharkhand a jati called by the name of *Gorait*.[11] But the zamindars known as ghatwals in this area are a different people. In other words, the ghatwals have nothing to do with any particular caste, much as the other zamindars do not belong to only one caste. Just as men of different castes and religions are zamindars, so too the ghatwals are of all castes. <30.11.41>

In Jharkhand we very often hear the word *ghati* or *ghat* referring to passes and valleys in the rugged mountain terrain of the region. In these hilly tracts, accessible roads are few and far between and historically people have followed river valleys as the main means of movement through these mountains. To do otherwise would have subjected the traveller to the dangers posed by the wild animals of the jungle. Now in modern times, even large mountains can be levelled by explosives, and roads and "tunnels" constructed. It is such tunnels which permit railway passage through the heart of Chotanagpur.

Consequently the rajas, maharajas and other rulers of the region found it necessary to guard these passes and valley routes. Otherwise, invading armies might at any moment gain control over these passes. It was therefore essential to have sentries posted at such points night and day. There was no other way of protecting these important access points. Those who were charged with this responsibility came to be known as *ghatwar* or *ghatwal*. The number of ghatwals depended upon the number of ghats or passes in a given area. Ghatwars were also found in the mountainous tracts in the southern parts of Bhagalpur, Monghyr and Gaya districts, instead of zamindars. Even now some ghatwars are still to be found in the area although their traditional functions have lost their meaning. In this scientific age many things have changed.

The ghatwars did not themselves perform their designated duties of protecting the passes. They employed a large number of chaukidars for this purpose. Just as today chaukidars are subordinate to *dafadars*, likewise there were similar gradations in rank in former times as well.[12] This was done to maintain close control on the regular performance of their duties by the chaukidars. And it was for the performance of their service functions and to cover whatever other expenditures might be incurred, that lands were granted to the ghatwars on *ghatwari* or *ghatwali* tenures. They paid only a nominal revenue to the government for such lands. Ordinarily speaking, the revenue paid by the zamindars of Bengal and Bihar was low and it was still lower on *ghatwali* land. This land revenue could neither be reduced nor increased, much like that in an *istamrari* settlement.[13] Even though that settlement is not common in Bihar, the *ghatwali* lands nevertheless were administered in this way. The Santal Pargana Inquiry Committee Report writes as follows about the ghatwals:

> In consideration of their performing certain duties in support of the police the ghatwals were granted a special status and protection. Their tenures were assessed to a low rent fixed in perpetuity and were declared inalienable and impartible. The ghatwals were precluded from granting any lease or creating any charge upon their estates beyond the term of their own life, except in case of leases for mining, irrigation or building, for which the Commissioner's consent is required, and for reclamation. The net result is that when a Ghatwal dies, his debts are simultaneously extinguished. [This special protection has enabled the ancient ghatwal families to survive; but only in a state of penury.][14]

It is further mentioned on page 62 of the Santal Parganas Report, that "the ghatwals are charged with the maintenance of chaukidars in their estates and on failure to meet these obligations are liable to dismissal." This clearly suggests that they are no longer required to keep watch on the ghats as in earlier days, nor do they have to maintain chaukidars for such work. Now instead of the villagers paying a chaukidari tax for the maintenance of chaukidars residing in the zamindari villages (*mauzas*) of the ghatwals, the latter have to pay their salary from their personal accounts. But a new practice has developed in Bihar, inasmuch as in all the mountainous regions of this province the ghatwals or zamindars have their personal retainers loosely called chaukidars stationed at every corner or street crossing. They are not official chaukidars, but personal servants of the ghatwals or zamindars. Their function is to charge poor people going to the jungle for cutting wood a fee or tax, which has come to be called *ghat*. I have personally seen this practice in operation. Poor kisans in the mountain tracts must necessarily go into the jungle for cutting wood, collecting grass, twigs, leaves, bamboos, fruits and flowers, either for their domestic use or for earning their livelihood. But unless they have paid the *ghatwala* tax they can have no access to these jungle. This oppression has multiplied many times over the years. Even outside Chotanagpur, that is to say in the forest areas of districts like Monghyr, the local kisans are regularly harassed on this account.

Apart from the Khas Mahal and ghatwali tenures, the third type of zamindari tenure in this area is similar to that in Bihar proper. As already suggested, there is no fundamental difference between the two. In the six districts of Jharkhand there are a good number of petty zamindars and ghatwals and only a very few big zamindars. I shall here recount the names of only some of the most prominent among them. But before doing so I find it necessary to refer to an account in the Hazaribagh Gazetteer of 1917 written by E. Lister, C.I.E., I.C.S. A statement on page 165 clearly shows that the revenue (*mal*) paid by the zamindars to government is nominal in the extreme. Most of the rent demand collected by the zamindars is in fact retained by themselves. The gazetteer description is clear on this fact:

> The demand of Rs. 47,260 (due in respect of seventy permanently held estates) represents about seven rupees a square mile, and the cash rent alone which landlords receive are twelve lakhs, on which sum the government revenue is less than four percent over and above the cash rent. The landlords have ex-

tensive areas in their own cultivation and also collect a considerable produce rent.[15]

This is open loot. No doubt, the ghatwals have to pay a nominal revenue to the government. But the case of the Jharkhand zamindars is very strange indeed and this is not the case only of Hazaribagh district but effectively in all the districts of the region. These zamindars do not pay to the government even four percent of the total cash demand realized from the kisans! What to speak of their income from *batai*, *bhaoli*, jungle produce, besides mica and coal? There is no proper accounting of incomes from all these sources. Moreover, these zamindars possess large areas of land under *zirat*, *kamat*, and *bakasht* tenures. *Salami* and *nazrana* are other forms of exactions as are illegal demands like *abwab*, *sood* [interest], and *tawan* [fines for delayed payment]! If this is not loot, what then shall we call it? And if any claims to the contrary are made by the kisans, it arouses the fury not only of the zamindars and ghatwals but of their friends, *dalals* [tout, broker, middleman] and government people as well. This is done in order to show that the zamindars are really suffering!

Now let us have a look at the prominent zamindars of each district. In the Santal Parganas, there are 1) Patsanda estate, 2) Manihari estate, 3) Balbadda estate, 4) Maheshpur estate, 5) the Ghatwali estate of Babhangawan, etc. In Hazaribagh there are 1) Satgawan (Chandradhari Singh) estate, 2) Garwan (*nawalig*, i.e., minor) estate, 3) Doranda estate, 4) Palganj estate, 5) Kunda estate, 6) Padma estate, 7) Dhanwar estate, etc. In Ranchi we have 1) Palkot, 2) Ratu, 3) Masmano Thakurgaon, 4) the zamindari of 84 villages of the Birla Brothers, 5) Kairogarh, etc. In Manbhum there are 1) Panchkot, 2) Barah Bazar, 3) Ichagarh, 4) Patkum, 5) Begum Kudar, 6) Jhalda, 7) Mau Bazar, 8) Katras, 9) Jharia, etc. In Singhbhum there are 1) Dalbhum estate, 2) Bandgaon, 3) Saranda, 4) Anandpur, 5) Chainpur, 6) Kewa, 7) Tata (Jamshedpur), etc. In Palamau there are 1) Ranka, 2) Chainpur, 3) Ladi, 4) Pathra, 5) Sonpura, 6) Nawa, 7) Bishrampur, 8) Tori, 9) Latehar, 10) Hami, 11) Nawadih, 12) Panki, 13) Balumath, 14)Kosiyara, 15) Nagar Utari, 16) Patan, 17) Hariharganj, etc. There are of course other big zamindars as well. I have listed here only some of the more prominent estate holders among them.[16]

Editor's Endnotes for Chapter IV

1 The correct Hindi and Sanskrit etymology is employed here by Sahajanand in the spelling of Nagvanshi. Much of the literature following the Bengali usage spells the name Nagbansi. One transliteration is obviously as legitimate as another. I have retained Sahajanand's usage in this translation.

2 As I have explained in the Introduction, this edited translation of Swami Sahajanand's 1941 *Jharkhand ke Kisan*, is meant to be precisely that and no more. It is neither a history of Jharkhand or the Chotanagpur districts and Santal Parganas which comprise it, nor an examination of the land system and forest policies which were developed before, during, and after British rule. And this edited translation is least of all a consideration of the politics of the Jharkhand movement in the 1990s. Inevitably all of these issues will intersect to some degree our primary interest in Sahajanand's perceptions of life and society in Jharkhand. But it is Sahajanand's reflective account of the kisans of Jharkhand in 1941 and what it reveals about the place and the people at that time, and significantly about Sahajanand himself, that makes this small political tract a document of historical interest.

We need to recall that Sahajanand was a major player in the politics of peasant activism in India in the 1930s and 40s, and certainly the central figure in that politics in Bihar, where the Kisan Sabha, at least until the time of his imprisonment, was a force in the political engagement of the day probably second only to the Indian National Congress. The question then inevitably arises, if the Bihar Provincial Kisan Sabha was so powerful an influence in the politics of Gangetic Bihar, why was its presence and role in Jharkhand so minimal. Sahajanand himself begins to answer that question in *Jharkhand ke Kisan*, and we will observe on the issue at appropriate points in the editorial endnotes to the chapters of this translation. At the moment, however, the point simply is to suggest that any document which serves to open a window on this fascinating history of the 1930s and 40s, involving the peasant actors who made so much of that history and one of their most articulate spokesmen, is of more than passing interest to the historian.

But as I have pointed out in the Editor's Introduction, that introduction itself and these editorial endnotes are meant to amplify, clarify, and provide bibliographic definition to Sahajanand's text. They are not concerned with rewriting or revising what Sahajanand has written but to make his text more accessible and hopefully more understandable. Accordingly, we are less concerned with the specific historical accuracy of what Sahajanand writes than presenting his perceptions of that history and social experience clearly and as consistent with the original Hindi text as is possible when working across two languages and 53 years of time. It will be obvious at this point that Part II of this book contains the original and unedited Hindi version of *Jharkhand ke Kisan.*

Finally, it needs to be said that the scholarship on the history of the Jharkhand region is wide and deep. What will be offered here is meant only as an introduction to a major literature on a major historical and cultural phenomenon. No bibliography, however brief, can begin without citing the pioneering work of K.S. Singh, whose 1985 collection of essays, *Tribal Society in India: An Anthropo-Historical Perspective* (New Delhi: Manohar Publications), is perhaps the most useful point of departure on the subject, especially considering that Dr. Singh's primary work has been done on and much of it in Chotanagpur. The first two essays, "History, Anthropology and Colonial Transformation," (pp. 1-26) and "State Formation," (pp. 27-52) are most directly relevant to the issues Sahajanand considers in the initial parts of the present chapter. Especially important for later chapters of Sahajanand's tract are the essays "Tribal Movements," (pp. 119-154), "The Freedom Movement and Tribal Sub-movements," (pp. 155-173), and 'From Ethnicity to Regionalism," (pp. 197-241). See also K.S. Singh, *The Dust Storm and the Hanging Mist: A Study of Birsa Munda and His Movement in Chotanagpur: 1874-1901* (Calcutta: Firma K.L. Mukhopadhyay, 1966); Sachchidananda, *The Changing Munda* (New Delhi: Concept Publishing, 1979); J.C. Jha, *The Kol Insurrection in Chotanagpur* (Calcutta: Thacker Spink, 1964); John McDougald, *Land or Religion? The Sardar and Kherwar Movements in Bihar, 1858-95* (Manohar Publications, 1985); D. Rothermund and D.C. Wadhwa, eds., *Zamindars, Mines and Peasants: Studies in the History of an Indian Coalfield and its Rural Hinterland* (New Delhi: Manohar Publications, 1978); Susana B.C. Devalle, *Discourses of Ethnicity: Culture and Protest in Jharkhand* (New Delhi: Sage Publications, 1992); and finally, and in many ways conceptually the most imaginative title, Ranajit Guha, *Elementary Aspects of Peasant Insurgency in Colonial India* (Delhi: Oxford University Press, 1983), where Guha relies heavily on Chotanagpur data to develop his argument about the nature of insurgency in 19th century India. For a useful and wide-ranging introduction see "Marginalised Tribals: A Symposium on the Situation of Tribals in Our Society," *Seminar* 412 (December 1993). Each of these titles has bibiliographies which extend this brief list of titles in many directions.

3 Sahajanand makes a fundamental point here about the nature of peasant activism at the local and regional level of India's political experience and its role both in defining its particular local interests while at the same time reinforcing the wider political movement of freedom. It is an insight about the autonomy of peasant activism and the perceptions which motivated it, and in a larger sense about peasant history and Indian history that is notable for its author's sensitivity to issues with which he was perhaps as familiar as anyone of his time, or after. The fact that it was an insight based in experience and expressed pointedly here, and in many other statements and writings throughout the 1930s, and this three decades and more before the idea became intellectually and politically fashionable, makes it all the more impressive.

4 Sahajanand's critique here derives from his negative reactions to Gandhi's attempt at accommodation between zamindars and peasants, his anxiety about Congressmen in general as opportunists who paraded as Gandhians, and finally his deep and visceral distrust of organized religion almost in any form. It might be noted of course, that the religious values of the peasants to which he attributes their faith in Gandhi, was certainly a factor in Sahajanand's symbiotic interaction with the peasants of Bihar and India through much of his career, albeit his saffron robe was only one element of the man's forceful personality as a peasant activist. His sharp and graphic tongue and his danda as an expression of peasant power were no less important. The danda is the staff which Sahajanand carried at all times identifying him as a Dandi Sannyasi of the Dasnami order. I will comment on its political importance in Sahajanand's hands in a later note.

5 While Sahajanand does not specifically identify it, this quote is obviously from Edward Tuite Dalton's major work, *Descriptive Ethnology of Bengal* (Calcutta: Superintendent Government Printing, 1872). Dalton was in the British Indian army and reached the rank of Colonel at the time of the Mutiny when he served both in Chotanagpur and Shahabad. He is referred to in this text both as Captain and Colonel, although during his long service as Commissioner of Chotanagpur following the Mutiny he reverted to civilian status and presumably did not retain his military rank, at least officially. The comments which Dalton appends to his own remarks were apparently modifications taken from the official record to which he certainly had access. That record, presently in the India Office Library and Records in London, now the Oriental and India Office Collections, is cited by Ranajit Guha, *Elementary Aspects* (1983), pp. 282-283 as follows, quoting Guha: "Bindrai, the Kol leader, spoke for all tribal insurgents of the nineteenth century when

he explained why his people had taken to arms in 1832: The Pathans had taken our Hoormut and the Sing our Sisters and the Koour, Harnath Sah had forcibly deprived us of our Estates of Twelve Villages which he had given to the Sing. Our Lives we considered of no Value, and being of one Caste and Brethern, it was agreed upon that we should commence to cut, plunder, murder and eat . . . It is with this resolution that we have been murdering and plundering those who have deprived us of both honour & homes. . ." Board's Collections 1363 (54227): Cuthbert & Wilkinson to Thomason (12 Feb. 1832).

Please note that Abwabs are illegal exactions or demands made on the peasant tenants by the zamindar or his agent, and Salami is a perquisite demand made by the superior claimant at the time of any transaction, a form of consideration money, so to speak. See also Glossary.

6 This is a theme to which Sahajanand returns again and again, reflecting on the possibilities neglected and the opportunities that might yet lie ahead in mobilizing the kisans of Jharkhand. His sense of the class consciousness of the Adivasi peasants as peasants follows his long experience and sense of peasants as a class in Gangetic Bihar and is also in keeping with some of the important writing on 19th century Chotanagpur, for example see Ranajit Guha, *Elementary Aspects* (1983).

7 Sahajanand is being uncharacteristically vague in these last three citations, we must presume because he did not have the documentation available to him in the Hazaribagh Central Jail. Normally he provides page numbers and often dates of his sources, but for Dalton, Hunter, and the Settlement Report he gives us none of these. For E.T. Dalton, see his *Descriptive Ethnology of Bengal* (Calcutta: Superitendent of Government Printing, 1872) from which this quote is certainly taken; and W.W. Hunter, *Annals of Rural Bengal* (London, 1866). Sahajanand's last quote appears to refer to a Santal Parganas Settlement Report, and if it was the last one as he mentions, it would be the 1936 Revisional Survey by J.F. Gantzer. There were more detailed Santal Parganas Settlement Reports also in 1912 and 1909. Full bibliographic details on these reports are given in Editor's Endnote 1, of Chapter VIII.

8 Apart from the "reserved" category mentioned here by Sahajanand, in 1941 when he was writing there was also a Protected Forests category, referring to those private forests in the control of zamindars or presumably other controlling interests. These forests vested in the state under the Bihar Land Reforms Act of 1950 and were thereafter defined as Protected Forests under the Indian Forests Act. There is a burgeoning literature on forests and deforestation and the social, politi-

cal, and economic implications of the use and misuse of this remarkable resource. Sahajanand devotes the longest chapter of this Jharkhand tract, that is Chapter VI to a more detailed consideration of the question, "who controls the jungle," and what meaning does this have for the Adivasi kisans of the region. I will cite some of the relevant literature at appropriate places in the Endnotes.

9 As I have indicated in the Editor's Introduction and the Glossary, Sahajanand frequently used English equivalents to reinforce or clarify meanings and most often put these English terms in quotation marks or sometimes parentheses. In the present instance, however, while using the quotation marks, he transliterates service tenure in the Devanagri, and uses the Hindi in the jagir quote. Sahajanand was least concerned with consistency of format and style, but rather with defining, describing, and then arguing his point to achieve the clearest representation of what in fact was happening in the lives of the kisans of Jharkhand.

10 Note that the chief administrative and revenue officer of a district is referred to as the Deputy Commissioner in Jharkhand. In Gangetic Bihar he is the District Magistrate or the Collector.

11 Gorait is most often a title for a village watchman or messenger, hence bearing some similarity to functions performed by the ghatwal, a term which literally means protector of the ghats or passes.

12 A dafadar may be a minor police official, or the head or leader of any group of persons he commands or directs.

13 Istamrari is a settlement or lease in perpetuity, granted by the government or a zamindar at a fixed rate.

14 I have added the sentence following the quotation Sahajanand has cited in order to reinforce the point he is making about the the condition of the ghatwals and what this means for the Adivasi kisans of Jharkhand. See SPICR (Patna, 1938), p. 61.

15 This volume appears in the Bihar and Orissa District Gazetteers series (Patna: Superintendent Government Printing, 1917). The other volume in this 1917 series was the Ranchi Gazetteer. For a useful guide to the gazetteers, see Henry Scholberg, *The District Gazetteers of British India: A Bibliography* (Zug, Switzerland: Inter Documentation Company, 1970), especially the Bengal, Bihar and Orissa, and Bihar sections, pp. 12-13, and 55-63.

16 The Garwan Estate in Hazaribagh which Sahajanand identifies with the term *nawalig*, that is minor, presumably means that this estate was under the management control of the Court of Wards at the time.

Chapter V

Peasant Landholding in Law and in Fact

[Sahajanand's Hindi title for this chapter translates literally, Land Related Hardships of the Kisans. I have taken the liberty of providing a title to reflect more explicitly what Sahajanand does here in one of the two longest chapters of this tract. The point is simple and direct, there is the tenancy law which is on the books, and then there is the law of the jungle so to speak. But it is not the law which has come down historically in the Adivasi cultural experience of the jungle and mountains of Jharkhand. The law in practice is neither the Chotanagpur Tenancy Act nor the inherited experience of Adivasi culture, but rather as Sahajanand repeats again and again, "it is the zamindar's will which is the law." Sahajanand covers the full range of peasant tenures, focussing most elaborately, however, on that process by which the Adivasi kisans have cleared the jungle to create fields from the forest, what is called korkar land. This process and the abuses to which the kisans of Jharkhand are subject by the zamindar in maintaining control of their land is the subject of the last half of this chapter. Ed.]

We will now consider the pattern of peasant landholding in Jharkhand which has features particular to this place. While it is true that some kinds of land tenure are common to both Bihar and Jharkhand, it is also the case that there are several special kinds of agricultural land in Jharkhand which are absolutely central to the lives of the peasants of the region and which we must understand. There are also peculiarities in the zirat holdings of the zamindars here which are uncommon in Bihar proper and which we will examine shortly. But first we will turn to a detailed consideration of the various kinds of agricultural landholding in Jharkhand.

In Section IV of the Bihar as well as the Chotanagpur Tenancy Act, we find reference to the various kinds of "tenants," that is kisans or peasants, some of which are common to both places. These include "tenure holders" and "under-tenure holders." A tenure holder is like a contractor (*thikedar*) of the zamindar who settles land with the kisan who cultivates it and who pays rent (*lagan*) to the thikedar. Ordinarily the tenure holder does not himself do cultivation, rather he collects rent from the kisan, pays a fixed share to the zamindar and retains the rest as his share. He may also hold the contract for settling unoccupied lands with other kisans. The person who then enters into a sub-contract with this thikedar on similar terms as the thikedar himself has with the zamindar is called an under-thikedar (*mathat thikedar*) or an under tenure holder. But the person who takes land from whosoever for doing cultivation, he is called a *raiyat* and whoever is under this raiyat is called an under-raiyat. This latter holding is defined as *shikmee*. This is the difference between a tenure holder and a raiyat. But all are "tenants," i.e., peasants. It is in this way that these four kinds of peasants or kisans have been identified in both the Chotanagpur and Bihar Tenancy Acts.[1]

Similarly, both the "occupancy" (*kayami*) kisans and "non-occupancy" (*gair kayami*) kisans are identified in these acts. In Bihar an occupancy tenant (*kayami kisan*) is considered to be the owner of his land. He has the right to plant trees and bamboos on this land, to make bricks and tiles and dig wells and tanks. He can also build a *pakka* house on that land as his residence. He cannot be dispossessed from his holding unless he has broken the conditions of the tenancy laws or his land is auctioned on account of nonpayment of land rent. But non-occupancy tenants have no such rights. Their rent can be easily increased. But it is with great difficulty that the rent of the occupancy tenant can be raised. But it must be noted that in Jharkhand even the occupancy tenants do not have the right to construct houses on their land, nor can they plant orchards or make bricks or tiles. This is a great injustice. Still these two categories of kisans are found in both Jharkhand and Gangetic Bihar.[2]

Now we will turn to the different kinds of tenures found in Jharkhand. In Bihar over and above the six categories of kisans already referred to there is a seventh category of kisan described as a "fixed rate" tenant. The rent of these *istamrari* tenants is permanently fixed; it can neither be enhanced nor decreased. But in the five districts of Chotanagpur, in place of *istamrari* kisans we come across various other kinds of tenancies, specifically three in number. These are 1) *bhuinhar* or *bhuinhari* landholders; 2) *khutkattidar* or *khutkatti* landholders; and 3). *Mundari khutkattidar* or *Mundari khutkatti* landholders. Ordinarily their land rent cannot be enhanced or decreased. But there are certain peculiarities in the Jharkhand system, which is why their istamrari landholdings are distinguished by these different names indicated here. We will consider the differences between the istamrari tenures of Bihar and khutkatti tenures of Chotanagpur momentarily. There is also another kind of kisan in Jharkhand. He is like the village *mukhiya* or a kind of *jeth raiyat* and is also called *pradhan*, *manjhi*, and *manki*. At some places these tenancies are also known as *ijaradar* or thikedar. The term pradhan is common in the Santal Parganas, Hazaribagh, and Ranchi; manjhi is common in Hazaribagh and Manbhum and manki is current in Manbhum and Singhbhum. These various peasant types are found in other places as well.[3]

It is said that those kisans who first came into the jungle and made it cultivable were called bhuinhars. This term is specifically common to Jharkhand and is not found elsewhere. Another version of this history is that the Mundas were the first to appear in Jharkhand and that they were followed by the Oraons. The latter were quick to seize the lands settled by the Mundas, who then moved deeper into the jungle and cut and cleared it for cultivation. These lands then came to be called Mundari khutkatti, whereas the fields they had previously owned were bhuinhari. Whatever may be the truth of these two historical accounts, the fact is that these two kinds of landholding came into being in Jharkhand. It is also the case that the bhuinhari lands are now generally held by the Oraons.

There is a third kind of land holding called *khutkatti* which is different from Mundari khutkatti. According to the Tenancy Act here, those who first cut the jungle, cleared the stubble and roots (*khunti*) and inhabited the new villages were known as khutkatti. Whatever the case, apparently the Mundas cleared the forest, settled these clearings and called it Mundari khutkatti. As with bhuinhari, these khutkatti lands are also generally held by the Oraons. Bhuinhari lands are also called bhuinhari patthargari, khutkatti lands khutkatti patthargari and Mundari lands are called Mundari patthargari. The term originated first in 1869, or about the time when the Survey and Settlement operations were begun. The boundaries of these different kinds of lands were demarcated by stone markers (*patthar*) thus to distinguish them one from the other, hence the name.

In earlier times the kisans also held two other kinds of land which was apparently seized from them, namely, *majhihas* and *bethkheta.* Majhihas literally means a part or share of the majhi, which is the technical term for mukhiya, or headman. The word suggests that just as now the pradhan, manki or majhi have their special land tenures, so also was the case in earlier times. Subsequently the zamindars seized these lands and made them their personal zirat land. Bethkheta means a plot of land given in *begar* [i.e., on forced labour, and most often without wages]. *Beth* is another word for begar. It seems that in former days the zamindar took personal services from begars as is still prevalent in the Damin area of the Santal Parganas. There all the villagers are generally made to render free services, that is, *begari* for building roads, and in return some lands are permanently settled with these begars on that account In the Damin area instead of paying road cess the villagers are obliged to render free services of this kind. The Santal Parganas Inquiry Committee has recommended that this practice be stopped. It is these lands which are called bethkheta. But now both these land tenures, namely majhihas and bethkheta are the personal property or zirat land of the zamindars. This fact is mentioned in Section 118 (b) of the Chotanagpur Tenancy Act. In Section 124 (b) of that Act it is also mentioned that those villages where bethkheta or majhihas land tenure had been recorded in the 1869 Survey Settlement, the zamindar there cannot claim any other land in the area to be his khas, zirat, or kamat land. In view of this history and the zamindar's personal claim, kisans can have no tenancy claim with either majhihas or bethkheta lands.[4]

There are other important systems of land holding, but before considering these let us examine in more detail the bhuinhari and other systems already mentioned. Bhuinhari was in fact the first kind of landholding. Its acreage remains fixed; it can neither be expanded nor decreased in size, and the rent demand on bhuinhari is minimal. I have been told that the rent is no more than four annas per bigha.[5] But the most important attribute of this system is that the land can under no circumstances be sold in auction by court decree. Secondly, the owner of that land cannot be jailed as a result of any court decree. Thirdly, if the land or any portion of it is given in lease to a thikedar, the latter cannot claim any "occupancy" right (*kayami*) over it. Fourthly, those castes [and tribes] which have been mentioned in the aforesaid two lists [in Chapter II] have no right to mortgage their lands with any cooperative society or in any other way into the hands of others for more than fifteen years, except in "usufructuary mortgage," (*bhogbandhak ya bhugutbandh*), or to divest them in any other way. In the same way they cannot under any circumstances give their land in lease or contract to anyone for more than five to seven years. Fifthly, the aforesaid Adivasi or backward castes can, however, either exchange or sell their lands within their *biradari* [brotherhood], i.e., "dal," within the same thana or police station. They can with the permission of the Deputy Commissioner, give land to their immediate kith and kin (*sage sambandhi*). These limitations are also applicable to the other lands of the bhuinhari landholders in those villages where the bhuinhari land system is in effect. Sixthly, no court decree can be obtained against the bhuinhari landholdings, nor can it be auctioned for sale on that account. Seventh, if a decree is passed against bhuinhari land on account of nonpayment of rent, it will be adjusted only by the produce of that land or from the movable property of that kisan. These points have been dealt with in sections 47, 48, 48 (a) and 184 (a) of the Chotanagpur Tenancy Act.[6]

The one particular fact about khutkatti land is that once the area of that land is recorded in the Survey Settlement it is fixed; it can neither be increased nor decreased in area. Secondly, if the rent at the time the land is declared khutkatti is not settled for further enhancement, then in that case all khutkatti holdings which were declared as such at least twenty years before 1908, cannot have their rent increased. Thirdly, if this is not the case, then the rent can be increased inasmuch as the land was declared khutkatti within the period of twenty years preceding 1908. In that case the total rent (*kul lagan*) of such land cannot be more than fifty percent of the rent of any occupancy land (*kayamee*) of the same category in the same *mauza* [revenue village] and having the same privileges. These facts have been described in Sections 37 and 134 of the Chotanagpur Tenancy Act. All such limitations which apply to the sale and purchase of other holdings of the peasants in this area are also applicable to their khutkatti land.[7]

Now we will consider the special features of the Mundari khutkatti system. First, once the acreage of the Mundari khutkatti land is recorded in the Survey no other land can be recorded under that heading. Secondly, that land cannot be put under any mortgage (*ijara*) and except the usufructuary mortgage (*bhugutbandh*) and that too under no circumstances for more than seven years. Thirdly, that land cannot be given in lease or contract to anyone other except to Munda raiyats for purposes of cultivation. Uncultivated land can be given on ordinary contract to such a raiyat or on fixed or permanent tenure (*mukarrari thike*) on condition that he bring that land under cultivation. Fourth, Mundari khutkatti land cannot be sold on account of any court decree. Fifth, the rent of that land cannot be enhanced without the permission of the Deputy Commissioner and even then it must be established that the question of increasing the land rent must be taken up within a period of twenty years from the time of that land being recorded as Mundari khutkatti. And if the rent is enhanced it will be within the limits prescribed for khutkatti land heretofore noted, that is, the enhancement, or total rent cannot be more than fifty percent of the existing rent [of similar land in the area]. Sixth, rent [arrears] on that land can be realized only by certificate or by seizure (*jabti kurkee*). But this is applicable only where the land has been recorded in the Survey register. But if the land has not been so recorded, the question of realizing the unpaid balance must be brought before a court of law and the court decree will be honoured by the balance being realized from the seizure of movable property or from any other such property which is liable for seizure. If these measures are not applicable the Deputy Commissioner can seize the land and arrange for the payment of the rent balance or any other such dues. As soon as the back dues are realized, the land is restored to its owner. These points have been dealt with in Sections 240, 243, 246, 248, and 256 of the Chotanagpur Tenancy Act.

Now we must turn to what is certainly the most important question for the kisans of Jharkhand, namely the availability of agricultural land in the jungle tracts. The fact is that in this mountainous region a given plot of land often becomes unfit for cultivation. Its productivity may decline or its cultivation must be discontinued under threat from animals of the jungle or because the natural supply of spring water or that provided by a mountain stream has either been diverted or literally dried up. Sometimes torrential rains in the hills and mountains cause land slides which can submerge fields in sand and stone forcing the kisans to give up their land. Often the oppressions of the zamindar or his agents become unbearable and at other times wood is no longer available in the jungle, and the kisan thus must move on, seeking new fields to maintain subsistence. In the jungle cultivable lands are seldom if ever found unutilized. And these new fields must always be cleared and prepared for cultivation.[8]

Sometimes the "holding" of a kisan consists in part of *dhankhar*, *dhankhet* or *dhani*, which are also called *don* land.[9] And some of these holdings may consist of sloping upland [often village waste land], defined as *unchi*, *bari*, or *tanr*. This land is often sown with spring (*rabi*) crops like gram, moong dal, [and other pulses], or allowed to remain fallow. Sometimes, however, these fields are ploughed, terraced, and prepared for paddy cultivation by constructing *aars* and *bandhs* [embankments] for capturing and storing water. This is then referred to as *don* land. Much the same is done in reclaiming fields which have otherwise become unfit for cultivation. Lands which are thus reclaimed are variously referred to as *korkar*, *aariyat*, *bahubala*, and *jalsasan*. The meaning of these terms is clear. The land is prepared by digging and ploughing. Without this process the land cannot be made fit for cultivation. Hence it is called *korkar*, for digging. As the land is surrounded by a bandh or *aar* for storing water, it is called *aariyat* and as the land is prepared by the strength of one's physical labour, it is call *bahubala* [that is, by the strength of one's arm]. And it is also called *jalshasan* or *jalsasan* because the fields are literally covered by water. After all it is a paddy field. It may also be called *khanrwat*. Very often water is stored in the paddy field and on occasion this water is released by breaching the bandh, and then closed to retain the water. These breaches are called *khanr*, hence paddy fields are sometimes referred to as *khanrwat*. Cultivation of paddy, of course, requires such procedures.

<1.12.41> In the districts of Palamau and Ranchi such lands are called *utkar*. Ordinarily there is little difference between *korkar* and *utkar*. But in practice lands which lie adjacent to *don* land or *tanr* within the same holding of the kisan and he digs and ploughs it for cultivation, this is called *korkar*. But when it falls outside his holding or is not near to his *don* land, but rather within the zamindar's personal holding and the kisan prepares this land for cultivation, it is called *utkar*. Mostly [coarse grain] crops like *gondli*, *sawan*, *marua*, *kurthi*, *makai*, etc., are grown on *utkar* land. In fact a large part of the cultivable land in Palamau is utkar and produces these crops.

A particular kind of cultivation is also found among the Paharias in the Damin area of the Santal Parganas. The Paharias are regarded as the oldest inhabitants of that area. It is said that the Santals first made their appearance here in about 1810. However, the Paharias were such vigorous fighters that they did not allow any outsiders to enter. Those who attempted to come into that area were brutally assaulted and driven away. The Paharias are in fact a very simple people. They do not possess any knowledge of plough cultivation with oxen, nor have they undertaken any other livelihood, nor has the government provided them any training to this end.

It is said that Warren Hastings was the first to take notice of the Paharias with the idea of subduing them. He initially sent a military force there under the command of one Captain Brown. Inasmuch as this conquering and civilizing mission failed, Hastings next sent two Englishmen, Messrs. James and Cleveland to learn more about the Paharias. It is said that Cleveland selected 1300 *sardars* [chiefs] from among them and sent these sardars to pursue the civilizing mission the British had in mind for the Paharias.[10] The sardars were paid a monthly allowance of rupees ten each. Even today these sardars or sirdars are found in these Adivasis areas. Cleveland further recommended certain measures for reforming and civilizing the Paharias, but the government made no effort to implement these recommendations.

The Paharias mostly live in the jungles and the mountains and hence they are called Paharias [for the term *pahar*, meaning hill or mountain]. Apart from subsisting on wild fruits, roots, and leaves, they carry on a kind of primitive cultivation not unlike that which was widely practised before the dawn of history and the introduction of the plough. After a few years of cultivation the land would become unproductive and they would clear the forest and prepare new fields, and this process would be repeated as each new field lost its fertility. Initially they used pointed sticks and then rough implements in planting seeds in the ground. Even today *diara* or sandy lands on river banks are cultivated in this way for producing *kharbooj*, *tarbooj*, *karaila*, and *kakri* [i.e., melons in the first two instances, a bitter vegetable, and finally, a cucumber-like vegetable, all of which grow especially well in sandy soil]. The seeds are simply placed in the soil and require no further cultivation.

The Paharias still carry on their cultivation in this way. They still make holes in the ground (*kund*, *surakh*, *chidra*) and sow them with *makai* [maize or corn], *jwar* [barley], *arhar* [a kind of dal or pulse] and *ghaghra*. In old Sanskrit texts such holes are called *kund*. As these were used for sowing seeds, so they came to be known as *kundchas* or *kunrawchas*. In Bengali, the word *chas* means cultivation and the word *chasi* means kisan. The word "*kund*" has become variously *kundwa*, *kudawn*, or *kurawn* and this kind of cultivation accordingly is often referred to as *kurawnchas*. The Santal Parganas Inquiry Committee Report uses the term "*kurwa*." It is also called *jhumchas*. I have read about the presence of "jhumland" in the jungle tracts of Bengal. The kisans cut down or burn the trees of the jungle and in this way clear the fields. Burning is the most effective method for clearing out the trees and brush, which then leaves a residue of ashes which serves to fertilize the newly planted crops. Fields prepared in this way are called *jhumchas* or *jhumland*. The Paharias prepare and cultivate their fields in this same way in the hilly terrain of the Damin in Santal Parganas.[11]

Now for the past five or seven years serious obstructions to this kind of agriculture have been placed in the way of the Paharias. The fact is that nearly forty years ago all these jungles were declared to be "reserved" forests. But out of fear of incurring the wrath of the Paharias, government did not immediately enforce the policy. This has now changed and the policy is now being rigorously enforced. Both the zamindars and the government now mercilessly prevent the Paharias from using the forest, a right they have enjoyed from times immemorial. It is easy for the government simply to declare the forest a reserved area. But then it must at the same time assure that the livelihood of these poor peasants is also not disturbed. Forests are reserved for the benefit of the people. But if people begin to starve because the forests are officially reserved, what kind of benefit is that? Will the wood be used for the funeral pyres of the Paharias who are in fact dying for lack of food or any source of livelihood? It would be like the practice of "Hari Bol" followed by the Hindus of Bengal. They often compelled a man on the point of death to utter the word "Hari" and immediately he did so, people would throw him into the Ganges or any other river to die! They felt they were doing the dying man a great service by sending him straight to heaven [with the word Hari, i.e., God on his lips]! It is strange indeed to starve people in an effort allegedly to benefit them by reserving the forest. It is in fact an effort at enforced civilization, literally by depriving the Paharias of their livelihood! And all of this when the government over these many years has made no effort whatsoever of providing an education for even a single Paharia child. How will they then be civilized, one might ask? But preventing them from cutting the trees of the forest which sustain them is an absolute cruelty.

This then is the condition of the Paharias none of whom can read or write. But the Mundas, Oraons, Santals, and others have benefitted from the work of the missionaries for the last so many years. Some among them have learned to read and write. But now their korkar and utkar lands are also coming under pressure and being grabbed. This is being done by manipulating the official statutes of government literally to usurp the rights of the Adivasis and seize their lands. Korkar and other categories of land rights are described in Section 3 (13) of the Tenancy Act. It is the special provisions found in Sections 64, 65, 66, 67, and 67 (a) of the Act which have used to deprive the kisans of their rights on korkar and utkar lands, rights which they had enjoyed for many years. They had inherited these rights well before there were zamindars or a zamindari system. Now systematic efforts are being made to deprive the Adivasis of their rights and their land. The laws in fact are both vague and complex. For example, Section 64 of the Tenancy Act suggests that the zamindar's concurrence is required for the enjoyment of rights on korkar and utkar lands. It is these and other provisions of the law which have adversely affected the position of the Adivasi kisans on the land which has been historically theirs.[12]

According to the provisions of the law, the kisan is free to convert several kinds of land into korkar and for which the zamindar's permission is not required. These include those lands which by custom do not require such permission and those uplands (*tanr* and *unchi*) on which the kisan holds occupancy rights and which are included in his raiyati land as a tenant. It is also laid down that lands other than the bethkheta and majhihas situated in the same revenue village and already recorded in the Survey register of the year 1867, that is to say the land is of bhuinhari type, and the kisans there own such bhuinhari lands, these kisans have the freedom to convert such land into korkar without taking the zamindar's permission. And similarly where the land has been recorded as Mundari khutkatti and is being cultivated by the Mundas, they too have the freedom to convert it into korkar without seeking the permission of the zamindar. The third circumstance mentioned in the same section of the Act is that even where the zamindar's permission is necessary and the kisan has started converting the land into utkar or korkar and unless the zamindar has applied to the Deputy Commissioner for the kisan's dispossession from that land within two years of beginning this process, it would be deemed that the kisan has been permitted by the zamindar to do so. Consequently the kisan cannot be dispossessed from that land at a later date inasmuch as if that "*dehi*" kisan living in any village creates a korkar plot in that very village, he cannot be dispossessed of that land without the order of the Deputy Commissioner, but even this cannot be done without a court order.[13]

It is Sections 65 and 66 of the Chotanagpur Tenancy Act which take up the issue of dispossession described here. When a petition for dispossession is filed, the Deputy Commissioner will make an enquiry and if he is satisfied on the merits of the case, he will issue orders for dispossession. In that case the kisan will not only be deprived of his land, but will be made to pay fines and other dues to the zamindar from his personal household account. Of course, if no order for dispossession is issued, the matter ends there. But is this likely in the circumstances we have been describing? It is written in the Act that agricultural land, homestead land and orchard land cannot be converted into korkar land. Is it even possible that anyone would attempt forcibly to occupy the land of others, cut down their orchard or pull down their houses and then literally by force convert these lands into korkar land? But these are precisely the possibilities which have been raised here, thereby holding out the threat that the kisans can be dispossessed of their korkar land on various legal pretexts. The zamindar can easily purchase false witnesses. In the meantime, what do these Adivasi kisans know about our complex legal formulations?

Let us examine the implications for the kisans of Jharkhand of these three sections of the Act. We have already dealt with Section 67 and found that its wording is rather vague and complicated. But the conditions laid down in the other two sections are no less dangerous. The requirement of consulting the zamindar is obviously wrong. It is sure to lead to deception and cheating. To suggest that if the practice is based on local custom it will require no consultation with the zamindar, is also misleading. The practice of forming korkar land was in use here long before there were zamindars. The Mundas, Oraons, and others were the first to come to the region, its original inhabitants. Thus, the very idea of local custom involving the zamindars is meaningless. When there were no zamindars the question of seeking their permission obviously did not arise. In these circumstances then, to raise the question of custom is to give the zamindars the opportunity to use force and money in their efforts at alienating the rightful land of the peasants. They will of course deny both Adivasi custom and practice and assert that the formation of korkar land is not possible without their permission. Of course it is expressly written that bhuinhari and Mundari khutkatti landholders living in bhuinhari and Mundari khutkatti villages do not have to take the permission of the zamindar. But this is relevant only when the Mundari peasant is in possession of other lands as well, otherwise he will have to seek the zamindar's permission. Hence as regards the bhuinhari and Mundari landholders living in such villages it is the responsibility of the zamindar to prove that the kisans must seek his permission. The core of the problem is that even where the permission of the zamindar is necessary, it is actually the latter's responsibility to demonstrate this fact. But even this condition has not been clearly laid down in the Tenancy Act, otherwise it would have been easier for the kisan and more difficult for the zamindar to proceed in these cases. The conditions of the Act are in fact hopeless inasmuch as they require that the zamindar must first be consulted and if he is ignored the kisan must show that prior consultation was not necessary. Thus the entire burden of proof rests with the kisan and this in fact acts to poison the whole system.

Much the same is true at the time of inquiry by the Deputy Commissioner. How can the poor kisan compete with the fraud and heavy expenses of the court? As I have said, he is ignorant of the intricacies of the law and of court procedures and is almost certain thereby to damage his case. He is not only deprived of his land, the *bahubala* land acquired by the sheer physical effort of his sweat and blood, but he is also obliged to pay compensation! No doubt this is done purposely in order to intimidate the Adivasi peasant so that out of fear he will worship the zamindar and offer him bribes. This is the real purpose of having to seek permission and consent from the zamindar, for doing anything having to do with the land. The whole idea frightens the kisan which is precisely why these vague procedures were adopted. Lands which were useless heretofore and were made fit for cultivation only by the ceaseless toil, by the sweat and blood of the family of the kisan, that land the zamindar now seizes by dispossessing him! The zamindar gains not only a plot of land which had been lying fallow and unused but the *nazrana* and rents in conveying it to another kisan. It is no mean achievement for the zamindar![14]

The public practitioners of the law should know that in accordance with Section 64 of the Act, an occupancy kisan need not have permission of the zamindar for converting any of his upland (*tanr*) lying within his raiyati holding, into utkar or korkar. But nevertheless, as soon as the kisan does so, the zamindar will seek to impose a new and separate rent on that korkar land. Let us leave aside the raiyati holding of the kisan, which may be held in various tenures. But even if a portion of his landholding is *don* and the other is *tanr* which is converted into *don*, the zamindar forcibly fixes a new rent on it and the tenant must pay it. If he fails to do so he is harassed (*tang*) in a thousand and one ways. After all the lathi enforces the principle that might is right ("*zabardast ki lathi sar par*"), and this is perhaps more true in Jharkhand than anywhere else. The peasants here are completely unaware of their rights. Hence until all these conditions which govern korkar land are removed, the kisan cannot breathe easily.[15] The harassments which the kisans must endure are endless. Among the foremost of these, as I have explained, is the insistence that the kisan must seek the zamindar's prior permission before converting his land to korkar. And if the kisan does so, he must then also pay *salami*, *nazrana* and other cesses as demanded by the zamindar under threat of intimidation and eviction. These coercive demands of the zamindar are quite beyond the comprehension of any outsider unfamiliar with the system.

But if the peasant, out of fear, does not first consult the zamindar, the zamindar's agents will certainly find him out. This is in fact their main business. And they must immediately be bribed, otherwise they will not only inform the zamindar but give the kisan a good beating as well. And even if they are bribed they do not hesitate to beat and assault the kisan and drag him to the zamindar's headquarters to undergo further physical abuse. But the zamindar must in the end realize sufficient nazrana and whatever rent he may demand. The peasant of course, tries to meet the zamindar's demands as best he can, thereby to avoid being dispossessed from his land. And occasionally, if the amla has been appropriately bribed, he may even plead the kisan's case and achieve some concessions on his behalf.

But if the kisan is bold enough to suggest that the zamindar has no rights in this issue under the law, then heaven help him. What use is the law in this case? In fact, it is the zamindar's will which is the law. The peasant will be forcibly deprived of his korkar and utkar lands. And if he resists there are hundreds of legal and extra-legal deceptions which will be employed to harass and ruin him. In fact, the kisan will have no respite until and unless he satisfies the demands of the zamindar.

As is clearly evident in Section 67 of the Chotanagpur Tenancy Act, as soon as land is formed into korkar or utkar, the kisan has occupancy rights over it. Generally twelve years of continuous cultivation of any landholding entitles a kisan to have occupancy rights over his land. But this condition does not apply to korkar land. Moreover the law does not require the kisan to have been a settled raiyat of the village. In accordance with Section 18 of the Act, kisans who, in addition to bhuinhari, Mundari khutkattidari holdings, or the zamindar's zirat [that is, his personal holding], cultivate in addition any other lands in the village, are by definition settled raiyats. But a korkar kisan needs only to have bhuinhari rights to be a settled raiyat. This is the peculiarity of the land system here in Chotanagpur. But will the zamindars permit matters to proceed in this way? In fact they and their agents make capital out of the ignorance of the kisans on these issues!

Section 67 (a) of the Tenancy Act deals with the rules governing rents on korkar and utkar land. There it is explained that rent can be assessed only four years after the first harvest has been completed, that is to say five years from the time the land is first brought under cultivation. No rent can be levied before that time. But who will observe this regulation which is designed to benefit only the kisan? Why should the zamindar observe it? Why should he care at all, inasmuch as he begins to suck the blood (*khoon choosne*) of the kisan even before the korkar land in question has been readied for cultivation. Who can expect silence on the part of the zamindar for a full five years?[16]

In the same section it is written that after the expiry of five years when the zamindar can legally levy rent on the land, it cannot exceed that paid on the least productive paddy field in the village. And if the practice obtaining in that village is such that the rent levied on any pre-existing korkar land is half that levied on third rate paddy land, then the zamindar will have to stay within these same limits. The zamindar will then submit all documentation to the Deputy Commissioner who will initiate an enquiry, including consultation with the kisan, before giving his approval to the zamindar's submission. Only then can the rent on the new korkar land be realized. But in practice this seldom happens, for here in Jharkhand a different Ganga flows [i.e., different rules apply]. I have met responsible kisans lamenting their fate at having to pay whatever rent the zamindar demanded. Who cares for the ruling of the Deputy Commissioner? Who cares about the many sections and subsections of the Tenancy Act?

Now let us consider the particular characteristics of utkar land. I have already said that this is another kind of korkar landholding. But it consists mainly of relatively infertile upland (*unchi ya bari*) in which *moong* and other pulses and grains are grown. It is mostly found in Palamau and to a lesser extent in the district of Ranchi. Some utkar lands are cultivated every year, but the rest is fit for cultivation only at intervals of two to three years. But the zamindars assess rent as they wish from the outset and do not grant receipts. They issue receipts only when they are paid the utkar land rent and the rent for other occupancy holdings of the kisan. But even then they issue a receipt only for the utkar land and not for the occupancy holdings in an obvious effort to place the kisan in debt and thereby put his occupancy rights at risk.[17] What does the kisan know of these fraudulent practices, or to read the receipt, assuming even that he could do so? In fact, the greatest difficulty with regard to these lands is the total ignorance of the kisan about the rules and regulations which govern the system, although once it so happened that nearly 500 kisans of Palamau District petitioned the Deputy Commissioner for revising their rent assessment. But, as it turned out, the appeal was denied.[18]

Payment of rent on utkar land is made both in cash (*nagdi*) and in kind (*bhaoli*). The rents for fertile lands are assessed in kind while those of barren lands are demanded in cash. In the case of rent in kind, the zamindar's share is often so high that it exceeds the entire crop produce of the tenant in a given season! The zamindars are past masters in these manipulations. For example, they assess a separate settlement on the Palas and Mahua trees grown on the utkar land and thereby realize a separate rent as well. As I have mentioned before, Mahua [flowers] are eaten by the Adivasis and Palas leaves are used for lac production. I have already explained that a settlement fee (*salami*) is extracted from the peasant while the utkar land is in process of preparation. If the kisan resists, he is not only assaulted but is forced to pay a penalty and is threatened with false cases. Sometimes legal cases are instituted as well. The assessment of rent is entirely arbitrary and is sometimes so exorbitant that the kisan is forced to quit his holding and flee. At other times kisans are simply dispossessed by force from their good utkar lands.

Editor's Endnotes to Chapter V

1 In this formal introduction to the law of landlord and tenant in Chotanagpur and Bihar, Sahajanand begins to describe the nature of subinfeudation, and the manner in which various kinds of subtenancies come into being. It is notable here that Sahajanand refers to both tenure holders and raiyats as kisans or peasants. That suggests the nature of the legal definitions which concern him here and also the great range of rights and tenancies potentially includable in the term peasant. Sahajanand was more aware of this certainly than anyone and his suggestion here is not to describe large thikedar contractors as peasants. For anyone uncertain of these terminological distictions and Sahajanand's perception of their meaning, I suggest a brief perusal of the *Khet Mazdoor* tract he completed only months before embarking on the *Jharkhand ke Kisan* effort of this volume. Nothing more needs to be said here about definitions, a subject about which far too much ink and print has already been committed over literally decades of speculation and refutation, both ideological and otherwise.

Having said that, I will take only a final moment of explanation for those few readers who might be unfamiliar with the terminology of land tenure in India. The term settlement, or settling the land which Sahajanand uses here literally refers to the contractual agreement by which a landlord or his agent comes to terms with a tenure holder or a peasant tenant. Accordingly the survey and settlement operations of the late nineteenth and early twentieth centuries, implementing provisions of the Bengal Tenancy Act of 1885, defined and documented the existing tenure relationships on the land. These legal definitions are recorded in the survey khatian or register in each administrative district of the province, and a final, published report on the survey and settlement operations was issued for each district as those operations were completed. These reports and the very extensive related documentation are among the more important sources of record for the historian of agrarian relations in India, whether social, economic, or political. The secondary literature is not only vast in its range and complexity but well beyond the scope of these explanatory endnotes. We will rest content with Sahajanand's descriptions, which are certainly a good beginning, and those few sources he cites to reinforce his argument, or titles which bear directly on specific issues he raises. Finally, to repeat one final time, a zamindar is a landlord; and a kisan is a peasant and a raiyat is a tenant. The terms in this peasant category are used interchangeably in this manuscript.

2 The distance between the formal provisions of the law which Sahajanand describes here and the reality on the ground is rather considerable, as Sahajanand's whole career of peasant activism and agitation in Bihar has made amply clear. For example, the stable condition of the occupancy raiyat as defined in the law in fact suffers from many pervasive intrusions in the fields of everyday experience. Many of these intrusions as they occur in Jharkhand are revealed in this and the remaining chapters of this 1941 tract. See for example Sahajanand's discussion later in this chapter of the complexities of korkar land, that is land which the Adivasi kisan brings under cultivation for the first time. See also Editor's Endnote 17 of this chapter. A pakka house is a house with a degree of permanence, solid, well-built, in all likelihood constructed of brick or cement.

3 The mukhiya category of tenancies to which Sahajanand refers here is most often a superior tenancy associated with place and position. A jeth raiyat is in fact a superior or substantial tenant of the village and hence often plays a critical intermediary role between the dominant land controller and the tenant. All the other terms Sahajanand gives here are variations of mukhiya or village head or chief, used in different parts of Jharkhand as Sahajanand reports.

4 Prabhu Prasad Mohapatra renders majhihas as manjhihas, for manjhi, that is pradhan or headman. He also points out that both these tenures are found only in Ranchi District. See his "Class Conflict and Agrarian Regimes in Chotanagpur, 1860-1950," *The Indian Economic and Social History Review* 28:1 (1991), pp. 1-42; "Land and Credit Market in Chotanagpur, 1880-1950," *Studies in History* 6:2 n.s. (1990), pp. 163-199; and especially his unpublished PhD thesis, "Aspects of Agrarian Economy of Chotanagpur, 1880-1950," Centre for Historical Studies, Jawaharlal Nehru University, 1990, which is certainly the most recent and most thorough examination of the agrarian economy of Chotanagpur. I thank Dr. Mohapatra for making a substantial part of this manuscript available to me while he was in the United States during the academic year 1993-94. Regretably his brief visit to the University of Virginia in April 1994 permitted us no more than a moment to probe these issues except at the most preliminary level. The thesis and the published essays I have cited bear on virtually all aspects of Sahajanand's discussion of land and tenure in the *Jharkhand ke Kisan* tract. At appropriate points I will attempt to make the bibliographic connection. A somewhat more technical piece of Dr. Mohapatra's, "Quantitative Estimate of Agricultural Output in Chotanagpur," appears

in Sumit Guha, ed., *Growth, Stagnation or Decline? Agricultural Productivity in British India* (Delhi: Oxford University Press, 1992), pp. 259-284. Prabhu Mohapatra is a Fellow at the Nehru Memorial Museum and Library in New Delhi. See the Glossary following Part II of this volume for definitions which are not obvious or otherwise identified in the text.

5 An anna was 1/16th part of a rupee, and a bigha is a variable measure of land, depending on region, and depending on the length of the local measuring rod or chain which is in use. The standard bigha in the Northwest Provinces was 5/8th of an acres, in Bengal the bigha was a little less than 1/3 of an acres, etc.

6 For the most thorough treatment of bhugutbandh and bhuinhari, see the appropriate entries in John Hoffmann and Arthur Van Emelen, *Encyclopaedia Mundarica*, In 16 Volumes (New Delhi Reprint Edition: Gian Publishing House, 1990), Vol. II, pp. 507-521, extracts from which I have cited in the Frontispiece of this edited translation. Hoffmann's seminal encyclopaedia will be cited in subsequent references simply as *Mundarica*. For a brief comment on the publication history of the *Mundarica*, see Editor's Endnote 6, Chapter III of this volume. On bhuinhari see also Mohapatra, "Class Conflict and Agrarian Regimes," *IESHR* 28:1 (1991).

7 On khutkatti see the reference in the *Mundarica*, Vol. VIII, pp. 2382-2387, and especially the "Special Memorandum on the Land System of the Munda Country," by Father Hoffmann and E. Lister, I.C.S., pp. 2388-2404, which Prabhu Mohapatra rightly refers to as the classic account of the khutkatti system. See also Mohapatra, "Class Conflict and Agrarian Regimes," *IESHR* 28:1 (1991); and S.C. Roy, *The Mundas and Their Country* (Calcutta: Kuntaline Press, 1912). Reissued by Asia Publishing House in Calcutta and New York in 1970). See especially his Ch. III.

8 The relationship between man, forests, and arable land is a complex issue involving a vast range of social and ecological consequences. I have touched on the issue in Endnote 9 of Chapter II, and refer here again to the essay by Richards, Hagen, and Haynes, "Changing Land Use," *MAS* 19:3 (1985), specifically as it relates to Bihar and Chotanagpur. See also P.P. Mohapatra, "Agrarian Economy," JNU Thesis (1990), especially Ch. III on arable expansion in Chotanagpur. For the wider all-India implications of this issue see *B.H. Farmer, Agricultural Colonization in India Since Independence* (London, 1974); and finally, Madhav Gadgil and Ramchandra Guha, *This Fissured Land: An Ecological History of India* (Delhi: Oxford University Press, 1990).

9 Rice, both as a crop or threshed but unhusked is called dhan, hence

the references here are clearly to rice cultivation. The English term for dhan is paddy.

10 Although Sahajanand is not explicit on who the sardars were, the assumption is that they were chosen from among the Paharias themselves. It seems unlikely that non-Paharias would have been brought in to work with and among the Paharias.

11 Although Sahajanand does not use the term, what he is describing here is apparently slash and burn agriculture.

12 The vast gulf between prevailing concepts of landownership on the one hand and that of the Mundas on the other, is described graphically by Father Hoffmann in his bhuinhari entry in *Mundarica*, Vol. II, especially pp. 514-515, where he explains that the Mundas have neither "room in their economic system nor a word in their language," for such a person as a landlord. When the concept was forced on them, "they did not trouble to coin a word for it nor did they, for a long time, deign to borrow the Hind[i] equivalents of the English word landlord, they simply called these people Diku, Hindu or alien." ". . . they were probably convinced that they had proved their case to the hilt when to the landlord's claims they had opposed their stereotyped sayings: We have snatched the fields from the jaw of the tiger and the fang of the snake, we have ploughed and sown, Singbonga sends the rain and sunshine! What has the Diku done that we should pay him anything?' and that other one: 'The burial stones are our title deeds.' Little did they suspect that the presupposition on which the whole force of these statements rests, namely that all the members of an original Mundari village were joint-owners of the whole village on account of their direct descent from the original founder, whose title rested solely on his being the first occupant and the first tiller of that spot, at a time when there was no raja of Chota Nagpur as yet, this presupposition, I say, did not exist in the English mind and would not have been accepted at once and without much argument by the English, even if it had been presented to them in clear and explicit terms." Etc.

More than six decades after these lines appeared in print, and probably more than seventy five years after they were written, the problem for the kisans of Jharkhand has not gone away. On July 7, 1994 the Chief Minister of Bihar, Mr. Laloo Prasad Yadav, announced in the State Assembly "that the Government would soon bring about a major amendment in the Chotanagpur-Santhal Parganas Tenancy Act to avoid transfer of lands belonging to tribals to outsiders." The Minister for Land Reforms and Revenue, Mr. Deonarayan Yadav, was reported to have said that he would immediately despatch a senior officer of the State Government "to investigate illegal settlements of tribal lands with the outsiders. The Minister admitted that the illegal settlement of tribal land worth Rs. 300 crore in Ranchi district had come to light." The Government claimed, however, that it "had cancelled the unlawful settlement of about 144.8 acres of tribal lands with outsiders in Ranchi district recently." See "Chotanagpur Tenancy Act to be Amended," in *The Hindustan Times*, Patna Edition, July 8, 1994, p. 1.

It needs to be noted that the issue of land alienation is not unique to Bihar. The Tripura Minister for Revenue and Industry, Mr. Samar Chowdhury indicated on July 24, 1994 that the Tripura State Government "had launched a massive drive to restore illegally alientated tribal land from non-tribals." The effort was to "rehabilitate the landless and homeless tribals in the restricted reserved and protected forest areas." See "Tripura Drive to Restore Tribals' Land," *The Times of India*, New Delhi Edition, July 25, 1994.

13 A dehi kisan is a settled raiyat, more specifically a tenant who has occupancy rights on the land he cultivates, giving him in legal terms a degree of permanence in his tenancy and the associated rights Sahajanand describes here, which attend that legal status. That it is a right which may be circumvented legally and by custom is the argument Sahajanand is making.

14 Nazrana is one of the many customary perquisites due to the zamindar on the most arcane of occasions, but in this case on allocating tenancy rights to a new peasant holder. On the complexities of the system from the experience of the Adivasi peasant, see again Hoffmann's *Mundarica.* As against the elaborate system of title deeds and grants existing historically in India and reinforced by British perceptions and policy, "the Mundas had no written laws, no written records of any kind and they were of course unable to explain their economic system in anything like clear terms and well reasoned expositions. What was worst of all is the fact that the little they could say to the new masters of their destiny had to be interpreted in the language of their enemies by those very enemies, who had no interest whatsoever to plead for them." *Mundarica*, Vol. II, p. 515.

15 Sahajanand returns here to one of his central sub-texts in this tract, namely the condition of the peasants of Jharkhand and how, because they have been educationally deprived and exploited in every other way, they do not have the political sensitivity to mobilize themselves in ways that would be effective in identifying and pursuing the rights which are justly theirs. This is obviously Sahajanand the peasant activist reflecting on what might have been and the role he could and should have played in this history. While reflecting on what he perceives as the latent possibilities for political mobilization among the kisans of

Jharkhand, Sahajanand nevertheless recognizes the force of character, the will, and the conditions which have driven the Adivasi kisans to an activism notable historically for its persistence. These are of course not inconsistent views inasmuch as both things may be true, that is the history of insurgency in the most extreme conditions, and the prospect for a wider and more vital mobilization in the contemporary present. If Sahajanand did not believe that was happening in the late 1930s, it has certainly been happening increasingly in the decades since, most notably in the 1980s and 1990s as the Jharkhand phenomenon moves in the direction of a more insistent demand for a wider and more sensitive recognition of its cultural, social, economic, and political identity.

16 Blood sucking zamindars and moneylenders is one of Sahajanand's favorite and more graphic metaphors in this tract and in much of his other writing and no less in his public speaking, across the length and breadth of much of Bihar and India in these years. In Endnote 6 of Chapter III, I refer to the remarkable similarity in the critiques Sahajanand and Father Hoffmann were making of the agrarian condition of Chotanagpur, albeit their observations were separated by as much as three decades in time. As example see Hoffmann in the *Mundarica*, Vol. II, p. 507 on moneylenders among the Mundas: "A full and detailed exposition of the practices resorted to by these vampires would hardly find credence among Europeans. Etc."

17 Sahajanand here makes the point I referred to in Endnote 2 at the beginning of this chapter in observing on the vast distance between the legal provisions of the law as Sahajanand was there describing them, and the on-the-ground realities to which he refers here. However generous the Chotanagpur Tenancy Act may appear in defining the rights of peasants with occupancy holdings, the apparent permanence of that right is in many respects illusory as Sahajanand shows in these last pages of Chapter V. The following paragraph reinforces this point in its brief description of the mechanisms of rent assessment on utkar holdings, whether in cash or kind.

18 This experience of the Palamau peasants reinforces Sahajanand's argument through much of this tract about the manner in which the Adivasi kisans are in effect driven against the wall, so to speak, and in this instance where they sought formal redress they were ignored or denied, or both. It is circumstances such as these which have moved the peasants of Jharkhand on more than one occasion historically, to resort to insurgent action in seeking redress. It is such activism Sahajanand apparently seeks by the very revelations he makes in the *Jharkhand ke Kisan* tract.

Chapter VI

Life in the Jungle, or Adivasi Kisans as Victims

[It is appropriate that the longest chapter in this political tract about the peasants of Jharkand deals with the jungle. The life and culture of the Adivasi peasants has been dominated by the jungle in both positive and negative terms. It is the place from which they have carved many of the fields which they cultivate, and its rich products have provided them the very sustenance of life. But it has also been in more recent historic times, a place of ruthless victimization and this chapter chronicles that victimization in the most graphic terms imaginable. The victims are the peasants, the perpetrators are the zamindars, their agents, the government and its agents, whether police, forest rangers, or any of the dozens of other petty officials who demand an unending array of fees, cesses, levies, taxes, and bribes to permit peasant access to the jungle. The degree of this exploitation moves Sahajanand to address the issue of peasant activism and mobilization more directly than anywhere in this tract. He concludes with an attack on the purveyors of religions, in this case the Christian missionaries whose work in education he admires, but whose attempts to separate Adivasi Christian kisans from the wider population he condemns. In the fight for human decency and justice for the rural poor, there is no place for this kind of religious hypocrisy, Sahajanand concludes. Ed.]

The problems inherent in the various forms of cultivation and landholding, such as *kurawnchas*, korkar, and utkar are countless and deeply felt by the peasants of Jharkhand. They would prefer death to the sufferings which are inflicted on them. Their daily lives are consumed by these problems of the land and its cultivation. But there are other problems as well and these are no less painful and together they grind the peasants as between a mill stone. One of the most important of these has to do with their access to the produce of the jungle, its fruits, flowers, wood, bamboo, grass, leaves, roots, water, etc. In the past the peasants may have experienced much suffering but never before had they been deprived of the natural products of the jungle which were always easily available. There was always sufficient water for drinking, bathing, water for their domestic animals, and for irrigation. Mahua, *Genthi* and *Kera* fruits and flowers were always easily available for eating. The Adivasis could also earn by selling the lac produced from the Palas and Kusum trees. There was also sufficient wood and bamboo for making carts, ploughs, and rooves for their houses, and for selling in the market. They would sell *pattals*, or plates made of leaves and prepare beautiful umbrellas from yet other leaves to protect themselves from the rain.

It must also be noted that the Adivasis have scarcely any clothing. The men use mostly a loin cloth or *langoti*, and the women too leave their bodies mostly uncovered! Where from are they to get sufficient clothing? So in the cold of the winter they warm themselves with wood fires and by covering their bodies with paddy straw (*pual*). And they protect themselves from the animals of the jungle by preparing deep enclosures of thorny bushes and thickets around their houses. These enclosures are then covered with creepers like *sem* beans [Phaseolus Magnus] which grow well in this setting. It is these adaptations to the jungle which have defined the life and culture of the Adivasis. But now everything has changed, for all the rights which they had enjoyed from the beginning have been withdrawn! The poor Adivasis are stunned by the calamity which has befallen them. They cannot understand why they have been deprived of their rights in the jungle.

The Survey operations led to the introduction of a *khatian*, i.e., a record of rights, and the zamindars and their agents gained possession over the jungle by bribing the settlement officers![1] For example, one of these jungles is the mountainous forest of the Parasnath Hills. This whole area is now recorded in the *khatian* as belonging to the zamindar. The Manjhis (Santals) living at the foot of those hills are completely debarred by the settlement from taking wood, bamboo, fruits, flowers, leaves, etc. from the jungle or from using even the drinking water of the hill streams! What idea have they about the khatian? They have little education and are simple people. At the time of the survey they had no idea as to what was happening. They did not dream that these wealthy, white-skinned Jains, who were governed by a vow of *ahimsa,* were so black of heart as to deprive them of their forest rights and would not even allow them or their animals to drink the water of the forest. Had they suspected that these two legged animals were at the same time so dangerous and wicked of motive, they would have dealt with them more directly at the time, whatever the consequences. This whole episode made their blood boil. When I attended their meetings at Pirtanr and Dumri they considered these tyrannies and how they might be ended. Despite police instruction to the contrary, they in fact invaded the jungle to reclaim their rights. And the Congress ministers in Patna were shaken. But they could not restore their rights to the kisans! This is yet another example of their concern for the people's welfare and their love for the peasantry![2]

I have already written how reserving the forests has curtailed the rights of the Adivasis, and now after the Survey Settlement still more forests are being reserved. In the process the difficulties of the Adivasis with regard to drinking water, jungle fruits, flowers, etc., are in effect multiplying. They do not know when they will be deprived of yet more rights. No doubt it is often said that their rights to the forest for their domestic use is recorded in the khatian. But I am more concerned with what happens in practice than in theory. These kisans are least concerned with the written word. For them the khatian and its specifications about the kinds of wood, its length and breadth, etc., conveys only confusion. They must first complete an engineering degree and carry with them appropriate scientific instruments, only then can they function in the jungle as the law demands. But they do not read and write. How then can they function in this increasingly complicated environment?

There is much more to be told. The kisans are victim to a continuing series of exploitations. For example, if they were able to meet their needs of wood from the jungle, then what would be left for the forest officials, great and small to do? In fact these "rangers," "foresters," "patrolmen," and others seek out any opportunity to oppress the people, very much like beasts of prey. If they are not bribed, their sole object is to harass the poor. My blood begins to boil when I recall the many stories told to me by the Adivasi kisans of the harassment they have had to endure at the hands of forest officers. The kisans of one village, whose name I cannot now remember, related to me such stories of harassment and intimidation. Their village was in Gawan thana (Hazaribagh) just across a narrow river on the road from Gawan to Hazaribagh. What can anyone know of this gradual torture without having experienced it? I have tried to understand the feelings of the kisans by entering into their hearts. Our educated friends [*babu log*] idle away their time in the Assembly and the Secretariat at Patna. If they were to be born a thousand times they could not understand the pain and sorrow of these afflicted Adivasis. In the end that requires a human heart.[3]

<2.12.41> Other than the ordinary jungle there is also the "protected" (*surakshit*) jungle and the "reserved" (*rakshit*) jungle, both of which have certain restrictions on their use. No one can enter into a "protected" jungle nor touch a blade of its grass. The kisan can, however, enter into a "reserved" jungle and take particular kinds and sizes of wood for certain domestic use. Moreover it is laid down in the jungle regulations that certain varieties of trees cannot be cut, nor can particular leaves and grasses be touched. It is a kind of Jungle Purana, defining [as in the ancient texts] what can and cannot be taken from the forest. These restrictions apply especially to the "reserved" forests, less so to the ordinary forests.[4] It is remarkable that in all the village khatians of the jungle area, specific distances and areas of access within the forests are defined. And the peculiarity is that the zamindar realizes an access tax for that entrance. This is called *tangkar* or *tangikar*. This tax is prevalent all over the area except in Mahuadand thana of the Palamau district. There was a great storm of agitation there over this issue. The Mahuadand thana had in fact become a rebel (*bagi*) area. The trouble continues and taxes are still taken. Every householder has to pay a tax of four annas annually, whether he cuts wood or not. Of course they can sell the wood collected from that forest. Residents of other thanas can only utilise the wood for their domestic purpose except what they can carry on their head.

Whether in Ranchi or in other places, this levy called tangkar or *vankar* is mercilessly realized by the zamindar. In Manbhum, Hazaribagh, and other districts, levies like tangkar, vankar, *patkar*, *lahkar*, *chulhakar*, are all the same tax called by different names in different places. Tangkar is for cutting wood by a *tangi* [axe], chulhakar is for using wood as fuel in a *chulha* [oven], patkar refers to the collection of leaves and vankar refers to the bringing wood from a *van* or forest. In the Ranchi district people formerly paid an annual one anna jungle fee. When the Survey operations began this levy was raised to four annas. Now one rupee and four annas must be paid annually. In addition to this the chaprasi and the jungle clerk (*muharir*) together get four annas for issuing the receipts for these fees. Chaprasis or *barkandazes* who are posted in the jungle also make cash demands, otherwise they too will harass the kisans. These levies go on increasing although this is never shown on paper and when the kisan resists payment, there is always trouble. The Ranka zamindars of Palamau realize the chulhakar tax forcibly. Then when the Survey Settlement began, these local zamindars fraudulently tried to get the levy recorded at four annas per annum, which the Survey officer refused to do. The zamindars of Mahuadand, however, were successful in getting this four anna tangkar levy recorded in the Survey khatian. But for some years they quietly ignored the levy and did not realize a paisa on this account. The kisans who had objected to any such tax presumed that the matter had been dropped. Then when some of these zamindaris came under the Court of Wards and the levy was again imposed, the kisans again raised vigorous objections. Though their reactions were restrained there was nevertheless a strong sense of dissatisfaction in the air. I witnessed this opposition to the tangkar tax when I visited this place in December 1939.

But these levies of four or eight annas are not uniform everywhere. In Hazaribagh and other places I have seen receipts indicating these variations. They show that separate levies are realized for different kinds of wood used for varying domestic purposes. There is no escape from these payments. And as has been indicated before, in reserved forests there are only certain areas where wood can be cut. Like the gates of a temple which opens and closes at fixed hours, these specified areas can be visited only at appointed times. Immediately the forest is opened there is a great rush to make payment and begin cutting. This is because once the forest closes, it may remain closed for as much as three years. So the effort is to collect sufficient fuel for that full three year period. It is also the case that kisans who live a great distance from the jungle must make particular provision to provide their needs thereby to avoid special hardship when the forest is closed.

Previously in Palamau people who maintained cows, water buffaloes, etc., had to pay an illegal exaction called *kharchari*, which was abolished with much difficulty. The zamindars of Ranka were specially known for realizing this illegal tax. I clearly remember the contents of the notice distributed by Mr. Godbole [Y. A. Godbole] now the Chief Secretary of the Government of Bihar. He was then the Deputy Commissioner of Palamau and had threatened the zamindars in that notice that unless they stopped realizing the illegal kharchari tax they would be brought to book. The cattle of the kisans were not allowed to enter the forest without paying kharchari tax. "Reserved jungles" and "protected forests" have the same grazing restrictions even today. Grasses may dry up in these areas, still no cattle are permitted to graze there. If they do, they would immediately be put into a cattle pound or pay the forest guard or the thikedar a bribe. Usually the zamindars farm out their jungle tracts to contractors or thikedars who impose these illegal exactions on the kisans. The zamindar says that he is unable to help inasmuch as he has farmed out the forest to a contractor. The poor kisan must then negotiate with the contractor over the kharchari tax in order to get wood. The zamindar cannot directly demand money from the kisan for fear of acting illegally outside the stipulations of the khatian. Hence he has cleverly adopted this method of making his demands through the agency of the thikedar.

Even where the kisans have legitimate rights to the wood and other products of the forest there too the zamindars and their agents engage in extortion. Unless they take permission from the zamindar or the forest guards and then pay a bribe, the Adivasi peasants will be endlessly harassed. In the jails I have come across prisoners who had been cutting wood in accordance with their rights. When they were stopped and then resisted to the point of violence and someone's death, they inevitably became involved in a criminal case. But because the court conceded the legitimacy of their forest rights they were not sentenced to capital punishment. But inasmuch as they had crossed the limits of acceptable "self-defence" they were sentenced to undergo imprisonment for extended terms! Why had this happened? The guilty parties were in fact the zamindar's agents. Had they not wrongly intervened in the just rights of the kisans, there would have been no encounter and no case.

During the first Congress Ministry the Santals and other kisans of Dumri and Pirtanr thanas in Hazaribagh forcibly started cutting wood in the jungles of the Parasnath Hills. A stormy scene ensued and the armed police were brought in to make arrests and to teach the kisans a lesson. I had earlier gone there on a whirlwind tour to participate in meetings organized by the kisans. When the kisans, in their local dialects and by physical expressions and gestures narrated their woeful tales, I was simply shocked. I was told that like the other zamindars, the Jain businessmen who had purchased that hill had made it clear in the Survey records that the kisans had no rights over streams and rivers, fruits and flowers, wood, and bamboos of the jungle. So without the permission of the Jains, and on payment, the kisans could touch nothing, just as though the air and the sun itself were reserved only for the zamindars![5] Do the kisans know when, why, and by whom these rights were prescribed in the khatian, and were the kisans given any opportunity to object? Had they been informed beforehand what was being done, the kisans certainly would have responded immediately. To punish them after clandestinely manipulating the khatian is absolutely wrong. They must have wood, bamboo, fruits, flowers, grass, leaves, and water to meet their basic subsistence needs. If they are to die a slow death in any event, they will have these rights at whatever cost.

There was much whispering that I had instigated the simple Manjhis [Santals] and they were thus intent on breaking the law! It was very strange! The Manjhis want no more than the basic necessities without which they cannot survive in the struggle for life. Yet it was said that they were being instigated![6] If they are provided the basic necessities, only then can one see whether they are being instigated. But if one insists in speaking in these terms then perhaps a brief encounter with world history will result in a more intelligent appraisal of human affairs. In fact the peasants of the world have done historically whatever was necessary to achieve their rights to the produce of the forest. I quote a short extract from the book *Evolution of Prop-*

erty by Paul Lafargue to shed some light on this wider experience. It runs thus:

> The forests were grabbed up more brutally: eschewing all legal formalities, the landlords adjudged to themselves the ownership of the woods and underwood; they enclosed the forests and forbade hunting, and abolished the right of estovers; the right of taking wood for fuel and for the repairs of houses, fences, implements, etc. The encroachments of the nobles on the forest-lands, which were the common property of the village, gave rise to terrible revolts of the peasants. The Jacqueries, which broke out in the middle of the fourteenth century (1357-58) in the provinces of the north and the centre of France, were in fact, occasioned by the pretentions of the nobles to forbid hunting and to interfere with the right of common in the forests, and the enjoyment of the rivers. Similar conflicts arose in Germany, such as the famous revolt of the Saxons against the Emperor Henry II, and that of the Suabian peasants, who, in the time of Luther, took up arms against the lords, who [had] debarred them from the enjoyment of the forests. These peasant insurrections compelled the lords on several occasions to respect the ancient rights of common, which consisted in the right -- limited only by the peasants' wants -- to take wood and brushwood for hedging, firing and repairing his implements (hedge-bote, fire-bote and plough-bote); and in the right of common pasture, or the right to send his cows, horses, swine and in some cases his goats to graze on the commons throughout the year, the month of May alone excepted. So firmly were rooted these rights that La Poix de Fréminville declared, in 1760, that even in the event of their abuse by the peasants they could not be taken away from them 'for the right of usage is perpetual, and being so, it is accorded alike to the actual inhabitants and to those who may come after them; one cannot strip of an acquired right even those who are as yet unborn.' But the revolutionary bourgeoisie of 1789 felt none of the feudal legists' respect for the peasants' rights and abolished them for the benefit of the landed proprietors.[7]

This extract requires little comment or reaction. Everything is reflected here as clearly as the image in a mirror. It seems as if the author has recorded these words after witnessing personally life in the Jharkhand tract! His description provides a remarkable picture of events here, almost word by word. The only difference is that in countries like France and Germany, the peasants after repeated insurrections and armed rebellions against the zamindars, were able to force them to come to terms, to desist from their inhumanity and openly to respect the rights of the peasants in the forests. But this has not happened in Jharkhand. If at all the kisans did anything here, it was largely peaceful and restrained, and only in a few cases were their actions more forceful and then most often they were suppressed. They could not, by their own power, compel the zamindars to desist from their actions or remove them. The stories of the restrictions imposed in the reserved forests, or at the Parasnath Hills are all fresh in our minds. The issue of forest rights has been a world-wide phenomenon. In Jharkhand, by one stroke of the pen the government of the capitalists has deprived the kisans of their ancient rights and made the zamindars their masters.

And there is yet another difference in our experience that must be noted before we continue. There was in France a great legal thinker who was very familiar with the legal rights of the feudal age and as early as 1760 wrote the following:

> whether the kisans misuse these rights, even then, they cannot be deprived of them. These rights are regarded so dear and are so deep-seated in the human heart that those still unborn shall benefit from them. These have come down in accordance with certain ancient customs and usages and not by virtue of ordinary laws. Hence they will exist forever and those yet to be born cannot be deprived of their benefits. This can never happen, etc.[8]

But here we do not come across such honest and learned legal scholars. At least their writings are not known to me.[9]

What a beautiful and natural idea it is that as the law does not entitle anyone to enjoy rights over the forests, so too the law cannot deprive anyone of these rights. These rights are inherited in accordance with custom and usage and have come down from generation to generation. Hence the function of the law here is only to affix an indelible stamp of approval on these rights and to proclaim their existence for all generations. These rights cannot be taken away. Even if the kisans should misuse these rights they cannot be deprived of them. Yet these days our so-called intellectuals and patriots argue not only that the kisans abuse these rights but that they should be stripped of them, or at least limited in their use. Then only two years ago, a learned scholar gave an appropriate reply to this formulation, explaining that any such restrictions would be sheer high handedness.[10] The kisans should be able to take as much grass, wood, and as many bamboos as they require. In the past we have been influenced by feudal attitudes before civilization had made much progress. But now this is an age of capitalism when we have made full inquiry into the origins and meanings of the peoples' rights, yet the same injustices and brutality are still to be found! So let us then see when and how the kisans can get back their ancient rights fully, those that have come down to them from the ages.

I shall proceed after discussing one further point about forest rights. As already stated, the rights of the kisans to the Palas and other kinds of trees from which lac is produced have been taken away. In almost all the districts of Jharkhand lac is produced to some degree or other. It is produced especially from the "jungle trees," Palas and Kusum and also from the Ber [plum] tree.[11] It is on these trees that lac worms are reared and from which lac is produced. I have personally witnessed this process in Palamau district and I was absolutely astonished at the exploitation of the kisans in the zamindari of Ranka! It seems that any sin or crime can be perpetrated on behalf of the zamindars!

It so happens that the Palas and other lac-producing trees grow on those lands which in the Survey khatian [register] are recorded as the occupancy land of the kisans. But it has been so arranged that the Palas trees growing on those fields have been separately recorded as lying under the possession of the zamindar! This is simply extraordinary. The peasants own all the lands in the area while not an inch of this land is the *khas*, *zirat*, or other personal land of the zamindar. The poor kisans have always cultivated these lands, produced crops on them, protected them, and literally have worked and died on these fields. Neither the zamindar nor his agents have ever set foot on this land! And yet the Palas trees growing on this land have been recorded as in the possession not of the peasant but of the landlord! This is an absolute injustice! It is not as though these trees were planted by the zamindar. They are in fact wild trees of the forest. But because someone once mentioned that these trees belong to the zamindar they were so entered in the Survey khatian. And since then even new trees growing on this land of the kisan are defined as belonging to the zamindar! This is nothing less than a tragedy! It is said that the survey officers made this determination after careful investigation. Is this in fact true, or were they under the influence of alcohol or was some other influence exerted on them?

This same is also true for the Mahua trees, except that unlike the Palas trees, which provide a reasonable income from their lac, Mahua flowers bring hardly four to eight annas. It is however, the staple diet for the poor people of the hilly areas and is an important source of sugar. These poverty-stricken people seldom get sugar or gur, or other foods for that matter. Hence they collect the sweet Mahua flowers, and dry and preserve them for use during the year as a basic food source. These dried flowers are very sweet and warming to the body as well. They are also used for making a local alcohol (*sharab*) called *hanriya* which is also made from boiled rice.[12]

With a heavy heart, I saw for the first time a kisan going to the forest quite early in the morning with an axe in hand and a handful of Mahua flowers tied at the end of his towel. I stopped him and asked as to where he was going. He replied that he was going to the forest to cut wood. When will he return, I inquired. He said that he would be back by night fall. Next morning he would sell the wood in the market and this would provide for his daily needs. And what was his day's meal, I asked? He showed me that handful of Mahua flowers. He also had one anna. I asked him the meaning of that anna. This, he replied, had to be paid at the ghat, i.e., the entrance to the forest, to the zamindar's watchman! This was a daily affair. He barely cut two annas worth of wood! To collect the wood and then dispose of it required two days of work, one day in the jungle and one day going and coming from the market! His income was thus one anna a day after so much of labour and one anna of this went to the zamindar! And there were also the food and clothing needs of his family. So it is not surprising that he had only a handful of Mahua flowers as his day's meal, nor that his bones were clearly visible! I was totally disheartened by this experience and left utterly speechless. My shame was so great at what I had witnessed that I wished that the earth would be rent asunder and I should be consumed in its bowels. Failing that, I must destroy the evil zamindari system and that society which permits such cruel injustice to be done!

This is a brief and painful account of the Mahua! The even more astounding fact is that the Mahua trees which grow not only in the fields of the kisans but elsewhere, are also all recorded as in the possession of the zamindar. But unlike the smaller Palas tree, Mahua trees are very large and cover a wide area, which means that crops cannot grow on at least a *kattha* of land surrounding the tree.[13] But nobody asks that the zamindar who owns these Mahua trees should compensate the kisan for the loss of his crop yield. He should at least remit the rent for that acreage which cannot produce a crop. But who dares raise these questions? The whole atmosphere is poisoned much as if *bhang* were put in the village well, so no one dares speak out![14] All are either the friends or *dalals* [touts, middlemen, agents] of the zamindar. And who will listen to the appeals of the Kisan Sabha? Its workers are viewed as rebels both by the zamindar and the government.[15]

The most painful fact is that our so-called gentlemen zamindars, instead of settling the Mahua and Palas trees with the kisans, seek to settle them first with outsiders. Why so? Simply because the kisans would not like others to enter their fields and so they are obliged to offer the zamindar a higher bid for the Mahua and Palas contract. This is merciless blood sucking much as the dogs try to suck blood from dry bones! The kisan may raise an incessant cry, but who is there to listen? For him not only the government is deaf, but also its courts, its officers, its police, its leaders, as well as the sadhus and mahatmas, gods and goddesses and even God himself, all are deaf to the cries of the kisans!

When they narrated to me the stories of these exploitations, I outlined for them in many "meetings" a firm course of action. I explained that

> if this brutal injustice of the zamindars continues, then let them settle the trees with others and we will remain quiet. But let it

> also be known openly that those who enter into such settlements with the zamindars shall have no access to our lands. Without our permission they have neither any moral or legal right to step into our fields. Be aware! Those who enter into contracts or settlements with the zamindar may come by air or magic to collect the lac and Mahua flowers. We shall permit this. But as soon as they step into our fields, we shall break their legs and in this act they shall be held guilty. The responsibility will not be ours, and they should never forget this fact, etc. etc.[16]

Only then will the kisans have victory. This is a clear and unfailing remedy. Even today, I can prescribe the same remedy for the kisans. I have no other remedy. Tyrants have no respect for humble prayers or quiet appeals. On the contrary, they only practice their tyranny more daringly. As soon as the kisans become self-reliant and are able to stand on their own feet, they are certain to win their rights. They must be prepared to die for these rights. They must forsake fear and organize themselves. The zamindars will have no fear of one, two or four kisans; they must be given a collective challenge on the issue of rights in the trees. Only with an organized and large scale opposition will the zamindars, their agents, and thikedars [contractors] finally lose heart.

<3.12.41> I am reminded of an important incident in connection with Mahua. During my tour of Palamau, I had come to Mahuadand in December 1939, and what I saw there was simply unforgettable. We were greeted by a great procession of Adivasi kisans, men, women, and their children, who had come from near and far proudly bearing their banners and flags.[17] It was there that I saw for the first time so many different flags. These peasants in their simplicity and innocence (*sidhe aur bhole*) created a scene by their numbers and their very presence, which could only evoke admiration.

And when I reached the meeting ground I found the rostrum erected in the large maidan of the Dak bungalow. It was constructed entirely from local materials and decorated with jungle leaves and branches. It was a very large gathering and people were sitting all around in groups. The Netarhat Hills lie adjacent to Mahuadand and at this time of the year this place is especially cold. Yet these kisans, men and women, were almost without clothes, which is in fact how they normally live. They are a black people, handsome and sturdy of body. I have always admired their beautiful, well-formed features. Had they been getting milk, ghee and other nutritious food, imagine how they would have looked then!

When I climbed onto the rostrum in this vast gathering of kisans, I found thirty or thirty-five kinds of fruits and flowers wrapped in large jungle leaves. On inquiry I learned that this is what the poor kisans eat, but even these fruits and roots of the jungle are taxed by the zamindars! Imagine! Even the roots, fruits, flowers, and leaves of the jungle have not been spared from the extractions of the zamindar. Some of these are so bitter and near poisonous, that they must first be boiled for hours before they can be eaten. But the hunger of the kisans must be satisfied and this too is their food. For example, 1) *genthi* is a jungle root which must be boiled four times and kept in water the whole of the night, only then can it be eaten. The same is the case with 2) *sarai*, a fruit which grows on the *sakhoo* tree [Sal] and is also very bitter. It must be boiled at least six times before it becomes edible. Other trees and edible forest products are: 3) *tend*, 4) *dinthora*, 5) *ber* [plum], 6) *goolar*, 7) *pipal*, 8) *bar* [Banyan fruit], 9) *goolar* fruit, 10) *pakar* fruit, 11) Mahua, 12) *chakaur* leaves, 13) *kyonar* leaves, etc. Because these are jungle trees, fruits, and leaves they do not require to be cultivated by the kisans. Those crops which are cultivated include: 14) *gondli*, 15) *surguja*, 16) *kodo* [a coarse grain], 17) *marua* [also a coarse grain], 18) *sawan*, 19) *kurthi* [dal], 20) *batra*, and 21) *jatangi* [an oil seed]. At some places pulses like 22) *rahar* [arhar], 23) *urad*, are also grown but in very small amounts. A jungle fruit called 24) *bel* is also a staple food of the Adivasis. There are as many as ten or twelve other such edible jungle products. The sight of these jungle foods, literally brought tears to my eyes. I thought that had there been a just and almighty God whose place it was to befriend the poor, his throne would have long since been threatened with destruction given the condition of these Adivasis. Who can be more poor and innocent than these people of the jungle?

While addressing the Mahuadand meeting (*sabha*) I lay bare my heart before these kisans. They listened with rapt attention. I am used to speaking in simple language which can be understood by the kisans of the jungle.[18] I have also worked with jungle kisans in Gujarat. While in the Mahuadand meeting ground I learned that the kisans of the neighbouring areas who had been converted to Christianity by the old "Roman Catholic Mission" in the locality, were prevented from coming to the Mahuadand meeting. I was beside myself with rage when I heard this. I frankly said that I am not at all concerned with religion. I simply want to meet the people, talk with them and help them better to understand their condition, whatever their religion. Hence I have no quarrel with the Christian religion. But when I learned of this particular incident I was angered. Do they want their converts to behave only like sheep of Jesus Christ? If so, this is wrong.

I was under the impression that the Christians were not only converting the Adivasis to their religion but also teaching them to fight for their rights. In fact we have seen cases where Chamars who had become Christians confronted their Hindu zamindars.[19] I had also thought that so long as the Adivasis were Hindus they possessed three attributes, namely, speaking the truth, and being moral and fearless.[20] But they lived like animals and this too the Hindus had brought them. When they became Christians, apparently these great virtues were lost to the demon of civilization. It flourishes on their ashes. But one presumes that the Christian Adivasis would also have become men of courage prepared to fight for their rights. We must recall that the Christian priests came from those very European states where the peasants had revolted and toppled their kings. As I have already stated, they had done everything for preserving their rights over the forests. The assumption is that the same teachings would have been imparted here as well.

But when I visited some neighbouring villages, I learned that the Adivasi Christians lived in a totally different world from the rest of the kisans. They were kept separately like lambs of Jesus Christ. I was pained to see this. It is not what I had expected. No sooner had they changed their religion than they cut all relationships with their Adivasi brothers in the neighbourhood and lived a completely separate life. This is not acceptable. It must be said that in this regard the missionaries are doing a great injustice! No purpose is served by instigating Christian kisans to quarrel with Hindu kisans in the name of religion! This is an old disease the world over and is widespread in this unfortunate land of ours. We want to be relieved of this problem and we were hopeful that these missionaries coming from the

Western countries might have brought a more enlightened attitude with them on this issue, moving the Christian kisans rather to fight for bread, land, and justice. But I was disappointed at the failure of the missionaries to have inculcated these values among the Adivasi converts to Christianity. This was the first opportunity I had personally to witness these unfortunate circumstances. Then when I visited other nearby villages to enquire into the condition of the kisans, I came across other strange practices.[21]

Firstly, one evening I met three or four children on the road going toward the Mission. I was curious to know where they were going at this hour. When one of my Kisan (*"kisan" jati wale*) companions asked them in their language, they replied that they were going to see the Father (*padri, guru*) "to confess their sins." I heard this answer from a young girl. I could not understand its meaning. I had known that at the time of death, Christian priests took "confessions" from the dying. But what was happening now? Later on I learned that there was a practice among the Christians to go daily, or at intervals of two to four days for making a confession of their sins before the Father. When the elder members of the family were not free, they sent the children to make confessions on their behalf! How strange! It is like using a good soap for washing off their daily misdeeds! Just as the Hindus wash away their sins by repeating an evening prayer or mantra (*sandhya gayatri*) and the Muslims by daily prayer (*namaz*), so too the Christians by doing confession! It would appear that in this regard history is repeating itself!

Secondly, I learned that just like Hindu gurus and Muslim pirs, these Christian priests (*padri guru*) visit their disciples (*chelon*) in every village each year, being fed and accepting offerings of rupees and clothing as a form of "*puja*."[22] When possible they also seek new converts on these tours! As I have suggested, this practice of moving from village to village seeking gifts is not unlike that of some Hindu priests and gurus! The missionaries do not preach on issues of contemporary importance to the families they visit, rather they practise hypocrisy in the name of religion! May God save them!

There is one more interesting experience in connection with the meeting at Mahuadand. Just after the meeting was over all the kisans who had come from distant places began an all night celebration. They had brought rice, wood, and cooking pots with them, and started preparing food in groups in the vicinity of the meeting ground. I had retired before they took their food, when suddenly I was awakened in the dead of night. What I heard was a beautiful melody sung with the accompaniment of a *mridang* [a kind of two-ended drum], and cymbals and other instruments. When I came out to watch, I saw men and women dancing and singing in groups! They went round and round, facing each other, singing and dancing in perfect rhythm. What a beautiful sight it was, I cannot describe it! It was dancing and singing as well as physical exercise and a kind of work, all at once! When I watched more closely I found a kind of competition going on between the male and the female groups, and this went on for the whole night! They knew no rest and only on the next morning would their dancing be over! None had had a wink of sleep! At first I had wondered how they would be able to spend this cold winter's night in an open field with so little clothing. But now I had the answer! Their dance was exercise, entertainment, and a display of art all at once, and above all it provided relief from the pangs of winter! What a remarkable achievement, combining all of this into one remarkably integrated performance. No doubt fires were kept burning at a few places but no one sat near them for any length of time! I can never forget this heaven-like sight! I have witnessed similar things in the jungle tracts of Gujarat when I was on tour in that province. And this same kind of thing obviously happens at other places as well!

One troublesome issue of great harshness and pain in the life of the jungle kisans remains to be considered. This involves the impounding of their cattle by the forest chaprasis and the *amlas* or agents of the zamindars. I have seen poor kisans beating their chests and crying aloud on this account. They are literally robbed, looted, and stripped of all their belongings in the process. The fact is that cattle pounds (*kanihaus*) are a regular feature of the forest areas where stray animals are locked up. These pounds are no less than slaughter houses. Animals there mostly die without food or water, even though a handfull of fodder is placed before them just for show. In fact cattle are effecively being killed there in this way! I have myself witnessed this sight. I cannot understand why these civilized slaughter houses are permitted at all to exist.

As soon as the jungle guards or the zamindar's agents have occasion to feel angry with the kisans, they search out their cattle and drive them into the pound! More than fifty or a hundred cattle are put into the pound at a time! The penalty which must then be paid for their release compels the kisans to sell their lands, household goods, etc. Laws are such that the kisans cannot oppose this practice, otherwise they are immediately involved in criminal cases! Four and twenty hours they must deal with the zamindar's agents and forest guards, supplying them with milk, curd, ghee, even bribes; otherwise, these guards will become enraged! Times without number the kisans have demanded the removal of these notorious cattle pounds so that they may finally breathe a sigh of relief!

Editor's Endnotes to Chapter VI

1 As I have explained in an earlier note, the Survey and Settlement operations were undertaken in the late nineteenth and early twentieth centuries in implementing provisions of the Bengal Tenancy Act of 1885. That Act applied to greater Bengal including Bihar and Chotanagpur with subsequent modifications in specific Tenancy Acts both for Gangetic Bihar and for Chotanagpur, and also for Santal Parganas as indicated by Sahajanand in earlier chapters of this tract, especially Chapter V. As example, dates for survey and settlement proceedings in some of the Chotanagpur districts are as follows: Ranchi, 1902-1910; Hazaribagh, 1908-1915; and Palamau, 1913-1920. There was a revisional survey and settlement in Ranchi during the years 1927-1935. It is these surveys to which Sahajanand refers in this and other chapters. In each instance a final published report on the survey and settlement operations was issued, generally a year or two following completion of the survey. The actual khatians or registers recording the results of the proceedings were/are functional land revenue records and maintained in the district record rooms of the several districts of the province at the time Sahajanand was writing and continuing so after Independence. See also Chapter VIII following where Sahajanand deals specifically and in some detail with provisions of the Chotanagpur Tenancy Act and its meaning for the kisans of Jharkhand. At the present writing I do not have immediate access to the Survey and Settlement literature for Chotanagpur and accordingly rely for the references in this Note on the published and unpublished work of P.P. Mohapatra cited in the Endnotes of the preceding chapter.

2 Dumri was/is in the immediate vicinity of Parasnath, and Pirtanr not far distant slightly to the north and east. All three places were in Hazaribagh district at the time Sahajanand was writing and in 1994 are in the new Giridih district. While Sahajanand had not spent much time in Jharkhand during the peak years of peasant activism in Gangetic Bihar where the meetings, rallies, and agitations in which he was involved numbered literally in the hundreds, he was not entirely absent from the Chotanagpur districts as this report on the Parasnath meetings suggests. But by comparison we are problably looking at numbers in the tens rather than the hundreds. The other point here is that by the late thirties, indeed during virtually the full period of the Congress Ministry in Bihar between mid-1937 and October 1939, Sahajanand and the Indian National Congress were in a sharply con-

frontational political relationship, a fact which explains the Swami's pointed criticisms of Congress actions or inactions throughout this tract.

3 Again, Sahajanand here is cynically critical of the politicians in the Legislative Assembly in Patna and the civil servants in the provincial Secretariat, also of course, in Patna. More notable perhaps is the deep, indeed emotional sensitivity Sahajanand feels and expresses here for the condition of the Adivasi kisans of Jharkhand, however limited his involvement with their lives had been in the decade before he wrote. He was in many ways a driven man, whether the kisans of his concern were the peasant tenants and agriculural labourers of Gangetic Bihar, or as in the present case the Adivasi kisans of Jharkhand. As we have suggested in the introduction it was this deep anxiety about achieving some measure of justice and human decency for all peasants, however defined, which moved Sahajanand perhaps to make political decisions that in the end did not serve his central object in ways that he might have liked. He wanted change sooner than later.

4 I have explained in an earlier Endnote that protected forests were those forests in private hands, and hence as Sahajanand explains, imposed the severest restrictions on their use. Next in order of severity is the forest reserved by the government, and it is this category of forest to which Sahajanand addresses most of his remarks in this chapter. We may infer from his infrequent mention of the third category of ordinary forests that they were fewer in number or relatively less important in the lives of the kisans of Jharkhand with whom Sahajanand is here concerned.

5 I cannot resist continuing here the comparisions between Sahajanand's perceptions of peasant reality and the cultural perceptions of that reality in the experience of the Adivasi kisans themselves, again as related by Father Hoffmann who was so powerfully influenced by and deeply sensitive to the Munda experience. Hoffmann quotes a Munda saying, which I have cited previously, which is an almost verbatim expression of the point Sahajanand makes here, to wit: "We have snatched the fields from the jaw of the tiger and the fang of the snake, we have ploughed and sown, Singbonga sends the rain and the sunshine! What has the Diku done that we should pay him anything?" *Mundarica*, Vol. II, p. 515. On Singbonga see Hoffmann's long entry both on Singbonga and on legends relating to Munda folklore, *Mundarica*, Vol. XIII, pp. 3973-3988. To quote briefly from that entry: "Singbonga, the spirit of light, the Supreme God of the Mundas, all-good, omniscient and omnipotent; maker, master and fosterer of all things living or inanimate. Etc." See also Editor's Endnote 6 of Chapter III and Endnote 9, following in this Chapter.

Sahajanand's uncanny sensitivity to the Adivasi's view of their world makes one believe that Sahajanand perhaps imbibed more deeply and more fully in the Jharkhand peasant experience than he reports or than we have previously thought. This does not alter the fact that his direct political involvement in mobilizing the peasants of Jharkhand was limited by comparison with what he was doing elsewhere, but it does suggest that only with the kind of emotional sensitivity he shows in this tract could he in fact have expressed the poignant regret which emerges in these pages that he was not a fuller and more active participant in the lives and politics of the kisans of Jharkhand.

6 Sahajanand makes a fundamental point here about the nature of peasant activism, namely that peasants whether in Gangetic Bihar or in Jharkhand are perfectly aware of their social and economic condition and do not require or depend on outside "instigators" to tell them they are being exploited and how that experience might affect their lives. This is a slight variation from Sahajanand's theme earlier in this tract that the "simple, backward" kisans of Jharkhand are so removed from contemporary political realities and techniques of mobilization that they have not been able to assert their just rights. These observations are not meant to suggest that on-the-ground peasant awareness is or should inevitably function independently of outside agents of mobilization. This is of course precisely the role Sahajanand played in Gangetic Bihar and the role he was playing in the Parasnath Hills area of Hazaribagh, namely to participate in moving the local awareness of rights denied to a more sophisticated level of consciousness about what might be done to redeem those rights. The relationship between the peasant in the villages and fields of conflict on the one hand, and the local and outside activist on the other, is after all a reciprocal one. Each facilitates and reinforces the consciousness, awareness, and understanding of the other in terms that at their most positive can only be described as symbiotic. It is that kind of symbiotic relationship Sahajanand had established with the peasants of Gangetic Bihar and which is clearly reflected in the sensitivity Sahajanand shows for the kisans of Jharkhand in these pages.

7 The term estover in this extract from Lafargue, as he himself explains, refers to a right guaranteed in law to necessary natural requirements of the peasants, as for example, to forest wood which a tenant may need for completing needed repairs to his implements or house, etc.

Sahajanand often provided dates and page numbers for the sources he cited, but in this case he did neither. The exceptions to this practice were most often to official publications of the British Indian Government for which Sahajanand provided fairly complete bibliographic data and which were presumably more easily available. We need to keep in mind of course, that even British jails did not have elaborate library facilities, and more importantly that Sahajanand was producing a political tract, not a historical monograph. It is in fact revealing of the man's attention to detail that he provided as much information as he did about the large numbers of references he used in these tracts to reinforce his argument. He obviously knew his sources well, quite apart from the richness of a remarkably full political career which was reflected in virtually everything he wrote.

In the case of the Lafargue title we can only estimate the particular edition of the book he might have had at his disposal in the Hazaribagh Central Jail. It is of course well known that a good range of Marxist literature was available to political prisoners in British Indian jails, the more so after the German attack on the Soviet Union in June 1941, but even before that date in keeping with the anti-Fascist sensibilities of the Raj. The full reference to the first edition of Lafargue is as follows: Paul Lafargue, *The Evolution of Property From Savagery to Civilization* (London: Swan Sonnenschein & Co., 1890). The book was issued again by the same publisher in 1890 and in 1894, and in that year also in New York: Scribner's Sons. An early twentieth century edition, which may have been the one Sahajanand used, was published in Calcutta: Bharati Library, 19—. We do not know the exact date of that edition, except as I have indicated that it was early in the century. A recent American edition is that edited by Richard Broadhead, ed., *Selected Marxist Writings of Paul Lafargue* (Berkeley: Center for Socialist History, c1984). One of the early editions reports that "Paul Lafargue was one of the two or three men who established a Marxist movement in France. He became its leading propagandist and educator." Lafargue's dates were 1842-1911.

8 Sahajanand gives only the Devanagri of this quote and provides no source but it is clearly from de Fréminville. It is obviously taken in part from the Lafargue quote cited above, with some minor continuation which does not appear in the extract from Lafargue. de Fréminville's full name was Edme de La Poix de Fréminville. His dates were 1683-1773.

9 The irony I refer to in Endnote 6 of Chapter III is compounded further by this statement of Sahajanand's and his appeal to an eighteenth century French legal scholar and a nineteenth century French Marxist publicist to reinforce his sense of the just rights of the kisans of Jharkhand to the forest and its products. The concepts which de Fréminville and Lafargue describe from the European experience are concepts embedded in the Adivasi cultural experience, albeit not in

written form. But that written form was provided not by a legal scholar but by Father John Hoffmann in his *Encyclopaedia Mundarica*, which certainly marks him as a deeply sensitive ethnologist, historian, linguist, and protagonist of Adivasi culture, a culture which enshrines the very rights to the jungle of which Sahajanand was more than aware and of which he writes here so forcefully. That Sahajanand was unaware of the *Mundarica*, published at Gulzarbagh literally only miles from Sahajanand's Sitaram Ashram at Bihta and both in Patna District, is an unfortunate coincidence of history. On the conceptual link in the thinking of Sahajanand and Father Hoffmann, apart from Endnote 6, Chapter III, see also Endnote 5 of this present chapter.

A contemporary of Sahajanand's and also deeply sensitive of Adivasi culture, especially that of the Santals was W.G. Archer, who was District Magistrate of Patna at the very time Sahajanand was in the Hazaribagh Central Jail. Archer's publications came much later, and whether he and Sahajanand knew one another we do not learn from Sahajanand's writing, and I have personally not had the opportunity of examining the Archer Papers in the Oriental and India Office Collections in London. Among Archer's many publications, see especially on the Santal, *Hill of Flutes: Life, Love and Poetry in Tribal India: A Portrait of the Santals* (London: George Allen Unwin, 1974), and *Tribal Law and Justice: A Report on the Santal* (New Delhi: Concept Publishing Company, 1984).

10 Sahajanand's tantalizing reference here to the words of a "learned scholar" writing or speaking in 1939, is regretably left incomplete. Sahajanand could conceivably have been referring to something W.G. Archer might have said on forest rights, although as an I.C.S. officer Archer might not be identified by Sahajanand as a "learned scholar." In any event, we will never know to whom Sahajanand was referring.

11 For the botanical names of the Palas, Kusum, and Ber trees see the entry for Lac in the Editor's Glossary following the Devanagri text in Part II of this volume. See also related entries for Mahua and Sal, other important trees of the jungle tracts of Jharkhand.

12 Sahajanand uses the term hanriya here in a generic sense for sharab or country liquor made variously from Mahua flowers or boiled rice. He refers again to hanriya in Chapter IX specifically as it is made from boiled rice. In the *Mundarica*, Hoffmann's Munda term for the drink made from Mahua flowers is arki, which is presumably derivative from the Arabic, Hindi, and Tamil arak, or araku, for spirit, juice, essence, or more specifically, a fermented liquor. See *Mundarica*, Vol. IX, p. 2743; and H.H. Wilson, *A Glossary of Judicial and Revenue Terms . . .* (London: Wm. H. Allen & Co., 1855), p. 30. Wilson was reissued

in 1968 in Delhi by Munshiram Manoharlal.

The description here and especially in the succeeding paragraph is as poignant and revealing a statement about the social and economic conditions of Adivasi culture in 1941 as is perhaps found in Sahajanand's tract. For an equally poignant statement on the phenomenon in 1994 see the long report by P. Sainath of *The Times of India* from Sarguja district in Madhya Pradesh bordering on Palamau and Gumla districts in Jharkhand. Sainath reports in part as follows, commenting on the local Adivasi Pandos: "The little agricultural produce they generate and the mahua flowers they collect go to the nearest moneylender who sells them for eight times what he pays them. 'Suppose we decide to stay for dinner?' 'We will feed you mahua wine,' says Puthuli, Budhram's wife, laughing, 'We have nothing else.' Budhram seems to pin his hopes on the education of their grandchildren. Perhaps if the children learned something, then we too can learn something from them, then maybe people can't treat us the way they do now.'" *The Times of India*, New Delhi Edition, August 3, 1994.

13 A kattha is 1/20th part of a bigha, which as I have explained earlier is a variable land measure, depending on the region and within a given locale on the length of the chain or rod used in making the measurement. Grierson gives a pakka bigha at 1,600 square yards, or a little less than 1/3rd of an English acre of 4,840 square yards. By this calculation a kattha would be the equivalent of 80 square yards, or 720 square feet. Other calculations put a bigha at 0.25 part of a hectare or 0.625 or an American acre of 4,800 square yards. Inasmuch as a hectare is 10,000 square meters, a bigha by this calculation would be 2500 square meters and a kattha 125 square meters, which would be 150 square yards, or 1350 square feet. These figures make the obvious point about wide regional variation in the concept bigha and kattha, but they do not alter Sahajanand's point here that whatever the measure, the peasant is losing valuable cultivable land by the presence of one tree or many trees on his fields.

14 Wilson describes bhang as "an intoxicating preparation of hemp (Cannabis Sativa), either an infusion of the leaves and capsules, or the leaves and stalks bruised and pounded, and chewed or smoked like tobacco. According to Mr. Elliot, the natives of Hindustan distinguish the Bhang from the Ganja plant; the former bearing female flowers only, the latter male. From Dr. O'Shaughnessy's description, the term Bhang properly applies to the larger leaves and capsules, and Ganja to the dried plant with the stalks. From Bhang is prepared the infusion bearing the same name. The Ganja is used for smoking." (p. 76). For Ganja quoting Wilson, "The hemp plant (Cannabis Sativa), or according to

some authorities, a different species (Cannabis Indica); according to others it is applicable to the plant only whilst young. . . In Bengal the [young flowers and leaves] are dried and pounded, and then used in smoking. The intoxicating property depends in either case upon the resinous exudation of the plant adhering to the vegetable substance." (p. 165). Grierson adds: "The hemp plant (Cannibus Sativa) is known as ganja when cultivated in Rajshahi, and bhang when wild elsewhere. The leaves are known as bhang, sabuja (north-west), or sabja (Patna and Gaya). A favourite way of taking the drug is in the form of a sweetmeat, called majum. Charas is the resin which exudes from the flowers and leaves." (p. 243). See also Crooke, who adds for hemp that "The plant itself is ganja. The leaves are known under the name of bhang, siddhi, patti, and sabzi or sabji. . . The male plant is marda, the female madi, and the hermaphrodite plants khasia. (p. 113). See H.H. Wilson, *A Glossary of Judicial and Revenue Terms* . . . (Delhi reprint of 1855 original edition: Munshiram Manoharlal, 1968); George A. Grierson, *Bihar Peasant Life* . . . (Delhi reprint of 1885 original: Cosmo Publications, 1975); and William Crooke, *A Glossary of North Indian Peasant Life* (Delhi reprint 1879 original: Oxford University Press, 1989), edited by Shahid Amin.

15 This is one of the more specific appeals Sahajanand makes in this tract to an active mobilization of the kisans of Jharkhand over a given issue, in this case that of control and access to the Mahua and Palas trees on the lands of the peasants. It is an issue in which he felt the kisans suffered grievous injustice and in which he obviously became directly involved. It is also one of the few occasions in this tract where he refers directly to the Kisan Sabha and its potential role in Jharkhand and its relations with both Government and the zamindars.

16 Following on the previous note, it is clear that Sahajanand was deeply exercised by the injustices the peasants suffered over the custom and law which had the zamindar controlling the trees on the land of the kisans. He issues here a specific call for action which, it should be noted, calls unapologetically for violence in the defence of peasant rights. The paraphrase he gives us suggests that he was perhaps more widely involved in this kind of agitation on behalf of the kisans of Jharkhand than we had heretofore thought, although this suggestion is based only on the evidence immediately at hand.

17 Sahajanand here specifically uses the term Adivasi kisan, a point I note because most often in the Adivasi setting which he writes about in this tract, he simply uses the term kisan or Adivasi, or a range of other Hindi terms for people, Adivasis, original inhabitants, etc., which in context are obviously references to Adivasi kisans, that is, the Adivasi peasants of Jharkhand.

18 As the pages of this tract make amply clear, Sahajanand always spoke in the language of the peasants, meaning that he addressed them in the local, colloquial, and hence familiar vernacular which was their language and which they best understood. The same is true in much of Sahajanand's writing, especially his political tracts, of which *Jharkhand ke Kisan* is a good example. The Hindi version of the original manuscript, duplicated verbatim and unedited in Part II, is written very much as Sahajanand spoke to his peasant audiences, what we may refer to as *bol chal ki bhasha*, i.e., language as spoken. And I have suggested more than once in these Endnotes that Sahajanand always spoke "from the heart," to use his term; he had not only a sensitivity to the peasants and the lived experience of their daily lives, in whatever terms we might want to define it, but a deep emotional commitment to understanding their condition, and to changing it. It was for him a total commitment and it consumed his total energy and effort whether in Gangetic Bihar, or as here in Palamau among the Adivasi kisans of Mahuadand. That commitment was unwavering and it was expressed not only in the language of the kisans but with a degree of candor and directness that left no one in doubt about where Sahajanand stood. The objects of his scorn were just as likely to be politicians as zamindars and moneylenders, or as in the remainder of this chapter, Christian missionaries, Hindu priests and purohits, or to use one of his favourite terms of derision, gurus. If the peasants were being victimized by whomever in Sahajanand's view, the perpetrators of that victimization were subject to his wrath and to the graphic and uncompromising language he used to express it.

Later in this chapter Sahajanand refers to an encounter he had with several young peasant children, with whom he spoke "in their language," through a local Adivasi companion. The question thus arises, what was the language in which Sahananand addressed the Adivasi kisans of Mahuadand, or of any other part of Jharkhand or India ? On his testimony we may presume that he conveyed his thoughts in ways that were understood by the kisans, whether through someone who translated his words or by his own tongue. We should remember that Sahajanand was a man of very substantial intellectual and linguistic achievement. Though I have no way of knowing this, I am assuming here that Sahajanand knew no Adivasi language. Several brief points of explanation then need to be made about the issue of communication in addressing the kisans of Jharkhand. On page 116 above, Sahajanand makes the not unimportant point about the kisans narrating their woeful tale both in their local dialects "and by physical gestures and expressions."

It must be further noted also, that despite his apparent language limitations in Jharkhand, this was nevertheless not totally unfamiliar territory for Sahajanand. He had made more than an occasional foray into the area, although to counter the logic I am developing, we might suggest that among other reasons for his more limited activity in Jharkhand as compared to Biharkhand, the problem of language might be one. However that may be, it is secondly the case that by 1961 the Adivasi population of Jharkhand was estimated to be in the range of one-third the plateau's population. (I have discussed these percentages in an Endnote to an earlier chapter.) Even assuming, based on Sahajanand's figures in the earlier part of this manuscript, that the percentage figures were somewhat higher when he was writing, we still have a substantial non-Adivasi population, many of whom, however, again following Sahajanand, are integrated into the local agrarian Adivasi culture and economy. These are the Sadans, and include significantly, agricultural castes like the Kurmis and Gwalas (Yadav or Ahir). This would help explain what is a third and further consideration, which is that there is a substantial degree of bilingualism in the Jharkhand region, the most relevant numbers for which are available in the 1931 and the 1961 Census Reports for Bihar. The 1931 Census shows a wide distribution of Hindustani speakers in the Chotanagpur districts and Santal Parganas, while the 1961 Census suggests a similar trend with as many as eighteen of Bihar's thirty enumerated Adivasi groups speaking a second (non-tribal) language, in most cases Sadani, which S.D. Prasad describes "as a form of Bhojpuri." While these eighteen include none of the major groups, it nevertheless suggests a pattern, which closer examination might suggest was already apparent in 1931 and which presumably continues. Sadani is clearly the first language for the Sadans of Jharkhand, namely those non-Adivasis whom we have referred to frequently in these Notes.

This bilingualism will be further reinforced by what is a fourth consideration, namely the distribution of Adivasi populations in the districts of Jharkhand. The 1961 Census for example reveals that while most (93.7 percent) of the Adivasi population of Bihar resides in the Jharkhand plateau districts, within that Jharkhand universe, 31 out of every 100 Adivasis are to be found in Ranchi, 24 in Santal Parganas, 23 in Singhbhum, 6 in Hazaribagh, 5 in Palamau, and 3 in Dhanbad. What these figures reveal are low Adivasi distributions in three of the six districts, including Palamau where Sahajanand was speaking in December 1939. Finally, it is also the case that the Kharwar, although in 1961 numbering only 109,357 but the fifth largest tribal group in Bihar were almost exclusively Hindu by Census definition and concentrated mainly in the Palamau District. A number of inferences about levels of language understanding may conceivably be drawn from these several factors, apart from Sahajanand's reactions, which we will address in a succeeding Endnote. For 1931 data, see Census of India, 1931, Vol. VII, *Bihar and Orissa, Part II, Tables* (Patna: Superintendent Government Printing, 1932), Table XV, Part II, Bilingualism, esp. pp. 120-121. For 1961 data see Census of India, 1961, Vol. IV, Bihar, Part V-A, *Special Tables for Scheduled Castes and Scheduled Tribes* (Patna: Superintendent of Census Operations, 1965), esp. pp. x, xi, and xxx. S.D. Prasad, I.A.S. was the Superintendent of Census Operations in 1961.

19 Chamars are on the lower fringes of Untouchability whose caste function it is to remove the carcasses of dead cattle. Hence they are also leather workers, and of course many are landless agricultural labourers or low end tenants, which is the point of Sahajanand's juxtaposing Christian Chamars and their Hindu zamindars in a confrontation over rights, thereby to demonstrate the courage which their new status as Christians had given them, or this was Sahajanand's assumption and hope.

20 Sahajanand's passing inference here suggesting that Adivasis are Hindu or were so before adopting Christianity in the case of Adivasi Christians, seems to pass over one of the fundamental elements of Adivasi culture, namely the importance of what S.D. Prasad, Superintendent of the 1961 Census in Bihar described as "tribal religion," and what Adivasis themselves and generations of scholars have defined as Sarna, in the case of the Munda and the Oraon, Jahera for the Santal, and Deshauli for the Ho, each of these terms referring to the Sacred Grove. I have referred earlier to other elements of Munda religious belief and practice in citing Father Hoffmann in the *Encyclopaedia Mundarica*. The 1961 Bihar Census percentages for all tribes is 72.1 percent Hindu, 17.4 percent "Tribal," and 10.5 percent Christian. At 73.3 percent, the Ho have the largest number of adherents of Adivasi religious beliefs, the Kharia with 61.4 percent the largest number of Christian believers, followed by the Munda with 26.3 percent, and the Oraon with 23.8 percent. The largest Adivasi group in Bihar, the Santal have Christian followers of 1.8 percent, Hinduism, 91.5 percent and Jahera, 6.7 percent.

Another possibilty in explaining Sahajanand's 1941 assertion is that if his experience was sigificantly in Mahuadand in Palamau or at Dumri and Pirtanr in Hazaribagh, he might well have presumed that Adivasis were indeed uniformly Hindu, given the heavy presence of the Kharwar in Palamau and the Santal in Dumri and Pirtanr area. Both the Kharwar and the Santal are singnificantly Hindu by Census definition.

While it is not directly germane to this discussion of 1941 perceptions, the most recent scholarship on the subject is that of Dr. K.S. Singh in the monumental People of India project, based on elaborate survey procedures and using 1981 Census data as well. Singh observes in the Scheduled Tribes volume that "there has also been a rise in the number of tribal followers of Christianity in Bihar (11.87 percent)," and "There has also been a return to the cult of the sacred grove (Sarna, Jahera) among the Munda, Ho and Santal. The 1981 census records the followers in Sarna in Bihar as being 18.95 percent." Singh concludes that "a major finding in terms of religion has been the continuance of the autonomy of the tribal religious system in spite of the tribes' close interaction with Christianity and Hinduism." He suggests that "This reflects, no matter how small the number of followers of the tribals' own religion may be, the nascent process of identity formation and identity assertion among the tribal communities." See K.S. Singh, *The Scheduled Tribes*, People of India, National Series Vol. III, Anthropological Survey of India (Delhi: Oxford University Press, 1994), pp. 11-12. See also Census of India, 1961, Vol. IV, Bihar, Part V-A, *Special Tables for Scheduled Castes and Scheduled Tribes* (Patna: Superintendent of Census Operations, 1965), pp. xxv-xxvi.

While Census figures and definitions are of course invaluable in our understanding the cultural and social profile of a given place, it is nevertheless ultimately what the people themselves do and say that is most critical to such understanding. The People of India project comes as close as a published source, certainly any recent source, can to revealing such attitudes on the printed page. Based on the unique data at his disposal, K.S. Singh makes two further observations which seem relevant in our consideration of Jharkhand in the 1930s and 40s. Singh tells us that "The tribes have generally remained outside the varna system. Therefore, only 11.8 percent of them recognize their place in it," and "Another 31.6 percent are only aware of the varna system." These figures, which reveal that apparently 56.6 percent of the Adivasi population of India neither places itself in nor is aware of the varna system, or put another way, that 88.2 percent of that population live their lives outside the framework of one of the central organizing principles of Hindu culture. This certainly suggests some qualification both of Sahajanand's sense of Jharkhand religious belief and practice in 1941 and other more recent observations of that phenomenon. In fact, Dr. Singh provides just such an explanation in what he describes as one of the major findings of his People of India project, namely, the spread of Hinduism occurring in two forms: "The first is the amorphous kind of Hinduism at the local level where both the tribal and folk forms blend, interact and integrate. Secondly, we have the Sanatana form of

Hinduism propagated by religious institutions." While Singh does not specifically make the point, one might reasonably presume that the same processes and results are at work in the experience of Christianity. In fact, the phenomenon Singh describes here reinforces another of his findings already alluded to, namely "the continuance of the autonomy of the tribal religious system in spite of the tribes' close interaction with Christianity and Hinduism," which he finds reflecting a "nascent process of identity formation and identity assertion among the tribal communities." See K.S. Singh, *The Scheduled Tribes*, People of India, National Series, Vol. III, 1994, pp. 7 and 12. I am also indebted to Professor D. Hamsda, Principal, Lal Bahadur Shastri College, Karandih, Jamshedpur for clarifying many of these issues for me in our conversation of June 21, 1994.

21 Sahajanand makes clear in these pages that his quarrel is not with missionaries or Christianity as such but with what he has described in other contexts as "purveyors of false religion." He has applied this term primarily to Hindu priests, purohits, and gurus who have been perhaps second only to zamindars and moneylenders as objects of derision as exploiters of the rural poor. There is an air of sadness in Sahajanand's tone here as he appeals to the humanity of Hindus and Christians alike in responding to the condition of the kisans of Jharkhand as he describes it in this tract. And there is also a remarkable denial of the place of communalism in human relations whatever religious beliefs and commitments one might have. Such attitudes and practices, Sahajanand writes, have no place in the India of 1941. His observation is notable for the time at which he made it and the fact that it was he, a Shaivite Dandi Sannyasi of the Dasnami sect, making it. He had one object in life which was to speak to the cause of justice and decency for the rural poor, whether peasants, agricultural labourers, or Adivasi kisans, wherever in India and Bihar they might be found.

22 Puja is a form of worship in Hinduism wherein the pujari or worshipper venerates the deity by the act of gift giving as an offering.

Chapter VII

The Suffering of the Kamiyas and Usury as Loot

[The kamiyas are the bonded labourers of Jharkhand and Bihar. In the initial pages of this relatively short chapter, Sahajanand explains the etymology and the social meaning of various kinds of bonded labour, which he likens to forms of slavery and serfdom. He then goes on to examine the connected phenomenon of moneylending and usury in Jharkhand with some fascinating detail about who the usurers are, where they come from, and how they operate. The degrees of extortion to which peasants are subject in this environment makes the Hindi term loot seem entirely appropriate, as is Sahajanand's use of it in the title of this chapter. He concludes with several specific examples of how the system affected peasants in the border villages of Hazaribagh and Manbhum districts. Ed.]

The condition of the agricultural labourers (*kheton ke mazdooron*) of Jharkhand, also called *kamiyas*, is hopelessly bad. In many places in Palamau district they are also called *sevakiyas*. The word sevakiya is derived from the word "*sevak*," the generally accepted meaning of which is slave (*gulam*). The word kamiya is also derived from "*kam*," i.e., work. Kam means the same thing as *seva* or *sevakai*. In Bihar kamiya is the word commonly used although in Manbhum and Hazaribagh the terms *munis* and *gharbhatua* are often used as well, although they are not identical in meaning. Those persons who do "temporary" work are generally called munis while those who are employed for a longer period are called gharbhatua. The origin of the word munis is not certain but the meaning of gharbhatua is clear. Those who employed these people must have served them a meal of plain boiled rice (*bhat*) at their home (*ghar*) or residence, hence the word gharbhatua. The gharbhatuas presumably went to their own houses at night to sleep, but throughout the day they were obliged to be at the house of their master (*malik*) where they were fed boiled rice, or bhat. The practice may not be current now but it must have been so some time earlier. There are also other terms for kamiyas but of these I have no knowledge. I cite the above terms only by way of illustration for a practice which is widespread. The kamiya system (*kamiauti*) is prevalent in Bihar and is so described, while in other provinces it is identified by other terms. I have discussed this phenomenon at greater length in the tract *Khet Mazdoor*.[1]

Let us first deal with the sevakiya. First, it must be said that in Jharkhand the sevakiyas, kamiyas, munis, and gharbhatuas are most often found in the employ of zamindars, *banias* and other so-called civilized persons who have come here from the outside.[2] Not a single kamiya can be found working for a true kisan (*asli kisan*) or Adivasi in this area. However, I cannot confirm this with regard to those persons who are gradually becoming civilized and have become zamindars or big landholders. But their numbers are few and far between. They commit the sin of retaining kamiyas because they have become civilized![3]

The fact is that sometimes a zamindar, bania, or some other such person will lend a few rupees to a poor kisan on the occasion of a marriage or for giving a special feast and in the process the borrower becomes a slave for life.[4] He is provided only food and clothing in return. And sometimes it happens that the son becomes a slave after the death of his father in discharging a loan of no more than ten or twenty rupees. If it is fifty or sixty rupees then it is an entirely different matter. The slavery will be inherited not only by the son but by the grandson as well. If it is a loan of five, ten, or twenty rupees then one life of slavery may be sufficient to discharge the kamiya of his bondage. Much of course depends on the attitude of the person making the loan (*karzdata*). He does not charge interest as such and if the kamiya is freed in his lifetime it is entirely at the will of the karzdata. What a generous man! If his attitude is different, then of course, the kamiya will suffer the consequences. Two other points must be noted. The kamiyas are generally given inferior food and clothing and it is also true that they are to be found especially in the most remote villages and jungle tracts. The absence of any means of communication in these places means that they are totally isolated and they work there literally like beasts of burden.

A munis is like an ordinary labourer (*mazdoor*) who is told to leave if there is no work. For his day's labour he is paid one seer of rice (*kaccha chawal*) and three seers of paddy (*dhan*) or other grains![5] Nothing more! Only with the greatest difficulty are he and his children able to sustain themselves in these circumstances. Sometimes he gets flattened dried rice (*chura*) in place of uncooked rice which is meant for his morning meal (*nashta*) while paddy or other grains are meant for his main meal. The question is how other family members can subsist on food sufficient for only one man?

In addition to a daily meal and clothing, the gharbhatua gets ten to fourteen maunds of paddy in a year. Mostly between Asarh and Magh [that is from mid-June/mid-July to mid-January/mid-February] they are obliged to live with their masters.[6] Sometimes during this period, if there is no work, the gharbhatua is let go until he is needed. In fact gharbhatuas and munis are field labourers and slaves. In an earlier day they were called "serfs." However, they are not like ordinary slaves or personal, multi-purpose servants (*khawas*), as found in other parts of Bihar. Thus when there is no work on the land they are relieved. However, as soon as agricultural operations resume, gharbhatuas must return. That is the agreement they have with their malik [master]. But the munis will accept employment wherever he finds it and he will generally go where he finds the best conditions. Gharbhatuas and munis are thus generally free from any indebtedness, unlike the sevakiyas and kamiyas who are always trapped in debt. They are real slaves. In fact the kamiya is a "serf." But the sevakiya is a real "slave". Their life is one of great misery; they live a hellish existence.

Now let us come to the issue of usury (*soodkhori*). A cunning moneylender will first ask the simple kisan, "How much interest will you pay? How much interest will you pay in a year? Twice compounded or thrice compounded?" And the kisan replies, "how much you will take"? If the moneylender is kind he will demand the compounding of interest only two times, otherwise three and sometimes four times, that is, he will calculate the interest and add this to the principal and then calculate the interest on this new principal amount at each interval of three or four months. This practice of charging compound interest upon interest is absolutely vicious. Is this kind of loot possible anywhere else other than Jharkhand at this time? I have seen such instances with my own eyes. In Palamau, for example, after the death of their father, small children are compelled to work day and night at the house of the moneylender, where they are often mistreated as well. Once it happened that a landless kisan took a loan in kind consisting of 25 seers of *makai* [maize, corn] and 40 seers of *jatangi* [an oil seed]. Its total value was only three rupees. As a basis of repayment the kisan worked for three years at the moneylender's house, yet strangely enough instead of the loan having been repaid, it had mounted to rupees sixteen in that time! How could this calculation of interest and principal have been done? Possibly the interest was compounded every month and the rate was a 150 percent. Hence, even after working for three years, a loan of rupees three mounted up to rupees sixteen! This was worse even than what a Kabuli moneylender would do.[7] However, our kisan friend rebuked that evil moneylender, who out of fear released him from his clutches.

These usurers usually ply their moneylending trade in the towns and villages of Jharkhand. But well-to-do cultivators and petty zamindars are also engaged in the business of moneylending. In addition to the Kabulis, they are joined by the Gosains [a Hindu sect], Mussalmans, Punjabis, Kanyakubjas, Bhumihars, Marwaris, and Agarwal Banias, all of whom do moneylending in the various districts of Jharkhand.[8] Gosains and Brahmans from Bihar proper come to Ranchi district to sell male water buffaloes (*kara*) which are used for ploughing the fields. They then lend the sale proceeds on interest and return home, always coming back to realize their loan with compound interest. Actually they go from house to house making small loans in amounts of two to four rupees which are more easily collected and on which much heavier interest can be charged. A larger loan does not earn maximum interest and it will also be more difficult to collect. As a rule, Adivasi kisans do not borrow large amounts. At particular times of the year they will mostly take small loans of a few rupees for purchasing seeds. When the Gosain and Brahman creditors come to collect their loans, like beggars they also take their meals with the

Adivasi kisans. They make threats and do *dharna* [a form of picketting] to force realization of the loans quickly. The innocent kisans are of course fearful of these actions. The Adivasi kisans are also honest and true to their word and hence there is seldom any serious problem in the moneylender's realization of his loan.

But the Gosains, Kabulis and Punjabis realize their money mercilessly and relentlessly. These criminals are on a constant watch for the moment the labourers get their wages or the kisans have sold their grains and then they snatch the loan amount from them by force. They literally pound on the thatched roofs of the houses of the kisans and physically assault them in demanding payment. The Punjabis come here to sell clothes and the Kabulis deal in *hing* [asafoetida]. As they sell their goods on credit they are able to treble the price in a matter of months. The poor kisans do not apprehend that they will be victimized in this way, yet their creditors will brook no delay in demanding repayment and are fully prepared to use any means of force (*latthbaji*) necessary to realize their ends.

The rate of interest is generally one to two annas per month. This practice is common in all the districts. However, sometimes the rate is as high as four, six, or even eight annas a month.[9] The rate of interest depends on the poverty and need of the kisans and is also determined by the sheer physical force the moneylender making the loan can bring to bear on the borrower. There is no written documentation of this transaction, thus the amount finally to be realized depends very much on the will and strength of the creditor. There is no question here of what is just or right under the law. In Ranchi and Palamau districts the practice of *barhi* or *baarhi* and *derhi* are found both in the realization of grain loans or money debt. Barhi means payment of double the principal amount and derhi means payment of one and one half times of the money advanced, either in three to four months or at the maximum, in six months. The practice of derhi is most common.[10]

The Marwari shopkeepers, Agarwal Banias, and Punjabis sell goods and make cash loans especially in Hazaribagh and Manbhum districts. Out of every hundred there are ten Punjabis, sixty Agarwals and thirty Marwaris. The ratio among Punjabis, Gosains and Kabulis is 40:40:20. Marwaris and Agarwals have taken to cultivation as well. The other three [namely Gosains, Kabulis, and Punjabis] have nothing to do with agriculture. This is the general state of affairs. It must however be noted that whereas Marwaris are small cultivators (*chote chote khetihar*), Kanyakubjas and Bhumihars are very substantial cultivators (*bare bare khetihar*). These latter two are not shopkeepers but they advance both grains and cash on interest. A large number of Muslims from Gaya district are well known here in Jharkhand as merchants (*saudagar*) who sell cloth and also advance money on interest. They seldom take to cultivation. At some places, *Yajurvedis* [another Hindu sect] and others also carry on these same trading and moneylending activities. In short, the people I have mentioned here constitute the bulk of the moneylenders of this place. I will now turn briefly to a consideration of their misdeeds.

Those who keep shops for selling cloth and food grains generally sell their goods on credit to the Santals and others, who agree to pay compound interest two or three times per year. The shopkeepers then note down one and one half the original price in their register. The shopkeepers also prefer repayment in grain rather than money. For every rupee and eight annas of debt, they demand repayment of three kinds of food grains, namely twenty seers each of makai [maize or corn], marua [a coarse grain], and kodo [also a coarse grain] to cover this amount. This rate of twenty seers of grain per eight annas [i.e., half a rupee] of loan is entirely arbitrary and bears no relationship to the market price. What does the poor Santal understand about what is happening? If the agreement takes place in Asarh [June-July], then the first instalment for repayment falls due in Ashwin [September-October], the second instalment in Pus Magh [December-February], and the third in Phagun Chait [February-April]. Immediately an instalment is not paid the principal and the interest are combined to form a new principal amount and future interest will be charged on this amount. If the interest is not paid in Ashwin, the principal amount of rupees one and one-half will be added to the interest of the same amount and the two together will form the new principal of rupees three. Similarly in Magh the debtor's default will double the amount again to rupees six and in Chait to rupees twelve. In order to earn even more interest the creditors often refuse to accept payment from the kisans even when they are prepared to pay! Interest realized after Phagun-Chait is called *dhurikari*. Alternatively, as already indicated, those making loans will often demand payment of interest every month by the open use of force. However illegal this may be, the courts do not intervene.[11]

A particular practice of the Kanyakubja and the Bhumihar moneylenders is to remain silent for two to four years without any effort on their part to realize outstanding loans. Only later when the debt has mounted to ten or twenty times the principal amount, they will then get all the lands of the peasant mortgaged, who in the process is reduced to becoming one form or another of bonded labourer (*kamiya ya munis*). The same principal amount is written in the register of the usurer and he also executes a "handnote." By this arrangement the same principal amount is shown in two places [as if in fact there were two loans]. The kisan whose land has been taken in auction continues to cultivate that land with his ploughs and oxen, but now for his new master, i.e., the usurer. The usurer keeps only two to four ploughs with him. If employed in *begar* [unpaid, forced labour], the kisan will get food for only one meal per day and this for his labour *and* the use of his plough and oxen. And if he works as a kamiya, then as described before, he will get at most one seer of rice (*chawal*) and two seers of paddy (*dhan*) per day. If in the meantime the kamiya takes one maund of paddy on loan from his malik, then in ten years time he will be liable to pay fifty to sixty maunds of paddy in settlement. In fact at Dumri in Hazaribagh, the kisans told me that for one maund of paddy they sometimes were held liable to make payment of eighty maunds. If the landowner gives some land for cultivation to the kisan on *batai* [sharecropping], then his share will be eight to ten annas and the kisan will get only six annas. As a matter of fact the zamindars cultivate paddy at many places. They have their offices (*kachhari*) called *bhandar* [store or storehouse] in every village where they hold land.[12] The kisan must always plough the zamindar's land first and only then his own and so too with the use of irrigation water. For example, the zamindar Raja Neelkanth Narayan Singh of Navagarh near Katras [then in Manbhum, now in Dhanbad] has his bhandar at Laloodih. The kisans there cannot cultivate their fields unless they have cultivated those of the raja first. This is everywhere the case.

I shall conclude this painful story with several well-known examples of how the moneylenders ruined kisans who lived near the border of the Hazaribagh and Manbhum districts.

1) Dularchand Sahu of Khukhra mauza, thana Pirtanr in Hazaribagh lent a few rupees to Khanre Manjhi of village Gamhara in the same thana. When Khanre died, Sahu deceived his wife and took land producing 300 maunds of paddy at auction purchase in settlement for that petty loan. Khanre's wife and three children are now destitute. 2) It was again Dularchand who got the lands of Jitoo Manjhi of Gamhara auctioned in settlement for a petty loan. This was land producing 250 maunds of paddy annually. Jitoo who is only 30 years old was left without any means of livelihood. 3) Again Dularchand gave a plot of land to one Mangar Mahto of Gamhara for cultivation after taking rupees sixty in payment. After some time he reclaimed the land but without refunding any of the rupees. He has done the same thing with two widows of that locality as well. 4) Shri Trilok Singh Punjabi of Topchanchi in Manbhum district is a shopkeeper who deals in cloth and rice. He bought at auction [presumably in settlement of a petty debt] the land of Mangra Manjhi of Ganespur also in thana Topchanchi. This land yielded 150 maunds of paddy annually. Manjhi was forced to flee to Kenhuwari mauza in Pirtanr to live in his wife's village. In the meantime, his aged mother has no source of livelihood. 5) Chunu Manjhi, Jhari Manjhi and Darban Manjhi of Ganespur together held 84 acres of *lakhiraj* [rent free] land. Only three or four years ago Babu Manbharan Singh of Karni mauza, thana Govindpur got that entire land auctioned in settlement for a Rs. 100/- loan which he had advanced to them. At first he got a mortgage (*ijara*) executed and thereafter he instituted a case and got an auction decree issued in his favour. The [annual] "cess" for that entire land is a mere one and one half rupees. He refused again and again efforts to repay that loan by instalment.

(If the manjhi engages a labourer he gives some land for the latter's private cultivation as well as paying one seer of rice and three seers of paddy as daily wages. Others do not give any land for private cultivation, but pay two seers of paddy and one meal daily.)[13]

Editor's Endnotes to Chapter VII

1 Sahajanand completed the writing of the *Khet Mazdoor* tract on August 3, 1941 and wrote the bulk of *Jharkhand ke Kisan* between November 24 and December 5, 1941. He was writing these lines of Chapter VII on either December 3 or 4, following his date notations in the margins of his manuscript copy book. Accordingly, Sahajanand had only very recently, that is four months previously, completed the writing of *Khet Mazdoor*. Sahajanand's date notations are retained at the appropriate places both in the edited English translation of Part I of this volume and in the unedited Hindi text in Part II, as they are of course also in the published edition of the *Khet Mazdoor* tract. For details see my edited translation of *Khet Mazdoor* with an Introduction, Editorial Endnotes and Glossary, and including the original Hindi text as well. Hauser, *Sahajanand on Agricultural Labour and the Rural Poor* (New Delhi: Manohar Publishers, 1994). On kamiauti or debt bondage, see especially Chapter III, pp. 77-80, and Endnotes 9 through 14 of that chapter, although the issue is touched on in other parts of that tract as well. There is a wide literature on kamiauti; here I will cite only the brief comments by Mohapatra in "Class Conflict and Agrarian Regimes in Chotanagpur," *IESHR*, (1990), esp. pp. 17-21, dealing especially with Palamau; and Gyan Prakash, *Bonded Histories: Geneologies of Labor Servitude in Colonial India* (Cambridge: Cambridge University Press, 1990), the best full length study on the subject and focussing specifically on Gaya district in Bihar.

2 While the term Bania refers to a specific Vaishya caste group, most generally merchants, traders, shopkeepers, or moneylenders, it is most often used in this context to mean moneylender. There are obviously also many other terms for moneylender, mahajan, sahukar, and soodkhor among them, just as there are many groups in addition to Banias engaging in trade and moneylending, a point which emerges on many pages of this chapter and book, as it does in the pages of *Khet Mazdoor*.

3 Sahajanand uses the term sabhya, that is civilized, most often as a term of derision for those outsiders who make pretensions of being modern by comparison to the kisans of Jharkhand, Adivasi or otherwise. He includes in this category not only zamindars, merchants, and moneylenders, but officials of Government, forest contractors, mine owners, missionaries in their prosletyzing efforts, and of course the industrialists, notably the Tatas and their representatives. The Adivasi term which

best captures the meaning of Sahajanand's idea here is diku, implying an outsider, an alien who exploits the local environment and its people. Diku is also spelled dikku, although in this edited translation except where context demands otherwise, I follow the reading of my specialist informants by using diku.

4 As the title of this chapter makes clear, the bondage of the kamiya is intimately linked with the complex and highly elaborated system of indebtedness in Jharkhand, Bihar, and India. Sahajanand qualifies later in this chapter and in other parts of the manuscript the explanation he provides for the causes of indebtedness and the resulting bondage of the borrower. But it needs to be noted that an obvious but often misunderstood aspect of indebtedness in rural India, is that in circumstances of unemployment, seasonal under-employment, below minimum wages, and under education, apart from the social and cultural stigma which attaches to agricultural labour and the rural poor more generally, whether in Jharkhand or Biharkhand, indebtedness is almost by definition a way of life. This is a caveat meant to qualify the common perception that ritual demands or alcohol are among the chief causes of indebtedness in rural India. The rural poor, Adivasi or otherwise certainly drink and they must inevitably meet the cultural and religious demands of life cycle events, but to suggest that these are somehow central causes of indebtedness misses a critical point, namely that the first demand on the human and material resources of the rural poor is subsistence, namely to stay alive. I might add parenthetically, that the attitudes to which I refer here, and the conditions of those on the social and economic margin of society are not somehow unique to Bihar or India. They are, sadly, a universal human phenomenon. Sahajanand touches on some of these issues as they relate to Jharkhand in particularly compelling terms in Chapter VIII of this manuscript as he does in the pages of *Khet Mazdoor* already cited.

5 Rice whether as a crop or threshed but unhusked is called dhan; when husked it is chawal; and when it is boiled plain it is bhat. The term kaccha chawal here refers to chawal, or to uncooked rice. By this definition pakka chawal would then be cooked rice or bhat. The English term for dhan is paddy.

6 This is obviously the peak agricultural season, that is from the onset of the monsoon rains to the time of the spring harvest. The best description of agricultural times and seasons for Bihar is found in George A. Grierson, *Bihar Peasant Life, Being a Discursive Catalogue . . .* (Delhi reprint of original 1885 edition: Cosmo Publications, 1975), pp. 271-285. Grierson indicates that 40 seers equals one maund, which is equal to 100 pounds Troy, or 82.286 pounds Avoirdupois. There are

various multiples of a seer or parts of a maund, as for example, a paseri is five seers. It should also be noted, however, as Grierson does that in local bazars these weights and measures vary greatly, not only by locality, but according to goods being weighed and sold. Grierson, p. 430.

7 The measure for exploitive usury in Bihar is often the Kabuli merchant, trader, and moneylender from Afghanistan, who has a notorious reputation in Bihar for charging exhorbitant interest on his loans.

8 Sahajanand provides here a list of those regions, groups, castes, and communities who are the source of many of the moneylenders of Jharkhand. He adds to this list local, exploiting moneylenders from among well-to-do zamindars and cultivators. Kanyakubjas are Brahmans of U.P. and Bihar and Bhumihars are among the important landowners of eastern U.P. and Bihar who have historically claimed Brahman status. Marwaris are a business and trading community from western India.

It is notable that moneylenders and moneylending as described here by Sahajanand has not gone away over time. The importance and persistence of moneylending in tribal India generally is affirmed in the most recent work of Dr. K.S. Singh who reports that "The tribal attitude towards saving is not favourable, and dependence on moneylenders and shopkeepers still continues to be substantial (43.4 per cent)." See Singh, *The Scheduled Tribes*, People of India, National Series, Vol. III, Anthropological Survey of India (Delhi: Oxford University Press, 1994), p. 15.

9 Keeping in mind that an anna is 1/16th part of rupee, these interest rates work out to percentages of 6.25, 12.5, 25, 37.5, and 50 per month.

10 A quick calculation of these interest rates reveals that in place of the monthly rates given immediately above, the derhi rate results in an interest of fifty percent every three or four months, rather than monthly. Sahajanand's point need not be repeated here, but lest the repetition of these figures on the printed page fails to reveal the enormity of these interest rates, compounded as they are, I will do so nevertheless. A loan of Rs. 100/- calculated at the derhi rate at four month intervals, i.e., three times a year would result in a compounded principal amount of Rs. 337.50 at year's end, namely a net increase of Rs. 237.50 on the initial loan of Rs. 100/- which thus comes to an annual rate of 237.5 percent.

11 One cannot help note that the degree and manner of compounding interest in this description is staggering almost beyond belief. But ultimately of course the evidence speaks for itself, which was the particular point of Sahajanand's *Jharkhand ke Kisan* tract in 1941 and our

point in making it a part of the historical record with this edited translation together with the original Hindi text.

12 The description in this paragraph makes clear the pervasive network of social, economic, and cultural control residing in the hands of the zamindar landowner who is also the moneylender, userer, and potential shopkeeper. But here the bhandar, whether store or storehouse or both depending on the background of the zamindar/userer, which is also his local headquarters, are distributed throughout the countryside, literally as Sahajanand tells us, in every village (mauza) where the zamindar holds land. In fact, he has all the resources to manipulate, manage, and control the local agrarian environment, from making loans in money and grain, to forcing exhorbitant repayment. He is in a position to store and sell grain and other goods from the bhandar, or to make further loans, thereby to escalate the process to new levels of exploitation and control.

The proportions Sahajanand refers to should the zamindar concede to a share cropping arrangement with the peasant is based on a rupee of sixteen annas. Accordingly, a ten anna share would be 10/16ths or a 62.5 percent share of the crop, leaving six annas or a 37.5 percent share for the bataidar, or sharecropper. It needs to be kept in mind that this is a gross figure, not net. In other words all of the peasant's costs of production come from his share. This is a fundamental element of the agrarian system in Jharkhand, Bihar, and presumably other parts of India, and the excessive demands it puts on the cultivating peasant is the central point of Chapter VIII of this manuscript where Sahajanand discusses the Chotanagpur Tenancy Act.

13 A manjhi is a headman in some parts of Jharkhand. P.P. Mohapatra explains in the glossary of his JNU thesis that manjhihas is a landlord's privileged land and found only in Ranchi district. See Mohapatra, "Aspects of Agrarian Economy," JNU thesis, 1990. This unattached paragraph at the conclusion of Chapter VII seems to be an after thought, which Sahajanand wished to record but without inserting it marginally in the main text of this chapter, as he had obviously done on other occasions where elaborations of an idea are interlineated and extended into the margins. But Sahajanand seemed to be working against time in completing this tract and hence he left this brief note at this point in the text, and to convey something of his style I have left it at this point of the text, enclosed in parenthesis.

Chapter VIII

The Tenancy Act and the Kisans of Jharkhand

[Much of what Sahajanand has written up to this point of Jharkhand ke Kisan has been descriptive in order better to convey to those unfamiliar with the region and its history what the lived experience of the peasants of Jharkhand is really like. The story has been told in graphic detail to convey not only images of poverty, exploitation, and rights denied, but with occasional suggestions for change. Chapter VIII provides a close examination of the plusses and minuses of the Chotanagpur Tenancy Act, often compared with the Bihar Tenancy Act and then concludes with a candid conceptual observation of the basic systemic inequities of the agrarian economy of Jharkhand. Sahajanand examines the "root causes" of rural poverty and land alienation, and suggests that until the central concern for rent as the "first charge" on production is displaced with a concern for the well-being of the peasant as a human being with fundamental economic needs of subsistence, change will be slow to come. Sahajanand is also more explicit in this chapter than anywhere in this tract about the mobilization of a peasant movement that would begin to represent peasant interests more effectively. Ed.]

It is remarkable that there is to date no proper legislation governing tenancy relations in Santal Parganas. Some old rules and "regulations" or farmans are the basis on which land settlements have been arrived at there. This is indeed a deplorable situation and it is a problem which the Inquiry Committee noted in recommending tenancy legislation along the same lines as that of Chotanagpur.[1]

Now we will turn to an examination of the Chotanagpur Tenancy Act.[2] I have been especially impressed with one of its provisions. There are in the Bihar Tenancy Act abominable provisions for seizing and attaching the standing crops of the kisans and those provisions have in fact been strengthened by the Congress Ministry. Its application has been made so easy that the zamindars are now in a position to rob the kisans of all their labour and investment. But this is not the case in Chotanagpur. Even before, such provisions did not exist in the Act and nothing has been added to alter this arrangement. So perhaps we should express our appreciation!

But at the same time dangerous principles dealing with the issue of certificate or attachment of property have been retained in the Chotanagpur Act. The Congress Ministry was compelled to delete such sections from the Bihar Tenancy Act, inasmuch as the Kisan Sabha raised a major agitation on this issue. But at that time we had no knowledge that these sections had not been deleted from the Chotanagpur Tenancy Act. As a matter of fact the Adivasi members in the Legislative Assembly were a peculiar group of people. Being elected on Congress tickets, they were silent on the issue. They did not even point out these facts to us! Or was it that they were unable to follow the implications of the certificate provisions of the Act? Thus this cup of poison escaped our notice in the confusion! These sections continue to grind harshly on the chests of the kisans of Jharkhand. Possibly in place of the seizure (*jabti kurkee*) of standing crops, the term "certificate" or attachment has been kept as a measure of propitiation! After all the zamindars had to be kept happy![3]

But more dangerous than these provisions which we could not follow at the time is Chapter XIII of that Act, technically called the chapter dealing with land related conditions. There are seventeen sections in that chapter. It is specifically called the "Chapter of Praedial Conditions." Its provisions have been dealt with at various places throughout the Act and in this long chapter a detailed description has been given. Terms like *begari* [unpaid, forced labour], etc., which have been loudly acclaimed as unlawful and for the abolition of which stormy protests have been undertaken in Bihar, are mentioned in this chapter as having the force of law. This is indeed strange. Practices which have been declared to be illegal and hence abolished like *abwabs* [illegal exactions], have here been declared as lawful under the seal of the Congress Ministry! The law also provides elaborate procedures for converting *bhaoli* [rent payment in kind] to cash (*nagdi*). This is done through filing appropriate petitions with the Deputy Commissioner.

As I have reported earlier, in the Damin area of the Santal Parganas we still find that in place of a road cess the kisans have to work without wages (*begari*) to repair the roads. In the same way the zamindars provide some land to the peasants for their private cultivation for which the kisans do various kinds of work involving the digging and maintenance of irrigation facilities, etc., with the idea that both the zamindar and the kisans will benefit. I have already referred to the practice of *bethkheta* [confined primarily to Ranchi] and in much the same way the lands described here must have been allotted to the kisans for helping the zamindars in their cultivation. In place of paying rent on this land, the kisan provides his labour in cultivating the zamindar's fields. The conditions for this arrangement are described in Section 101 (a) of the Act. This was a common practice in the feudal age (*samant yug*), but at present rent has been fixed in cash or kind and the old practice has been abolished. But in Chotanagpur both rent and the earlier practice are still common. If the kisan so desires he can agree to make a lump sum payment to extricate himself from this labour commitment! What a tragedy! Here we still have "feudal levies" of by gone days! Could not the members of the Legislative Assembly elected from this area help abolish this practice? Or were they under some pressure?

In this connection I am reminded of a conversation I had in jail with two Members of the Legislative Assembly [MLAs] from Jharkhand about the practice of an 18:22 division of *bhaoli* rent shares in Chotanagpur! Both replied that the relevant legislation applied only to Bihar and not to Chotanagpur! I was surprised but not convinced and began consulting the Chotanagpur Tenancy Act! After much searching I came across sections 79 (a) and (b) where I found precisely the same description of this issue as appears in the Bihar Tenancy Act. I showed it to my friends and explained that in Chotanagpur the zamindar had no *danabandi* rights over occupancy lands (*kayami*) of the peasant. He can take no more than 18 seers out of one maund of the produce of the land! If he goes beyond that limit a suit may be brought against him! They were stunned and could say nothing! What could they have said? When they themselves were not aware of the law it is foolish to presume that the zamindars would abide by it. In fact I was later given to understand that nowhere in Chotanagpur do the zamindars accept an 18:22 division of the crop share as rent payment! Their slogan is, "whatever it was before, so it will remain." This is known as English law and justice and is widely proclaimed throughout the land.[4]

Let me cite an example of the losses which the kisans suffer on this account. I have no up-to-date statistics with me just now, but while going through the *Hazaribagh Gazetteer* of 1917, I have noted on page 127 an account of those lands whose rent is realized in kind and not in cash. In terms of acreage it is as follows: 1) khutkattidar, paddy land, 29.15 and *bhith* or *bari*, 25.86; 2) settled raiyat, paddy land, 9331.90 and bari, 7934.30; 3) occupancy holdings, 452.89 and 694.94; 4) non-occupancy holdings, 815.97 and 1278.60; and 5) under raiyat holdings, 2084.51 and 3233.37. Thus we find that both paddy fields and bari land taken together measure 20,000 acres. The danabandi settlement of these holdings should be stopped. And by now that acreage must certainly have increased. There was only 7,000 acres of non-occupancy (*gair kayami*) or under raiyat (*shikmee*) land where the restrictions on the 18:22 crop division was not applicable. It is possible that this also might have increased. So we find that the losses suffered by the kisans and the irregularities practised by the zamindars are largely a result of our ignorance of the tenancy laws.[5]

Section 118 of the Act dealing with the zirat or "private" land of the zamindar is also unacceptable. This issue should have been dealt with in Chotanagpur much as has been done in the Bihar Tenancy Act. Firstly, Subsection 1 (b) of this section which declares *majhihas* and *bethkheta* as zirat land is simply unjust. At most it should have been designated as *bakasht* or otherwise as the raiyati land of the kisans. There is no sound reason for declaring it as zirat land. As mentioned earlier, this type of land is defined in Bihar as "jagir" or by other names. And if it has not been defined as *kamat* of zirat there, it is not proper to mention it as such here in Chotanagpur.[6]

Secondly, Subsection 1 (a) of Section 118 is especially suspect. Formerly it consisted of the same provisions found in the Bihar Tenancy Act. But the reforms introduced in 1920 have made it much more dangerous. The Bihar Tenancy Act indicates that if a particular plot is let on *patta* [a deed of lease] by the zamindar for a year or several years, the land would still be the zirat of the zamindar as soon as the period of the patta expires. A patta is a document registering a piece of land in the court. Without such written registration, that is by oral agreement, no one can be described as a *pattedar*, [i.e., the holder of a patta]. But the Chotanagpur Act was amended in 1920 to the effect that "a written or oral patta [could be] made for less than a year." The greatest flaw in this amendment is that a patta can be executed orally without any documentary registration in the court. This is a very damaging clause. It is explained in Subsection (2), [Section 118] of the Act that the government will fix a date after which no oral patta which is of more than a year can be recognised. This in effect confirms that an oral patta is acceptable under the law. In this way those who cultivate the zirat land of the zamindar for more than a year on the basis of verbal agreement and without any registered patta, cannot claim any occupancy right over it in accordance with Section 19 of the Act. But as defined in Section 118 of the original Act this was possible. Another problem for the kisan is that with the possibility of the patta being concluded verbally for a year or less without any registration, why would the zamindar want to engage anyone with a registered patta? At most he will conclude a patta for a year and renew it annually, so that his right of zirat will not be infringed. When registration was required, he could not have done so. In accordance with the provisions of Section 19, under the earlier system, the kisan would be in a position to achieve occupancy rights. It is thus clear that this amendment was introduced specifically to benefit the zamindars. This is absolutely unjust and at the very least this provision should have been removed during the time of the Congress Ministry.[7]

This is a complicated issue and hence requires some further clarification. In accordance with the provisions laid down in Section 20 of the Bihar Tenancy Act and Section 17 of the Chotanagpur Tenancy Act, it has been broadly accepted that if a kisan cultivates a plot continuously for twelve years in a certain village, he thereby becomes a settled raiyat or *dehi* kisan of that village. It is not necessary that he should have been continuously cultivating a particular plot for twelve years, or that he should be doing so in *kayami*, i.e., in an occupancy status. Whether held as a sharecropper [*batai*] or on cash rent, etc., will make no differece in determiing the accrual of occupancy rights so long as the kisan or any of his family members have been continuously cultivating land in the village for twelve years, however many generations of the kisan's family may have been connected with its cultivation.[8]

In accordance with Section 21 of the Bihar Tenancy Act and Section 19 of the Chotanagpur Tenancy Act, if he meets these conditions, a settled kisan (*dehi raiyat*) will come to have occupancy rights over that land whatever its category, whether zirat or bakasht, and the zamindar cannot of his own will dispossess him. He can only realize a just rent (*uchit lagan*). Of course, zamindars resort to thousands of ways to shield themselves from these sections of the tenancy law. They indulge in forgery, fraud, and deception in this effort. It should be pointed out, however, that there is some legal protection for the zamindars provided in Section 120 of the Bihar Tenancy Act and Section 118 of the Chotanagpur Tenancy Act covering their zirat holdings.

It should also be realized that the acreage of the zamindar's zirat land is fixed and cannot be increased. The first survey which was undertaken after the passage of the first tenancy act determined that the zamindars had been cultivating many of their plots with their own ploughs and oxen for more than twelve years. Such lands were then and there defined as zirat. But where any variations from this pattern were identified, those lands were declared to be bakasht or *khudkasht*. Thereafter whatever lands the zamindars may have come to occupy have been identified as bakasht and not zirat land.

Now in accordance with Section 19 of the Chotanagpur Tenancy Act and Section 21 of the Bihar Tenancy Act, if a dehi kisan, that is a settled raiyat, ploughs any bakasht land, he automatically has an occupancy right over that land. Of course, he should not take his plough and oxen on the land surreptitiously or without permission and no kisan would dare to do so. But when the zamindar out of necessity for whatever reason, allows the kisan to cultivate that land, even if it was formerly the land of the kisan and bought at auction by the zamindar, the dehi kisan will then gain occupancy rights on that land.

But with regard to zirat land there is some difficulty. A dehi kisan, as soon as he starts cultivating zirat land assumes occupancy rights over that land. But if the zamindar has settled his zirat land by a registered patta with the kisan, the kisan will not gain occupancy rights over it. As soon as the term of the patta expires, the zamindar's ownership will revert to him in the form of zirat. The general practice is that the zamindar gives such land for cultivation on verbal agreement and without a registered patta. Who is there to raise questions about this procedure? But the danger for the zamindar is that the kisan may attempt to make it his raiyati land [namely with occupancy status]. To avoid this possibility, the Chotanagpur Tenancy Act has been amended accordingly, laying down that even an unregistered oral patta will be legally recognised as a valid patta or lease. We want that this provision which gives an oral patta the force of law to be removed and the rules regarding zirat land should be made uniform both in Bihar and Chotanagpur.

I was surprised to find that whereas under the Bihar Tenancy Act the kisans have the right to plant trees and bamboos and to cut them down, to construct houses, to make bricks and tiles, to dig wells and tanks on their *kayami* [occupancy] land, and to use it for any domestic purpose, here [in Chotanagpur] the Tenancy Act does not mention any of this. And in the Santal Parganas this confusion is even greater inasmuch as there is no formal tenancy act in that place.[9] This is one of the reasons why the zamindars in Chotanagpur harass the kisans as soon as they plant orchards on their holdings. The zamindars not only seek to dispossess them of their land but assess countless cesses and fines on them as well. These problems came up in the area of Godda in the Santal Parganas during the Congress Ministry but the kisans finally lost that case in the High Court.

In Bihar proper we had to wage a series of major struggles (*bari laraiyan*) to win these rights. This is widely known and it is only through these efforts that these rights have been achieved. The Bihar Provincial Kisan Sabha was born in the experience of this struggle. But it is a matter of regret that whereas the peasants of one part of the province have achieved this right, those of the other part of the same province have been denied these same rights till now. This is totally and absolutely unjust. I had not then studied the Chotanagpur Act as thoroughly as I should have. Hence I was unaware of these issues. It is not that the people of Chotanagpur or the Santal Parganas do not require the benefit of this legislation. Their need in fact is extremely urgent.[10]

On another issue, here in Chotanagpur the kisans feel great difficulty in making rent payment by "money order." In the tenancy acts of both Bihar and Chotanagpur, it has been accepted that the kisans could make their rent payment to the zamindar by postal money order. Sometimes the zamindar would not accept the payment, remain silent for some time and then harass the kisan by quietly instigating a case for non-payment of rent, get a decree from the court and try to take possession of the kisan's land. It is because the zamindars do not grant receipts on accepting the rent that the right to send rent by money order was in fact bestowed upon the kisans in the first place.

But there were still problems. It happened that the zamindar would not accept the money order payment and then sue for arrears. If the kisan produced the money order "coupon," it would be shown to be forged. Consequently the "postman" would be required to appear as a witness and the kisan was put to great difficulty. Who was the postman at the time? Where is he at the moment? Is he subject to the influence of the zamindar or has he been tranferred to some remote place? All such difficulties were there. Hence a movement was initiated to modify the law and as a consequence, Subsection (3) was added to Section 54 of the Bihar Tenancy Act. This subsection now legitimizes the money order "coupon." There is no longer any need to bring the postman as a witness. But in Chotanagpur nothing was added to Section 53 which deals with the despatch of rent by money order! This is very strange!

The time limit of one year for realization of rent arrears described in Section 231 of the Chotanagpur Act is clearly a good feature of the law. In Bihar the same is true for rent paid in kind, that is, bhaoli. But in the case of nagdi or cash rent [in Bihar] the time limit of three years is unjust. The Santal Parganas Inquiry Committee in paragraph 150, page 56 of its report have argued in favour of a one year time limit in order to protect the kisans from the harassment of the *pradhans* which exists there.[11] This practice of a one year limit is prevalent everywhere. We urge the government and the zamindars to reconsider this issue in these terms and our request would be found to be just. Thus the rule obtaining here in this connection is good. But the regret is that in Section 234, the time limit for the Mundari khutkattidars has been set at three years. Why this is the case is not clear. It is wrong and should be changed.[12]

Section 60 of the Chotanagpur Act holds that the "first charge" on the kisan's production is the payment of land rent. The same position is taken in Section 64 of the Bihar Tenancy Act. But the principle is wrong and I am strongly opposed to it. Justice demands that the total expenditure of all agricultural operations should be the first charge on production. Thereafter the kisan's subsistence and that of his family must be taken into account and payment of lagan, or rent should come only after this. No one can be expected to pay rent if they are naked and starving. Not even Government or the zamindars can openly subscribe to this view. It is indispensible that the cost of agricultural production come first, and this includes necessary preliminary activities like ploughing and sowing. It is a principle which should be accepted legally as well as in fact. If not, it should be candidly stated that the land rent will have to be paid, no matter whether the peasant cultivator is starving, naked or dying for lack of medicine. It is one thing to talk but quite another to live in these circumstnces. There should be no fraud. It must be stopped.[13]

Conditions have been laid down in the Tenancy Act here which forbids others from purchasing or procuring by mortgage lands belonging to the real kisans -- the Adivasis and backward people (*asli kisanon-Adivasiyon tatha pichre logon*) of Jharkhand.[14] The land may be conveyed to their own kinsmen from the same thana for periods not exceeding five to seven years. It is however the case that on the whole these lands, by specific legal requirement must be restored to the kisans and this is as it should be. The clear objective of these regulations is that the kisans of Jharkhand should not be deprived of their lands either by moneylenders, the rich and wealthy, or outsiders. Are these goals and objectives being fulfilled? I do not at present have the documentary evidence to show that this is in fact the case.[15]

At the beginning of the twentieth century the Government of the Punjab passed its Land Alienation Act with the same objective in view. The Act laid down certain conditions to prevent persons who were not kisans from buying the lands of the Punjab kisans. But was this objective achieved? Not at all. By forgery and other false means (*benami*), non-kisans were able to grab the lands of the kisans. Also other peasants purchased these lands and in this way they proved to be more dangerous than the Bania mahajan moneylenders themselves. Of course anyone can take to moneylending. At the beginning there were no moneylenders. The people who became moneylenders did not have horns and tails. It was only after indulging in these practices that they became dangerous and were then described as Banias and moneylenders. So why should some kisans not follow the same profession? That is why very recently the Punjab Government has introduced a number of provisions to check this fraud and deception. But will these measures be effective?

As a matter of fact few observers go to the root of the problem. Does the peasant sell his land because he wants to? Those who believe this are badly misinformed. As though he has no love for the land whose fruits have been enjoyed by his ancestors and forefathers and who have given their blood like water to make it productive. As a matter of fact his love for the land is so deeprooted that to part with even one inch of that land will break his heart. But finally he is helpless. What can he do? Bad economic conditions often force him to part with his land. After all hunger bordering on starvation will compel a man to sell or even to kill his children, his dearest possession on this earth. And much the same thing applies to his land. Laws against dispossession alone will not help. When the economic conditions of the kisans are improved beyond the level of absolute poverty, we will then see whether the sale of land stops or not. Then it would be appropriate to impose restrictions on the sale of the land of the peasants. This is ultimately the root of the problem.

But here [in Chotanagpur] it seems, the concern is more for the zamindars. How will they get their rent? It matters little whether the crop has failed or the kisan's family is naked or starving. Payment of the rent is inevitably considered the "first charge," the first demand to be made, and this often means, despite vigorous efforts to the contrary, that in difficult times the kisan's land will be sold at auction to meet the rent demand. This will change only when the zamindar knows that unless the productivity of land increases he will not get his rent. Only then will he strive to arrange for the supply of good seeds, manures and necessary irrigation facilities. Only then will he and the government be ready to provide to the kisan some other source of income over and above his cultivation, so that his financial position may improve and the rent payment may be regularly made. This is the real crux of the problem. Have the government, zamindars, or our leaders cared to think honestly about these fundamental issues?

Have they ever sincerely tried to improve the conditions of the kisans and hence the economy itself? Even if the land is not to be put up for auction, often the entire standing crop is seized and sold at auction. This is even more deplorable. That is why neither in Punjab nor elsewhere have measures to control this problem been successful. The standing crops, which are barely adequate for the basic subsistence of the kisans must never be auctioned or seized. In the United Provinces some modest effort has been made to limit seizure and attachment. But it is only a half way measure. In Jharkhand it is frequently asserted that the rent must be paid out of the peasant's share of the produce of the land. It is never considered how the kisan and his family members will sustain themselves. As a matter of fact anything which provides basic sustenance for the peasant and his family cannot be touched even by God himself. Unless this is the spirit of any legislation on this issue, it will not work. In fact, there is no other way out.

There is one very good element in the Chotanagpur Tenancy Act, found in Section 58. If one minor improvement is made it would be an especially effective measure. Section 58 indicates that generally an interest of one anna per rupee is to be charged annually on rent arrears [i.e., 6.25 percent]. But if the kisan pays the arrears before the expiry of a year, then the interest on the remaining balance will be at the rate of two pice per rupee annually [or 3.125 percent].[16] In the Bihar Tenancy Act, there is no mention of this two pice interest, hence the Chotanagpur Act is better in this respect. As a matter of fact no interest at all should be charged if the kisan is able to pay the rent within a year. There should be no interest charge if the rent is paid during that first year. My intention is clear; the kisan should be given the opportunity of paying the rent within the period of one year without penalty. Only thereafter should efforts be made, either by instituting a case or in some other manner to realize the rent. This should not be done for any period of less than a year. On the part of the kisan there should not be any great delay in making payment inasmuch as if such delay reaches one to three years or more there will be much difficulty for the kisan. The amount will also multiply like anything and it cannot easily be paid off.

Whatever I have written here about the Chotanagpur Tenancy Act and its application to the Jharkhand has mainly been concerned with identifying certain of its special features. These are issues on which there is broad general agreement. There are in fact many other issues in the Act which need to be considered and improved upon. But it is not here our purpose to analyse the whole of the law.

Editor's Endnotes to Chapter VIII

1 The regulations to which Sahajanand refers here are the Santal Parganas Settlement Regulation of 1872 and the Santal Parganas Rent Regulation of 1886. He mentions these in his Introduction and reports that the Santal Pargana Manual which was the operative tenancy document in the district was largely based on these regulations. It is also the case that in 1908 the Santal Parganas Settlement (Amendment) Regulation introduced restrictions on the transfer of land in the district, an issue which would recur again and again, as I suggest below. The Santal Parganas Tenancy Act of 1949 was enacted shortly after Independence during the Congress Ministry of Shri Krishna Singh. Tenancy legislation is of course an ongoing process as I indicate in an earlier Endnote referring to recent proposals in Bihar. The Janata Dal Ministry of Laloo Prasad Yadav announced in early July that "the Government would soon bring about a major amendment in the Chotanagpur-Santal Parganas Tenancy Act to avoid transfer of lands belonging to tribals to outsiders." See "Chotanagpur Tenancy Act to be Amended," *Hindustan Times*, Patna Edition, July 8, 1994.

In pre-Independence India three survey and settlement operations had been carried out in Santal Parganas. It was possibly the most recent of these, published in 1936, which Sahajanand was using in 1941, but considering its brevity, he may indeed have used one of the two earlier documents. See J.F. Gantzer, *Final Report on the Revision Survey and Settlement Operations in the District of Santal Parganas, 1922-35* (Patna: Superintendent of Government Printing, 1936). This was a relatively brief revision report of 79 pages. The two reports which preceded it were H.L.L. Allanson, *Final Report on the Survey and Settlement Operations in the District of Sontal Parganas* (Third Programme), 1898-1910 (Calcutta: Bengal Secreariat Book Depot, 1912), pp. 130; and H. McPherson, *Final Report on the Survey and Settlement Operations in the District of Sontal Parganas, 1889-1907* (Calcutta: Bengal Secretariat Book Depot, 1909), pp. 266. The Inquiry Committee Report to which Sahajanand refers here is the Santal Parganas Inquiry Committee Report of 1938, which I have cited in Endnotes of earlier chapters. Sahajanand cites it often in this tract.

2 The operative Act which was being amended during the Congress Ministry and before and since, was the Chotanagpur Tenancy Act of 1908, with earlier related measures in 1859, 1869, 1879, and 1903.

3 In this paragraph Sahajanand reveals much about the direction of Kisan

Sabha activism in the 1930s and his involvement in it. First, of course, the fact that almost throughout the term of the Congress Ministry from mid-1937 to October 1939, the Kisan Sabha and the Congress, and hence Sahajanand and the major players in Congress politics in Bihar and in India, were at serious odds about the nature and extent of tenancy legislation in the province Given the candor which Sahajanand reveals in this tract and in everything he wrote and said, he cannot hide his sarcasm in assessing the reasons for Congress actions. Rather it is a basic part of his very being in these years. It is a point which bears directly on the position he himself would assume only months after these lines were written in calling for restraint in mounting anti-zamindar agitations in Bihar following the People's War policy which he and the Communist Party of India were adopting at almost this very time. This is an issue which is obviously beyond the scope of this Endnote or this book, but it is nevertheless a matter of considerable interest in adding perspective to our understanding of this endlessly complex man.

Again, Sahajanand also allows here as he does throughout this tract that there was much happening in Chotanagpur with which he was not familiar, and this he clearly regrets as he looks back on what might have been. He was the central player in the politics of peasant activism in Gangetic Bihar and though this tract reveals his more extensive involvement in Chotanagpur and Santal Parganas than we had heretofore presumed, nevertheless his participation in mobilizing the kisans of Jharkhand in the 1930s, certainly by comparison with other parts of Bihar, was marginal.

4 The discussion here has to do with one of the key elements of landlord tenant relations, namely the manner and proportion in which rent payment in kind described as bhaoli, is made. One way of making the assessment is based on an estimate of the standing crop in the field before harvest, and obviously leaves the peasant tenant open to a wide range of possible manipulations. This method of estimating the crop rather than dividing the cut and threshed crop is referred to as danabandi. Occupancy rights are designed in law to provide the peasant a high degree of security in his tenancy, and is obviously a preferred status, albeit nevertheless a potentially risky one as the present discussion indicates. A maund is a local measure of weight equal to forty seers, a seer being something over two pounds. These weight measures vary widely from region to region. See earlier references and for specifics see Grierson, *Bihar Peasant Life*, 1975 Reprint Edition, p. 430.

It is also interesting to note here that while Sahajanand concedes throughout this tract his own weakness in understanding the law and conditions under which the kisans of Jharkhand live and work, he is also in this case making the point that the elected representatives of the area were little better informed and by his estimate open to political pressures from the Indian National Congress whose candidates and MLAs they were. One might also observe that this encounter took place in the Hazaribagh Central Jail, which apart from incarcerating political prisonsers, served as a critical contact point for information, the exchange of ideas, and a wide range of intellectual and political interaction.

5. The gazetteer which Sahajanand cites here is E. Lister, *Hazaribagh District Gazetteer* (Patna: Bihar and Orissa Government Press, 1917), which means of course that the figures he provides apply specifically to Hazaribagh. The example nevertheless makes his point. Please note that most of the various kinds of holdings and tenures indicted here are identified or described in some detail in Chapter V and Chapter VI of this tract. See also the work of P.P. Mohapatra already cited, especially his "Aspects of Agrarian Economy of Chotanagpur," JNU, (1990), and "Class Conflict and Agrarian Regimes in Chotanagpur," *IESHR* 28:1 (1991). See Grierson, *Bihar Peasant Life*, 1975 Reprint Edition, for definitions of *bhith* and *bari* referring to soil types, location, crop use, and moisture retention capabilities, esp. pp. 167, 168, 174, 248, and 326. Note that *Bari* is also described in this text as upland. Finally again, to note that while Sahajanand did not have major sources of data at his disposal in the Central Jail while he was writing, he did seem to have available the 1917 Hazaribagh District Gazetteer, among a substantial number of other titles already mentioned, and that he made maximum use of those books and publication which indeed were available, many of them publications of the Bihar Government Press at Gulzarbagh, it turns out.

6 Majhihas and bethkheta are tenancies similar to zirat, that is the private land of the zamindar or landowner. These holdings are not normally let out on tenancy, but Sahajanand explains in the succeeding pages of this chapter, how that process nevertheless is possible specifically with respect to zirat. Mohapatra describes majhihas and bethkheta as being confined to Ranchi district and explains that bethkheta is land on which a peasant will render only labour services. See the glossary of his "Aspects of Agrarian Economy of Chotanagpur," JNU Thesis (1990); and also Chapter V of this tract. Bakasht is land technically cultivated by the landowner himself, but which is also let out on tenancy. Kamat is a personal, i.e., zirat holding of the zamindar but which may be remote from his village or main holding. See also Wilson, *A Glossary of Judicial and Revenue Terms*, 1968 reprint edi-

tion, p. 254, for more on kamat.

7 The central issue here continues to be the question of the provisions in the law which assure or deny occupancy rights to the peasant tenant. If his patta or lease agreement with the zamindar is registered, the kisan would thereby be accruing the time necessary to achieve occupancy status. As Sahajanand explains in chapters V and VI, that time varies with the nature of the original holding. The issue is discussed further in the pages immediately following. The critical consideration from the point of view of the peasant tenant is to achieve the substantial permanence on his holding which occupancy status conveys. We constantly need to remind ourselves that the discussion here is about legal rights rather than who wields power and exercises control in these relationships. Sahajanand has raised those fundamental questions in earlier chapters. For more details on patta, see Wilson, *A Glossary of Judicial and Revenue Terms*, 1968 Reprint Edition, p. 408.

8 Dehi literally means resident, in this case as explained, it refers to a settled raiyat, that is peasant tenant living in a mauza or village and cultivating land in that place. See Grierson, *Bihar Peasant Life*, 1975 Reprint Edition, pp. 325, 326.

9 The Santal Parganas Tenancy Act became law in 1949, eight years after Sahajanand was writing and only a year before his death. See Editor's Endnote 1 of this chapter for a brief comment on the the history of the regulations which governed landlord tenant relations in Santal Parganas district.

We have referred at length to Sahajanand's limited activity in Jharkhand in the 1930s during the peak years of the peasant movement in Gangetic Bihar, and we have recounted with Sahajanand the occasions on which he in fact moved into that Adivasi jungle arena. It is perhaps worth noting in this connection that Sahajanand was a political prisoner at the Hazaribagh Central Jail, firmly located in Chotanagpur and Jharkhand and that when he writes as he does in this paragraph, he naturally refers to what is happening "here," meaning in Chotanagpur and the Jharkhand plateau. The encounter in the Central Jail was not a long one but it certainly placed Sahajanand in the social, cultural, and natural environment about which he was now reflecting and writing, apart from the human contacts he made there and to which he has referred more than once.

10 Sahajanand refers again and again to the relationship between Gangetic Bihar, which he knew so well and which was the primary arena of his activism, and to Jharkhand where he was both less familiar and less active by far. What is impressive here is not that Sahajanand passed over Jharkhand as a field of peasant mobilization in the 1930s, although

that fact in itself is of course important. Rather what is notable about this tract is the degree of self awareness reflected on many of its pages and no more candidly than in this paragraph about what did and didn't happen and what should have happened. At times like this, one sees a Sahajanand who had not only a clear sense of the kisans of Jharkhand and their trauma, but of himself. Because he was a man both of action and of ideas, and constantly on the move in a direction he perceived to be on the leading edge of change and justice for the rural poor, one does not always see that clarity and sensitivity in the decisions he took and the actions which followed. But as with so much else in the life of this man, that is another longer story. For the moment, his interest and ours are focussed on the peasants of Jharkhand in 1941.

It is also relevant at this point to observe on Sahajanand's assessment of the activism of the Bihar Provincial Kisan Sabha on the issue of occupancy rights for peasant tenants, and that it was literally "in the experience of this struggle," that the Kisan Sabha was born. The question put simply as he does in this section, is what rights do peasants have in the land which they legally hold? It is these rights which did not exist in Chotanagpur at the time Sahajanand was writing and which he felt must be a fundamental part of the tenancy law there. This is obviously a complex issue about which Sahajanand has written much. For a review of the issues and his views, see my forthcoming book, *Sahajanand and the Politics of Peasant Activism in Twentieth Century India.*

11 If my reading of this paragraph is correct, Sahajanand glosses the report of the Committee a bit differently than a close reading of that paragraph suggests. In its Chapter XIII, the Committee is concerned with The Pradhani System and the Collection of Rents, and in the paragraph Sahajanand cites the issue is how one or three year limits in rent realization would affect the pradhans. There is no more than a passing reference here to the raiyats, from whom the pradhan, representing the village community collects the rent to be conveyed to the zamindar. Of course the same logic applies in both cases. As Sahajanand explains at the very end of this chapter, a delay in payment of rent dues only extends and elaborates the opportunities for harassment, whether by the zamindar of the pradhan, or the pradhan of the Adivasi kisan. The Committee explains very clearly that the pradhan in Santal Parganas performs a triple function; first as head of the village community, then to represent village interests in dealings with the landlord, and finally as the link with government. Sahajanand's interpretation may of course be closer to reality than the Committee's, inasmuch as the pradhan may

well function in some instances as a kind of thikedar or jeth raiyat agent of the zamindar, and inasmuch as it is his function to make certain the rent is collected from the peasants, lest he be subject to pressures from the zamindar, the harassments of which Sahajanand speaks are certainly in the realm of the possible. See *SPICR*, Patna, 1938, esp. pp. 52-57.

12 Sahajanand discusses Mundari khutkatti in Chapter V of this manuscript. See also my Endnote 7 in that chapter for further references to khutkatti in the *Mundarica*, and in the work of Prabhu Mohapatra and S.C. Roy. It is a system, most specifically among the Munda related to the first clearing of the jungle for purposes of cultivation and its subsequent corporate ownership.

13 In the remaining pages of this chapter Sahajanand raises what he describes as the root causes or fundamental problems characterizing the political economy of Jharkhand, Bihar, and India. Those root causes have to do with poverty alleviation which relates directly to issues of production and land alienation. This is as explicit and sensitive a statement of the systemic inequities of this agrarian environment or any other which Sahajanand has put on paper, or at least which I have read. Selling land to maintain subsistence, dispossession, and alienation don't just happen, he tells us. They have causes and it is those causes which demand our urgent attention. The larger, overarching issue is one of the condition of the agrarian economy and the poverty it forces on the peasants of Jharkhand. Another more local, but equally critical issue is what Sahajanand refers to as the "first charge" on production, which is inevitably rent in this environment. So long as that is the case there is no inducement on the part of land controllers to enhance production or to make any efforts in that direction. If the welfare of the peasant who does the work is not taken into account as the first charge, things will not change Sahajanand allows. This is an old and familiar story, but the candor, directness, and emotion with which it is put here suggests a sensitivity to the real conditions of real peasants in Jharkhand which makes it difficult to believe Sahajanand did not have a deep and profound understanding of the kisans of Jharkhand.

14 I return here to Sahajanand's point in defining the Adivasis of the fields and forests of Jharkhand as peasants. In earlier notes I have referred to Sahajanand's specific use of the term Adivasi kisan and here he reinforces the concept by adding the adjective asli, to characterize them as real kisans together with the other backward people of the region, meaning here as he uses the term, poor non-Adivasi peasants. In other words, the real peasants of Jharkhand are the Adivasis kisans and the non-Adivasi kisans whose lives as peasants are not significantly distin-

guishable as they labour in the fields and forests of Chotanagpur and Santal Parganas.

15 The evidence which Sahajanand cites in the next paragraph for the Punjab and the evidence which has been mounting consistently in the fifty three years since these words were written, suggests that there is still little evidence that the goal of restricting land alienation to non-Adivasis has been met. That it is one of the central issues in the politics of 1994 is obvious in any daily newspaper whether in New Delhi or Patna, and I have mentioned in an earlier note that it continues to be a matter of concern to the Bihar Government which in early July reported that it would "soon bring about a major amendment in the Chotanagpur-Santal Parganas Tenancy Act to avoid transfer of lands belonging to tribals to outsiders." See *Hindustan Times*, Patna Edition, "Chotanagpur Tenancy Act to be Amended," July 8, 1994.

16 At the time Sahajanand was writing the Indian rupee was equal to sixteen annas, and the anna equal to four pice. Accordingly, the percentages of 6.25 on an interest rate of one anna, and 3.125 percent on an interest rate of two pice or half an anna.

Chapter IX

Other Basic Needs of the Kisans

[The land and the jungle provide the peasants of Jharkhand their livelihood and their agony, as Sahajanand has described it in the foregoing chapters of this book. But there is more to their suffering, and it is these questions which Sahajanand considers in this brief chapter. The issues are adequate irrigation water in an otherwise inhospitable terrain for agriculture and adequate and disease-free drinking water. Sahajanand then turns to another problem of drinking, that of country made alcohol which is central to the lives of the Adivasi kisans, as it is presumably to others. Sahajanand is both sensitive and rational in commenting on the production, use, and prohibition of hanriya. Two other issues concern him here, namely the urgent need for informing the kisans of legislation ostensibly designed to benefit them, and providing friend-of-the-kisan legal assistance which would get the peasants beyond the clutches of legal professionals, whom they can neither trust nor understand. Ed.]

The sufferings of the kisans which have thus far been described do not begin to exhaust the story of their misery. They experience other hardships, the cumulative effect of which is no less alarming. It is some of the more important of these to which I now turn.

When I consider these issues, the most striking is perhaps that of irrigation. Of course there is no dearth of mountains and rivers in Jharkhand. And in the rainy season there is an abundance of water which comes down from these mountains. Thus there is good opportunity for collecting water in large reservoirs (*ahars*) which can provide more than sufficient irrigation for both paddy and rabi crops. If the ahars are built in good number and are well placed they can easily meet local needs. But what to speak of building new ahars, even the old ones have disappeared for lack of proper maintenance and repair. Neither government nor the zamindars have any concern in this matter inasmuch their revenue and rent are forthcoming quite independently of any such investment.[1]

Where there are no reservoirs or these are not sufficient in number or size, then rivers and streams can be utilized in constructing embankments and a minor system of canals (*pains*) thereby to provide necessary irrigation. I have seen this myself at several places. But this too is costly and where will the poor kisan find the money to undertake such projects? And I have already said that the zamindar has no interest in this kind of development! And excepting the limited area at the foot of the hills, generally speaking the land in Jharkhand is not especially fertile. Most of the land is of quite ordinary quality and unless appropriate irrigation is provided, productivity is not good. This point is made at pages 72-73 of the *Hazaribagh Gazetteer* cited above:

> It is, however, certain that the soil is for the most part inherently infertile. Extensive irrigation works of a character beyond the means and equipment of local agriculturists might render some of the waste land cultivable. But the poverty of the soil and the irregularity of the surface make the chances of profit very doubtful.[2]

There are a number of significant points here to which I have already alluded. First, that a large area of the land is infertile, essentially wasteland and that its surface is uneven. Only if arrangements are made for extensive irrigation works, can more tracts be effectively utilised for cultivation. But this is certainly beyond the means of the kisans who can barely cover the minimum costs of production as is! And we have explained the lack of interest on the part of the zamindars in such projects. In fact proper irrigation is perhaps the most urgent requirement in alleviating the poverty and hunger of the kisans.

Closely related to the general problem of water availability is that of sufficient disease-free drinking water for the kisans and their animals. For this a network of wells providing safe drinking water is urgently required. I have myself seen the helplessness of the kisans in quenching their thirst by drinking water which seeps from water arteries in the fields and on hilly tracts. In Ranchi and its contiguous areas these arteries are referred to as *pajhra.* In some places it is called *don* water which is most often available only in the rainy season. But this water is not pure and is not safe for drinking. But what are the poor kisans to do? They have no alternative. In mountainous tracts, digging a well would require more than a thousand rupees and layers of rock would have to be drilled. Hence at some places *kaccha* wells are dug in the fields and sometimes thirst is quenched by digging in sandy soil until water is reached.[3]

Another serious problem for the kisans is the absence of proper legal assistance. In jail I have met thousands of prisoners from Jharkhand who would not have lost their lands or been imprisoned if only they had been given proper legal advice.[4] It is neither my intention of demeaning *vakils* and *mukhtars* nor of abusing their profession, but from my personal experience I can say with confidence that the legal profession is spoiled mainly due to the malpractices indulged in by the vakils.[5] Gradually the legal profession is becoming overcrowded in this country with the result that everyone must find something to do to justify his existence. Accordingly many vakils engage in whatever methods are necessary to maintain themselves, including fraud, deception and other dishonest means. I have seen cases which convinced me that the vakils are responsible for duping the poor kisans. The problem is compounded by the fact that neither the local peasants nor the vakils can adequately understand one another's language. Hence misgivings arise. Often it has happened that the client's evidence was not put forward by the vakil. The Santal Parganas Inquiry Committee has admitted this fact and has mentioned it in paragraph 55 of its Report as follows: "unrestricted recruitment would probably lead to touting, the fostering of litigation and other malpractices."[6]

These things of course happen in other parts of Bihar but less frequently. The kisans here are simple people (*nire sidhe*). There is much they do not understand and they have an implicit trust in everyone. And education has made little headway here. Hence these evils are rampant. To my mind it would be a great service to the country if in every court some vakils and mukhtars were specially appointed to help the Adivasi kisans. They should not be overly concerned for their fees and should be of a sacrificing temperament. They should be satisfied with earning a livelihood and rendering help to the poor. It is clear that a large number of the kisans here lose their cases because of their inability to pay vakil's fees.[7]

Fourthly, there is the problem of country made liquor (*deshi ya pahari sharab*) called *hanriya*. It has long been made and drunk in Jharkhand and has become an inseparable part of the lives of the people. Its absence would be regarded by them as a kind of death. But legal obstacles have been placed in the way of its production and use. Moreover, the opening of government liquor shops in the countryside has led to the widespread consumption of this government liquor as well. Just as the availability of mill made cloth has damaged the production of less costly *khadi*, so also is the case with *hanriya*.[8] Government sponsored liquor shops have endangered the very existence of *hanriya* and its disappearance is imminent. Unless all restrictions are removed on *hanriya* and so long as the government shops are not removed from the villages the difficulties of the kisans on this issue will not disappear. English and government liquor shops may be allowed to function in the cities. Then a "census" of those who drink this liquor should be made and they should be provided with a "certificate," and only they should be eligible to buy this alcohol. Others should be excluded and no Adivasis or backward kisans should be issued a liquor certificate. Only then will this scheme work.

This does not mean that I am against prohibition. It should be and must be implemented. But it should not be done by force as the government is attempting. Also prohibition should not become another source of government or illegal income. It should not provide a pretext for earning money. Secondly, those whose lives are indisolubly connected with *hanriya* should experience no hindrance in its use. It can be prepared easily from boiled rice. The kisans should have the right to prepare and use *hanriya* or *toddy* and at the same time be persuaded to abstain from its use.[9] Prohibition cannot be enforced with a lathi or a sword which will only move people to drink secretly. It is a different matter to apply moral force and persuasion. For example, the Tana movement whose primary field of activity was Jharkhand used religious persuasion to limit the use of alcohol and even meat eating. Meat is a staple element of the diet here yet the Tanas gave up meat eating of their own accord. This could not have been achieved by legislation, which is why I am opposed to legislation as a means for introducing prohibition.

Finally, it is important that whatever laws are enacted for the benefit of the kisans be done so with full and effective publicity. On the one hand the government considers Jharkhand to be backward while on the other it does not engage in serious efforts to inform the kisans of those laws which have ostensibly been introduced for their benefit. For example, the legislation which defined the ratio of sharing the produce of the land at 18:22, was never properly circulated. Leave alone the kisans, even Members of the Legislative Assembly from Jharkhand had no knowledge of this legislation.

Editor's Endnotes to Chapter IX

1 Sahajanand picks up almost immediately on the theme he raised in the last pages of Chapter VIII, namely, who draws down first on the productive capacity of the land and with what responsibilities. Sahajanand's point was that so long as rent was the "first charge" on the product of the land, the resultant poverty of the peasants would never be ended. He now reinforces that point by explaining the other obvious and well-documented fact, that so long as rent and revenue are forthcoming to zamindar and government, the likelihood of their investing in any project to enhance production would be minimal.

2 The gazetteer Sahajanand cites here and earlier is E. Lister, *Hazaribagh District Gazetteer* (Patna: Government of Bihar and Orissa Press, 1917). It might also be noted that Lister was the co-author with Father Hoffmann of the note in the *Mundarica*, titled "Special Memorandum on the Land System of the Munda Country," Vol. VIII, pp. 2388-2404, which is an especially rich source on the khutkatti or khuntkatti system found primarily among the Mundas. That Sahajanand was using Lister's gazetteer but not the *Mundarica* as I have noted earlier, suggests that the distribution of the encyclopaedia may have been limited. The difference in availability and distribution at the time Sahajanand was writing may also have had to do with the fact that one publication was official while the *Mundarica* clearly was not. We know of course that apart from using the gazetteers, Sahajanand made extensive use of the *Santal Parganas Inquiry Committee Report*, various Survey and Settlement Reports, and appropriate Census volumes, all of which were government publications, and all available at the Gulzarbagh press, which was almost certainly Sahajanand's source. It should be pointed out incidentally that the initial volumes of the *Mundarica* were in print as early as 1930 and most were published by 1938.

3 A kaccha well would be a rough, crudely dug, temporary well with no brickwork surrounding its interior walls.

4 I have written earlier about jail as a point of contact, communication, and information, and here Sahajanand provides us further evidence of this critical fact during this period of political activism and agitation.

5 The most common term for a trained legal professional in India is advocate. Earlier and at the time Sahajanand was writing the terms vakil and pleader were in use as well and these were the persons who most often functioned in the courts of a district town or the next higher level. The mukhtar practised law at a more local judicial level.

6 The section of the *Santal Parganas Inquiry Committee Report* which Sahajanand cites is titled "The Position of Pleaders," and in fact makes extended comment on the over supply of legal practitioners in the district and whether to limit the number of "pleaders and mukhtars," in order to avoid the result which Sahajanand cites in his quote. The Committee's decision then was to restrict access of outsiders but to make an exception "in favour of qualified persons who are genuinely native to or domiciled in the district." See *SPICR* (Patna, 1938), pp. 23-24 both for the paragraph 55 to which Sahajanand refers, and for the quote cited here. The full chapter dealing with pleaders in the district appears at pp. 22-26.

7 In 1994 the thought of public defenders for those unable to sustain normal court costs does not appear an especially imaginative idea. But in 1941 when Sahajanand was making the suggestion it was certainly a much less familiar one, leave alone its implementation. One cannot help but reflect on Sahajanand's reactions to the various public service civil liberties groups active in 1994 to represent precisely the kinds of interests Sahajanand felt were being unattended in 1941. On the other hand, given his commitment and candor, one might not want to contemplate his reactions to other aspects of life and society in the late twentieth century.

8 Khadi is hand spun and hand woven fabric whose production during the Freedom Movement became a complex and important symbol of independence and self-sufficiency, especially of course, as propagated by Gandhi the Mahatma. At the time it may well have been a cheaper fabric as Sahajanand suggests, but in 1994, certainly in its finer qualities, it is rather more costly than mill cloth.

9 Toddy is the liquid secreted from the toddy palm. It is generally collected in the morning in earthen pots attached the previous evening, and in the evening in the pots attached that morning. The juice taken in the evening which has thus been exposed to the sun the full day will be fermented. Fermented toddy has the consistency and alcoholic quality of beer. It is whitish in colour, approximating in that sense, heavily watered milk.

Chapter X

The True Behaviour of the Cooperative Societies

[Sahajanand and the Bihar Provincial Kisan Sabha were never friends of the cooperative credit societies in Gangetic Bihar and the Swami reinforces that image in his reactions to what has happened and is likely to continue happening in Jharkhand. He cites evidence from his experience primarily in Darbhanga and Monghyr and then makes the Jharkhand case with a long and critical extract from the official Congress Ministry report of the Santal Parganas Inquiry Committee of 1938. If the cooperative societies were run into bankruptcy by self-serving manipulators (yaars) in Gangetic Bihar, can anything more positive be expected in Jharkhand, Sahajanand asks rhetorically. The cooperative system is in need of dramatic overhaul, "otherwise it is certain to fail," Sahajanand concludes. Ed.]

It is necessary now to comment on the nature and role of the "co-operative credit societies" in Jharkhand. I find that special concessions have been given to these societies in the Chotanagpur Tenancy Act. Let me first examine Section 46 (2a) of the Act. Whereas the Adivasi kisans are permitted to mortgage their land as security to others for a period of no more than seven years, they can mortgage land to these cooperative societies for a period of fifteen years. There are other such instances which suggest that these societies have great importance in the eyes of government and the lawmakers. Not only are they viewed as important in theory but also in the daily lives of the people. No doubt these cooperative societies have noble goals.

But the real question is whether they actually serve any useful purpose for the kisans.

Actually I have had many bitter experiences with these societies in Darbhanga, Monghyr, Patna and other districts of Bihar. These districts are not as backward as those of Jharkhand. But when I remember the activities of these cooperative committees and societies vis-a-vis the kisans of these districts, I can only shudder with fright. The slashing criticisms of these committees by the Bihar Provincial Kisan Sabha not only enraged their architects but obliged them to deny the truth of our allegations. But we are not so weak as to be frightened by the idle chatterings of monkies (*bandar ghurkee*). Hence the Kisan Sabha maintained its position firmly and forcefully on this issue.

While trying to save our co-workers from the oppressions of these societies in Jamui [in Monghyr District], we learned of the corruptions (*dhandhli*) they practise on the poor kisans. This information was conveyed to us by our vakil friends in that area. I have come across similar stories in Patna and other districts and will relate here my personal experiences in Darbhanga. I was coming back after addressing a "meeting" at Girija Asthan near Dhanusha. Some kisans had taken me to their village which lay by the side of the road on a bus route. I do not now remember the name of the village but when we reached their house they related to me their problems and pointed out a large man (*mushchana*) standing nearby carrying a *danda*.[1] I learned that he had been deputed by the "society" to collect the dues from the kisans. He will come daily until payment is made on the kisan's loan, and in the meantime also take a meal from the kisan, if necessary by force. And this for realizing a balance of only one rupee. If the balance is even a little more, five men will come for collecting and they will assess annas six per head for their meals! This all in the name of the law. But what is the poor kisan to do? This fine of six annas will continue to mount, like a heavy weight on the chest of the kisan!

After all why have these societies failed? Some cunning persons (*yaar*) and learned vakils saw here an opportunity to serve their best self interest![2] One individual could manage to become the group "secretary" of eight cooperative societies at a time! Neither the kisans nor the people fully realized what was happening in these cooperative societies (in the villages it is called as *susayiti*).[3] They believed only that an organization had come as a new kind of mahajan to provide them loans! That is what they thought! And so they were looted. The true nature of these societies was neither understood nor explained to them! Formal explanations do not help. In order to persuade the unlettered villagers serious efforts must be made and this was not done! But who cares? In fact, elaborate "reports" were published describing the vigorous efforts undertaken by the cooperative societies to improve the economic condition of the villages! But these served no purpose, except that some politicians involved with the societies used it as a propaganda opportunity to procure votes during the general elections! Accordingly the cooperative effort was certain to end in bankruptcy!

If this was the case with the more progressive people [of Bihar], one can well imagine what must have happened among the relatively more backward people of Jharkhand. One might say "*andhe ki gaiya, Ram rakhvaiya*" that is, if a blind man has a cow, then only Ram can take care of that cow.[4] So there is no surprise at the fate of these societies. When the provisions of the tenancy law designed to benefit the kisans have been rendered ineffective without anyone being aware of it, then the failure of the cooperatives should come as no surprise. What to speak of others, even the government sponsored Santal Parganas Inquiry Committee has made pointed reference to the failings of the cooperative societies. And whatever the Inquiry Committee has written on this issue applies with equal force to the whole of Jharkhand. <5.12.41>

In paragraph 93 on pages 36 and 37 the committee has written as follows on this issue:

> Cooperative societies do not exist in many parts of the district, and even where they do they do not seem to have helped very much. We were struck by the amount of criticism of the cooperative societies that we received. It was not possible for us to investigate the working of these societies and the evidence that we have heard came mainly from those who have complaints to make, but many people feel that the rates of interest are too high and that they are nearly as oppressive in realising their debts as the Mahajans themselves. This is largely inevitable since land is inalienable and the only method of recovering debts is by

> attachment of crops. The Santal law does not allow attachment of standing crops for [meeting] Mahajan's debts. Even in the case of rent decrees attachment of standing crops is restricted to the amount sufficient to cover one year's rent, but under Section 35 of the Cooperative Societies Act there is no limit to the extent to which standing crops can be attached to recover a society's debts. Since the cooperative societies must recover their loans if they are to function at all, and since they have had to resort increasingly to this procedure, borrowers feel that they are being as harshly treated by the cooperative societies as they would have been by the Mahajans. There is also much complaint that in the Rajmahal Subdivision where the right of transfer exists, too little care and discrimination is used when putting property to sale for the recovery of cooperative dues, and that excessive areas are sold. The movement is distrusted. If it is to make further progress in the district, it will require remodelling. At present it is identified with all the oppressions of the mahajan and there is no constructive side to its work. If it is to succeed it will be necessary to reduce the rates of interest, to insure that much more care is taken in granting of loans and to develop the constructive side of cooperation.[5]

No further comment on this issue is required. The activities of the Kisan Sabha to which I have referred earlier, had examined all of these questions in detail. Of course, had the case been a different one or more complex, some of the facts might have escaped our attention. But everywhere the same awkward story is repeated and the same oppressions continue. For a petty loan, a large plot of land is mercilessly auctioned off and the kisan is ruined. Only then is he aware of what has happened! The real function of these societies is to benefit the kisans in some constructive and positive way, and it is this idea which must be conveyed to the people. The cooperative societies can be successful only if the people are fully aware of their current procedures on the one hand and their true purposes on the other. Otherwise they are certain to fail. Unfortunately, there is no one to take the initiative in improving the working of these societies. The sponsors (*yaars*) who have manipulated the system would only suffer in such an effort. In reality, loans were made indiscriminately. But in a cooperative society even bad loans are the collective responsibility of the society as a whole. In English the term is "collective liability." Such loans were sufficient in number so that the whole system has become bankrupt and failed. Actually, those yaars familiar with the workings of the societies have benefitted and the people for whom they were intended were sold out.

It should also be borne in mind that the evidence taken and the witnesses recorded by the Santal Parganas Inquiry Committee did not include any participation by the Kisan Sabha. It has been mentioned in the report that there were 230 written replies to queries and that 111 witnesses recorded oral evidence, including however, only government officers, vakils, zamindars, ghatwals and their village committees, and MLAs, pradhans, sirdars, and parganaits.[6]

Editor's Endnotes to Chapter X

1 A mushchand can best be described in American colloquial English as an enforcer. In the Indian context, he has the bearing of a pahalwan, or wrestler, meaning that he is large, heavily-built and hence threatening in carrying out his assigned duties, like collecting cooperative society dues. His threatening appearance is further enhanced by the weapon of choice in these cases, namely the danda, which is best described as a large truncheon, except that it is generally at least six feet in length, most often made of heavy bamboo and is likely to have metal tips at each end. It is a formidable instrument when used to beat the roof of the peasant's house or the peasant himself. Sahajanand uses the word danda here interchangeably with lathi, which is the normal term for the weapon I have described. Danda in this context is not to be confused with the danda or the ritually symbolic staff carried by Sahajanand himself as a Dandi Sannyasi of the Dasnami order. Although it should be pointed out that Sahajanand played on this very confusion during the activist conflicts of the late 1930s when he invoked his danda as an instrument of peasant power meant to change the corrupt and exploitative zamindari system. For a brief consideration of this issue see my essay, "Swami Sahajanand and the Politics of Social Reform, 1907-1950," *Indian Historical Review* 18:1-2 (July 1991-January 1992). A more thorough examination of the issue by Sahajanand himself appears in his memoirs, *Mera Jivan Sangharsh* (Bihta, Patna: Shri Sitaram Ashram, 1952), reissued by the People's Publishing House, New Delhi, in 1985.

2 Sahajanand here uses the term yaar, literally dripping with sarcasm, to describe that person who moves into any social or political situation to serve his best self interest, using any means necessary in the process. That Sahajanand should use the term in this context, suggests the contempt in which he held the cooperative societies of rural Bihar and Jharkhand and everyone who was involved in their operation.

3 The fact that Sahajanand himself adds this note about the spoken language of the villagers confirms the importance of a point I have made in the Introduction and elsewhere in this translation, namely that Sahajanand was not only aware of the qualities of locally spoken Hindi, but used it both in his own speech in that peasant environment and in his writing when that was his audience. It is precisely this *bol chal ki bhasha*, that is, language as spoken, which Sahajanand employs in the

Jharkhand ke Kisan tract. I emphasize the point to caution the reader who consults the Hindi text in Part II of this book, that what is found there is exactly what Sahajanand wrote. It is not "incorrect" Hindi. The point is also important because it tells us something about Sahajanand's intended audience, as I have already indicated. That this tract did not see print in Sahajanand's lifetime is another story which I have mentioned in passing in the Introduction and elsewhere in these Notes.

4 In other words, God help the peasants of Jharkhand when they have any dealings with the cooperative credit societies.

5 Two points need to be made here. First, that it is clear from Sahajanand's frequent reference to the *Santal Parganas Inquiry Committee Report* that he had the document close at hand in the Hazaribagh Jail while he was writing. It might also be noted that there was no similar official document available at the time for Chotanagpur as a whole, so it was almost inevitable that Sahajanand needed to draw precisely these kinds of inferences, reinforced by his personal experience in Gangetic Bihar and in Jharkhand. I have already mentioned that Sahajanand had apparently not used the *Encyclopaedia Mundarica,* which, however valuable, was in any event not an official document commenting on the contemporary issues with which Sahajanand was here concerned.

Secondly, his suggestion that the report's description and logic might apply with equal force to Jharkhand as a whole does in fact have some merit. A full reading of the Chapter XI on Economic Conditions and Rents, confirms Sahajanand's assessment in general terms, as does the subsection on credit, from which he quotes. Furthermore, in a comparison of rents in the Chotanagpur districts and Santal Parganas, the committee's figures reveal that for first class rice land only Palamau had a higher maximum rent than Santal Parganas, with Manbhum and Hazaribagh somewhat lower and Ranchi and Singhbhum substantially lower. The minimum rents for this land showed Palamau and Manbhum higher, Santal Parganas and Hazaribagh almost identical, with Ranchi and Singhbhum again lower. On first class upland, rents were higher in Palamau and Hazaribagh, lower in Manbhum and substantially so in Ranchi and Singhbhum. The minimum rents for this category of land were essentially identical in Santal Parganas, Ranchi and Singhbhum, and substantially higher in Palamau, Manbhum and Hazaribagh. While these figures would need closer examination to make more elaborate inferences, it would appear that Sahajanand's suggestion about general comparability certainly holds. See *SPICR* (Patna, 1938), p. 46 on rents, and pp. 34-46 for the full chapter on economic conditions and rents. On the levels and logic of rent in the Chotanagpur districts see P.P. Mohapatra, especially his "Class Conflict and Agrarian Regimes," *IESHR*, 28:1 (1991); and Chapter VI of his 1990 JNU PhD thesis, "Aspects of Agrarian Economy of Chotanagpur, 1880-1950."

6 Sahajanand's point here is well taken, inasmuch as the witnesses who appeared before the committee or were otherwise respondents included only officials, politicians, specifically Members of the Legislative Assembly, zamindars, and several categories of village headmen, many of whom it might be presumed would not want to be critical of the system. But even assuming some sypathetic testimony from among these witnesses, the critical quality of the note on cooperative societies is accordingly even more compelling. And while Sahajanand was not a prominent activist in Santal Parganas, neither were all members of the committee, nor certainly many of the respondents. That he was not called as an expert witness on cooperatives or any of a range of other agrarian questions, given the sponsorship of the inquiry by the Congress Ministry in Bihar, and the presence of a number of prominent Congress political figures on the committee, suggests that from the very outset of the Ministry, the confrontation between the Indian National Congress and Sahajanand was already very much at work. It may be recalled that the Ministry accepted office in July 1937, the Inquiry Committee was appointed in early September 1937, and its report was issued a year later in September 1938.

Chapter XI

Some Noteworthy Qualities of Life in Jharkhand

[Sahajanand is normally the critic of much he surveys in the world of rural India and this has certainly been apparent in his consideration of Jharkhand. But in this very short chapter he also finds among the kisans of Jharkhand things he admires. Among these the village community of Santal Parganas and the corporate ownership of land is particularly appealing. He then quickly examines a range of local Adivasi, and increasingly, non-Adivasi officials from the pradhan to the parganait to the sirdar. Inasmuch as he relies heavily on the Santal Parganas Inquiry Committee Report of 1938, his examples are drawn almost exclusively from that district. Ed.]

Here I must write about a number of features of life in Jharkhand which are particularly attractive and well worth emulating. The most interesting of these is that the lands in the villages of the Santal Parganas are not held individually or by a group of individuals. On the contrary the land is considered to be the common property of the village society as a whole. At one time this must have been the practice in other districts as well. But it is now to be found only in Santal Parganas and is absent from the remaining five districts.[1] Hence if anybody dies in Santal Parganas without heirs or leaves the place permanently his land becomes the property of the whole village and is again settled with anyone in that village who has no land or little land. During the period before the land is settled again it is managed by the mukhiya, who in Santal Parganas is referred to as the pradhan. During that time the pradhan cultivates these new fields.

In dealing with the cooperative societies we have just seen that no one has the right to sell his land. But if somebody does so quietly, for example to the moneylender, then the moneylender will lose possession of that land under the law and simultaneously the seller also loses possession of that land and it becomes the common property of the entire village. In the same way not only a particular kisan is sued for arrears of rent but the kisans of the village as a whole are held liable. Ordinarily the zamindar sues the pradhan as he is considered liable for payment of any outstanding balance of rent. But in practice the pradhan holds the kisans of the whole village responsible for this payment. Thus we find that the worldwide practice of having panchayats or "communes" is still functioning here, although its role in this sense is gradually being limited.

Another important element of Jharkhand life is the institution of the pradhan. The pradhan performs three important functions which have all been described in the report of the Inquiry Committee.[2] First, he is regarded as the mukhiya or head of the village society having all the powers of local self government. No doubt the old freedom associated with that function has practically disappeared. Being the president of the panchayat he performs many social and religious duties as well and decides petty disputes. Second, on behalf of the entire village it is only the pradhan who deals with the zamindar and pays the land rent of the village. As the zamindars do not deal directly with the peasant tenants, the latter do not in theory fall under the pressure of the zamindar or his amla [agent] for illegal exactions or otherwise. As a matter of fact amlas do not exist in this system. *Gair majarua* or *lavaris* lands are under his charge as well and it is he who settles such lands under the supervision of the Subdivisional Officer [SDO].[3] The third function of the pradhan is to be in regular contact with the local magistrate about all village affairs. He realizes cess, chaukidari tax and informs the magistrate about local crimes, thefts, and assaults. He is also charged with the arrest of absconders and is meant to look after the village forest and to assure that no one's rights are violated. Finally, he is also charged with the maintenance and repair of village roads and canals.

For the timely realization of rent the pradhan receives one anna per rupee as his commission from the zamindar and one anna from the kisan. In the event of non-realization of the rent he loses this commission. Moreover, he holds two kinds of agricultural land. First, in his capacity as pradhan, he holds a certain amount of personal land (*khas*) which is rent free. The purpose behind this privilege is that if the peasant fails to pay his rent in time, the pradhan would pay the due amount from the produce of such khas land and realize any due amount from the peasant afterwards. The Inquiry Committee has recommended that the pradhan should be given an amount of khas land sufficient to cover 1/12th of the land rent of the village. And if this allotment is insufficient to cover any outstanding rent balance, then the remaining balance should be met from the produce of the pradhan's *kisani* land for which he would get proportionate relief in the rent payment normally due on that land.[4] Like others he has to pay rent on his kisani land which is his raiyati holding and which he cultivates. On the contrary if he is removed from office or resigns as pradhan, his pradhani land is also liquidated and the next person who becomes pradhan will come to occupy that land. The practice of having a pradhan is found among the Santals and among other Adivasis, although it is no longer common.

Apart from the pradhan the office of mukhiya is also found among the Santals especially in the Damin area of the district. The office is technically titled as *parganait*. It seems that there was earlier a pradhan for every village and the head of a *pargana* was known as the parganait. For administrative convenience, Damin was divided into several *tahsils* or *thanas*. Each area had a government office or "bungalow" with a parganait belonging to that area as its head.[5] Over and above the realization of *mal* [or revenue] the parganait could hear local revenue and criminal cases and he assisted the police in various capacities. In fact it is these latter functions with which he is now primarily concerned. The parganait conveys all official news from the magistrate, locally called *hakim*, to the village. The offices of pradhan and parganait are hereditary but this is not an absolute requirement. Sometimes if able successors are not available new candidates may be sought out and sitting parganaits may also be removed. As a matter of fact, the system has degenerated because of its hereditary nature. The parganaits are paid proportionately on the realization of revenue at the rate of two percent. Moreover the parganait gets one rupee and ten annas annually from every village. But he holds no parganait land as is the case with the pradhan. They are now more or less regarded as police *darogas* although they are not directly involved in administering a police thana in their area.[6]

Officers called sirdars are found in Dumka, Jamtara, and Godda in Santal Parganas. The function of a sirdar is essentially that of policeman. In Godda the sirdars discharge the duties of *chaukidari sarpanch.*[7] They receive twelve rupees as their monthly salary. They work primarily in the Adivasi areas but now that practice is changing. Still it is difficult to work and move among the Adivasis and Santals without the help of the sirdars. We also find sirdars among the Paharias. As a matter of fact parganaits, pradhans and sirdars were earlier selected from among Adivasis, but now others can hold these offices as well, although Adivasis continue to serve as parganaits and pradhans. The practice of involving others in these local administrative fuctions has become possible because of the emergence of a mixed Adivasi and non-Adivasi population. The more advanced persons among the non-Adivasi population are known as *dikus* in the Santali language. As I have indicated, the practice of having pradhans, if properly exercised, has many worthwhile features.

There are also pradhans and *mankis* in the remaining five districts of Chotanagpur as well. But now they have little more significance than the jeth raiyat, or chaukidar in Bihar. And now chaukidari panches are being elected as well.[8] There are also persons like the *pahan* and the *deokali* in Chotanagpur but these have no significance in any modern sense. Pahans are like our priests and know the appropriate mantras for driving out evil spirits. Deokalis are specifically described as *ojhas*. Their function is to drive out particular evil spirits or to welcome others. It is the duty of the village people to arrange for the meal of the deokali. Unlike the pradhans these local priests have no claim on any land in the village.

The most important development of the present century in most of the districts of the region is the exploitation of mineral wealth like iron, mica, and coal. Workshops producing cement have also sprung up. The Japla Cement Factory in the district of Palamau is a well known example. Hundreds of thousands of labourers are employed in these factories, many of them of course from the surrounding villages. Under such circumstances both the kisans and factory workers can cooperate and assist one another in their respective struggles. Their full cooperation is of great importance in the present political climate. It is important not only on paper but has great potential if creatively implemented.[9] There are of course many problems for the kisans which I have not examined, as for example those on fields below which mines are worked. And the kisans of the interior have their own problems which we have already discussed. And the miseries of the factory labourers are already well known.

Editor's Endnotes to Chapter XI

1 This is obviously not the place for a consideration of the nature of property rights in Jharkhand, but Sahajanand raises questions which are relevant historically and in the contemporary present both in Santal Parganas and in Chotanagpur. For the districts of Chotanagpur we are fortunate to have the fine work of P.P. Mohapatra which I will cite briefly to indicate the nature of the issues involved. Quoting T.S. Mcpherson, a prominent revenue administrator in the area writing in 1905, Mohapatra then observes: "Mcpherson was only articulating the opinion of a considerable section of officialdom at the turn of the century, which held that beneath the legally recognised proprietary rights of zamindars . . . there existed in many areas of Chotanagpur much older customary and community rights over land. The locus of these rights was the village, and the origins of these rights were traced to the foundation of these villages through reclamation of the jungle. At the end of the nineteenth century, however, these village-based community and customary rights had been eroded to a great extent by incessant struggles with landlordism and the attendant concept of absolute property rights." Mohapatra then comments in a footnote that "There was a veritable discovery of the `village commmuity' at the turn of the century amongst officials. Father Hoffmann, the pioneer anthropologist and missionary, and author of the *Encyclopaedia Mundarica* was an important influence." See Mohapatra, "Class Conflict and Agrarian Regimes," *IESHR* 28:1 (1991), p. 7; and also his 1990 JNU thesis, "Aspects of Agrarian Economy of Chotanagpur," especially Chapter V. I have cited Hoffmann's *Mundarica* in earlier chapters and here repeat only in part one of the many references which reinforce Mohapatra's assessment of Hoffmann's likely influence on official thinking: ". . . the members of an original Mundari village were the joint-owners of the whole village on account of their direct descent from the original founder, whose title rested solely on his being the first occupant and the first tiller of that spot, etc." *Mundarica* Vol. II, p. 515. It is clearly this sense of the village community which had filtered into Sahajanand's own thinking, presumably through the official revenue settlement literature with which he was familiar. I have already suggested that it is my sense that he had not read the *Mundarica* itself. It is also useful to note, however, that Sahajanand follows the history which Mohapatra reports, namely, "that the practice is absent from the remaining five districts," that is, Chotanagpur.

2 See especially *SPICR* (Patna, 1938), p. 52 for a discussion of these pradhani functions, and pp. 52 to 57, which constitutes Chapter XIII of the Report and considers the system in detail. It is appropriately titled, The Pradhani System and the Collection of Rents. This is one of Sahajanand's primary sources for the issues he raises in these pages. See also Chapter VIII of *Jharkhand ke Kisan*, and my Endnote 11 of that chapter with specific reference to the issue of the time allowed for the realization of rent dues.

3 The Inquiry Committee Report refers to *gair majarua* or alternatively *gair mazarua* as waste land. Mazarua technically is a tilled field, hence gair mazarua would be an untilled or unused field. *Lavaris* literally means heirless, that is having no heir and Wilson reports that the term is laxly used to mean having no claimant. In place of lavaris, the Committee uses the terms *fauti* and *ferari* holdings, which mean respectively, the property of someone who dies intestate, and the property of a fugitive who has abandoned his lands. For more detail on these definitions see Wilson, *A Glossary of Judicial and Revenue Terms,* Delhi Reprint Edition, 1968, pp. 155, 159, 310, and 337. Other specifics can be found in the *SPICR* (Patna, 1938) at p. 52. The Subdivisional Officer holds administrative charge over a subdivision of a district whose responsibile administrative officer is the District Magistrate or District Collector. In Chotanagpur this officer is generally denominated Deputy Commissioner. The Commmissioner is the responsible officer in a division which is comprised of several districts.

4 Kisani land here refers to the regular tenancy land of the kisan, or peasant, and may also be called raiyati land or his raiyat holding. In other words, this is that land the pradhan holds as a peasant tenant or raiyat of the village apart from the land he holds in his official capacity.

5 The pargana, tahsil, and thana are all local level administrative subdivisions of a district. The terms are used variously depending on the locale, and the heads of these offices may also have varying responsibilities from one place to another.

6 A daroga is a very local level police official, whose rank and status will vary regionally.

7 This too is a police, or more accurately, a watchman function.

8 As indicated previously a jeth raiyat is a substantial and hence prominent raiyat or tenant, functioning formally or informally in some village administrative capacity, including the possibility that he may represent the zamindar's interest in the village with others of that zamindar's lesser tenants. A chaukidar is a watchman, and a panch is a local functionary of the village, sometimes elected, and ideally in a non-chaukidar capacity he may sit on the village panchayat, or council

of five, which is literally what the word panch means.

9 The relationship between local peasants and agricultural labourers on the land and in the mines and factories of Jharkhand is not one Sahajanand explores in this manuscript. He raises the issue more directly in his *Khet Mazdoor* tract when he considers definitions and distinctions among different categories of labourers. See my edited translation of this tract, *Sahajanand on Agricultural Labour and the Rural Poor* (New Delhi: Manohar Publishers, 1994), especially Chapter II, "Labourer or Kisan?" There is a very substantial literature on this subject which I cannot begin to cite in this note. A good beginning and one of the best treatments is Dietmar Rothermund and D.C. Wadhwa, eds., *Zamindars, Mines and Peasants: Studies in the History of an Indian Coalfield in Its Rural Hinterland* (New Delhi: Manohar Publications, 1978). There have also been many government commissions dealing with labour and agricultural labour over the years. As example, see The Report of the National Commission on Labour (1969), which includes a chapter dealing specifically with agricultural labourers. The report is doubly important inasmuch as this particular chapter was written by Dr. K.S. Singh, a senior Government of India administrative officer and an eminent historian of Chotanagpur as well.

Chapter XII

The Tatas and Mr. Homi

[In the last substantive chapter of this tract, Sahajanand invokes three pieces of evidence to demonstrate the role of the Tatas in the 1920s and 30s in exploiting the kisans of Jharkhand. He explains at the outset that it is the Tata's presence in Singhbhum as zamindars, not as industrialists that is his concern. In these few pages he relies significantly on his personal experience at Ghatshila, Jamshedpur, and Mango village itself, on the reactions of the Adivasi peasants and others of the rural poor he encountered in those places, and finally on two judgements by the District Magistrate and a Subdivisional Officer in Manbhum condemning the actions of Mr. Manik Homi, a key Tata agent in the 1920s. Ed.]

Without providing an account of the Tatas our story of Jharkhand will remain only half told. We have already dealt with the misdeeds of the wealthy Jains in connection with their domination of the Parasnath Hills. But the story of the Tatas is of much greater significance for all of Jharkhand. Their power and influence derives from their being both the local zamindar and the financial capital behind the Tata enterprise. Lakhs of workmen are under their influence and many leaders and organizers are under their direct control.[1] The magic of their wealth is so powerful that leaders, both great and small, feel intimidated and lose their identity in Jamshedpur. It is precisely for this reason that many labour leaders who have made their way to Jamshedpur to organize the workers have been unsuccessful. And accordingly, no where are the labourers so distrustful of their leaders as they are in this place. And few leaders have the patience to overcome this attitude of distrust. This is a prime example of the cleverness of the Tatas and their practical approach in manipulating the labourers of Jamshedpur.

But as a protagonist of the Kisan Sabha I am concerned here primarily with those activities of the Tatas which have a direct bearing on the peasants and the people more generally (*sarva sadharan*).[2] This is of course the aim of this book, as its title makes clear, and not to give an account of factory labourers and the conditions in which they work.[3] I also have no special knowledge of this subject. But the question of giving government aid to the Tatas was raised in the Central Assembly and the Swarajya Party of the [Indian National] Congress supported this measure. However, it opposed the proposal that the Tatas should undertake guarantees for the welfare of their workers as a precondition of such government assistance. In other words the Swarajya Party wanted that government aid should be unconditional. When we see such proposals being made by these powerful organizations *vis-a-vis* the labourers, some of us are puzzled. Yet, as I have said, we are not directly concerned with these issues here, but rather with resolving the problems of the peasants. These are the most immediate issues before us in this book. For example, we will have occasion to remember Mr. Homi, the old labour "leader" of Jamshedpur, in connection with the kisans. In order to make his role more clear, I shall quote at length from the speech I delivered on the occasion of the Singhbhum District Kisan Conference held at Ghatshila on July 3 and 4, 1939. That speech runs as follows:

> To the world outside, the Tatas are generally known for the manufacture of steel and thus represent a great capitalist enterprise. Few people who are in close contact with the Tatas and even few of us who are concerned for the welfare of the kisans know that this company is also a zamindar. Some twenty villages, large and small, in and around Jamshedpur pay rent to the Tatas amounting to Rs. 20 to 25 lakhs [that is, Rs. 2,000,000 to Rs. 2,500,000]. The names of these villages are Uliyan, Bhatiya, Gobharogora, Sonari, Khutari, Belari, Jojabera, Sakchi, Bara, Baridih, Maharara, Murkati, Nildi, Kalimati, Susnigariya, Golmuri, Siddhgora, and others. Their sufferings are beyond description.

In 1919-20 the government took control of these villages on behalf of the Tatas. Some of the horrible sufferings (*bhayankar kashton*) of these villages are described here in the words of the local people themselves. These reactions were given to me in writing during my tour of Jamshedpur in April [1939]. They reported to me the following:

'Jamshedpur and the neighbouring villages were formerly under the possession of the Raja of Dalbhum and were inhabited by us. The government on behalf of the Company acquired these villages as well as others in 1919-20 from the Raja. The Company urged us to remain in our villages as before, inasmuch as it would require our services as workers, cartmen, vegetable growers, etc. Hence the liquidation of the Raja's control over these villages was merely a paper transaction. It would produce no basic change from before.'

'The rent of these villages, which had been fixed by the Survey of 1906-09 was gradually enhanced after they were acquired by the Company. It then started realizing heavy rent from our lands. At the time we were able to tolerate this inasmuch as the price of rice, vegetables, etc., was then very high.'

'After some years, when the Company was able to manage its affairs without our help, it began attempting to drive us out from our hearth and home and take our lands for their own work. In the process we were being harassed continuously and in many ways. Then in 1932, cases were instituted against us for non-payment of land rent. But we won all these cases and could not be legally dispossessed. Then force began to be applied against us by the Company which was responsible for the administration of the town and its representative was also the chairman of the Notified Area Committee. He was cited in a number of criminal cases for illegal occupation and entry and the decree of the Lower Court against him was upheld by the High Court. Thereafter many criminal cases were instituted against us under Section 145 but fortunately these decrees always went in our favour.'

'Now the Company has started harassing us through the Jamshedpur [Notified] Area Committee. It is argued that we are residing within the limits of this Area Committee. But we enjoy no benefits of any kind from this municipality. In fact, it has only aggravated our problems and difficulties.'

'We are asked to take the Committee's approval by submitting a house plan even for minor work like repairing the thatched rooves of our houses. We are not provided with clean drinking water, rather the impure water is causing us to fall seriously ill. And yet we are not permitted to dig wells! Nor do we have any roads, lighting, or scavengers. Nor are there any facilities at all for teaching our children in schools.'

'Fallow lands which we formerly used for grazing our cattle are now let out to contractors by the Company for making bricks. Effectively this means that we must kill our cattle, inasmuch as we cannot take them out for fear of their being driven to the cattle pound. This action on the part of the Company has done us the greatest harm, because we cannot cultivate our fields without the use of our cattle. Consequently, we may literally have to desert our villages and seek shelter elsewhere. All of this coupled with the enhancement of rent has made it virtually impossible for us to pay the rent. As a result, many of our plots have been auctioned off in rent suits. This is because the present rent rate is four times higher than that of the existing rate in Dalbhum, and it is ten times more than the rent fixed at the time of the Survey! The following table will make this fact clear. Separate rents have been fixed for the paddy (*dhani*) fields and for the bari or bhith (*gorha*) fields.

Per bigha rent in Dalbhum		Per bigha Company rent	
Abbal (I) Paddy Field Rs.	1/-	(I) Paddy Field Rs.	4/-
Doyam (II) Paddy Field	8/-	(II) " "	3/-
Soyam (III) " "	6/-	(III) " "	2/-
Gorha Fields	2/-	Gorha Fields	3/-

Lands growing vegetables pay Rs. 8/-. The rent fixed by the Company differs from village to village.'

[*Note*: Abbal, Doyam and Soyam define three different categories of paddy land, in terms of quality.]

'Sakchi is a part of Jamshedpur town. Hence its inhabitants enjoy the facility of a good market, proper irrigation, and better roads. Other villages lack these facilities. Still the rents in Sakchi are relatively lower than in other villages as can be seen in the following table.

Indeed, one of the Company's officers has accepted that the difficulties of the kisans in other villages are greater than those of Sakchi.

Per bigha rent of paddy land in selected villages:

Abbal (I)	Sakchi Rs. 3/-	Ulyan, Mantiya, Gobharagora Rs.		4/-
Doyam (II)	" 2/4/-	" "	"	3/-
Soyam (III)	" ---	" "	"	2/-

Per bigha rent of gorha land in these same villages:

Abbal (I)	Sakchi Rs. 1/8/-	Ulyan, Mantiya, Gobharagora		3/-
Doyam (II)	" -/7/-	" "	"	3/-
Soyam (III)	" -/2/3	" "	"	3/-

Lands growing vegetables at Rs. 8/-'

'Water flowing out of the Tata Company mill destroys the sanitary condition of the river water so that the kisans cannot use this water to irrigate their fields. In addition bullock carts must pay regular tax. And the tax of Rs. 5/- which is levied for the removal of dead animal carcasses is ruinous.'

'Formerly people had irrigation facilities but now these no longer exist. Nor do the kisans get receipts on the payment of their rent. Only six months ago, we presented a memorandum on these conditions to the Finance Minister and thereafter to the Prime Minister.[of Bihar]. But these efforts have produced no results!'[4]

It is quite unnecessary to comment on this lengthy report of the kisans. So now let us hear about Mr. Homi. It has long been known that Mr. Homi claims to be the leader of the local factory workers while there are others who dispute this claim. Of course it is the business of the workers to decide the question of their leadership. Here I present him as a zamindar or *mukarraridar* of village Mango in Potamba thana of district Manbhum and report something of his activity in that capacity.[5] The village of Mango lies across the Subarnarekha River and is accordingly quite near to Jamshedpur. It was on my last visit to that place that I learned about his claim to be the mukarraridar of Mango and that this had resulted in great hardship for the local kisans and kamiyas. The oppressions and humiliations (*satate aur jalil*) committed in that village by the agents of Shri

Manik Homi were related to me in painful detail by Shri Kristo Gaur Pradhan and the men and women of Mango. Without adding a word to the atrocities (*julum* or *zulum*) committed there, I shall simply quote a few lines from two court judgements and the real circumstances will be self evident. This village lies on the border of the Manbhum district and is sixteen miles from the *thana*.[6] It is in an area where any clever person (*yaar*) can exploit the local Ho and Bhumij Adivasis and others at will. The first judgement was delivered in English by Mr. S.K. Ahsan, the then Subdivisional Officer, Purulia. The second judgement was delivered on 5.9.1927 by Mr. B.K. Gokhale, the District Magistrate of Manbhum. The first judgement runs as follows

> A complaint was lodged in the Police Report that Homi and his people had oppressed the kisans in many ways. They had threatened, assaulted, and forcibly extracted money from them. On behalf of himself and his people he has frankly agreed that they shall not hereafter employ force nor oppress anyone as has been the complaint, and that they shall only use legal processes. Hence I do not proceed against them at this time. However, I clearly warn Mr. Homi and his associates, not to intimidate or harass the kisans or whosoever in any way. A copy of this order should be sent to the officer in charge, Potamba Thana so that if they break their pledge, he will report against them.

The second judgement appears as Case No. 309 in a 1936 collection of well-known cases and reads as follows:

> It is clear to me from the evidence that Mr. Homi regards the jungle and its trees as his own property. He feels he can cut these down whenever he likes but he wants to prevent the villagers, who have by custom and from generation to generation, enjoyed such rights over the jungle and its trees, from doing so. Similarly he wants to stop the peasants from working the uncultivated land. There is no doubt that in accordance with pradhani usage, they have the right to cultivate these lands on payment of reasonable rent. Mr. Homi in his statement admits ignorance of the fact that the peasants are prepared to make rent payments for the lands they cultivate. This suggests that he has

> no contact with the people who have been settled there for generations but on the contrary wants to settle his own men on these lands. This is why all the villagers are strongly opposed to his scheme. It is mentioned in the fifth paragraph of the letter written by Mr. Homi on 26.1.1927 to the Superintendent of Police that 'the 2,000 acres of land acquired by me was to be converted into a model farm based on new techniques.' I regret that Mr. Homi had no knowledge of the special conditions attached to the land in question. He had in fact selected a pradhani village over which the entire village has special rights and these are being fully exercised. It would really be in his own interest if Mr. Homi were to give up the sooner the better, his idea of acting against the customs practised by the villagers from generation to generation. It would be a good action on his part for the preservation of peace and tranquility which is so much my concern as well.[7]

Any attempt to elaborate the points covered in these judgements is quite unnecessary. They convey a true picture of Mr. Manik Homi's ideal of service to the people. To become the leader of the workers means to serve them well. But Mr. Homi's sense of service is dangerous at best. He has erected a bungalow in Mango village as his personal residence. At the outset the villagers might have thought that a servant of the poor, concerned with their welfare, would live there. Later they learned that he was in fact a wolf in sheep's clothing.[8] But by then it was too late and he had firmly established himself. Until the poor people gather sufficient strength to protect their rights they will have to endure the bitter taste of Mr. Homi's will. But that strength is bound to come, and it must come soon.[9]

Editor's Endnotes to Chapter XII

1 Again, to remind anyone who might be unfamiliar with large number definitions in India, a lakh is 100,000, written as 1,00,000.

2 In order to locate Sahajanand's position in this chapter vis-a-vis the Tatas, I have translated the words Kisan Sabha *karyakartta* as "protagonist of the Kisan Sabha," but it is interesting to note that a more literal translation would be "worker of the Kisan Sabha," which was obviously Sahajanand's image of who he was and the nature of the politics in which he was engaged.

3 While Sahajanand avoids the subject here, he devoted a chapter to defining the distinctions between factory labourers and agricultural labourers in his earlier *Khet Mazdoor* tract. See my edited translation, *Sahajanand on Agricultural Labour and the Rural Poor* (New Delhi: Manohar Publishers, 1994), esp. Chapter II, "Labourer or Kisan," pp. 44-71.

4 Sahajanand is of course quite right to suggest that this extract from his 1939 speech at Ghatshila with extended reactions from the peasants of the villages in and around Jamshedpur in the early days of the Tata enterprise, requires little further comment. The peasants essentially speak for themselves and certainly make a compelling case. I will add here only two or three definitions and references. In the comparative rent tables which are provided, two sets of figures are given in each case, those for dhani or paddy land and those for bari, bhith, or gorha land. The normal inference is that the latter category is land planted with spring crops, which is the rabi crop, as opposed to the monsoon, or kharif crop, which in the official literature of the time is sometimes called the autumn crop. That crop is almost inevitably paddy, hence dhan or dhani in Hindi and in Bihar is harvested in November or December. The normal comparisons are with the rabi crops which are planted following the monsoon rains and harvested in the first three or four months of the year, generally in March or April. These are pulse crops, including the various dals as well as wheat, among other grains. Grierson specifically explains that bhith is a light friable soil suitable for these [spring] crops (p. 168). Both bhith and gorha are also described as being older land of the village, sometimes on raised ground in that belt near the homestead, better manured and more carefully cultivated. In this tract bari is also defined as upland. Note also that I have retained Sahajanand's spellings of village names

as he varies them in his Hindi text. On these several definitions of land and soil types see Grierson, *Bihar Peasant Life*, Delhi Reprint Edition, esp. p. 168; Crooke, *A Glossary of North Indian Peasant Life*, Delhi Reprint Edition, 1989, esp. p. 55; and Wilson, *A Glossary of Judicial and Revenue Terms*, Delhi Reprint Edition, 1968, esp. 168. Sahajanand also discusses some of these issues in his Chapter VIII, and there are additional references in my Editor's Endnote 5 of that chapter. The rent comparisons made between Dalbhum and Tata Company lands refers to that subdivision or pargana at the southeast end of Singhbhum district. Jamshedpur is situated in the northwest corner of that subdivision. The best official discussion of the land system of Dalbhum is W.G. Lacey, *Final Report on the Revisional Survey and Settlement Operations of Pargana Dhalbhum in the District of Singhbhum (1934-38)* (Patna: Superintendent Government Printing, 1942). As the date of publication indicates, this document was not yet in print when Sahajanand was writing in 1941.

Sahajanand's peasant informants indicate that six months before they spoke with him, they had submitted a memorandum to the Finance Minister and Prime Minister. These would have been members of the Congress Ministry in Bihar, and we surmise that the memorandum was submitted sometime in 1938. The Finance Minister at the time was Anugrah Narayan Sinha, and the Prime Minister was Shri Krishna Singh. That office is now referred to as Chief Minister. The comment about a case being upheld in the High Court refers to the highest court of appeal in the province, namely the Patna High Court. The reference to criminal cases being brought under Section 145, clearly relates to that section in the Criminal Procedure Code, 1898 dealing with procedures where disputes concerning land, water, etc. are likely to cause a breach of the peace. It was commonly employed in land litigation in the 1930s. For details see Government of India, *The Code of Criminal Procedure, 1898 (5 of 1898), As Modified up to the 1st January, 1962),* (New Delhi: Ministry of Law, 1962), pp. 54-56. A bigha, as I have explained many times in these notes is a locally variable measure of land.

5 A mukarrari is a fixed and permanent tenure, hence a mukarraridar is the holder of such a tenure, whether a zamindar in relation to the government, or a subsidiary tenure holder in relation to a zamindar. See Wilson, *A Glossary of Judicial and Revenue Terms*, New Delhi Reprint Edition, 1968, p. 352.

6 In this case Sahajanand uses the term thana to refer to the headquarters town of Potamba thana, which in the 1951 District Census Handbook is referred to as Patamda. See Census of India, 1951, *District*

Census Handbook for Purulia (Patna: Government of Bihar, 1956), especially the Population Map of District Purulia insert. A thana may refer to a local revenue and administrative subdivision or to a police station. At the time Sahajanand was writing Potamba thana was in the Manbhum district as he indicates. See my Endnote 3 of Sahajanand's Introduction and the map in the early pages of this volume for details on the 1956 border adjustments between Manbhum and Singhbhum districts following the recommendations of the States Reorganization Commission.

7 While only the Gokhale judgement is dated, it is nevertheless apparent from the context in which these judgements were delivered that they are both 1927 cases. Whereas Sahajanand normally provides the English text for all English quotes he uses, in this case he uses only his immediate Hindi translation.

8 The Hindi rendering of the idea expressed in this English colloquialism is equally revealing, namely *muni na hoy yah nishichar ghora,* that is, a horse of the night cannot become a saint by morning. Mr. Manik Homi does not emerge very favourably in either case.

9 This is Sahajanand's final appeal that the Adivasi kisans and the rural poor of Jharkhand must mobilize to avoid the exploitations to which they are victim. And he ends on a positive note, assuring us that they indeed have the strength to protect their just rights, and that they will invoke it in that cause sooner than later.

Chapter XIII

The Principal Demands of the Peasants

[In this concluding chapter Sahajanand summarizes his findings by way of making recommendations about what needs to be done to improve the quality of life for the kisans of Jharkhand. He provides eighteen such recommendations or demands, most of which are examined in some detail in the preceding chapters of this book. For Sahajanand as peasant activist, change can happen only when a sufficiently sensitive degree of awareness and understanding is brought to bear on the conditions in which the peasants of Jharkhand, or any other place in India live their lives. "Only then will we be in a position to deal constructively with their problems," he suggests. Such understanding is a precondition for mobilization, and the process, Sahajanand tells us throughout this book, is an ongoing one. Ed.]

Whatever I have had to say I have now said. There is nothing further to report. I have considered in detail some of the major grievances of the kisans of Jharkhand and now wish to present a summary statement of their demands based on these grievances with the aim of providing a set of proposals for those workers who wish to serve the cause of the poor. We must first familiarize ourselves with the long history of the Jharkhand experience and then by moving through the villages to learn things which may well have escaped our attention initially. The object is to achieve as complete an awareness and understanding of the problems as possible and only then will we be in a position to deal with them constructively. But in any case, it is important to focus first on those issues which are most painful and begin seeking solutions there rather than to be distracted by lesser problems. Hence in the remainder of this concluding chapter I will concentrate on those demands of the kisans I consider to be most significant.

1) The first and the foremost issue to be resolved in benefitting the kisans of Jharkhand has to do with their cultivation of korkar, utkar, and other similar kinds of land. It is critical to put a stop to the zamindar's interference in the kisan's cultivation of these lands by whatever legal and administrative means are necessary. Furthermore, the rent on these lands should be fixed only after five years from the time the land has been prepared for cultivation and put into production. And under no circumstances should the rent of these lands be more than that on the worst agricultural land neighbouring these new fields. Generally, it should be half the rent of such land.[1]

2) There should be no restrictions on the kisans' use of jungle products for their daily domestic use and otherwise for maintaining their livelihood. This includes the cutting of wood and bamboos, the collecting of leaves, grass, stones, sand, bushes, fruits, flowers, roots, honey, etc. The kisans should have full freedom to collect Mahua flowers, whether the trees are in the jungle or in the fields and this right should not be taxed. They should also be free to use Palas, Kusum and Ber trees in their fields for producing lac and selling it without payment of any levy. And whatever impositions might have existed on such activity should be abolished immediately by law or other administrative measures. Finally, exactions like tangkar, patkar, vankar, chulhakar or kharchari and other notorious taxes should be declared illegal forthwith.

3) Immediate arrangements should be made for providing pure drinking water for the kisans and their cattle and necessary wells should be dug at fixed locations throughout the region. There should be no restrictions on the kisans or their cattle to access streams and springs for quenching their thirst. If any such stream or spring lies in a reserved or protected area, an access path should be built with a strong, high barricade on both sides so that neither man nor animal can easily cross into the protected jungle.

4) All cattle pounds in the whole of Jharkhand should be removed and dismantled one by one.

5) As compared to the land revenue paid by the zamindar to government, the rent paid by the kisans to the zamindar is excessive. Inasmuch as it is 30 to 40 times greater than the revenue which the zamindar pays, it has become intolerable. Hence it should be reduced to a level which will cover the amount of government revenue, plus the cost of realization, plus an amount equal to that of the revenue itself, which will be the zamindar's profit.[2]

6) The Paharias in the Damin region of the Santal Parganas should have full freedom of kurawn or jhumchas cultivation and whatever obstacles there might be for such cultivation should be removed at once.

7) Immediate arrangements should be made to educate the Adivasis and other backward people and kisans in their own languages. Elementary education in their own languages should be made compulsory. Moreover quick steps should be taken to provide facilities for higher education free of cost.

8) Full irrigation facilities should be provided to the kisans immediately and the zamindars should be fully responsible for doing so, failing which they will not be permitted to realize even a paisa of rent. And it is the obligation of government to see that this responsibility of the zamindars is fully implemented. If the zamindars fail to do so, the government itself should provide necessary irrigation facilities and realize necessary rent from the kisans. However, if the zamindars are again invested with the power to realize the rent, this right should be subject to some penalty fine which will go on increasing so long as costs for proper and full irrigation facilities are not provided.

9) Arrears of rent may be realized by attachment or sale of the crops only after providing the kisan and his family with one year's requirement of food grains from his standing crops.

10) Kisans can be sued only for one year's arrear of rent, neither more nor less. If the kisan pays his rent before the expiry of the year, he need not pay a single paisa of interest.

11) There should be one uniform Tenancy Act for all the districts of Jharkhand and it should be similar to that of the Bihar Tenancy Act. Consequently there should be one law for the whole of the province. No doubt sections guaranteeing special rights to the Adivasis or backward kisans must be incorporated in such a law. Finally, the zamindar should not have the power of seizing, issuing certificates or

attaching standing crops of the kisans in settlement of suits. And all "praedial conditions" with regard to land must be abolished.

12) Government should provide loans to the kisans at a maximum interest of three percent per annum. Under no circumstances should the charging of compound interest be accepted as legal. Any interest above three percent should be illegal and no court should pass a decree for any amount more than double the principal sum advanced. And there should be strict enforcement of laws to stop the practice of usury.

13) Sevakai, kamiauti, and any form of slavery and the kamiya system should be declared illegal and its complete abolition must be enforced.

14) Arrangements should be made with all speed so that only government officials having a thorough knowledge of the languages of the Adivasis and the backward kisans as well as their culture, should try their cases. Consequently, such officers should receive appropriate training as quickly as possible. It would be still better if these officers were to be recruited from amongst the Adivasis themselves.

15) Special regulations should be laid down governing the conduct of those vakils, mukhtars and other legal advisers working with Adivasis to assure that they are not subject to fraud and deception. Hence there should be close supervision of the conduct of all such legal professionals.

16) Whatever laws, enactments, or other measures are adopted which affect the kisans, these should be given full publicity and announced promptly from door to door and village to village, thereby fully to inform the kisans of their rights.

17) Laws relating to the punishment of those kisans and poor people, on the pretext of theft, who collect and sell mica lying on the surface, all such laws should be declared null and void. And whatever difficulties subsurface coal mines cause to the agricultural fields of the kisans, should be appropriately resolved by government.[3]

18) Because there is only one Judicial Commissioner for several districts in Jharkhand, much time is lost in disposing of sessions cases. These delays must be eliminated by whatever means necessary.[4]

Editor's Endnotes to Chapter XIII

1 Inasmuch as this is a summary chapter and most of the issues Sahajanand raises have been examined in some detail in the text itself, I will not here be defining terms or, excepting one or two instances, providing explanatory endnotes.

2 It is important to note here that although Sahajanand had long been calling for the abolition of zamindari as a non-productive intermediate system of exploitation, he was nevertheless not talking about expropriation. Indeed, the suggestion made here is much more a recommendation of reform than it is of systemic structural change. As I have explained before, he was writing just at the time he and the Communist Party of India were deciding their policy response to Hitler's invasion of the Soviet Union, which as we know resulted in defining World War II as a People's War rather than an Imperialist's War. The point here is that this policy resulted in a softening of Kisan Sabha activism against zamindars, but my sense is that these policy decisions and the actions which followed were not yet reflected in Sahajanand's writing of *Jharkhand ke Kisan*, nor in this particular recommendation on limiting the rent income of zamindars. It is probably more likely that in terms of the package of proposals as a whole, Sahajanand in this case as in all the others, was trying to be candid, yet practical and realistic.

3 Although he touches on the mineral wealth of Jharkhand and its exploitation by outsiders, Sahajanand does not devote much space in this short tract either to the mica issue he raises here or more specifically to the damage subsurface mining may cause to cultivation on the surface. The fact that he raises the issue in this series of recommendations and demands, suggests that the problem is perhaps more important than might otherwise be supposed, especially in those districts of heavy coal mining activity.

4 In this concluding Endnote we need to return to where we began in the Editor's Introduction, to remind ourselves that this is a historical tract of its time. Sahajanand was making recommendations and demands he felt were not only justified but compelling when he was writing in 1941. But with all the changes that more than five decades have wrought, and they have been many, nevertheless there is much about life in 1994 that resonates with what Sahajanand was writing in 1941. Anyone who doubts that fact need not pursue an advanced de-

gree in anthropology, economics, or political science. A casual reading of any metropolitan or provincial daily newspaper will provide more than sufficient justification for Sahajanand's concern in 1941 and those of his successor activists in the political arenas of this remarkably open democratic society.

We need not be reminded that in the meantime there has been massive social change, much of it state sponsored, some of it privately funded. Among the rural development schemes some have begun to respond to Sahajanand's concerns, zamindari has of course long since been abolished, and government agencies have proliferated in many directions, perhaps most positively in the arena of education, where important institutions of higher learning, universities and colleges, medical colleges, agricultural colleges, management institutes, and institutes of technology have begun to provide an infrastructure for meaningful change of the kind Sahajanand had in mind in 1941. And while much of this has been a function of government both at the Centre and in the State as I have suggested, some of course has also been private. There are far too many non-government organizations active in the region even to begin listing them, and Sahajanand might be surprised to find Tata engaged in a range of rural development schemes that are impressive by any standard, whatever their limitations. And there would certainly be satisfaction in his knowing that at Ranchi University, in the very heart of Jharkhand there has existed for some years a prominent and active Department of Tribal and Regional Languages. Finally, of course, it must be said that the issues Sahajanand was contemplating in 1941 were not problems limited to Jharkhand, Bihar or India. They were human problems and that is as true in 1994 as it was in 1941. It is a fact of which Sahajanand's 1941 essay is a grim reminder, however active we may be in pursuing his goal of improving the human condition.

Part II

Jharkhand ke Kisan

Swami Sahajanand Saraswati

[As explained in the Editor's Preface and the Editor's Introduction, what follows is the original Hindi text of Jharkhand ke Kisan, exactly as it was written by Sahajanand in 1941. There are no editorial interventions or emendations in the pages which follow. It should, however, be noted that this is most often rural, colloquial Hindi as it was spoken by the kisans of Bihar and presumably understood most widely by Sahajanand's intended audience. This is essentially bol chal ki bhasha, i.e., spoken Hindi conveyed here by Sahajanand on the written and printed page. What may appear as misprints or spelling errors in this text are in fact neither; they are exactly what Sahajanand wrote and what he intended. We need to remind ourselves that Sahajanand as a Dasnami sannyasi was entirely at home with Sanskrit and with shuddh Hindi, i.e., Hindi in its purest form. What appears in the pages of this Devanagri text is the language of Sahajanand the peasant activist. Ed.]

रास्ता भी निकाल लेते। इधर तो उन्हें पता ही नहीं है उस सवाल से
सभायें उन पर लाद जाती हैं। जेल में रहके उन लोगों से रहने और उनके
साथ बातचीत करने मिलने पर पता चलता है कि वे किस जाल में
फँस गये हैं। उनके पास इसका सबूत उनके पास मौजूद है नहीं। किसी भी
असेम्बली या कौंसिल के मुताबिक वे हाकिम के सामने परेशान रहते हैं
और लद गये। मगर वे इन कायदे कानूनों को जानने आ गये? उन्हें किसने
ये बातें सिखाने की कोशिश की? कानून बनते हैं अंग्रेजी में और आम
जनता की तो बात ही नहीं, उनके जो खास सदस्य असेम्बलियों में चुने गये
हैं उनमें शायद ही एकाध अंग्रेजी जानते हैं। बाकियों की तो हालत ज्यादातर
"किंकर्तव्यविमूढ़" जैसी ही है। थोड़ी बहुत हिन्दी जानने से भी तो काम नहीं
चलता।

ऐसी दशा में आगे जो कुछ लिखा जा रहा है वह सबों की जानकारी
के ही लिये। किसी दल या पार्टी या सम्प्रदाय के खंडन मंडन से हमारा
मतलब नहीं है। हमें तो अपना काम करना है। यदि हम झारखंड की जनता
की और खासकर वहाँ के किसानों की कुछ भी सच्ची सेवा करना चाहते
हैं तो सबसे पहले उसे इस अंधेरे से, उस अन्धेरी गुफा — No man's land —
की भूल भुलैया से निकालना और परिस्थिति समझा देना जरूरी है। नहीं तो भटक
जाने की पूरी संभावना है। वैसी हालत में केवल दो चार अच्छी बातों से
हम सबको अकड़ के नाते में फँसाने की कोशिश भी नहीं कर सकते हैं। कह नहीं
सकता कि हमें इसमें कहाँ तक सफलता मिलेगी।

सेन्ट्रल जेल, हजारीबाग
नवम्बर दिवाली, शुक्रवार (७-११-४१)

स्वामी सहजानन्द सरस्वती

झारखंड के किसान

स्वामी सहजानन्द सरस्वती

यह काम किस लिये ?

बिहार प्रान्त को असल में ''बिहार और छोटानागपुर'' के नाम से ही पुकारा जाता है। यों कभी कभी संक्षेप में केवल ''बिहार'' भी कह देते हैं। जब उड़ीसा का सम्बन्ध बिहार से था तब तो ''बिहार और उड़ीसा'' अकसर कहा जाता था। मगर उड़ीसा के अलग हो जाने के बाद केवल ''बिहार'' के बजाय ''बिहार और छोटानागपुर'' कहना हीं उचित प्रतीत होता है। यों तो उड़ीसा के मिले रहने पर भी कभी-कभी केवल ''बिहार'' ही कहते थे। चाहे जो भी हो, छोटानागपुर का महत्त्व काफी है और जान या अनजान में इसकी याद हमेशा बनी रही है।

बात असल यह है कि इस प्रान्त के कुल सोलह जिलों में सिर्फ सारन, चम्पारन, दरभंगा, मुजफ्फरपुर और पूर्णियां यही पांच ऐसे हैं जहां पहाड़ नहीं हैं । शेष ग्यारह में तो कमवेश पहाड़ पाये ही जाते हैं। यह ठीक है कि छोटानागपुर के पांच जिलों — पलामू, रांची, हजारीबाग, मानभूम और सिंहभूम — तथा संथाल परगना, इन छः जिलों की भूमि जिस प्रकार पार्वत्य या पहाड़मयी है वैसी गया, मुंगेर आदि की नहीं है। ये छः तो पहाड़ों और जंगलों से घिरे हैं। मगर गया वगैरः के कुछी हिस्से पहाड़ी हैं। फिर भी यह बात सही है कि ये जिले भी अपने भीतर कुछ न कुछ जंगल और पहाड़ रखते ही हैं। पटना जिले में ही सब से कम पहाड़ और जंगल हैं। इस प्रकार जंगलों की प्रधानता का खयाल करके ही पलामू आदि छः जिलों को बहुत पहले से झारखंड कहते चले आते हैं। बाकी जो ग्यारह जिले बच जाते हैं उनमें या तो जंगल पहाड़ हई नहीं, या बहुत ज्यादा नहीं हैं। यह भी बात है कि उनमें बौद्धकाल में बौद्ध भिक्षुओं के रहने और पढ़ने आदि के लिये जगह जगह मठ या मकान प्रायः बने रहते थे जिन्हें बौद्ध सम्प्रदाय में विहार कहते हैं। इसीलिये वे ग्यारह जिले विहार कहे जाने लगे। असल में तो इस लम्बे सूबे को दो भागों में बांटकर जैसे जंगली भाग को झारखंड कहते थे वैसे ही दूसरे भाग को विहार खंड ही कहना उचित था। मगर जाने क्यों केवल ''विहार'' ही कहा जाता था।

इस प्रकार बिहार या विहार खंड और झारखंड के नाम से दो भागों में बंटे इस सूबे में विहार खंड के किसानों की दशा सुधारने की कोशिशें तो इधर

बहुत हुई हैं। मगर यह बात झारखंड के बारे में नहीं हुई है। बिहार प्रान्तीय किसान सभा ने भी उतना ध्यान इस ओर नहीं दिया है जितना बिहार खंड की ओर। फलतः और तो और, बाहरी लोगों को यहां के किसानों की समस्याओं तथा मुसीबतों की जानकारी तक प्रायः हुई नहीं! थोड़ी बहुत टूटीफूटी बातें ही लोग जानते हैं। कभी कभी कोई उथल पुथल हो जाने पर ही कुछ नई बातें मालूम हो पाती हैं। जिसे पक्की और ब्यौरे की जानकारी कहते हैं वह तो फिर भी नहीं होती। वहां के असली निवासी, जिन्हें आदिवासी भी कहते हैं, आमतौर से मूक जैसे हैं। पढ़ने लिखने की तो बात ही जाने दीजिये। उनकी भाषा ऐसी है कि दूसरे लोग समझी नहीं सकते। उनके रस्म रिवाज भी निराले ही हैं। वे सीधे भी हद से ज्यादा हैं।

यह प्रान्त तो बड़ा है नहीं। कुल सोलह जिले हैं। जनसंख्या भी प्रायः साढ़े तीन (३६३४००००) करोड़ ही है। मगर जहांतक किसानों की बात है, यहां तीन तरह के काश्तकारी कानून लागू है। बिहार काश्तकारी कानून –Bihar Tenancy Act– सिर्फ विहार खंड के दस जिलों में ही लागू हैं। उसका ताल्लुक झारखंड से हई नहीं। झारखंड में भी दो कानून हैं। संथाल परगने को छोड़ बाकी पांच जिलों में छोटानागपुर काश्तकारी कानून –Chotanagpur Tenancy Act– प्रचलित है और उसी के अनुसार वहां काम होता है। मगर संथाल परगने की तो निराली ही हालत - मुरारेस्तृतीयः - पन्थाः है। इन दोनों में एक भी वहां लागू नहीं है। उस जिले के लिये एक तीसरी ही कानूनी व्यवस्था है जिसे संथाल परगना मैनुअल –Santhal Pargana Manual– कहते हैं। उसी के अनुसार वहां का इन्तजाम होता है। यह मैनुअल भी बना है ज्यादातर १८७२ और १८८६ के नियमकायदों (Regulations) के आधार पर ही। झारखंड की पेचीदगी इसीलिये और भी बढ़ जाती है।

बदकिस्मती की बात यह भी है कि वहां के मूल निवासियों का नेतृत्व दूसरों के ही हाथ में है। ईसाइयों के जानें कितने हीं मिशन वहां बहुत दिनों से काम करते हैं। उनने ईसाइयत का प्रचार भी वहां काफी किया है। अतएव एक तो वही लोग वहां के किसानों का नेतृत्व करते आये हैं। उनके सिवाय समय समय पर सूबे के उत्तरी भाग या विहार खंड से भी पढ़े लिखे सूदखोर बनिये या व्यापारी लोग वहां समय समय पर बसते गये हैं। वकील, मुखतार या और तरह के पढ़े लिखे लोग, या तो वही हैं या बंगाली। अबरक, कोयला, लोहा वगैरः के कारबार और लाह या लकड़ी के रोजगार के सिलसिले में भी सभी तरह के लोग भारत के कोने कोने से ही नहीं, बल्कि दूसरे देशों से भी आके

वहां बस गये हैं। इसलिये स्वभावतः ऐसे लोग उन गरीबों के अगुवा बनने की कोशिश करते हैं। कांग्रेस जैसी प्रभावशाली संस्था के जितने प्रमुख नेता झारखंड में हैं वे सभी बाहर वाले ही हैं।

आदिवासी आन्दोलन के रूप में आज एक संस्था वहां खड़ी हो गई है सही और उसका नेतृत्व भी आदिवासियों के हाथ में ही बताया जाता है। कई ऐसे लोग भी हैं जो आदिवसी ही हैं और किसान सभा के नाम पर उनने एक संस्था भी बना ली है। मगर उनका नेतृत्व निहायत लचर और अवसरवादी है। वे किसानों को उठाना नहीं चाहते। किन्तु अपना काम निकालना चाहते हैं। आदिवासी आन्दोलन की कनी यह है कि शुद्ध मध्यवर्गीय ढंग से ही चालू हो रहा है। यदि वह किसानों के वर्ग स्वार्थों के ही आधार पर चालू होता तो उसमें अपार शक्ति आ जाती और वह सचमुच झारखंड वासियों का निस्तार ही कर देता।

यही कारण है कि असलियत का पता नहीं लग पाता और घपले बढ़ गये हैं। मैं शुद्ध किसान हित के खयाल से ही वहां की स्थिति पर प्रकाश डालना चाहता हूँ ताकि उस अन्धेरी गुफा की झांकी हमें मिले। हमें और हमारे कार्यकर्त्ताओं को सबसे बड़ी दिक्कत यह है कि वहां के निवासियों के अभाव-अभियोगों को जानते ही नहीं। वहां के काश्तकारी कानून की खास बात क्या है और उसमें क्या कमी है यह बात हमें मालूम नहीं। फिर उसके सुधार का आन्दोलन भी किया जाय तो कैसे? बाहरी लोगों की दृष्टि से वहां के काश्तकारी कानून में पेचीदगियां हैं। कांग्रेसी मंत्रियों के समय वहां का कानून भी बहुत कुछ सुधारा गया ठीक बिहार के काश्तकारी कानून के ही ढंग पर। मगर कितने मेम्बरों ने असेम्बली में उसे समझा भी, यह एक सवाल है। सिर्फ रस्मअदाई के खयाल से या दो चार लोगों के कहने से ही जो कानून बने उससे हम लोगों का फायदा कहां तक कर सकते हैं? विहार के कितने कांग्रेसी नेता हैं जो उन कानूनों को समझते हैं।

जब तक हम वहां की असली परिस्थिति न जानें, लोगों की सबसे चुभने वाली मांगों की हमें पूरी जानकारी न हो, सरकारी महकमे वहां कैसे कान करते हैं, कचहरियां कहां तक किस तरह उन गरीबों के साथ मौजूदा कानून के अनुसार भी न्याय कर पाती हैं, इत्यादि बातें हम न समझें उनके लिये कुछ भी कर सकते हैं क्या और कैसे? आदिवासियों की भाषा न तो हाकिम समझते और न दूसरे ही लोग। बाहरी वकील मुखतार भी सिर्फ काम चलाऊ बातें ही जानते हैं। नतीजा यह होता है कि वे बेचारे बहुत बार नाहक लद जाते हैं। अंग्रेजी कानूनों

की पेचीदगियां वे क्या जानने गये? यदि जानते तो बचाव का रास्ता भी निकालते। इधर तो उन्हें पता ही नहीं है उधर सख्त से सख्त सजायें उन पर लद जाती हैं। जेल में रहके उनसे बातें करने और उनके साथ बार बार हिलने मिलने पर पता चलता है कि वे किस बला में फंस गये हैं। अपने पक्ष का सबूत उनके पास मौजूद है सही। फिर भी ठीक समय पर या कायदे के मुताबिक वे हाकिम के सामने पेश न कर सके और लद गये! मगर वे इन कायदे कानूनों को जानने क्या गये? उन्हें किसने ये बातें सिखाने की कोशिश कीं? कानून बनते हैं अंग्रेजी में और आदि जनता की तो बात ही नहीं, उनके जो खास सदस्य असेम्बली में चुने गये हैं उनमें शायद ही एकाध अंग्रेजी जानते हैं । बाकियों की तो हालत ज्यादातर 'लिख लोढ़ा पढ़ पत्थर'' जैसी ही है। थोड़ी बहुत हिन्दी जानने से भी काम तो नहीं चलता।

ऐसी दशा में आगे जो कुछ लिखा जायगा वह सबों की जानकारी के ही लिये। किसी दल या पार्टी या सम्प्रदाय के खंडन-मंडन से हमारा मतलब नहीं है। हमें तो अपना काम करना है। यदि हम झारखंड की जनता की और खासकर वहां के किसानों की कुछ भी सच्ची सेवा करना चाहते हैं तो सबसे पहले उस क्षेत्र की, उस अन्धेरी गुफा –no man's land– की झांकी लगाना और परिस्थिति समझ लेना जरूरी है। नहीं तो भटक जाने की पूरी संभावना है । वैसी हालत में केवल दो चार ऊपरी बातों से ही हम सन्तोष कर के तह में घुसने की कोशिश करी नहीं सकते हैं। कहा नहीं जा सकता कि हमें इसमें सफलता कहां तक मिलेगी।

सेन्ट्रल जेल, हजारीबाग — स्वामी सहजानन्द सरस्वती

नवम्बर दिवस, शुक्रवार 7-11-41

(१)

झारखंड की भूमि

<24.11.41> विहार और छोटानागपुर सूबे का दक्षिणी हिस्सा ही झारखंड कहा जाता है। यह पुराना नाम है। संस्कृत में वनखंड या वनषंड शब्द जंगली या पहाड़ी भूभाग के लिये बार बार पुरानी पोथियों में आया है। आज भी चलती भाषा में झाड़ शब्द पेड़ों के ही मानी में आता है। ''झार'' और ''झाड़'' इन दोनों में कोई फर्क नहीं है। ''झाड़'' की ही जगह पहले ''झार'' बोलते थे। इस प्रकार संथाल परगना और छोटानागपुर के पांच जिले इस प्रान्त के जंगल प्रधान भूभाग को लेकर ही बने हैं। शाहाबाद के सहसराम सबडिविजन के कुछ हिस्से, गया का अधिकांश दक्षिणी हिस्सा, मुंगेर और भागलपुर के भी दक्षिणी भाग का बहुत कुछ अंश इसी झारखंड से मिलकर इसे और भी विस्तृत बनाता है। इसी झारखंड के सिंहभूम जिले के पश्चिमी हिस्से से एक ओर उत्कल के गांगपुर स्टेट का मेल हो जाता है और दूसरी ओर दक्षिणी भाग में उत्कल या उड़ीसा के सूबे के मयूरभंज, बोनाई, क्योंझर रियासतों का। पलामू के साथ युक्तप्रान्त के मिर्जापुर का भी गंठजोड़ा है। और सरगुजा स्टेट का। रांची के साथ सरगुजा, जशपुर और गांगपुर राज्यों का सम्बन्द्ध हो जाता है। सिंहभूम तथा मानभूम के पूर्वी हिस्से बंगाल से जुट जाते हैं। संथाल परगना तो दक्षिण और पूर्व में बंगाल से जुटा हुआ हई । खूबी तो यह है कि बंगाल, उत्कल, मध्यप्रान्त या युक्तप्रान्त के जिन हिस्सों से इस झारखंड का सम्बन्ध जुटा है वे सभी इसी तरह पर्वत तथा जंगल मय हैं। फलतः चारों ओर अपने जैसे ही भूभागों से घिरे होने के कारण यह झारखंड अत्यन्त विस्तृत हो जाने के साथ ही दुष्प्रवेश और अगम –no man's land– बन जाता है।

यही कारण है कि यहां के निवासियों की अपनी निराली दुनियां मानी जाती थी। जैसे अथाह समुद्र के भीतर के जीवजंतु अपने आपको सुरक्षित समझते हैं वैसे ही ये लोग अपने को कम सुरक्षित नहीं मानते थे। इनने ठेठ प्रकृति माता की गोद में ही बसेरा समुद्री मच्छ कच्छपों की तरह लिया था।

इन भयंकर कांटे कुसों से घिरे, निबिड़ और दुष्प्रवेश प्रदेश में उन्हें सताने के लिये जाने की हिम्मत किसे होती? अगर कांटे कुशों की पर्वा कोई न भी करता तो भी भयानक सिंह व्याघ्रों और भालू भेड़ियों की याद से तो दुश्मनों के देवता ही कूच कर जाते। प्रकृति माता ने अपने इन पुत्रों की रक्षा के लिये अपने हाथों बनाये इस गढ़ के भीषण सन्तरी के रूप में इन खूंखार जानवरों को काफी तादाद में चारों ओर रख छोड़ा था, ताकि उसमें घुसने की हिम्मत करने वालों से दूर से ही ये चिग्घाड़ मार के कह दें, डांट दें कि खबरदार, कौन आ रहा है –who comes there ? इसीलिये तो दिन रात इनका पहरा पड़ता रहता है।

मगर क्या इतने पर भी इनकी जान बच सकी है? क्या इस अभेद्य दुर्ग के भीतर भी शत्रु लोग घुस नहीं आये? उनने इनकी लूटपाट क्या खूब ही नहीं की है? क्या अब भी नहीं कर रहे हैं? इसी का कुछ कुछ पता तो आगे मिलेगा। इस वर्णन में और तो कुछ है नहीं सिवाय इस लूट के संक्षिप्त वर्णन के। जैसे अथाह और अतल सागर के गर्भ में क्रीड़ा करने वाले जीवजंतुओं को फंसाने के लिये मनुष्य के दिमाग ने महाजाल तैयार किया है; जिस प्रकार गहरे पानी के बीच रहने वाली मछलियों को फंसाने के लिये बंशी तैयार की गई है, ठीक उसी प्रकार इन झारखंड वासियों को फंसाने और इनका रक्तमांस वगैरः सभी कुछ चाट जाने के लिये सैंकड़ों उपाय चतुर खिलाड़ियों और काइंया यारों ने ढूंढ निकाले हैं। ऐसे ऐसे जाल बिछाये गये हैं कि यदि एक से बचे तो दूसरे, नहीं तो तीसरे, चौथे में तो खामखाह फंसेंगे ही। ज्यादातर तो ऐसा होता है कि एके बाद दीगरे कई जालों में ये बेचारे सीधे सादे लोग फंसके छट्टपट्ट करते और तलमला के मरते रहते हैं। खूबी तो यह है कि जितना हीं दक्षिण बढ़ते जाइये उतना हीं शोषण ज्यादा मिलेगा, हालांकि उसी तरफ अपार धनराशि है – कोयला है, अबरक है, लोहा है और क्या क्या नहीं है।

ऐसा क्यों होता है यह जानने के पूर्व इस झारखंड के दक्षिणी या यों कहिये कि दक्षिणी, पूर्वी और पश्चिमी हिस्सों की रचना पर थोड़ा ध्यान देना जरूरी है। इसके लिये नक्शे को देखना होगा। उड़ीसा की रियासतों का जिक्र तो पहले किया ही है। उन रियासतों ने समूचा दक्षिणी हिस्सा तो घेरी लिया है। वह पश्चिमी हिस्से का भी अधिकांश घेरे पड़ी है और मध्यप्रान्त के सरगुजा ने भी कुछ पश्चिमी हिस्से को छेंक लिया है। उत्कल की सरायकेला, करायकेला और खरसवां – इन तीनों – रियासतों की तो यहां तक हालत

है कि सिंहभूम के पेट में घुस गई हैं। या यों कहिये कि इस जिले को ही काट के ये तीनों बनी हैं। सिंहभूम जिले के पूर्वी सबडिविजन दलभूम (धल या ढलभूम भी कहते हैं) को पश्चिम के सदर या चाईबासा सबडिविजन के बीच में ही सरायकेला है और उसी से मिली उससे छोटी रियासत खरसवां है जो उससे पश्चिम है। इस प्रकार जिले को दो हिस्सों में बेलाग बांट देने (क्योंकि सिंहभूम में तो दोई सबडिविजन हैं) के बाद भी सन्तोष नहीं हुआ अैर चाईबासा के उत्तरी हिस्से को काट के एक नन्हीं सी रियासत करायकेला नाम की उसकी छाती पर बिठा दी गई है।

इसके बाद दलभूम के दक्षिण पूर्व से बंगाल की सीमा शुरू होती है जिसका पहला जिला मिदनापुर उसके दक्षिण-पूर्व और पूर्व में है। मानभूम के पूर्व में बांकुड़ा और बर्दवान का कुछ हिस्सा है। संथाल परगने के पूर्व दक्षिण कुछ हिस्से में बर्दवान और उसके पूर्व वीरभूम, मुर्शिदाबाद और मालदा का कुछ भाग पड़ता है। इस प्रकार समस्त छोटानागपुर का पूर्वी हिस्सा बंगाल के अनेक जिलों से घिरा है। यही कारग है कि छोटानागपुर (झारखंड के पूर्वी जिले या उनके पूर्वी हिस्से बंगालियों की भूमि जैसे बन गये हैं और उनमें या तो सीधे बंगाली लोग या बंगलाभाषी दूसरे लोग बसते हैं। ये हिस्से विहार की अपेक्षा बंगाल से ज्यादा निलते और उसी के भाग मालूम पड़ते हैं। वहां जो आदिवासी लोग हैं उनकी भाषा भी खिचड़ी सी हो गई है और उनकी अपनी तथा बंगला भाषा की खिदमत मिदमत के करते अजीब सी मालूम पड़ती है। उसे अकसर खोरठा बोली भी कहा करते हैं।

अब जहां तक सरगुजा या उत्कल की रियासतों का ताल्लुक है, उनमें तो निरंकुश शासन टांगें तोड़ के बैठ गया है। उनके लिये तो बीसवीं सदी मालूम होता है, आई ही नहीं है। मध्ययुग के अन्धकाराच्छन समय से ही वे रियासतें गुजरती हैं जहां तक जनता के अधिकारों और लोकशासन का ताल्लुक है। उनके राजे खुद तो मोटर, रेडियो वगैरः सभी अपटुडेट चीजें रखते हैं। मगर जनता को पशु की जिन्दगी बिताने पर ही विवश करते हैं। उत्कल राज्यपरिषद के मंत्री श्री शाड्र्गधर दास ने जो जांच कमिटी की रिपोर्ट छपवाई है उसे पढ़के तो पता लगता है कि वहां दूसरी ही दुनियां है। जहां विवाह शादी, सभा सोसाइटी, पंचायत और मृतक जलाने तक पर भी कर लगते हों या सरकारी आज्ञा की जरूरत हो और जहां पान वगैरः की बिक्री पर टैक्स लगे हों उन राज्यों की जनता का तो खुदा हाफिज। तीन चार साल पूर्व उत्कल की कई रियासतों में जो गोली कांड हुआ था और सिंहभूम के पड़ोसी

राज्य गांगपुर में ऐसी ही घटना हुई थी उसका चित्र तो हमारी आंखों के सामने ताजा ही है। और जब वही रियासतें न सिर्फ झारखंड को बहुत दूर तक घेरे हुई हैं, बल्कि उसके पेट तक में घुस गई हैं तब यहां के लोगों की दशा यदि अत्यन्त पिछड़ी न हो और इनका यदि कोई सच्चा पुर्सा हाल न हो तो इसमें आश्चर्य होई क्या सकता है? पड़ोसी का असर तो होना हीं चाहिये।

बंगाल से घिरे होने के कारण भी इनकी अजीब दशा इसलिये है कि यहां रोज खींचतान बनी रहती है कि यह बंगाल में रहे या बिहार में। जमशेदपुर, रांची, पुरूलिया आदि शहरों में तो इसकी धूम बराबर ही रहती है। बदकिसमती से बिहार में बंगाली-बिहारी झमेला उठ खड़ा हुआ है। उसका सबसे बुरा नतीजा इस झारखंड को ही भोगना पड़ता है। यह साझे का खेत जो ठहरा। बिहार के बाकी जिले तो ऐसे हैं नहीं। मगर यहां कुछ ऐसी बात है कि कई लोग इन पर दावेदार हैं। नतीजा यह है कि प्रगति का असली काम हो पाता नहीं। साझे की जमीन तो हमेशा पड़ती ही रहा करती है। उसमें उपज कोई हो कैसे? इधर एक तीसरे दावेदार हो गये हैं आदिवासी आन्दोलन वाले मध्यमवर्गीय लोग। जिस प्रकार वंगाली — विहारी समस्या मध्यमवर्गीय बाबुओं और पढ़े लिखों की है, ठीक वैसी ही यह भी है। इनने देखा कि हमीं क्यों चूकें जबकि हमारे दो प्रतिद्वन्दी आपस में लड़ते हैं तो हम उससे फायदा क्यों न उठा लें। क्योंकि ''जबकि दो मूजियों में हो खटपट। अपने बचने की फिक्र कर झटपट''। इस तरह इस तेहरी लड़ाई –triangular fight– के बीच यह झारखंड पिस रहा है।

<25.11.41> झारखंड के संथाल परगना जिले की तो यह हालत है कि वह प्रायः सब ओर से सभ्य कहे जाने वाले लोगों से घिरा है। बंगाल के जिलों के सिवाय बिहार के भागलपुर और मुंगेर ने दूसरी ओर से घेर लिया है। यह ठीक है कि जो भाग भागलपुर और मुंगेर का संथाल परगना या हजारीबाग से मिलता है उसमें बहुत कुछ आदिवासी भी रहते हैं। मगर वे एक तो दूसरों से मिले जुले हैं। दूसरे सभ्य लोग नजदीक ही तो हैं जो आसानी से सर्वत्र घुस जाते हैं। यही बात बाकी हिस्से की है जो गया, पटना और शाहाबाद आदि जिलों से सटे हुए हैं। उनसे मिला हुआ इन जिलों का हिस्सा पहाड़ी और जंगली जरूर है और उसमें कुछ असभ्य या अर्द्धअसभ्य कहे जाने लोग बसते हैं। मगर सभ्य बाबू लोग भी वहां तथा नजदीक में ही पड़े होने के कारण भीतर घुस गये हैं, घुसते जाते और इन भोलेभाले लोगों

को हर तरह लूटते हैं। इस प्रकार चारों ओर से उनकी जमीनें और कमाई लुट रही है और वे तबाह हो रहे हैं। इस बात की ज्यादा जानकारी आगे होगी कि लूट के तरीके कौन कौन से हैं।

मगर इतना तो साफ है कि इन झारखंड वासियों के साथ दूसरे शोषक लोग महाजन, सूदखोर आदि के रूप में मिल के इन्हें तबाह करते आ रहे हैं। यदि इस तरह के सभ्य कहे जाने वाले इलाकों से इनका सम्बन्ध नहीं होता, तो यह दुर्दशा तो हर्गिज नहीं होती, और अगर होती भी तो थोड़ी-थोड़ी, सो भी बहुत धीरे धीरे। यह विस्तार और तेजी उस तबाही की हर्गिज नहीं होती। पहले तो संथाल परगने के बारे में ही ऐसा खयाल किया जाता था कि सभ्य लोग उसके भीतर घुस के वहां के मूल निवासियों को तबाह करते हैं। सरकार का तो कम से कम ऐसा ही कहना है। इसीलिये उस जिले के लिये खासतौर की शासन व्यवस्था बनाई गई बताई जाती है। हो सकता है, हिन्दुओं का एक प्रधान तीर्थ स्थान होने के कारण यह बात वहां पहले ज्यादा रही हो और भक्ति के बहाने भगवान को ठगने वाले वहां ज्यादा संख्या में पहुंच के इन भोले भाले लोगों को भी बहुत पहले ठगने लगे हों। मगर अब तो यह बात कमवेश सभी जिलों में एक ही तरह की पाई जाती है। सर्वत्र जमीनों पर दूसरे लोग काबिज हो गये और होते जा रहे हैं धड़ाधड़। इसलिये कांग्रेसी मंत्रियों के जमाने की जांच कमिटी की रिपोर्ट के चौथे पृष्ठ में जो बात इस सम्बन्ध में कही गई है वह सर्वत्र लागू है। वहां लिखा है कि, "The system was designed and created to meet the needs of an area which contains a large proportion of somewhat primitive aboriginals and semi-aboriginals intermingled in varying proportions with a more advanced population. The problems arising out of this mixture of population are intensified by the fact that, unlike the other large aboriginal tracts in the province, the district is almost surrounded by areas inhabited by more advanced people and suffering from an excessive pressure of population on the soil. This has throughout the last century produced a steady tendency for the surrounding population to encroach upon the land of the aboriginals and to exploit that population."

"खास ढंग की जो शासन प्रणाली यहां बनाई गई वह इस इलाके की जरूरतों को पूरा करने के ही लिये बनी। क्योंकि यहां एक खासी तादाद मूल आदिवासियों तथा अर्द्ध आदिवासियों की है जिसके साथ कहीं कम, कहीं ज्यादा इस तरह प्रगतिशील लोग मिले हुए हैं। इस तरह की खिचड़ी जनसंख्या

को लेकर जो समस्याएं खड़ी हुई हैं वह और भी पेचीदा इसलिये हो गई हैं कि इस प्रान्त के और आदिवासियों के निवास स्थान स्वरूप बड़े हिस्सों के विपरीत यह जिला प्रायः चारों ओर ऐसे इलाकों से घिरा है जहां ज्यादा प्रगतिशील और सभ्य लोग बसते हैं और उनकी आवादी घनी होने के कारण जमीन जोतने पर ज्यादा जोर देते हैं। इसी का फल है कि गत समूची शताब्दी में इर्दगिर्द के लोगों ने यहां के आदिवासियों की जमीनों को दबाया है और इनका शोषण करने पर वे ज्यादा झुके हैं।''

यह कहना कि यह बात केवल संथाल परगने के लिये है, बेबुनियाद है। हजारीबाग या मानभूम की जनसंख्या का विश्लेषण करने से पता लग जाता है कि वहां भी बहुसंख्य ऐसे लोग पाये जाते हैं जो आदिवासी नहीं हैं और किसी न किसी रूप में वहां के मूल निवासियों के शोषक के रूप में ही वहां जा बसे हैं। आज भी उनका शोषण अविच्छिन्न रूप से जारी है। अधिकांश जमीनें उनने हथियाली हैं। पारसनाथ पहाड़ और उसके पास की जमीनों तथा जंगल झाड़ियों की कहानी यदि आज सुनाई जाय तो सहृदय लोगों के खून के आंसू बह निकलें। जैसे वैद्यनाथ धाम हिन्दुओं का तीर्थ स्थान है वैसे ही वह जैनियों का। मगर जीव हिंसा से भागने वाले तथा जीव दया के बड़े हामी कहे जाने वाले जैनी मालदारों ने वहां के संथालों तथा दूसरे निवासियों को जितना सताया है, आज भी वे उन्हें जितना सता रहे हैं वह वर्णनातीत है। उनने पहाड़ और पास के जंगल, झरने खरीद लिये हैं और सर्वे में सब पर अपना पूरा कब्जा लिखवा लिया है। भोले भाले गरीब लोग सर्वे क्या जानने गये? मगर उसी के बल पर कानून की छत्रछाया में संथाल लोग पानी, घास, पात, लकड़ी, जलावन, फल, फूल आदि वहां के सभी पदार्थों से बुरी तरह वञ्चित कर दिये गये हैं। उनकी दुर्दशा ऐसी है कि उनकी खबर लेने वाला कोई दीखता नहीं। यहां तक कांग्रेसी मंत्रिमंडल के जमाने में भी उनकी सुनवाई नहीं हो सकी! ऐसे बहुतेरे दृष्टान्त हैं। इसलिये अब संथाल परगने को छोटानागपुर के और जिलों से इस मामले में जुदा बताया जा सकता है नहीं। ऐसा कहना सरासर गलत है। ताता की लूट तो आगे बतायेंगे।

एक बात जरूर हुई है कि बंगाली विहारी झमेले के चलते और विहारखंड तथा झारखंड की सीमा पर सर्वत्र पहाड़ी इलाके दूर तक फैले रहने के कारण विहार से भी आदिवासियों तथा झारखंड के किसानों एवं जनता की जागृति का काम ठीक ठीक हो नहीं सका है। जब हम खुद गया, पटना, मुंगेर, भागलपुर आदि के दक्षिणी पहाड़ी हिस्सों में ही पूरा काम नहीं कर पाते

जिससे और भागों की अपेक्षा वे पिछड़े हुए हैं तो और आगे बढ़ के झारखंड वासियों में जन-जागरण कैसे कर सकते हैं? मेरा तो निजी अनुभव है कि इन दक्षिणी भागों में ज्यादा जा नहीं सका हूँ। कुछ स्थान तो ऐसे हैं जहां एक बार भी जाना हो नहीं सका है, हालांकि ऐसे स्थान इने गिने ही हैं। इनके दक्षिण जाके आदिवासियों में विशेष काम मैं खुद नहीं कर सका हूँ। गोकि मेरे दौरे प्रायः सर्वत्र हुए हैं। मगर वे तो बहुत ही नाकाफी हैं। उनसे काम करने का रास्ता ही तैयार हो सका है, न कि ज्यादा कुछ। खैर, यह तो एक बात है।

झारखंड की भूमि, जैसा कि कही चुके हैं, जंगल और पर्वत की ही भूमि है। पलामू के कुछ हिस्सों में और हजारीबाग, मानभूम के भी कुछ भाग में समतल जमीन मिलती है। समतल के मानी सिर्फ इतना हीं, कि पहाड़ों की श्रेणियां नहीं मिलती हैं। सिर्फ कहीं कहीं पहाड़ियां खड़ी मिलती हैं। संथाल परगने की भी कुछ ऐसी बात है। फिर भी विहार की तरह उपजाऊ और समतल भूमि कहीं भी क्यों मिलने लगी? नदी नाले तो सर्वत्र मिलते ही हैं जो न सिर्फ जमीन को ऊखड़ खाबड़ बना देते हैं, बल्कि उसे धोधा के साफ और प्रायः निर्जीव कर देते हैं। इसीलिये जमीन में पैदावार बहुत ही कम होती है। पलामू की तो यह दशा है कि जमीन बहुत ही रद्दी है। पहाड़ें के बीच की ही जमीनें कुछ अच्छी और पैदावार हैं। पहाड़ी इलाके तो पैदावार के लिहाज से बहुत ही चौपट हैं। फिर चाहे वह झारखंड में हैं, या दूसरी जगह। जिस प्रकार चीन की जमीनें धान की उपज के लिये बहुत ही अच्छी मानी जाती हैं वह बात यहां नहीं है। इसीलिये यहां के किसान बहुत ही गरीब और भूखे हैं।

हजारीबाग और रांची जिले के कुछ हिस्से काफी ऊंचे और ठडे भी हैं। इसीलिये गवर्नर वगैरः गर्मियों में रांची में रहमे और नेतरहाट भी चले जाते हैं। नेतरहाट तो पलामू के महुवाडांड थाने के सिवाने पर ही है। इसीलिये पलामू का वह हिस्सा भी ठंडा है। विहार की अपेक्षा छोटानागपुर तो ठंडा हई। क्योंकि यह समस्त भूखंड कछुवे रीढ़ की तरह ऊंचा है। इसी ठंडक और यहां की पिछड़ी दशा ने शोषकों को मौका दिया कि वे इसके भीतर हजार बहानेबाजी से घुस के मूक जनता का वस्त्रमोच करें और उन्हें जबह करें।

लेकिन यह भूमि देखने के लिये ऊपर से जितनी हीं रूखी, नीरस और रद्दी प्रतीत होती है, भीतर से उतनी हीं सरस, बहुमूल्य, सरस तथा वाञ्छनीय

है। यहीं कोयले का अपार भंडार है जिसके बिना आज के कल कारखाने, हमारी रेलें और सारा का सारा शासन यंत्र ही रुक जाय। इस कोयले को काला सोना (Black Gold) कहते हैं और यह अरक्षः सही है। इस दुनियां का तो सारा कारबार ही आज बन्द हो जाय यदि यह अमूल्य पदार्थ न हो। वर्त्तमान पूंजीवाद की नींव इसी कोयले, पेट्रोल, लोहे और रबर आदि से ही बनी है। अबरक भी उनमें एक है। इसीलिये इस दृष्टि से इस भू भाग को अमूल्य कह सकते हैं। यह सारे सूबे का प्राण है यह कहना कोई अत्युक्ति नहीं है। संथाल परगना, मानभूम, हजारीबाग और रांची के कुछ भाग में यह बहुतायत से पाया जाता है । कतरास, झरिया की कोयले की खानें तो संसार में प्रसिद्ध हैं।

लोहा भी यहां काफी है। ताता का जो जमशेदपुर में बड़ा भारी लोहे का कारखाना है और उसी के हाथ जो और भी दर्जनों कारखानें हैं वह आखिर इस झारखंड में ही तो हैं। सिंहभूम जिले के दलभूम सबडिविजन का ही हेडक्वार्टर जमशेदपुर है। वहां लोहे के सिवाय दूसरी चीजें भी तैयार होती हैं। तांबा और पीतल ये दो चीजें भी उसी सबडिविजन के जमशेदपुर और घाटशिला के इलाके में तैयार होती हैं। लोहे का यह कारबार तो भारत में सबसे बड़ा है। ऐसा कारखाना और कहीं नहीं है।

अबरक भी यहां बहुत है। ज्यादातर हजारीबाग जिले के उत्तरी हिस्से में इसकी खानें जगह जगह पाई जाती हैं। वह सारी की सारी भूमि अबरक को ही अपने गर्भ में रखे पड़ी है। कोडरमा अबरक का बड़ा सेन्टर माना जाता है। यहां से वह देश विदेश भेजा जाता है। असल में हजारीबाग का गिरिडीह सबडिविजन इस अबरक के लिये काफी प्रसिद्ध है। उसकी जमीन के भीतर यह अमूल्य पदार्थ बहुतायत से पाया जाता है। उस इलाके में हमने कदम कदम पर इसकी खानें और कारखानें देखे हैं। अमेरिका आदि देशों के लोगों ने भी यहां खाने ले रखी हैं। गिरिडीह में तो कोयले की भी बड़ी भारी खान है।

यह तो हुई जमीन के भीतर की बात। मगर जमीन के ऊपर जो साखू वगैरः की लकड़ियों की अपार राशि है वह कम मूल्य की चीज नहीं है। सभी तरह के जंगल यहां हैं और तरह तरह के काष्ठयें उनमें पाये जाते हैं। आजकल बांस से कागज बनता है और उन बांसों की बहुतायत यहीं पर है। पत्थरों का तो पूछिये मत। तरह तरह के पत्थर यहां भरे पड़े हैं। जिस लाख (लाह) की बड़ी कीमत है वह भी तो यहीं पैदा होती है। पलास, कुसुम और

बेर इन तीन वृक्षों पर ही खासतौर से यह चीज पैदा होती है और ये वृक्ष मानभूम, पलामू, रांची, संथाल परगना आदि सभी जिलों में बहुतायत से पाये जाते हैं। यहां लाह की यह उपज काफी है। इसके करते किसानों की कम परीशानी नहीं होती। जमीदार लोग लाह के पेड़ों पर जबर्दस्ती अपना कब्जा किये बैठे हैं। खेत है किसान का। मगर उसी खेत में जो पलास है और जिस पर लाह के कीड़े लगते हैं वह जमीदार का माना जाता है! सिर्फ जबानी ही यह हिसाब नहीं है। सर्वे खतियान में भी दर्ज है! यह बात अक्ल में तो आने की नहीं। मगर कागज में तो आई गई है। फलतः हाकिमों के दिमाग में भी आसानी से आ जाती है। इस कागज के मुकाबिले में सोचने की कोई कीमत वे नहीं करते और आंखमूंद के फैसला देते हैं! फिर तो किसान की खुदा ही खैर करे! उसे पूछता भी कौन है?

<26.11.41> इस तरह हमने देखा कि झारखंड की भूमि तो, सोना पैदा करती है, अपार सम्पत्ति देती है। इसका अबरक, इसका कोयला, इसका लोहा, इसकी लाह इसकी बहुमूल्य लकड़ियां और इसके रंग बिरंगे पत्थरों के चलते देश विदेश के लोग करोड़पति बन बैठे हैं, बनते चले जा रहे हैं। तमाम खानें दूसरों के हाथों में हैं। बम्बई से ताता ने असंख्य धन कमाया है - लूटा है। मगर पांव तले अन्धेरा है। खुद इसी इलाके के लोग दरिद्र के दरिद्र हैं। कहते हैं महादेव झारखंडी कहलाते हैं, झाड़ों और जंगलों में रहते जो हैं। वे स्वयं तो दरिद्र हैं। मगर सेवकों को कुबेर बनाते हैं। ठीक यही बात इन झारखंडियों की है। खुद दरिद्र हैं। मगर गैरों को मालामाल बना दिया है।

(२)

जनसंख्या, भाषा आदि

इस झारखंड का विस्तार करीब उतना ही है जितना विहार खंड का। कोई भी नक्शा देख के ही यह बात बता दे सकता है। समूचे विहार छोटानागपुर का क्षेत्रफल है ७०१८१ वर्गमील, जिसमें विहार खंड का है ३७५६० वर्गमील और झारखंड का ३२६२१ वर्गमील। दोनों के विस्तार या क्षेत्रफल में पांच हजार वर्गमील का भी तो अन्तर है नहीं। इसीलिये हमें यह कहने में क्यों संकोच हो कि दोनों का विस्तार प्रायः समान हीं है। जाने क्यों संथाल परगना की जांच कमिटी ने अपनी रिपोर्ट में कैसे लिख दिया है कि आदिवासियों का इलाका समूचे सूबे के एक तिहाई से ज्यादा है। ऐसा कहने में तो भारी अन्याय हो जाता है जबकि दोनों ही इलाके करीब करीब बराबर हैं।

जनसंख्या की हालत यह है कि जहां समूचे सूबे के लोगों की तादाद १९३१ में ३२३७१००० थीं, तहां १९४१ में बढ़कर ३६३४०००० हो गई है। इसमें झारखंड की संख्या बहुत ही कम है। दोनों का विस्तार बराबर देख के खयाल हो सकता है कि जनसंख्या भी कमबेश वैसी ही होगी। मगर यहां तो उल्टी गंगा बहती है। संथाल परगने को मिलाकर इन कुल छः जिलों की जनसंख्या सिर्फ ९७५०००० यानी पूरी एक करोड़ भी नहीं है। ढाई लाख की उसमें भी कमी रह जाती है! इसका सीधा मतलब यही है कि सारे सूबे की जनसंख्या की एक चौथाई से कुछी ज्यादा तादाद यहां के कुल लोगों की है। इसी में आदिवासी और दूसरे सभी शामिल हैं! इससे स्पष्ट हो जाता है कि यहां का जीवन कष्टमय होने के कारण ही ज्यादा लोग यहां रह नहीं सके हैं। जहां की जमीन पैदावार हो वहां खामखा जनसंख्या ज्यादा होती ही है।

बिहार प्रान्त के चार ही जिले ऐसे माने जाते हैं जिनकी जनसंख्या प्रति वर्गमील साढ़े सात सौ से ज्यादा मानी जाती है। ये हैं मुजफ्फरपुर, दरभंगा, सारन और पटना। अब अगर इनके क्षेत्रफल और जनसंख्या को देखें तो यहां यह बात यों भी साफ हो जाती है। मुजफ्फरपुर का विस्तार है ३४४४ वर्गमील और जनसंख्या ३२४४६५१; दरभंगा की संख्या ३४५७०७० और क्षेत्रफल

३४५१ वर्गमील; सारन की संख्या २८६०५३७ और क्षेत्रफल २६१३ तथा पटने की संख्या २१६२००८ और २०७९ है। इन जिलों की जमीनों की हालत यह है कि सबसे ज्यादा पैदावार दरभंगा और मुजफ्फरपुर हैं। दरभंगे में तो वागमती और कमला नदियों के चलते बहुत ज्यादा जमीन खराब हो जाती है। यह बात मुजफ्फरपुर में नहीं है। इसीलिये मुजफ्फरपुर की आबादी दरभंगे से भी घनी है जैसा कि संख्यायें बताती हैं। इन दोनों की अपेक्षा सारन कम पैदावार है। यहां ज्यादा जमीन माट या दोरस है और उसकी उत्पादन शक्ति जाती रही है। पटने की हालत सारन से शायद कुछ अच्छी है। यहां दाल और धान की जमीनें काफी पैदावार हैं और नहरों के करते भी इसमें बहुत कुछ मदद मिलती है। मगर एक बात यह है कि पटना शहर और दानापुर की जनसंख्या बहुत ज्यादा है और ढाई और तीन लाख के बीच है। यदि इसे निकाल दिया जाय तो साफ हो जाता है कि सारन से भी कम पैदावार पटना है। ठीक भी यही है। क्योंकि आमतौर से उत्तर बिहार, जो गंगा से उत्तर है, ज्यादा पैदावार माना जाता है। पटने में नहरें भी बहुत ही थोड़े हिस्से में हैं। चार सबडिविजनों में केवल दानापुर में ही नहरें हैं। सो भी समूचे में वहां भी नहीं हैं।

मगर हमें तो सिर्फ झारखंड के ही जिलों पर अलग अलग विचार करने से यही बात सिद्ध हो जाती है। इनमें संथाल परगने की आबादी कुल २२३४४९७ और क्षेत्र ५५१२ वर्गमील है; मानभूम की २०३२१४६ और ४२०४; हजारीबाग की १७५१३३९ और ७०५९; रांची की १६७५४१३ और ७०९९; सिंहभूम की ११४४७१७ तथा ३८७९ और पलामू की ९१२७३४ तथा ४८६८ है। ये आंकड़े साफ बताते हैं कि कौन जिला कैसा है। पलामू की जमीन सबसे रद्दी है। सिवाय धान की थोड़ी सी जमीनों के बाकी टांड या बारी है और उपज उसमें बहुत ही कम होती है। सर्वे की रिपोर्टों ने यह बात कबूल की है। नतीजा यह है कि उसकी जनसंख्या सबसे कम है — प्रति वर्गमील १०० से २०० तक ही है। बाकी बचे पांच जिले इनमें रांची, हजारीबाग और सिंहभूम इन तीनों की पैदावार प्रायः समान है और जनसंख्या भी २०० के ऊपर से ३५० तक ही प्रति वर्गमील है। बाकी दो जिलों — मानभूम और संथाल परगने की हालत यह है कि इनकी जनसंख्या ३५१ से ५०० तक प्रति वर्गमील है। संथाल परगने की जांच कमिटी ने यही बात अपनी रिपोर्ट में स्वीकार की है। उसने हर जिले की धान और रबी वगैरः की सभी तरह की जमीनों की उपज का मुकाबिला करके भी यही बात दिखाई है। यों तो जरामरा फर्क रहता ही है। इसीलिये संथाल परगना और मानभूम बाकियों (तीनों) से आबादी में कुछ घने हैं।

बेशक विहार खंड का एक ही जिला है जो इन मानभूम और संथाल परगना नामक दो जिलों जैसी ही आवादी वाला है और वह है शाहाबाद। यदि वहां गंगा के दियारे की जमीनें न होतीं तो शायद वह इनसे भी नीचे जा पड़ता और पलामू के ही टक्कर का या उससे बहुत कुछ हिलता मिलता हो जाता। मगर दियारे की जमीनों के करते और बहुत से हिस्सों में नहरों के हो जाने से — क्योंकि एक भबुआ को छोड़ शेष तीन सबडिविजनों में नहरें पाई जाती हैं — उसकी पैदावार कुछ अच्छी है। इसीलिये जनसंख्या प्रति वर्गमील ३५१ से लेकर ५०० तक है। उसका कुल क्षेत्रफल ४३७२ वर्गमील और जनसंख्या २३२८५८१ है।

रह गये विहार के मुंगेर, भागलपुर, चम्पारन और गया — ये चार जिले। सो तो इनकी दशा प्रायः एक सी हीं है। इनकी आबादी समान रूप से प्रति वर्गमील ५०१ से लेकर ७५० तक है। हां, पूर्णियां भी शाहाबाद जैसा ही है और उसकी जनसंख्या भी ३५१ से लेकर ५०० तक ही वर्गमील के हिसाब से है। पूर्णियां पैदावार है सही। मगर कोसी और दूसरी नदियों के करते उसकी तबाही ऐसी है कि पूरी तरह आबाद होई नहीं सकता। इसीलिये गंगा के दक्षिण सूबे का पश्चिमी जिला शाहाबाद और गंगा के उत्तर पूर्वी जिला — पूर्णियां ये दोनों ही जनसंख्या में भी मिल जाते हैं। पूर्णियां की आवादी भी २३९०१०५ है। मगर क्षेत्रफल थोड़ा ज्यादा, यानी ५१७५ वर्गमील है। फिर भी इस मामूली अन्तर के करते प्रति वर्गमील जनसंख्या में कोई महत्वपूर्ण अन्तर नहीं आता। दोनों ही समान हैं।

भागलपुर की आवादी कुल २४०८८७९ और क्षेत्रफल ४२२६ वर्गमील है। मुंगेर की संख्या २५६४५४४ और क्षेत्रफल ४०८९; चम्पारन की २३९७५६९ और ३४२२ तथा गया की २७७५३६१ और ४६८९ है। यों देखने से कुछ कुछ अन्तर मालूम होता है सही। फिर भी सभी बातें मिलाकर देखने से इनमें एक तरह की समानता है। सरकारी रिपोर्टों ने यही बात मानी है। इन चार जिलों को एक ही साथ जनसंख्या के लिहाज से रखा है। कहीं जमीनें अच्छी हो जाने से आबादी बहुत ज्यादा है तो कहीं बहुत ही कम। इसीलिये सब जगहों की औसत प्रायः मिल जाती है।

इस प्रकार विहार के सभी जिलों की संक्षिप्त आवादी आदि का मुकाबिला करने से पता चल जाता है कि गरीबी के पलड़े में झारखंड ही सबसे नीचे है। इसका एक जिला, पलामू तो सबसे ज्यादा गरीब है। और उसके बाद ही स्थान है इसी के हजारीबाग, रांची और सिंहभूम का। केवल इसके दोई जिले —

मानभूम और संथाल परगना ऐसे हैं जो विहार खंड के सबसे निचले जिलों - शाहाबाद और पूर्णियां - से मिलते जुलते हैं। फलतः विहार तो इस छोटानागपुर की अपेक्षा हर तरह से सुखी सम्पन्न है। हालांकि असली सम्पत्ति का केन्द्र स्थान छोटानागपुर ही है। यदि इसे बिहार से जुदा कर दिया तो उसकी मौत ही समझिये। यह ठीक है कि झारखंड की सम्पत्ति ज्यादातर दूसरे ही लूटते हैं। वह तो आज बिहारियों को बहुत ही नाममात्र को मिलती है। मगर समय आने वाला है जब यह बाहरी लूट रुकेगी - जब ताता और दूसरे यह धन लूट के बम्बई, पंजाब, गुजरात या देश के बाहर ले जा न सकेंगे। किन्तु उन्हें अपनी अय का तो बहुत कुछ अंश विहार को ही देना पड़ेगा, या अपना विस्तर यहां से बांधना होगा। क्योंकि बिना ऐसा हुए बिहार की गरीबी दूर होगी ही नहीं। उस समय यदि कहीं यह झारखंड बिहार से अलग हो गया, जिसके लिये आज सख्त आन्दोलन चालू है, तब तो विहार की मौत होई जायगी। लेकिन यदि यह बात हो गई तो विहार ने आज तक झारखंडियों के प्रति जो उपेक्षा अपने कर्त्तव्य की की है उसी के फलस्वरूप यह बात होगी। अभी भी समय है कि यह बात होने न पाये। मगर इसके लिये बहुत कुछ करना होगा।

यह तो हुआ यहां के जनसंख्या का साधारण दिग्दर्शन। मगर इतने से तो काम चलेगा नहीं, जब तक इसका कुछ विशेष ब्योरा मालूम न हो जाय। गोकि यहां की आवादी बिहार के शेष इलाके की आवादी की प्रायः तिहाई है। फिर भी यहां के लोग तो एक प्रकार से मूक हैं, गूंगे हैं। इन्हें जबान नहीं कि अपना दुःखदर्द सुना सकें। आज के तरीके से अपने अभाव अभियोगों के सुनने तथा अपने दावे पेश करने का माद्दा इनमें हई नहीं। नहीं तो कम होते हुए भी सारे सूबे को अपनी पुकारों तथा हलचलों से गुंजा देते, थर्रा देते। असल में ये इतने पिछड़े हैं, इतने अन्धकार में पड़े हैं कि नऐ ढंग के प्रदर्शन, नई तरह की मीटिंगें ये खुद कर नहीं सकते - करना जानते ही नहीं। इसीलिये जो मीटिंगें होती हैं, जो प्रदर्शन किये जाते भी है उन पर इनके असली अभाव-अभियोगों की, दर्द की छाप नहीं होती। वे मीटिंगें किसानों या शोषित पीड़ितों की चुभती हुई मांगों और बेधती हुई पुकारों को प्रकट कर सकती हैं नहीं, प्रतिबिम्बित कर नहीं सकती हैं। इसीलिये इनकी दृष्टि से उनमें कृत्रिमता ही कृत्रिमता नजर आती है। उनमें इनका दर्द, इनकी चीख पुकार सुनाई नहीं पड़ती है। वहां तो मध्यमवर्गीयों के झमेले ही दीखते हैं — वही नौकरियों की बात, वही अलग प्रतिनिधित्व की चर्चा, वही बोर्डों और असेम्बली की सीटों की हाय तोबा और वही राजभक्ति की उफान!

यदि यहां के अधिवासियों में जागृति होती, वर्ग चेतना होगी, अपने अधिकारों तथा हकों की जानकारी के साथ ही उन्हें निर्भयता पूर्वक सफाई के साथ पेश करने की योग्यता होगी और अगर ये लोग अपनी मांगों को प्रभावशाली बनाना जानते तो यह बात नहीं होती। यद्यपि विहार के भी किसानों की और दूसरे प्रान्त वालों की भी अभी कुछ ऐसी ही हालत है कि वे खुद अपने पांवों बखूबी खड़े हो सकते नहीं। फिर भी वे बहुत कुछ कर सकते हैं। बहुत आगे बढ़ चुके हैं। मगर यहां वाले तो अवनति के गढ़े में ही पड़े हैं। इन्हें जानबूझ कर ऐसे ही रहने देने की कोशिश की गई है, गुट्टबन्दी हुई है ऐसा मालूम पड़ता है। नहीं तो इन्हें शिक्षित क्यों नहीं बनाया गया? जहां इसी झारखंड की रहने वाली प्रगतिशील जातियों की शिक्षा-वृद्धि की भरपूर कोशिश की गई है, तहां आदिवासियों के प्रति भयंकर उपेक्षा से काम लिया गया है। इस सम्बन्ध में ज्यादा बातें तो आगे कहेंगे। मगर संथाल परगना की सरकारी जांच कमिटी की रिपोर्ट का ही एक अंश यहां लिख देना जरूरी है। उसके ४४ वें पृष्ठ में लिखा है, "There has been no development of aboriginal schools in recent years; in fact the position is now worse than it was 15 years ago. There is not a single school for the 60,000 Paharias in the Damin Hills. In fifteen years the number of Santal children attending school has risen only from 12020 to 13448. The number of Santal primary schools has actually decreased from 465 to 403. This was largely due to the financial straits of the District Committee during the period of economic depression which affected all classes of schools. But the salient fact emerges that while between 1922 and 1937 the total number of schools have been reduced by 73, 62 of these were Santal schools. In fact, the most of the education retrenchment of the District Committee has been at the cost of the Santals."

<27.11.41> "इधर कुछ साल के भीतर आदिवासियों के स्कूलों में वृद्धि नहीं हुई है। दरअसल १५ साल पूर्व की अपेक्षा आज की हालत खराब है। दामिन पहाड़ों के साठ हजार पहड़िया लोगों के लिये तो एक भी स्कूल है नहीं। पन्द्रह साल के भीतर स्कूल जाने वाले संताली लड़कों की तादाद सिर्फ १२०२० से १३४४८ ही हुई है। संथालों के प्राइमरी स्कूलों की संख्या ४६५ से ४०३ हो गई है। अर्थसंकट के जमाने में जिला कमिटी जो डिस्ट्रिक्ट बोर्ड की जगह थी - की आर्थिक दशा खराब होने से ही अधिकांश यह बात हुई है, जिसका सभी तरह के स्कूलों पर असर हुआ। लेकिन एक बात साफ हो गई है कि

१९२२ और १९३७ के दर्म्यान जो कुल ७३ स्कूल इस तरह बन्द हुए उनमें ६२ तो केवल संतालों के ही थे। असलियत तो यह है कि जिला कमिटी ने जो शिक्षा में कमी की है उसका अधिक हिस्सा सन्तालों के ही माथे पड़ा है''!

यह कहने से तो काम चलने का नहीं कि अंग्रेजी सरकार और उसकी कमिटी ने ही ऐसा किया है। आखिर अंग्रेजी सरकार को हमेशा यहां रहना है नहीं। जल्द या देर से अब जो सरकार इस प्रान्त में बनेगी वह तो बिहारियों की — इसी सूबे वालों की — ही होगी। फलतः नतीजा उसे ही भुगतना होगा। अपने ही शरीर के किसी अंग को रोगी, कमजोर या लकवा-ग्रस्त रहने देने का नतीजा क्या किसी और को भोगना होता है? हमने इन पिछड़े भाइयों की जो खबर अब तक प्रायः नहीं ली है उसी का नतीजा यह है कि एक ओर छोटानागपुर को बंगाल में मिलाने की कोशिश होती है, तो दूसरी ओर अलग प्रान्त बनाने हीं की। इन कोशिशों के लिये मसाला आखिर आया है कहां से? अब तक की गई लापर्वाही को ही तो सामने रखके भोले भाले लोगों को समझाया जाता है कि जब तक बिहार के पुछल्ले बने रहोगे कोई न पूछेगा। क्या यह दलील पेश नहीं की जाती है कि सारा खजाना यहीं होने पर तथा विस्तार में विहार के बराबर रहने पर भी आदिवासियों का एक भी आदमी कांग्रेसी जमाने में मंत्री नहीं बनाया गया? क्या बिहारी लोग बराबर इस बात का विरोध नहीं करते रहे कि बिहार सरकार रांची में कतई जाय ही नहीं? और क्या इसी बात को लेके उनके माथे दोष लगाया नहीं जाता? क्या कांग्रेसी मंत्रियों के समय में एक पार्लिमेन्टरी सेक्रेटरी साहब ने, जो छोटानागपुर में ही रहते हैं, रांची में असेम्बली की बैठक का विरोध नहीं किया था?

हां, तो हम झारखंड के लोगों की बात कह रहे थे कि ये पिछड़े हैं। इसका एक जो बहुत पक्का सबूत है वह यही है कि यद्यपि ब्राह्मण, क्षत्रिय, बनिया महाजन, कायस्थ वगैरः आगे बढ़ी जातियों के लोग भी यहां लाखों की तादाद में पाये जाते हैं। फिर भी एक करोड़ की जनसंख्या में ऐसे लोग बहुत हो कम हैं। कहें तो कह सकते हैं कि दाल में नमक की तरह हैं। हम इस झमेले में नहीं पड़ते कि आदिवासी कौन हैं, कौन नहीं। हमें बाल की खाल नहीं खींचनी है और नुक्ताचीनी के लिये बारीकियां ढूंढनी हैं। हम तो इतना ही जानते हैं कि जो लोग पिछड़े हुए हैं और अपनी आवाज बिहारियों या बंगालियों की तरह खुद उठा नहीं सकते उनकी संख्या अस्सी फीसदी से कम नहीं है। हमें तो असली किसानों से मतलब है जो छोटानागपुर में पाये जाते हैं। जो लोग आगे बढ़े हुए हैं वे तो बाहर से यहां लूटने आये हैं। यदि और लोगों से मिलके वे भी गुजर

करते, तो हमें कुछ कहना नहीं था। तब तो इन्हीं जैसे वे भी खामखा बन जाते। तब शोषण की बात ही क्यों उठती? कहा जाता है, उरांव लोग रोहतासगढ़ से यहां पीछे आये। यह भी माना जाता है कि संथाल परगने में पहले तो पहड़िया लोग ही रहते थे। संथाल तो पहले पहले १८१० में ही आये। मगर यह तो नहीं कहा जाता है कि ये लोग शोषक बनके आये। चाहे जब जैसे आये गुजर करने के ही लिये आये और हिलमिल के एक हो गये।

भारत में शक, हूण आदि भी आये, मुसलमान भी पहुंचे और अंग्रेज भी। मगर शक, हुण और मुसलमान वगैरः यहीं हिलमिल के रह गये। उन्हें बाहरियों की तरह शोषण करना न था, किन्तु गुजर करना। लेकिन अंग्रेज तो शोषक बन के ही आये। इसीलिये कभी हिलेमिले नहीं। ठीक यही दशा उन सभ्य, शिक्षित और ऊंची कहे जाने वाली जातियों की है जो केवल शोषक बन के ही झारखंड में आईं और बसीं। भले ही अंग्रेजों की तरह उनका बाहर ताल्लुक अब न भी हो। फिर भी उनका शोषण तो अखंड रूप से जारी ही है। बाहर भी बिबाह शादी आदि के जरिये सम्बन्ध सभी का हई। मगर जिनने अपने को यहां के आदिवासियों जैसा बना लिया वे शोषक न होके इन्हीं जैसे पिछड़े हुए हैं। ऐसे लोगों में ग्वाले और कुर्मी आदि लोग हैं। गाय भैंसे पालने के लिये या खेती करने के ही लिये ये लोग यहां आये। मगर यहीं के हो गये। कुर्मी लोगों के बारे में तो और भी बातें कहीं जाती हैं कि वे बिहारी कुर्मियों से निराले ही हैं। मगर हमें इससे कोई मतलब नहीं। हम यह मानते भी नहीं। चाहे वे यहीं के हैं या बाहर से आये। मगर हर हालत में आदिवासियों से हिलमिल गये। यही कारण है कि सब मिलाके पिछड़े लोगों की संख्या अस्सी ले लेकर नब्बे फीसदी तक हो जाती है।

सरकार ने इस बारे में एक और ही रास्ता निकाला है और आदिवासियों की बात को लेके झगड़ने वाले दोनों दलों को खुश करते हुए अपना काम निकाल लिया है। साथ ही कुछ झमेला भी खड़ा कर दिया है। यहां की पिछड़ी जातियों की जमीनें दूसरी जाति के लोग इजारा ले या खरीद न सकें इसके लिये काश्तकारी कानून में कुछ धारायें ज़ोड़ी गई हैं। छोटानागपुर काश्तकारी कानून (Chotanagpur Tenancy Act) की ४८, २०८ तथा २४० और २४२ धाराओं में यह बात पाई जाती है। ये जातियां कौन कौन सी हैं इनकी एक सूची सरकार ने खुद तैयार की है। विहार के काश्तकारी कानून में भी कुछ ऐसी धारायें हैं और कुछ जातियों की सूची वहां भी दी गई है। वह सूची आदिवासियों तथा पिछड़ी जातियों की ही कहके बनी है। इनमें आदिवासियों में ये जातियां

लिखी गई हैं, (१) असुर, (२) बनजारा (३) बठुड़ी (४) बेंटकार (५) विनझिया (६) बिरहोर (७) बियाजिया (८) चेरो (९) चिक बरैक (१०) गोड़ाबा (११) घटवार (१२) गोंड (१३) गोड़ाइत (१४) हो (१५) जुआंग (१६) करमाली (१७) खरिया (१८) खरवार (१९) खेतौरी (२०) खोंड़ (२१) किसान (२२) कोली (२३) कोड़ा (२४) कोड़वा (२५) महली (२६) मलपहड़िया (२७) मुंडा (२८) उरांव (२९) पढ़िया (३०) संताल (३१) सौरिया पहड़िया (३२) शबर (३३) थारू।

पिछड़ी जातियों की जो तालिका दी गई है वह यों है, (१) चमार (२) चौपाल (३) धोबी (४) दुसाध (५) डोम (६) हलालखोर (७) हारी (८) कंजर (९) कुड़रियार (१०) लालबेगी (११) मोची (१२) मुसहर (१३) नट (१४) पासी (१५) बौरी (१६) भोक्ता (१७) भुइयां (१८) भूमिज (१९) घासी (२०) पान (२१) रजवार (२२) तूड़ी।

बेशक कोइरी, ग्वाला, कुर्मी वगैरह को इसमें नहीं गिनाया है और शायद इन जातियों के कुछ पढ़े लिखे लोग इसमें अपनी शान समझते हों कि हम पिछड़ी जातियों के नहीं हैं। शायद उन्हें शर्म भी मालूम होती हो कि पासी, चमार आदि के साथ ही कैसे अपनी जातियों को गिनायें। मगर यह तो भूल है। असलियत को छिपाने से क्या लाभ? जब शिक्षा आदि का विचार किया जाय तो आंखें खुल जाती हैं। अगर असेम्बली और बोर्डों की सीटों का सवाल उठे या नौकरियों की बात आये तो वे लोग भी खामखा रिआयतें चाहते और पिछड़ी जाति वाले कहके खास सलूक चाहते हैं। तब इस तरह की बात के लिये गुंजाइश है कहां?

इस जनसंख्या के साथ ही उनकी बोली और भाषा का भी प्रश्न आता है। यह तो ठीक ही है कि जो वंगाली और बिहारी यहां बस गये हैं उनकी भाषा वंगला और हिन्दी हुई। यह ठीक है कि विहार के विभिन्न जिलों से आकर बसने के कारण मगही और भोजपुरी भाषायें भी वे लोग बोलते और कैथी अक्षरों में चिट्ठी पत्री वगैरः लिखते हैं। यहां की सर्वे खतियान तो कैथी अक्षरों में ही लिखी गई है। इसका साफ मतलब है कि विहार की छाप झारखंड पर लगा दी गई है। हालांकि ऐसा करने का हक किसी को भी न था। जो यहां के मूल निवासी हैं और जिनका बहुमत है वे कैथी क्या जानने गये? मगर जो मूक हैं, बोल नहीं सकते उनकी पर्वा करने जाता है कौन? मुट्ठीभर पढ़े लिखों की ही तो पर्वा सर्वत्र की जाती है। क्योंकि वे बोलना और तूफान मचाना जनते हैं। जब इसकी याद उन गरीबों को होती है तो उनके कलेजे पर सांप लोट जाता जरूर

है। वे कोई बात समझ नहीं पाते और आह मारके रह जाते हैं। इन्हीं कैथी की खतियानों के आधार पर उनके जंगल के सभी हक छिन गये! ये खतियानें वेद, बाइबिल और कुरान से भी बढ़ के प्रामाणिक मानी जाती हैं जहां तक जमीन वगैरः के हक का सवाल है! क्या अंधेर है!

लेकिन उनकी अपनी भाषा और बोली तो कुछ और ही है। संथाल, उरांव और मुंडा अपनी निजी भाषा रखते हैं। यों तो हो लोगों की भी अपनी जुदा भाषा है। फिर भी उरांव और हो की भाषा न जानके भी किसी कदर काम चलाया जा सकता है यदि संथाली और मुंडारी भाषा का ज्ञान हो। उरांव भाषा का या हो भाषा का भी ज्ञान होने पर भी उनसे किसी तरह काम चल जाता है। ये दोनों भाषायें थोड़ी बहुत उनसे मिलती जुलती हैं ऐसा कहा जाता है। मगर सच बात तो यह है कि संथाली, मुंडारी, उरांव की और हो लोगों की — ये चारों भाषायें अपना स्वतंत्र अस्तित्व रखती हैं और जब इन भाषाओं के बोलने वाले किसान ठेठ अपनी भाषा में ही परस्पर बातचीत करते हैं तो एक भाषा वाले भी दूसरी वाले की बातें समझ नहीं पाते। यों तो एकाध शब्दों के मेलजोल से हिन्दी या बंगाली भाषा के जानकार भी दस बीस बातों में शायद एकाध को अन्दाज़ से समझ लें। मगर किसी प्रकार काम चलाना और बात है और भाषा को समझना दूसरी। जब साधारण लोग एक दूसरे की भाषा न समझ सकें तो मानना ही होगा कि उनकी भाषायें जुदी हैं।

यद्यपि मुण्डा और उरांव दोनों को ही कोल शब्द से पुकारा जाता है। तथापि ये दोनों दो जुदी जातियां हैं और इन दोनों का परस्पर कोई मेल नहीं है। इसी प्रकार संथाल इन दोनों से ही निराले और हो इन तीनों से जुदे हैं। उनकी भाषायें इतनी जुदी हैं और रस्मरिवाज भी बहुत कुछ ऐसे भिन्न हैं कि ये लोग ज्यादातर जुदेजुले अञ्चलों में पाये जाते हैं। संथालों की ही तरह पहड़िया लोग भी निराले हैं। उनकी भाषा भी भिन्न ही है। वे तो ज्यादातर संथाल परगने के दामिने कोह या दामिन इलाके में, जो खासमहाल या सरकारी जमींदारी है, पाये जाते हैं। गोड्डा, राजमहाल, पाकौड़ और दुमका — इन चार — सबडिविजनों के जो हिस्से एक दूसरे से मिल जाते या बीच में पड़ जाते हैं उन्हीं को एक जगह मिला के यह दामिन की सरकारी का इलाका है। यह बिल्कुल ही पर्वतों की तराई में उन्हीं से घिरा हुआ इलाका है। कोह कहते हैं फारसी में पहाड़ को और दामन नाम है उसकी कोख या बगल या तरीका। इसी से दामिने या दामने कोह का मतलब है पहाड़ की तरी या तराई। दामन को ही दामिन कह देते हैं। दामन और कोह के बीच जो ''इ'' या ''ए'' है उसका अर्थ फारसी में होता

है ''का''। इसी से कोह का दामन मतलब लगाते हैं। फारसी में उलटे ही ''का'' का सम्बन्ध जुटता है — ''दामन'' के बजाय ''कोह'' से ही ''का'' जोड़ते हैं।

संथाल लोग संथाल परगने में तो हईं। हजारीबाग के उत्तर-पूर्वी हिस्से में और उसी से मिलते जुलते मानभूम के भागों में भी ज्यादातर पाये जाते हैं। यों तो प्रायः सारा का सारा हजारीबाग जिला भी संथालों का ही है। पार्श्वनाथ पहाड़ की तली में वही लोग हैं और धनबाद के इलाके में भी। दक्षिणी हजारी-बाग के कुछ भाग में कहीं कहीं और उससे मिले रांची के बहुत बड़े हिस्से में बीच से और पच्छिम में उरांव लोग ज्यादातर पाये जाते हैं। मुण्डा लोग रांची के दक्षिण पश्चिमी हिस्से में ज्यादा हैं और उससे मिले सिंहभूम के भागों में। बाकी सिंहभूम में और खास कर दलभूम सबडिविजन में हो लोगों की बस्ती अधिक है। पहड़िया लोग तो ज्यादातर दामिन इलाके में ही हैं। पलामू और रांची की सरहदें जहां मिलती हैं वहां दोनों ही जिले में उरांव लोग ही ज्यादातर हैं और दूसरे भी पाये जाते हैं। पलामू का महुवाडांड़ थाना और रांची के लोहारदागा ये दोनों इलाके जहां मिलते हैं वहीं पर ''किसान'' कहे जाने वाले भी कुछ लोग पाये जाते हैं। मैंने उनसे महुवाडांड़ में खुद बातें की हैं। पलामू के पश्चिमी, दक्षिणी, पूर्वी, दक्षिणपूर्वी, दक्षिण पश्चिमी भागों में और पूर्वोत्तर तथा पश्चिमोत्तर के भी कुछ अंशों में आदिवासियों की ही आबादी है। हजारीबाग से मिले मानभूम के बहुत हिस्सों में और हजारीबाग में भी कुर्मी लोग ज्यादातर मिलते हैं। यों तो जहां तहां सभी जातियां एक दूसरे के सगम स्थान पर हिलमिल के भी रहती हैं।

एक बात जो सबसे ज्यादा जरूरी लिखने की है वह यह है कि यद्यपि झारखंड के आदिवासी लोग पिछड़े हुए हैं। तथापि इनकी दशा विहार खंड या दूसरे स्थानों के पिछड़े हुए लोगों जैसी नहीं है। और जगह के ऐसे लोग निरे खेत मजदूर जैसे ही हैं सिवाय उन जगहों के जहां उनकी संख्या ज्यादा है और जमीनें रखते हैं। मगर मुंडा, उरांव वगैरः सब के सब पक्के किसान हैं। ये लोग जन्म से ही पुश्त दर पुश्त से ऐसे ही हैं। इन्हें जमीन से बड़ी मुहब्बत है — वैसी ही जैसी जंगल से। इन दोनों के बिना ये रह नहीं सकते। इनके पास जो काश्तकारी जमीनें हैं उनकी अनेक किस्में इस बात का पक्का सबूत हैं। उनके बारे में आगे लिखा गया है।

इसीलिये ''किसान'' नाम की एक जाति ही यहां पाई जाती है। झारखंड के सिवाय हमें एक ही जगह और भी ''किसान'' जाति मिली है जो युक्त प्रान्त

के फर्रुखाबाद में पाई जाती है। संथाल परगना में ''कृशानी'' शब्द कुछ इसी अर्थ में बोला भी जाता है। वहां भावली या बंटाई की ही तरह की खेती को ''कृशानी'' कहते हैं। इसका जिक्र वहां की जांच कमिटी की रिपोर्ट में आया है। यही कारण है कि हमने ''झारखंड के निवासी'' की जगह इस पुस्तक का नाम भी ''झारखंड के किसान'' लिखा है। यहां के निवासी तो दूसरे हईं नहीं। कुर्मी या ग्वाले लोग भी पक्के किसान ही हैं। यहां के आदिवासियों की नाड़ियों में अभी गर्मी भी काफी है। वे हरिजनों की तरह कुचले जा सके हैं नहीं। इसीलिये यदि इनका वर्ग हित के आधार पर संगठन किया जाय तो एक अपूर्व शक्ति ये लोग बन जायंगे जिसे कोई दबा नहीं सकता। इनकी आजादी भी अभी-अभी छिनी है। इसीलिये इनके खून में उसका अंश शेष है।

(३)

शिक्षा का सवाल

इन लोगों की शिक्षा की बात पहले कुछ कही गई है। मगर उस पर कुछ ज्यादा विचार करना निहायत जरूरी है। वस्तुस्थिति पर पूरा प्रकाश पड़ने के लिये यह आवश्यक है। इसी के साथ यह भी जरूरी है कि विहार के दूसरे जिलों और विहार खंड समूचे का भी मुकाबिला शिक्षा के बारे में इस झारखंड के साथ किया जाय। हम इस सम्बन्ध में और ज्यादा बातें नहीं कहके कांग्रेसी मंत्रियों के जमाने में १९३८ में प्रकाशित आंकड़ों को ही पेश करेंगे और उन्हीं के आधार पर विचार करके अपना काम पूरा करेंगे। उन आंकड़ों के ऊपर कुछ कहना जरूरी होगा। नहीं तो असलियत पर पूरा प्रकाश पड़ नहीं सकता।

<28.11.41> सबसे पहली बात जो इस सम्बन्ध में कहने की है वह यही कि जहां विहार खंड में कुल मिलाके १७३ हाई इंगलिश स्कूल, ६३० मिड्ल स्कूल, २५०२ अपर प्राइमरी और १३२१९ लोअर प्राइमरी स्कूल हैं तहां झारखंड में सब मिलाके सिर्फ ४० हाई स्कूल, १६७ मिड्ल स्कूल, ६९० अपर और ४३४४ लोअर प्राइमरी स्कूल हैं। वहां के मिड्ल स्कूलों और यहां के अपर प्राइमरी स्कूलों का तादाद प्रायः बराबर है। ६३० और ६९० में कोई ज्यादा फर्क तो है नहीं। यह याद रखना चाहिये कि विहार की अपेक्षा यहां की जनसंख्या आधी से कम और तिहाई से ज्यादा - आधी और तिहाई के बीच में है जैसा कि पहले कहा जा चुका है। मगर सिवा लोअर प्राइमरी स्कूलों के जिनकी संख्या यहां वहां से प्रायः एक तिहाई है, शेष सभी हाई, मिड्ल या अपर स्कूलों की तादाद यहां वहां के मुकाबिले में आमतौर से करीब करीब चौथाई है। हाई स्कूल तो यहां चौथाई से भी कम हैं! वहां पूरे १७३ और यहां सिर्फ ४० हैं! यह इतनी साफ बात है कि इस पर ज्यादा टीका टिप्पणी बेकार है।

अब अगर जिलेवार यह बात देखी जाय तो और भी मजेदार है। विहार का सिर्फ एक ही जिला - चम्पारन — ऐसा है जो यहां के शिक्षा में सबसे बढ़े तीन जिलों - रांची, मानभूम और संथाल परगना — के साथ करीब करीब

टक्कर लेता है। फिर भी बहुत अंशों में कहीं बढ़ा चढ़ा है। उसके बाद ही पूर्णियां का नाम आता है, जो चम्पारन से कहीं अधिक बढ़ा हुआ है। बिहार के ये दो अभागे जिले भी यहां के सर्वोन्नत जिलों से बहुत ज्यादा आगे हैं, यही सबसे बड़ी खूबी है। रांची में हाई स्कूल १०, मिड्ल ४४, अपर १४६ और लोअर १०९४ हैं; मानभूम में ये क्रमशः ११, ४१, १६१ और ९८१ हैं ; संथाल परगने में क्रमशः १०, ३१, १६८ ओर ९४७ हैं। खूबी तो यह है कि जहां लोअर स्कूल बढ़े हैं वहां बाकियों में उसी हिसाब से कमी आ गई है और जहां लोअर स्कूल नहीं बढ़े हैं वहां बाकी भी प्रायः सभी ज्यादा हैं। रांची के साथ बाकी दो के आंकड़ों को मिलाने से यह बात साफ हो जाती है। मगर जब क्षेत्रफल और जनसंख्या की मिलान करते हैं तब तो कुछ और ही बात दीखने लगती है। रांची की जनसंख्या इन दोनों से कम होने के कारण इनकी अपेक्षा वह प्रगतिशील प्रतीत होता है। क्योंकि विस्तार तो उसका इन दोनों से ज्यादा है। मगर आबादी कम है। उसकी प्रगति की बात पर आगे विचार करेंगे।

लेकिन बिहार के उन दोनों जिलों को भी तो जरा देख लें। चम्पारन में हाई स्कूल १०, मिड्ल ४९, अपर २२० और लोअर ८६६ है और पूर्णियां में इनकी संख्या क्रमशः ९, ४३, १७३ और ११३६ है। यद्यपि जनसंख्या दोनों की ही बराबर ही है और वह है २३ लाख से कुछी ज्यादा। मगर क्षेत्रफल में बहुत ज्यादा फर्क है। इस दृष्टि से तो चम्पारन से भी गया गुजरा प्रतीत होता है। क्योंकि चम्पारन से इसका विस्तार डयोढ़ा होने पर भी यहां लोअर को छोड़ सभी तरह के स्कूलों में चम्पारन से कमी है। हां, लोअर स्कूल कुछ ज्यादा हैं।

यह तो हुई इन दो पिछड़े जिलों की बात जिन्हें गांधीजी के अनुयायी होने का सब से ज्यादा दावा और फख्र होते हुए भी यह नहीं सूझता कि आम लोगों को शिक्षित तो बनायें। केवल चर्खा चलाना यदि गांधी-भक्ति की पहचान है तब तो खुदा हाफिज! अब हमें विहार के शेष आठ जिलों की भी दशा का सिंहावलोकन कर लेना है। यहां दरभंगा जिला सबसे आगे है। उसके बाद गया वगैरः जिले आते हैं। मगर यह बात केवल लोअर आदि स्कूलों की संख्या की ही दृष्टि से है। यों तो यदि क्षेत्रफल और आवादी का विचार करके स्कूलों की संख्या पर गौर करें तो पटना ही सबसे बढ़ा चढ़ा है। जनसंख्या और क्षेत्रफल तो पहले ही बता चुके हैं। पटना में हाई स्कूल २६, मिड्ल ५९, अपर २४९ और लोअर १४०० हैं ; गया में क्रमशः १५, ४१, १६२ और १७०१; शाहाबाद में १७, ५८, २४९ और ११२९; मुंगेर में १७, ७७, २४४ और १४३७; भागलपुर में १८, ५३, २७० और १२१०; सारन में २५, ८८,

२३८, और ११२५; मुजफ्फरपुर में १९, ७७, ३०६ और १४७०, दरभंगा में १७, ८५, ३८८ और १७४५। यह याद रखना होगा कि चम्पारन में प्राइमरी शिक्षा मुफ्त दी जाती है।

हमें अब और पहलुवों से भी यह बात देखनी है। पहली बात तो यह है कि झारखंड में जो जर्मन, इंगलिश और रोमन कैथलिक मिशनों के मुख्य अड्डे हैं और एकाध और भी हैं उनने अपने खयाल से बहुत ज्यादा खोल रखे हैं। जर्मन मिशन के प्रायः दो सौ, इंगलिश मिशन के प्रायः डेढ़ सौ और कैथलिक तथा औरों के मिलाके भी करीब सैंकड़ों स्कूल यहां खुले हैं। इस तरह चार पांच सौ स्कूलों का श्रेय तो इन ईसाई मिशनों को ही है। हजारीबाग, रांची, संथाल परगना में इनका अधिक स्कूल है। कालिज भी तो जो यहां केवल हजारीबाग में एक है वह मिशन का ही है। यही कारण है कि रांची सबसे बढ़ा चढ़ा है। खूबी तो यह है कि इनने तो इतने ज्यादा स्कूल खोले हैं। मगर जमशेदपुर से ताता और दूसरे पूंजीपति साल में आठ दस करोड़ के लगभग रुपये ढो ले जाते हैं और उदारता की दम भी खूब ही भरते हैं। मगर उनने एक भी कालिज वहां नहीं खोला है। ये लोग आखिर हिन्दुस्तानी किस बात के हैं? उनसे तो ये पादरी, ये मिशन, ये चर्च अच्छे निकले जो यहां तब आये जब किसी भी हिन्दू पण्डित या मौलवी की हिम्मत भी न थी कि यहां आता। सैंकड़ों साल पहले - १८४५ में — यहां आके इनने अपना काम शुरू किया। फलतः ये पादरी, ये मिशन ताता वगैरः से कहीं अच्छे हैं जो यहां से कमाते तो एक कौड़ी नहीं। लेकिन शिक्षा, औषधालय आदि में लाखों रुपये हर साल खर्चते हैं। यह ठीक है कि उनका उद्देश्य है ईसाईयों की संख्या बढ़ाना और इस प्रकार साम्राज्यवाद और विदेशी पूंजीवाद को मजबूत करना। मगर ताता और उनके दोस्त लोग भी क्यों नहीं उन्हीं की देखादेखी स्वदेशी पूंजीवाद को मजबूत करते हैं? ये पादरी और मिशन यहां के लोगों को ईसाई बनाते हैं सही। मगर उसी के साथ इन्हें आदमी भी तो बनाते हैं! हमने तो इन्हें पशु से भी बदतर बना रखा था और रखा है। ईसाईयों और मिशनों से हमें इस बात में कोई झगड़ा नहीं हैं और अगर कोई झगड़ा है तो वह दूसरी ही बात में है जिसका जिक्र आगे करेंगे। यदि हिन्दुओं या औरों को यह बात बुरी लगती है तो अपने कामों के जरिये उन मिशनों से बाजी क्यों नहीं मार ले जाते? सिर्फ धर्म धर्म चिल्लाने से कोई न सुनेगा। वह जमाना लद गया।

हां, यहां जो भी शिक्षा है उसका बहुत हिस्सा तो मिशनों के चलते है न कि विहारियों या विहार सरकार के चलते। सरकार का क्या यह काम न था कि

जमशेदपुर, रांची और हजारीबाग में तो जरूर ही कालिज खोल देती। आज बीसियों साल से यहां सरकार के शिक्षा सचिव तो हिन्दुस्तानी हीं होते आये हैं। मगर उनने यहां के मूक किसानों की आंखें खोलने के लिये क्या किया? कितनी कोशिश उनने की? कितने रुपये खर्चने के लिये सरकार को मजबूर किया? मेम्बर तो ज्यादातर विहारी ही रहे कौंसिलों के। उनने क्या इधर दृष्टि डाली? दृष्टि से मेरा मतलब है उचित और जैसी चाहिये वैसी दृष्टि से। कसम खाने के लिये कुछ कर देने से मेरा मतलब नहीं है।

दूसरी बात यह देखने की है कि जो भी स्कूल हैं यहां हैं उनसे कितना लाभ यहां के पिछड़े लोगों का होता है— उनमें उनके कितने लड़के पढ़ते हैं, लड़कियों की तो बात ही दूर रहे। यदि झारखंड के मुख्य मुख्य शहरों और बड़े बड़े गांवों का, जहां ज्यादातर बाहरी या प्रगतिशील लोग, शोषक लोग ही बसते हैं हिसाब लगाया जाय तो पता चलेगा कि जो भी स्कूल खुले हैं इनसे ज्यादा फायदा - बहुत अधिक लाभ वही लोग उठाते हैं। आदिवासी या दूसरे पिछड़े लोग तो बहुत ही कम पढ़ते हैं। इनमें से यदि ईसाईयों को निकाल दें तो और भी कमी हो जाय। क्योंकि ईसाईयों के पढ़ाने का श्रेय तो हमें प्रायः हई नहीं। उन्हें तो मिशन वाले ही पढ़ाते हैं। हमने तो थाने के हिसाब से देखा है कि प्रधान शहरों में ही बहुत ज्यादा स्कूल हैं या बाजारों में। इससे साफ हो जाता है कि आदिवासियों और उनके साथियों के प्रति - यहां के असली किसानों के प्रति कितनी लापर्वाही शिक्षा के मामले में की जाती है। संथाल परगने के बारे में जो जांच कमिटी की बात पहले लिखी गई है उससे तो स्पष्ट हो जाता है कि पिछड़े लोगों की शिक्षा पर ही छुरी चला के बाकियों की शिक्षा का यहां प्रबन्ध किया जाता है।

सब से ज्यादा खटकने वाली तो तीसरी बात है जिससे बखूबी पता लग जाता है कि यहां के सच्चे किसानों और मूक जनता की शिक्षा पर हम लोग कितना ध्यान देते हैं। हमें यह जानकर आश्चर्य हुआ कि आज तक संथाली, उरांव, मुण्डा और हो की भाषाओं के एक भी स्कूल नहीं खोले गये हैं! हिन्दी भाषा जानने वालों के लिये कलकत्ते और बम्बई में भी स्कूल होने हीं चाहिये। नहीं तो तूफान होगा। मुसलमान लोग और नहीं, तो धर्म के नाम पर ही उर्दू के स्कूल खुलवा के ही छोड़ते हैं। बंगालियों का तो पूछिये मत। उनने तो अपना प्रबन्ध सर्वत्र किया ही है। झारखंड में जिन जिलों में उनकी संख्या ज्यादा है वहां वंगला पढ़ने पढ़ाने का प्रबन्ध हई। मानभूम के डिस्ट्रिक्ट बोर्ड की तरफ से तो वंगला पढ़ाने का ही प्रबन्ध है। अब धनबाद वगैरः में कुछ हिन्दी भाषा

भाषियों की बात ले के हिन्दी के लिये वाबेला मचा है। इसी प्रकार हजारीबाग के रामगढ़, गोला, पेटरबार वगैरः इलाकों में भी वंगला पढ़ाई जाती है और जब हजारीबाग का बोर्ड उसकी जगह हिन्दी करना चाहता है तो भी वाबेला खड़ा होता है। ठीक ही है। बच्चे बच्चियों को तो खामखा मातृभाषा में हो शिक्षा देना ठीक है। जो ऐसा नहीं करते वे घोर अन्याय ही नहीं करते, बल्कि चाहते नहीं कि दूसरे भाषा के बोलने वाले उठ सकें ही न। आखिर यहां अंग्रेजी के बजाय मातृभाषा को ही माध्यम बना के जो अंग्रेजी की तालीम देने का आन्दोलन बहुत दिनों से चालू है और उसे सफलता भी मिल रही है उसका भी तो यही मतलब है न?

आखिर जब प्रगतिशील और सभ्य कहे जाने वाले लोग अपनी मातृभाषा में ही बच्चों की शिक्षा के लिये और तो और इस झारखंड में ही कुश्तम कुश्ता कर रहे हैं, जैसा कि बंगाली और हिन्दी के सम्बन्ध के हाल के कोलाहलों और झमेलों से मालूम होता है, तो इन गरीब आदिवासियों ने ही क्या बिगाड़ा है कि इनके बच्चों की या तो शिक्षा का प्रबन्ध हई नहीं, या अगर थोड़ा बहुत है भी तो हिन्दी या बंगला में ही? एक तो ये यों ही पिछड़े हैं। फलतः इनके बच्चे कुछ भी जानते ही नहीं। दूसरे उन्हें वैसी भाषा में पढ़ाना जिससे उन्हें कोई भी संसर्ग जन्म से हुआ ही नहीं, कितनी अन्धेर है! ऐसी शिक्षा तो इनके लिये जहर का ही काम करती है। इसके फलस्वरूप एक तो इनका दिमाग कुन्द हो जाता है। बहुत ज्यादा मिहनत जो करनी पड़ती है। दूसरे वे अध कचरे बन के रह जाते हैं। वह शिक्षा इनके किसी भी काम की नहीं होती। व्यवहार में तो काम आती नहीं और ज्यादा दूर तक पढ़ने का इन्हें सौभाग्य नहीं कि आगे काम दे सके। इस तरह ये न तो घर के रह जाते और न घाट के।

सोवियट रूस में भारत की सरहद पर ही कई छोटे छोटे प्रजातंत्र हैं - बहुत ही नन्हें नन्हें। उनमें ऐसी जातियां हैं जो ताजिक आदि के नाम से प्रसिद्ध हैं। उनके न तो अक्षर थे और न लिखी पुस्तकें उनके पास थीं। मगर आज सोवियट शासन के चलते उनके लिये नई वर्णमाला तैयार हो के उसी में सभी तरह की किताबें उनकी अपनी भाषा में ही लिखी जा चुकी हैं। उनके स्कूल कालिजों में वही किताबें पढ़ाई जाती हैं। उनका शासन भी अपनी भाषा में ही चलता है और कारबार भी। सोवियट ने देखा कि इनकी अपनी भाषा का प्रसार हुए बिना न तो ये जिन्दा रह सकते और न आगे बढ़ सकते हैं। इसलिये उसने सब से पहले यही काम किया। आखिर वह सचमुच ही जनता की - किसानों

और मजदूरों की - अपनी सरकार जो ठहरी। अतएव वैसा करती क्यों नहीं?

मगर यहां तो हम बेगाने ठहरे और ये झारखंडवासी दूसरे ही हैं। हम तो इन्हें जबर्दस्ती सभ्य बनाने पर तुले बैठे हैं - ठोंक-पीट के बैद्यराज बनाने पर कटिबद्ध हैं। फिर हमें पर्वा क्या कि किस भाषा में इनकी पढ़ाई होती है? इनकी तो अपनी भाषा असभ्य है और हमें बनाना है इन्हें सभ्य। इसीलिये हिन्दी, बंगला, अंग्रेजी कोई भी सभ्य भाषा इन्हें पढ़ना हीं पड़ेगा! यही है हमारी नीच मनोवृत्ति का गया गुजरा नमूना और इसी के बल पर हम बाबू जयपाल सिंह के आदिवासी आन्दोलन का मुकाबिला करना और छोटानागपुर को अपनी दुम से बांध रखना चाहते हैं! निश्चय ही यदि वंगला की पढ़ाई न रहती तो न तो मानभूम वगैरः में ही उतने स्कूल होते और न बाकी जिलों में ही हिन्दी के रहने पर उतने मिलते जितने पाये जाते हैं! तब तो विहारियों और बंगालियों को यहां की शिक्षा में और भी कोई दिलचस्पी रही नहीं जाती! ये इतने भी स्कूल तो सिर्फ इसीलिये पाये जाते हैं कि बंगला, हिन्दी और अंग्रेजी ही इनमें पढ़ाई जाती है। अतः हम तो निस्संकोच यही कह सकते हैं यहां के असली निवासी किसानों और मूक जनता को पढ़ाने का कोई भी यत्न नहीं किया गया है और जो कुछ किया गया है वह निरी धोखेबाजी है।

अकेले दामिने कोह में केवल पहड़िया हैं पूरे साठ हजार। मगर उनके बच्चों के लिये एक भी स्कूल नहीं है! हम नहीं कहते हैं। यह तो सरकारी कमिटी की सरकारी रिपोर्ट कहती है। खूबी तो यह कि दामिन का इलाका सरकारी जमींदारी है। दूसरा जमीदार वहां हैं नहीं और उसी की यह हालत है! चिराग तले अन्धेरा और क्या हो सकता है? रिपोर्ट ने यों तो हिसाब दिखाने के लिये यहां तक कह डाला है कि सरकारी जमींदारी या खासमहाल की कुल आय का एक प्रतिशत और पूरे अट्ठारह हजार रुपये सालाना शिक्षा में खर्च होते हैं! मगर किनके लिये? जो खुद भी पढ़ सकते हैं उन्हीं के लिये? यदि नहीं तो जब वही रिपोर्ट खुद कबूल करती है कि दामिन के बाशिन्दे तो ८५ फीसदी कोरे आदि और अत्यन्त पिछड़े हैं - "In which is 85 percent aboriginal, which is very primitive." (page 64). मगर यह हिसाब तो वही मुंशीजी वाला हिसाब है जिसके अनुसार ''नापे जो खे थाहे। लड़के डूबे काहे?'' जरा उसी रिपोर्ट की एक बात और सुनिये जो मजेदार है और जो कही गई है संथालों को ही लक्ष्य करके। मगर वह कमवैश समस्त छोटानागपुर और संथाल परगने पर ही लागू है। वह यों है :— "The first essential for the aboriginals is more education. Until they have advanced in this respect they cannot hope to compete with their Dikku neighbours or improve their own conditions. The percentage of literacy recorded in the district at the last census of 1931 is very low indeed, being only 2.90 against a provincial average of 5.2. The figures for aboriginals are even lower. While the percentage of literacy among Dikkus is 4.72 it was only 0.40 among the aboriginals. The wastage is also abnormal. For, although the educational returns show that an average of over 13,800 Santal children have attended school annually during the last 15 years the census figures show that there were in 1931 only 3490 literate Santals." (page 44).

"आदिवासियों के लिये सब से पहली जरूरी चीज है वह है अधिक शिक्षा। जब तक वे इसमें प्रगति नहीं कर लेते, न तो अपनी दशा सुधारने की ही आशा कर सकते हैं और न अपने पड़ोसी दिक्कू (प्रगतिशील) लोगों से मुकाबिला ही कर सकते हैं। १९३१ की मर्दुमशुमारी में जिले में पठितों की संख्या बेशक बहुत ही कम यानी केवल २.९ प्रतिशत बताई गई है जबकि समूचे प्रान्त की ५.२ है। लेकिन आदिवासियों के आंकड़े तो और भी नीचे हैं। जहां दिक्कुओं में पढ़े लिखों की संख्या प्रतिशत ४.७२ है तहां आदिवासियों की सिर्फ .४ यानी ढाई सौ में एक है! बेकार खर्च भी असाधारण है। क्योंकि यद्यपि शिक्षा सम्बन्धी रिपोर्टों के आंकड़ों से पता चलता है कि गत १५ साल के भीतर औसतन १३८०० संताल लड़के हर साल स्कूल में जाते रहे हैं। तथापि १९३१ की मनुष्यगणना के अंकों से पता चलता है कि उस साल सिर्फ ३४९० संताल ही कमवेश पढ़े लिखे थे!"

जैसा कि पहले कहा जा चुका है, संथाल परगना शिक्षा में झारखंड के और जिलों से पीछे नहीं है। किन्तु उनके मुकाबिले का ही है। यदि रांची और मानभूम से कुछ पीछे है, तो सिंहभूम, हजारीबाग और पलामू से कहीं आगे है। इसलिये सब मिला के औसतन उनसे कुछ न कुछ आगे ही माना जा सकता है। उनके बराबर तो हर हालत में ही है। ऐसी दशा में यदि यहां आदिवासियों के अक्षर ज्ञान (literacy) की यह हालत है कि पूरे ढाई सौ में से केवल एक ही पढ़ा है - अक्षर कट्टू - अक्षरज्ञ - है तो छोटानागपुर की औसत तो इससे भी गिरी यानी प्रायः तीन सौ में एक ही अक्षर कट्टू मिलेगा! विपरीत इसके विहार की औसत करीब सवा पांच प्रतिशत बताई गई है। यह तो जमीन आसमान का अन्तर हो जाता है! विहार की अपेक्षा छोटानागपुर (झारखंड) पढ़ने लिखने इस हिसाब से पन्द्रहवां हिस्सा है - झारखंड से विहार पन्द्रह गुना बढ़ा है! यह

है शिक्षा की असलियत!

पहले जो चौथाई वाला आंकड़ा दिखाया गया था उसकी असलियत का पता अब चल जाता है। हमने तो वहां भी कहा था कि प्रगतिशील जातियों को निकाल देने पर आदिवासी किसानों की दशा बहुत पीछे पड़ जायगी। उसका रहस्य अब मालूम हो गया। हमने जो अभी विहार को झारखंड से पन्द्रह गुना आगे बताया है वह समूचे प्रान्त की बात है। क्योंकि समूचे सूबे की, जिसमें झारखंड भी शामिल है, औसत ५.२ है। मगर अगर सिर्फ विहार के दस जिलों से ही शेष इन छः का मुकाबिला करें और इनमें से भी बढ़ी जातियों को उन दस जिलों में ही शामिल करके केवल आदिवासियों और पिछड़ी जातियों के ही साथ शेष सबों की मिलान करें तो बहुत ज्यादा फर्क हो जायगा और शेष सबों की अपेक्षा ये लोग पच्चीसवां भाग ही पढ़े लिखे या अक्षर कट्टू सिद्ध होंगे! यह है कठोर और अप्रिय सत्य।

देखने से चौथाई के करीब और असलियत में पच्चीसवां हिस्सा! ऐसा क्यों? इसका उत्तर कहा जा चुका है कि और जातियों के साथ मिला देने पर चौथाई प्रतीत होता है। मगर दरअसल इन्हें जो अपनी मातृभाषा में शिक्षा नहीं दी जाती है उसी का यह भयंकर नतीजा है कि स्कूल जा के भी इनके बच्चे कुछ पढ़ लिख नहीं सकते। उनके माथे पर पहाड़ पड़ जाता है। एक तो अस्वाभाविक चीज में उनका मन नहीं लगता। दूसरे बहुत ज्यादा परिश्रम करने की जरूरत होती है। तीसरे ये खुद पिछड़े हैं और इनमें उसके लिये - पढ़ने के लिये लगन और रूचि पैदा करने की जगह विदेशी - बेगानी - भाषा पढ़ने के लिये इन्हें मजबूर किया जाता है। यही बात संथाल परगने की कमिटी की रिपोर्ट में बेकार खर्च या बरबादी (wastage) कहा है। यह न सिर्फ पैसे की ही बरबादी है, बल्कि उनके देह, दिमाग और सबों के परिश्रम की भी। सारी चीजें बेकार चली जाती हैं और नतीजा होता है निहायत ही हानिकारक। क्योंकि इसका बुरा असर उन बच्चों पर पड़ता है। अफसोस है कि इस मोटी सी बात को हमने आज तक नहीं समझा। रिपोर्ट के लेखकों ने भी, जिनमें बहुतेरे जवाबदेह कांग्रेसी हैं, यह बात लिख के भी ठीक समझी नहीं। नतीजा सामने है।

(४)

किसान और जमींदार

मगर किसानों की असली हालत और उनसे ताल्लुक रखने वाले काश्तकारी कानून (Tenancy Act) को जानने के लिये उसमें क्या दोष गुण हैं, हमें यहां की जमीन के बन्दोबस्त (Land tenure) का जान लेना जरूरी है। शिक्षा वगैरः की कमी तो उसी हालत को और भी बदतर कर देती है। बेशक, यदि किसानों में हक के लिये लड़ने और मर मिटने की माद्दा हो, भाव हो तो शिक्षा उन्हें ऐसा बना देती है कि आसानी से ही जल्द से जल्द अपना हक हासिल कर लेते हैं। और अगर यह माद्दा उनमें न हो तो भी शिक्षा के फलस्वरूप धीरे धीरे उस ओर बढ़ते हैं। इसीलिये हर हालत में शिक्षा निहायत जरूरी है, उनकी प्रगति की जान (essential) है, जैसा कि कहा गया है। मगर झारखंडी किसान तो बड़े ही बहादुर और जमीन के सच्चे प्रेमी हैं यह बात पहले कही जा चुकी है।

इनके जमीन सम्बन्धी प्रेम और इनकी बहादुरी के बहुत से दृष्टांत पाये जाते हैं। कहा जाता है कि यहां के नागवंशी राजे, जिनके हाथ में पहले यहां का शासन था, इन्हीं के — यहां के मूल निवासियों के ही — वंश के थे। पुरानी पंचायती प्रथा के अनुसार ही इनने उन्हें अपना सरदार और मुखिया चुना, जो समय पाके इनके मालिक बन गये, जैसा कि सामन्तशाही का इतिहास सभी देशों में पाया जाता है और जमींदारी प्रथा की बुनियाद जिससे कायम हुई है। मुगल जमाने तक तो बात ठीक पाई गई बताई जाती है। मगर पीछे दिल्ली दरबार में जाने आने का सिलसिला खतरनाक साबित हुआ। जब तक इन जंगलों में वे लोग रहे तब तक तो राजसी ठांटबाट और व्यसन की वैसी बात थी नहीं। मगर वहां जाने पर साज सामान और घोड़े हाथी वगैरह का शौक देखा देखी जरूरी था। ऐयाशी भी सूझी। फिर तो इन सामानों और हथी घोड़ों को पहुंचाने वाले लोगों का प्रसार यहां होना जरूरी था। पश्चिमी प्रान्तों से सिख, पठान और दूसरे कारबारी पहुंचने लगे और दरबारी सामान वगैरः पहुंचा के माल लूटने लगे। जब सामान के बदले रुपये नहीं मिलते तो गांव के गांव

ठेके पर दे दिये जाते। इस प्रकार बाहरी जमींदारों का यहां पदार्पण हो गया। दूसरे तरीकों से भी कुछ लोग पहुंचे ही थे। दोस्ती और लड़ाई के जरिये भी, जैसा कि पहले होता था, बहुतेरे लोग आ गये। मुगलों की खुशामद और अंग्रेजों की सेवा के बल पर भी १७६५ के बाद कुछ लोगों का यहां पहुंच जाना जरूरी था। अब तो खरीद बिक्री के जरिये भी कितने हीं आ गये हैं। बिवाह शादी और नाते रिश्ते के करते भी पहले ही बहुतेरे आये। दुर्भेद्य जंगलों में गढ़ बना के रहने के लिये भी कुछ लोग पहुंची गये।

इस प्रकार जब धीरे धीरे बाहरी शोषक लोग यहां जम के किसानों का दोहन और शोषण करने लगे तो ये घबराये और इनकी आंखें खुली कि यह क्या? मारवाड़ी साहुकारों और दूसरे बनिये महाजनों ने भी इन्हें कम नहीं लूटा। इनके खेती से गाढ़ी कमाई जो भी मिलती सब की सब इन जमींदारों, मारवाड़ियों और सूदखोर बनियों के पेट में चली जाती। यहां तक कि इनकी इज्जत आबरू तक पर आ बनती। नये अंग्रेजी कानूनों की शरण लेके इन भोलेभाले किसानों का रक्त चूसा जाता, जमीनें छीनी जातीं और ये गुलाम बना लिये जाते। जेलों में भी बन्द हो जाने की नौबत बार बार आती थी। इससे ऊबकर छोटानागपुर के किसानों ने १८२० और १८३१-३२ में तथा उसके बाद भी जानें कितनी बार बगावतें कीं, लूटपाट की। १८५५ की ३०वीं जून से प्रस्थान करके पहले पहल ७ वीं जूलाई को वीरभूम में तीस हजार संथालों के दल ने जो पुलिसवालों पर हमले किये और लूटपाट की वह इसी अत्याचार से ऊब जाने के बाद ही हुई। १८८९—९० से लेकर फिर जो गड़बड़ी हुई और १८९५ में जो वीरसा आन्दोलन रांची जिले में शुरू होके आग की तरह चारों ओर बात की बात में फैल गया उसके भीतर भी यही बात थी। सबसे आखिर में जो "टानाभगत" आन्दोलन १९१४ के यूरोपीय महासमर के शुरू होने पर जारी होके १९२१ के असहयोग के समय तक काफी तेज था वह तो साफ ही किसान आन्दोलन था। टाना लोगों का एक जबर्दस्त दल जमींदारों को लगान देने से साफ इन्कार करता, जेल जाता, तबाह होता और जमीनें नीलाम करवाता था।

जबकि भारत में रौलटऐक्ट और पंजाब के मार्शल ला की बातें लेकर तथा खिलाफत के मसले पर भी राजनीतिक आन्दोलन बड़े बड़े धुरन्धर नेता चालू कर रहे थे। उसी समय झारखंड के भोले-भाले, पर बहादुर किसान अपने ही ढंग से ऐसा जबर्दस्त किसान आन्दोलन और लगान-बन्दी तथा कर बन्दी की जबर्दस्त लड़ाई चला रहे थे कि देखते ही बनता था। हमारी असली लड़ाई का रूप तो उनने ही खड़ा किया और सारे मुल्क का प्रदर्शन वे लोग जबान से

नहीं, अपने कामों से कर रहे थे। वे तो मूक ठहरे। शिक्षा तो उन्हें दी गई न थी। फिर बोलते क्या? बोलने का काम तो देश के दूसरे दूसरे कोने में नेता लोग करी रहे थे। बोलना ज्यादातर उनका काम था और काम करना इनका। असल में टानाभगतों की वह लगान-बन्दी हर्गिज नहीं रुकती, यदि १९२१ के अश्विन में गांधीजी खुद रांची में आके उन्हें अपनी जबान से नहीं रोकते और पीछे कांग्रेस के कार्यकर्त्ता लोग घूमघूम के प्रचार नहीं करते कि जमींदार का लगान जरूर दे दो! यह है हमारी राजनीति का नमूना और यह है यहां के किसानों की लड़ाई का सच्चा रूप। ये सीधे और भोले किसान तो धर्म में साधु महात्मा में विश्वास करते थे। ये लोग भगत तो कहे जाते ही थे। बस गांधीजी को महात्मा समझ इनने उनकी आज्ञा मान कर-बन्दी बन्द कर दी।

जब इनकी नाकों दम हो जाता है ये सीधे लोग तभी उभड़ते हैं। नहीं तो जहां तक हो सकता है जुल्मों को चुपचाप पशु की तरह बर्दाश्त करते जाते हैं। १८२० और १८३१-३२ के जमाने में ये कैसे सताये गये तब इनने क्या किया इसके बारे में कुछ पंक्तियां हम कैप्टन डालटन के शब्दों में लिखते हैं जो उस समय छोटानागपुर के प्रबंधक थे। वे लिखते हैं कि "The oppressions of these men (Jagirdars) were however borne with courage, but a far worse class of men had obtained a footing in the country about the year 1820, when the late Maharaja Jagarnath Sahi Deo obtained his ancestral gadi on the death of his father in July of that year. These men were Musalmans, Sikhs and some others who came to the country as horse dealers, and shawl and brocade merchants, fetched enormous offers for their goods from the Nagvanshi Chiefs and obtained farms of villages instead of cash, of which latter the Chiefs were always in want. The foreign farmers having but a temporary interest in the villages squeezed as much as possible from the ryots in the shape of rents, abwabs and salami. But this was not all. They proved their yoke to be galling indeed and rendered true the very name thikadar in Chotanagpur in farms."

"The Pathans have taken our hoormat and the Sikhs our sisters, our lives are of no value, and being of one caste let us stand fast to each other and commence to plunder, murder and loot," thus said they.

"जागरीदारों के जुल्मों को तो इन लोगों ने किसी प्रकार हिम्मत करके बर्दाश्त किया। मगर १८२० की जुलाई में अपने पिता के मरने पर भूतपूर्व महाराजा जगरनाथ शाही देव को जब गद्दी मिली उस समय एक दूसरे ही दल

के लोगों को इस प्रदेश में जगह मिल गई। ये लोग थे मुसलमान, सिख और कुछ दूसरे जो घोड़ों कार चोबी की चीजों और शाल दुशालों के सौदागर थे। इन्हें अपने माल के लिये इन नागवंशी राजाओं से काफी पैसे मिलते थे। मगर पास में पैसे न होने से ये राजे अपने गांव इन्हें ठीके में दे दिया करते थे। इन बाहरी ठीकेदारों का गावों और क्या स्वार्थ था सिवाय इसके कि थोड़ी ही मुद्दत में ज्यादा से ज्यादा पैसे किसानों से लगान, अबवाब और सलामी के रूप में जबर्दस्ती चूसें? लेकिन इतना ही न था। सचमुच उनने किसानों को सता सता के अपना ठीकेंदार नाम छोटानागपुर में सार्थक कर दिया! ऊब कर किसानों ने कहा कि ''पठानों ने हमारी इज्जत (हुर्मत) और सिखों ने हमारी बहनें ले लीं। हमारी जिन्दगी अब बेकार है। हम तो एक ही वर्ग (जाति) के हैं। इसीलिये आइये परस्पर एक दूसरे से खूब मिल जांय और लूटमार, कत्ल और डाका शुरू कर दें।''

उनने जो कुछ भी ऊबकर किया यहां उसके खंडन मंडन से हमारा मतलब नहीं है। उनने तो उसका नतीजा खुद भोगा। हमें तो सिर्फ यही दिखाना है कि जब कोई रास्ता यहां के किसानों को नहीं सूझता तो हथेली पर जान लेके खड़े हो जाते हैं और लूटमार शुरू करके स्वयं भी तबाह हो जाते हैं। और रास्ता तो अब तक उन्हें मालूम न था। इसीलिये उनने कहा कि हमारा जीना धिक्कार है। यहां पर जो उनका यह कहना लिखा है कि हम एक ही जाति या वर्ग के हैं, बड़े ही मार्के का है। इससे पता चलता है कि उनमें वर्ग चेतना (class consciousness) बहुत पहले से ही है। यह ठीक है कि वह पुराने ढंग की है और उसे नये सांचे में ढालना होगा। वे संगठन भी बड़ा पक्का करते हैं और लाखों की तादाद में एक ही साथ इसीलिये उठ खड़े होते हैं। यही तो उनका असली बल है। मगर इसका प्रयोग ठीक रास्ते पर तथा उचित नेतृत्व में होना चाहिये। ऐसे समयोपयोगी नेतृत्व का उनमें एकदम अभाव है। इसे पैदा करना हमारा काम है।

इसी प्रकार हन्टर ने जो अपनी किताब ''बंगाल की देहातों के इतिहास'' (**Annals of Rural Bengal** by W.W. Hunter) में संथालों के १८५५ वाले विद्रोह के बारे में लिखा है उसकी भी कुछ पंक्तियां यहां जानकारी के लिये लिख देना जरूरी है। उनसे उन गरीबों की लूट और उन पर होने वाले अत्याचारों का पता चलता है। वहां लिखा है कि, "They cheated the poor Santal in every transaction. The forestor brought his jars of clarified butter for sale, the Hindus measured in vessels for salt, oil, cloth and gunpowder; the Hindu used heavy weights in ascertaining the quantity of grain, light ones in weighing out the articles given in return. If the Santal remonstrated, he was told that salt, being and excisable commodity, had a set of weights and measures peculiar to itself. The fortunes made by trafic in produce were augmented by usury.

The Hindu dealer gave them a few shillings worth of rice, and seized the land as soon as they had cleared it and sown the crop. Another family, in a fit of hospitality, feasted away their whole harvest, and then opened an account at the grain dealers, who advanced enough to keep them above starvation during the rest of the year. From the moment the peasant touched the borrowed rice, he and his children were the serfs of the corn merchant. No matter what economy the family practised, no matter what effort they made to extricate themselves, stint as they might, toil as they might, the Hindu claimed this whole crop, and carried on a balance to be paid out of the next harvest."

"Year after year Santhals sweated for his oppressor. If the victim threatened to run off into the jungle, the userer instituted a suit in the courts, taking care that the Santhal should know nothing of it till the decree had been obtained and execution taken out Without the slightest warning, the poor husbandman's buffaloes, cows and little homestead were sold, not omitting the bronze household vessels which formed the sole heirloom of the family. Even the cheap iron ornaments, outward tokens of female respectability among the Santhals, were torn from the wife's wrists."

"ये बनिये हर बात में संथालों को ठगते थे। जंगली लोग घड़े भर के शुद्ध घी लाते थे और हिन्दु बनिये उसे नमक, तेल, कपड़ा और बारूद तौलने के बर्त्तनों से (क्योंकि पहले तराजू की जगह बर्त्तनों से ही तौल होती थी और आज भी संथाल वगैरः ऐसा ही करते हैं) ही तौलते थे। बनियें अपनी चीजों को हलके बाटों से और संथाल किसानों के गल्ले को वजनी बाटों से तौलते थे। यदि संथाल इस पर कुछ हो हल्ला करते तो चट उन्हें कह देते कि नमक पर तो टैक्स लगता है। इसीलिये उसके तौलने के बाट वगैरः और ही है। इस प्रकार चीजों की लेन देन में जो नफा वे कमाते थे उसे सूदखोरी के जरिये और भी बढ़ाते थे।

"हिन्दू बनिये संथालों को कुछी रुपयों के चावल देकर उनकी सारी जमीनों

को फौरन हथिया लेते जिन्हें साफ करके उनमें वे फसल बोते थे। कोई घर ऐसा होता कि खिलाने पिलाने की उमंग में सारी पैदावार खर्च कर देता और उसके बाद गल्ला वेंचने वालों से उधार अन्न खर्च के लिये लेता था। ये गल्ले वाले अन्न देकर साल के बाकी दिनों में उन्हें भूखों मरने से बचा लेते थे सही। मगर ज्योंही किसान ने उनसे चावल वगैरः उधार लिया कि वे और उनके बाल बच्चे बनियों के गुलाम बन गये! फिर चाहे कितनी ही किफायत से खर्च करें और बनिये से पिंड छुड़ाने के लिए हजार कोशिश करें, जितनी भी कंजूसी करें और कलेजा फाड़ के मिहनत करें। मगर बनियां उनकी सारी फसल का दावीदार बनने के साथ ही आगे के लिये कुछ न कुछ बकाया भी रख छोड़ता था।

"प्रति साल इन जालिमों के लिये संताल खून को पसीना बनाते रहते थे। यदि ऊबकर जंगल में भाग जाना चाहते तो सूदखोर उन पर अदालतों में केस करते थे। मगर यह काम इस चालाकी से किया जाता था कि जब तक डिग्री होके दखल दिहानी जारी न हो जाय तब तक बेचारे संथाल को इसका जरा भी पता चले ही न। फिर तो बिना कहे सुने ही उस गरीब की भैंसें, गायें और घरबार सभी चीजें नीलाम कर ली जाती थीं, यहां तक कि बापदादों के वक्त के जो कांसे के बर्त्तन होते वे भी न बच पाते। गरीब संथाल की औरत की इज्जत की निशानी के रूप में उसकी कलाइयों में लोहे के जेवर होते वे भी जबर्दस्ती छीन लिये जाते थे!"

इसी का नतीजा था वह १८५५ के मध्य का संथाल-विद्रोह जिसका जिक्र पहले कर चुके हैं। हजारीबाग वगैरः के बारे में तो पहले ही कह चुके हैं। गत सर्वे की रिपोर्ट में भी उनके बारे में यही लिखा है कि उनने जो विद्रोह किया था वह इन सूदखोरों और जालिमों से ही बचने के लिये। जैसे १८५५ में तीस हजार संथालों ने जमा होके यह काम किया। ठीक उसी तरह १८३१ में छोटानागपुर वालों ने भी गरोह बांध के यही काम किया था। साफ लिखा है कि, "They unnaturally became excited by the weakening of the authority and thought the occasion opportune for squaring with the oppressive money lenders and others. Several bands of Santals collected for marauding purposes." "जैसा कि आमतौर से नहीं होता वैसी गर्मी उनमें आ गई जबकि शासन सूत्र की कमजोरी का उन्हें अन्दाज लगा। उनने सोचा कि यही मौका है कि जालिम बनियों, सूदखोरों और दूसरों से बदला सधा लिया जाय। फलतः गिरोह के गिरोह संथाल लूटपाट वगैरह के लिये जमा हो गये"!

यहां तो सरकार की कमजोरी का जिक्र है। मगर संथाल परगने के संथालों

के सम्बन्ध में तो लिखा गया है कि वे कलकत्ते जाके लाट साहब को अर्जी देना चाहते थे कि जुल्म होता है और आपकी अदालतें भी हमें सताती हैं। चाहे बात कुछ भी क्यों न हो। मगर जब उनने देखा कि न्याय के नाम पर अंग्रेज, कानून और अदालतें उनका खून कर रही हैं और शोषक मालदारों का ही साथ दे रही हैं तो सरकार के ऊपर भी उनका गुस्सा जरूरी हो गया। नतीजा यह हुआ सरकार को तमाचे लगे और उसने सोचा कि इनके साथ दूसरे ढंग से पेश आना चाहिये। इनकी अपनी रहन सहन और रीति रिवाज पर ध्यान देना उसने जरूरी समझा। चाहे वह उनकी यथार्थतः रक्षा भले ही न कर सकी, और उसके लिये यह संभव भी न था। फिर भी उसी तरह की कानूनी व्यवस्था क इन्तजाम उसने करना शुरू कर दिया। एक ओर सभ्यता के शिखर पर बैठी सरकार और दूसरी ओर अवनति के अतलगर्त्त में गिरे ये किसान! फिर दोनों का मेल हो तो कैसे? चाहे वह हजार कहे कि हमें इन आदिवासियों की सामाजिक व्यवस्था के ही अनुसार चलना है। फिर भी वह भारत में जिस काम के लिये आई वह तो शोषण की बुनियाद पर ही चल सकता है। इसीलिये घुमाफिरा के इनका भी शोषण होई जाता है। फिर भी १८६९ के छोटानागपुर टेन्योर्स ऐक्ट, १८७९ के छोटानागपुर लैंडलोर्ड टेनेन्ट प्रोसीजर ऐक्ट, १८९७ के छोटानुगपुर कम्यूटेशन ऐक्ट, १९०३, १९०५ और १९०८ के छोटानागपुर टेनेन्सी ऐक्ट्स वगैरह के जरिये यहां का शासन कुछ दूसरे ही ढंग से चलाया जाने लगा ताकि वैसी लूट न हो सके। इसी तरह १८५५, १८५९, १८७२, १८८८ आदि के खास ढंग के नियमों और विधानों के ही अनुसार संथाल परगना का शासन होने लगा। संथाल परगना को सब तरह के साधारण विधानों से बाहर (non-regulation) और छोटानागपुर को पिछड़ा हुआ (backward) इलाका भी तभी से घोषित किया गया जो आज तक यह बात किसी न किसी रूप में मौजूद है। लेकिन किसानों के त्याग और बलिदान ने इतना कर तो दिया। इससे आगे का रास्ता भी साफ हो गया।

किसानों की समय समय की बेचैनी और उत्तेजना को जानने के साथ ही यहाँ की जमीन की बन्दोबस्ती व्यवस्था कैसी है यह भी जानना जरूरी है। उसमें भी किसानों की काश्तकारी जमीनें कितनी तरह की हैं इसका तो आगे स्वतंत्र वर्णन करेंगे। क्योंकि यह यहाँ की खास बात है और इससे स्थिति का कुछ खास पता चलता है। यहाँ सिर्फ जमींदारी या जमीन की मलिकाई पर ही प्रकाश डालना है। किसानों की असली लड़ाई तो इसी जमींदारी प्रथा से है। अतएव उसके बारे में एवं तत्संबंधी कानूनों के बारे में जो कुछ आगे कहा जायगा उसे

समझने के लिए यहाँ यह जान लेना है कि यहाँ के प्रधान जमींदार कैसे और कौन कौन से हैं।

झारखंड के कुल छः जिलों में तीन तरह के जमींदार पाये जाते हैं। विहार की भी यही हालत है। मगर यहां जो कुछ विशेषता है वह यह है कि सरकार यहां सबसे बड़ा जमींदार है। दामिने कोह, संथाल परगना की बात तो पहले ही कही जा चुकी है। घने पर्वतों के बीच के बहुत बड़े भूभाग पर, जिसका क्षेत्र समूचे जिले के क्षेत्रफल का प्रायः एक चौथाई है और करीब डेढ़ हजार वर्गमील में जो फैला है, सरकारी जमींदारी या खासमहाल है जिसे गवर्नमेन्ट इस्टेट भी कहते हैं। यह सबसे पिछड़ा इलाका है। इसी में साठ हजार पहड़िया लोग बसते हैं जिनके एक बच्चे के भी पढ़ने का प्रबन्ध खासमहाल ने अब तक नहीं किया है। यह सरकार दूसरे जमींदारों को क्या कहेगी जब खुद जमींदार बन के कुछ नहीं करती। पहड़िया लोगों की खास तकलीफ तो आगे लिखी जायगी।

सिंहभूम के दलभूम सबडिविजन का एक बहुत बड़ा भाग भी, जिसे कोल्हान कहते हैं, खासमहाल ही है। उसी सबडिविजन का प्रधान नगर जमशेदपुर या ताता नगर है। यह कोल्हान भी वैसा ही पिछड़ा हुआ है जैसा कि दामिन का इलाका। यहां के किसान भी प्रधान रूप से वही आदिवासी लोग ही हैं जिन्हें जबान मिली ही नहीं है। और अंग्रेजों की तो हालत यह है कि इनने खुद तूफान खड़ा करके ही अपने लिये स्वराज्य हासिल किया है। इसीलिये ये तो वैसे ही आन्दोलन को समझते और उसके सामने सर झुकाते हैं। यों तो छोटेमोटे और भी इलाके खासमहाल के हैं। इन्कम्बर्ड इस्टेट्स ऐक्ट के अनुसार जानें कितनी हीं जमीदारियों का इन्तजाम भी खुद सरकार ही अपने कोर्ट औफ वार्ड्स नामक विभाग के जरिये करती है। सरकार की यह दूसरी चीज है।

सरकार की एक तीसरी चीज और है। यहां के बहुत से घने जंगल भी ठेठ सरकार के ही हाथ में हैं और उनका इन्तजाम वह खुद करती है। यों तो जमींदारों के भी अपने जंगल हैं जो सुरक्षित (reserved) हैं और जिनके भीतर कोई आदमी या पशु पांव तक नहीं दे सकते। मगर सरकारी सुरक्षित जंगल (reserved forest) बहुत ज्यादा हैं। इन सुरक्षित जंगलों के करते और तकलीफें तो हईं जिन्हें आगे बतायेंगे। मगर इनके पास के किसान और उनके पशु खासकर गर्मियों में पानी के बिना मर जाते हैं। असल में पानी के सोते ऐसे ही जंगलों में होते हैं जो घने, आबाद और सुरक्षित होते हैं। पहाड़ों में कूआं खोदना भी किसानों के बिसात के बाहर की बात है। जमींदार या सरकार को तो इसकी पर्वा होती ही नहीं। अब अगर वे या उनके पशु पानी पीने के लिये रक्षित जंगलों

के झरनों पर जायें तो कानून के अनुसार फौरन उन पर केस चले। यह तो आम बात है और किसान इसके चलते खून के आंसू रोते रहते हैं। इस पर आगे ज्यादा कहेंगे।

अब रहे गैर सरकारी जमींदार। वे भी दो तरह के हैं। एक तो घटवार और दूसरे साधारण जमींदार। ये साधारण या आमतौर के जमींदार तो वही हैं जो विहार में पाये जाते हैं। उनमें और इनमें, जहां तक इनका किसानों से ताल्लुक है, कोई बुनियादी फर्क नहीं है। हां, इनके खास अधिकार हैं जो गवर्नमेन्ट से इन्हें प्राप्त हैं, जैसा कि कर्ज में डूबने पर खासतौर से उसकी जांच वगैरह करके असल कर्ज का पता लगाना और उसके चुकाने के लिये सरकार के द्वारा जमींदारी का प्रबन्ध अपने हाथ में लिया जाना इत्यादि। इसी तरह की कुछ और भी बातें हैं। मगर यह कोई मौलिक या बुनियादी फर्क है नहीं। इस फर्क से किसानों का कोई मतलब भी नहीं है।

मगर घटवार या घटवाल तो निराले ढंग के जमींदार हैं। उन्हें यह जमींदारी तो खास तरह के काम या सेवा के लिये ही दी गई है। इसीलिये इसे अंग्रेजी में ''सर्विस टेन्योर'' या ''काम के लिये दी गई जागीर'' कहते हैं। जिस प्रकार जमींदार या किसान चौकीदार, नाऊ, पुरोहित आदि को पहले कुछ जमीनें जागीर के रूप में दे देते थे। ठीक उसी तरह की यह चीज है, जागीर है। फर्क इतना ही है कि यह खुद सरकार के द्वारा दी गई चीज है। इसीलिये उसी जागीर की तरह यह भी छिनी जा सकती है यदि घटवाल अपनी ड्यूटी समय पर अदा न करे। यहां के डिप्टी कमिश्नरों की जरा भी नजर बिगड़ी और यह घटवाली गई! झारखंड में घटवार नाम की एक जाति भी है। शायद उस जाति के लोग पहले वही काम करते हों जो पीछे इन घटवारों को दे दिये गये। इसीलिये तो गोड़ाइत नामक एक और भी जाति यहां हो गई है। मगर ये जो जमींदार के रूप में घटवाल आज पाये जाते हैं वह दूसरे ही हैं। उनका घटवार जाति से कोई ताल्लुक नहीं है। <30.11.41> यह ठीक है कि वे लोग किसी खास जाति के नहीं हैं ठीक जैसे जमींदारों की कोई एक जाति नहीं है। किन्तु सभी जाति और धर्म के लोग जमींदार हैं। घटवाल भी सभी जाति के हैं।

घाटी का नाम तो अकसर पढ़ा सुना जाता है। पहाड़ों में जहां उतार चढ़ाव ज्यादा होता है और इसीलिये पार करने में दिक्कत होती है उसे ही घाटी कहते हैं। घाट भी उसी का नाम है। पहाड़ी इलाकों में प्रवेश करने और जाने के रास्ते यों तो आमतौर से होते नहीं। जहां कहीं नदियों के गुजरने से पहाड़ कटे से मालूम पड़ते हैं वहीं से इधर-उधर आ जा सकते हैं। आजकल तो डिनामाइट

नाम की बारूद को लगाके तथा और भी वैज्ञानिक ढंगों का प्रयोग करके बड़े से बड़े पहाड़ों को काट के, उड़ा के, फाड़ के उनके बीच से रास्ते बनाये जाते हैं,, सुरंगे (tunnels) बनती हैं जिनसे होके रेलें पास करती हैं। मगर पहले तो नदियों के किनारों को पकड़ के ही, या दो पहाड़ों के बीच के भारी चढ़ाव-उतार वाले रास्तों के जरिये ही पहाड़ी प्रदेशों में आना जाना संभव था। यदि ऐसा न किया जाता तो खूंखार जानवर खा जाते और पहाड़ों के ऊपर चढ़ना गैर मुमकिन हो जाता। यों भी पहाड़ों पर चढ़ना असंभव ही होता है। इसलिये पहले के जमाने में घाटों या घाटियों के ही जरिये आ जा सकते थे।

इसीलिये राजे महाराजाओं और शासकों को इस बात की जरूरत बनी रहती थी कि इन घाटों की निगरानी की जाय, चौकसी और देखभाल बराबर की जाय, पहरेदारी हो। नहीं तो दुश्मनों या हमला करने वालों का गिरोह जानें किस रास्ते कब भीतर घुस जाय और दखल जमा ले। दिन रात इन घाटों पर पहरा दिये विना काम नहीं चल सकता था। दूसरा उपाय था भी नहीं। इसीलिये इस बात की जिम्मेवारी जिन लोगों पर रखी जाती थी वे घटवार या घटवाल कहे जाने लगे। पर्वतीय प्रदेश में घाटों की संख्या के ही हिसाब से कम या ज्यादा घटवाल तैनात किये जाते थे। भागलपुर, मुंगेर या गया जिले के भी दक्षिणी पहाड़ी इलाकों में जमींदार के बजाय घटवार ही रहते थे। आज भी कुछ न कुछ पाये जाते हैं। हालांकि उनके वह काम अब कहीं भी शायद ही पाये जाते हैं। अब तो इस वैज्ञानिक युग में सभी बातें बदल चुकी हैं।

मगर घटवार लोग यह काम खुद तो करते न थे। वे इसी काम के लिये काफी तादाद में चौकीदार रखते थे। और जैसे आज चौकीदारों के ऊपर दफादार होते हैं उसी तरह पहले भी रखे जाते थे। ताकि चौकीदारों के काम की देखभाल ठिकाने से होती रहे। इन्हीं सब कामों और उनके खर्च के लिये जो जमीनें घटवारों को दी जाती थीं उन्हें घटवारी या घटवाली कहते हैं। उन्हें इन जमीनों के लिये सरकार को माल या मालगुजारी बहुत ही कम देनी होती थी। एक तो बंगाल और विहार के जमींदारों की मालगुजारी यों ही कम ठहरी। तिस पर भी तुर्रा यह कि घटवाली जमीनों पर और भी कम लगती थी। यह मालगुजारी घटती बढ़ती भी न थी। जहां कहीं इस्तमरारी बन्दोबस्त नहीं है वहां तो मालगुजारी घटती बढ़ती है और इस सूबे में भी कहीं कहीं ऐसा पाया जाता है । मगर जब यह इस्तमरारी बन्दोबस्त न था तब भी घटवाली जमीनें इस्तमरारी ही थीं। संथाल परगने की जांच की रिपोर्ट में घटवालों के बारे में यों लिखा है :—

"In consideration of their preforming certain duties in support of the police the ghatwals were granted a special status and protection. Their tenures were assessed to a low rent fixed in perpetuity and were declared inalienable and impartible. The ghatwals were precluded from granting any lease or creating any charge upon their estates beyond the term of their own life, except in case of leases for mining, irrigation or building, for which the commissioner's consent is required, and for reclamation. The net result is that when a ghatwal dies, his debts are simultaneously extinguished" (page 61).

''पुलिस की मदद के लिये कुछ खास ढंग के कामों के करने के कारण ही घटवालों को विशेष स्थान दिया गया है और उनकी रक्षा का भी खास प्रबन्ध है। उन्हें दी गई जमीनों पर बहुत ही कम लगान या माल देना पड़ता है जो घटता बढ़ता नहीं। वे जमीनें न तो बिक सकती हैं और न उनका बंटवारा किया जा सकता है। जैसा कि मुश्तरका खान्दान में जुदाई होने पर और जमीनों का होता है। घटवालों को अधिकार नहीं है कि अपनी जमीनें आमतौर से पट्टे पर दे दें। वे किसी तरह का ऐसा खर्च या कर्ज भी उन जमीनों पर ले नहीं सकते जो उनकी मौत के बाद कायम रह जाय। हां, खानों, सिंचाई के कामों और मकानों के ही लिये पट्टे पर जमीनें दे सकते हैं। मगर इसमें भी कमिश्नर की मंजूरी जरूरी होती है। जंगल, पड़ती आदि गैर आबाद जमीनों को आबाद करने के लिए पट्टा जरूर दे सकते हैं। इन सब बन्धनों का सम्मिलित परिणाम यह है कि ज्यों ही कोई घटवाल मरा कि उसका कर्ज भी अपने आप खत्म हो गया।''

आगे चलके ६२ वें पृष्ठ में यह भी लिखा है कि "The ghatwals are charged with the maintenance of chaukidars in their estates and on failure to meet these obligations are liable to the dismissal." ''घटवालों को अपनी जमींदारी में चौकीदारों को रखना और तनखाह देना पड़ता है और ऐसा न करने पर उनकी घटवाली छीन ली जा सकती है''। इसका सीधा अर्थ यही है कि अब पुराने ढंग से न तो उन्हें घाटों की रक्षा करनी पड़ती है और न चौकीदार वगैरह रखने पड़ते हैं। अब तो सिर्फ यही होता है कि जिस घटवाल की जमींदारी के मौजों में जितने चौकीदार हों उनके वेतन के लिये उन गांव वालों से चौकीदारी टैक्स नही वसूला जाकर घटवालों को ही अपने पास से वह वेतन चुकाना पड़ता है। मगर एक बात जरूर हो गई है कि बिहार प्रान्त के सभी पहाड़ी इलाकों में घटवाल या जमींदार जगह जगह रास्तों के नाकों पर अपने खास नौकर या चौकीदार रखते हैं। ये पुलिस वाले चौकीदार नहीं होके

घटवालों और जमींदारों के निजी नौकर होते हैं। इनका काम यही होता है कि गरीब लोग जब पास के जंगलों में लकड़ी काटने जाते हैं तो उनसे पैसे वसूला करते हैं। इन्हीं पैसों या टैक्सों को अब घाट कहने लगे हैं। हमने यह दृश्य खुद देखा है। जंगली इलाकों के किसानों और गरीबों को अपने घरेलू काम के लिये और अकसर बेंचकर जीविका करने के लिये भी जंगल से प्रतिदिन लकड़ी, पत्ता, घास, बांस, फल, फूल वगैरह लेना जरूरी होता है। मगर जब तक घाटवाला टैक्स पहले ही चुकता न कर लें जंगलों में वे घुसने पाते ही नहीं। यह अत्याचार बहुत ही बढ़ा चढ़ा है। छोटानागपुर के बाहर भी मुंगेर आदि जिलों के पहाड़ी इलाकों के किसान इससे तबाह हैं।

खासमहाल और घटवालों के अलावे तीसरे ढंग के जमींदार तो यहां वैसे ही हैं जैसे विहार खंड में। इनमें कोई बुनियादी फर्क नहीं है जैसा कि कही चुके हैं। इन छओं जिलों में यों तो छोटे मोटे जमींदार और घटवाल बहुतेरे हैं। मगर बड़े बड़ों की संख्या बहुत ज्यादा नहीं है। हम जानकारी के लिये यहां कुछ प्रमुख लोगों को ही गिना देना चाहते हैं। मगर ऐसा करने के पूर्व हजारीबाग के १९१७ के गजेटियर की एक बात लिखना जरूरी समझते हैं। उसके लेखक हैं ई० लिस्टर, सी.आई.ई., आई.सी.एस.। उसके १६५ पृष्ठ में जमींदारों के बारे में जो कुछ लिखा गया है उससे साफ है कि उन्हें बहुत ही नाममात्र के लिये सरकार को माल देना पड़ता है। वे लोग खूब मजा मारते हैं। वहां लिखा है — "The demand of Rs. 47620 (due in respect of seventy permanently held estates) represents about seven rupees a square mile, and the cash rent alone which landlords receive are twelve lakhs, on which sum the government revenue is less than four percent over and above the cash rent. The landlords have extensive areas in their own cultivation and also collect a considerable produce rent."

''इस्तमरारी बन्दोबस्त (परमानेन्ट सेट्लमेन्ट) वाली सत्तर जमींदारियों से जो कुल ४७२६० रुपये सरकारी मालगुजारी में मिलते हैं वह प्रति वर्गमील सात रुपये के हिसाब से पड़ते हैं। मगर उनके बदले जमीदार लोग जो सिर्फ नगद लगान किसानों से वसूल करते हैं वह बारह लाख रुपया है। इसके मानी हैं यह कि नगद लगान के ४ प्रतिशत से भी कम वे लोग सरकार को देते हैं! इसके सिवाय उनकी अपनी खेती की भी बहुत ज्यादा जमीनें हैं और बंटाई या भावली लगान भी काफी वसूल करते हैं''।

यह तो लूट है। घटवालों को कम माल देना पड़ता है सही। मगर झारखंडी जमींदारों की तो देखिये। यह कोई हजारीबाग जिले की खास बात थोड़े ही है।

यही दशा सभी जिलों में है। किसानों से जो नगद वसूली करते हैं उसका चार सैकड़ा भी सरकार को नहीं देते! बटाई, भावली, जंगल की आमदनी और कोयला, अबरक वगैरः की आय की तो बात ही जाने दीजिये। उसका तो हिसाब ही नहीं कि कितनी है। जिरात, कामत और बकाश्त के नाम पर भी बहुत ज्यादा जमीनें पड़ी हैं। सलामी और नजराना का कुछ कहना हीं नहीं। अनेक अबवाब और सूद, तावान वगैरः जुदे ही ठहरे! यह लूट नहीं है, तो है क्या? फिर भी जब किसानों की ओर से कोई भी दावा पेश हो तो न सिर्फ जमींदार और घटवाल, बल्कि उनके दोस्त, दलाल और सरकारी आदमी भी हाय तोबा मचाने लगते हैं, जिससे पता चलता है कि जमींदार मरे जा रहे हैं!

अच्छा तो अब कुछ प्रमुख जमींदारों को हर जिले के हिसाब से गिना के आगे बढ़ेंगे। संथाल परगने में ये हैं (१) पत्संडा इस्टेट (२) मनिहारी इस्टेट (३) बलबड्डा इस्टेट (४) महेशपुर इस्टेट (५) बभनगांवा की घटवाली इस्टेट वगैरह। हजारीबाग में, (१) सतगांवा (चन्द्रधारी सिंह) इस्टेट (२) गरवां (नाबालिग) इस्टेट (३) दोरंडा इस्टेट (४) पालगंज इस्टेट (५) कुंदा इस्टेट (६) पद्मा इस्टेट (७) धनवार इस्टेट वगैरह। रांची में, (१) पालकोट (२) रातू (३) मसमानो ठाकुर गांव (४) बिड़ला ब्रदर्स की चौरासी गांव की जमींदारी (५) कैरोगढ़ वगैरह। मानभूम में (१) पंचकोट (२) बराहबाजार (३) ईचागढ़ (४) पाटकुम (५) बेगम कुदार (६) झालदा (७) मऊवाजर (८) कतरास (९) झरिया वगैरह। सिंहभूम में, (१) दलभूम इस्टेट (२) बन्दगांव (३) सरंडा (४) आनंदपुर (५) चैनपुर (६) केवा (७) ताता (जमशेदपुर) वगैरह । पलामू में, (१) रांका (२) चैनपुर (३) लादी (४) पथरा (५) सोनपुरा (६) नावा (७) विश्रामपुर (८) टोरी (९) लटेहार (१०) हामी (११) नवाडीह (१२) पांकी (१३) वालूमठ (१४) कोसियारा (१५) नगर उटारी (१६) पाटन (१७) हरिहरगंज वगैरह। और भी अनेक बड़े जमींदार हैं।

(५)

किसानों की जमीनें और उनकी तकलीफें

हमें आगे बढ़ने के पहले यहां के किसानों की जमीनें कितनी तरह की हैं यह बात भी जान लेना जरूरी है। झारखंड के किसानों की यह खास बात है। यों तो विहार के किसानों की जमीनें कई तरह की होती हैं और वे झारखंड में भी पाई जाती हैं। मगर उनके अलावे कुछ खास ढंग की भी काश्तकारी जमीनें हैं और यहीं हैं यहां के किसानों के प्राण स्वरूप। बेशक जमींदारों की जिरात जमीनों के बारे में भी विहार की अपेक्षा यहां कुछ विशेषता है। इसलिये उसे भी जान लेना जरूरी है। मगर यह बात पीछे कही जायगी। अभी तो काश्तकारी जमीनों की खास बातों पर ही पहले विचार कर लेना है।

बिहार तथा छोटानागपुर के काश्तकारी कानूनों की चौथी धारा में किसानों (tenants) की कई किस्में बताई गई हैं। दोनों कानूनों की चौथी ही धारा में यह बात लिखी है। कुछ किस्में तो दोनों में एक ही हैं। टेन्योर होल्डर या अन्डर टेन्योर होल्डर दोनों ही में आते हैं। टेन्योर होल्डर कहते हैं जमींदार के ठेकेदार को जो आमतौर से लगान की वसूली के लिये जमीन पर किसानों को आवाद करता है। साधारणतः वह खेती नहीं करता। किन्तु लगान किसानों से लेके जमींदार का हिस्से देता है और बाकी खुद लेता है। वह गैर आबाद जमीन को भी वहां किसान बसा के आबाद करवाने का ठीका लेता है। उस ठेकेदार से जो फिर वैसा ही ठीका ले वही मातहत ठेकेदार या अन्डर टेन्योर होल्डर कहा जाता है। मगर जो आदमी किसी से भी जमीन लेता है आमतौर से सिर्फ खेती करने के लिये वही रैयत कहा जाता है। जो उसके मातहत होगा वह अन्डर रैयत या शिकमी कहा जाता है। इस तरह टेन्योर होल्डर और रैयत में अन्तर है। मगर टेनेन्ट (किसान) तो सभी हैं। इस तरह दोनों कानूनों में ये चार तरह के किसान बताये गये हैं।

इसी तरह दोनों ही में कायमी (occupancy) और गैर कायमी (non-occupancy) किसान भी कहे गये हैं। कायमी किसान की जमीन अपनी मानी जाती है और उसे विहार में अपनी जमीन पर पेड़, बांस वगैरह लगाने, ईंट,

खपड़ा बनाने और कूआं, तालाब खोदने का हक प्राप्त है। उस पर वह अपने घर गिरस्ती के लिये पक्के मकान भी बनवा सकता है। इसी प्रकार बिना काश्तकारी कानून की शर्त्तें तोड़े या वाकी लगान की डिग्री में नीलाम कराये वह जमीन से बेदखल भी नहीं किया जा सकता है। मगर गैरकायमी किसान को ये कोई भी हक प्राप्त नहीं है। उसका लगान भी आसानी से बढ़ाया जा सकता है। मगर कायमी का लगान बढ़ाना कठिन है — दिक्कत से होता है। यह ठीक है कि झारखंड के कायमी किसान को मकान वगैरह बनाने का हक नहीं प्राप्त है और यह भारी अन्याय है। वह बाग भी लगा नहीं सकता और न ईंट, खपड़े बना सकता है। फिर भी ये दोनों ही किस्म के किसान भी दोनों जगह हैं।

इसके बाद फर्क चलता है। विहार में पूर्वोक्त छे तरह के किसानों के अलावे एक सातवें प्रकार का किसान है जिसे "फिक्स्डरेट" (fixed rate) या गुजश्तेदार किसान कहते हैं। उसका लगान इस्तमरारी होता है, जो न कभी बढ़ता है और न घटता है। मगर झारखंड के छोटानागपुर के पांच जिलों में इस्तमरारी किसान की जगह कई और तरह के किसान पाये जाते हैं। वे तीन तरह के हैं (१) भुंइहर या भुंइहरी जमीन वाले, (२) खुंटकट्टीदार या खुटकट्टी जमीन वाले, और (३) मुंडारी खुटकट्टीदार या मुंडारी खुदटकट्टी जमीन वाले। इन तीनों का लगान आमतौर से घटता बढ़ता नहीं है। मगर इनमें कुछ कुछ खास बातें हैं। इसीलिये ये तीनों ही जुदा जुदा हैं। इसीलिये इनकी ये इस्तमरारी जमीनें भी भुंइहरी, खुटकट्टी और मुंडारी खुटकट्टी के नाम से क्रमशः विख्यात हैं। इस्तमरारी जमीनों में और खुटकट्टी में जो थोड़ा अन्तर है वह आगे मालूम हो जायगा। झारखंड में एक तरह के और भी किसान होते हैं जो गांव के मुखिया या जेठरैयत की किस्म के होते हैं और जिन्हें प्रधान, मांझी और मानकी कहते हैं। कहीं कहीं ठीकेदार और इजारादार के नाम से भी वे लोग पुकारे जाते हैं। प्रधान तो संथाल परगना, हजारीबाग, रांची में और मांझी हजारीबाग, मानभूम में तथा मानकी नानभूम और सिंहभूम में आमतौर से पाये जाते हैं। यों तो इधर उधर भी मिल सकते हैं।

कहते हैं कि जंगलों में पहले पहल जो किसान आये उनने जगह जगह खेती वगैरह के लिये जमीनें चुन लीं, ठीक कर लीं और आबाद कर लीं। वही भुंइहर कहाये। यह झारखंड का खास शब्द है। और जगह यह शब्द बोला नहीं जाता। यह भी कहा जाता है कि यहां पहले मुंडा लोग आये और उनके पीछे आये उरांव लोग। इसलिये मुंडा लोगों की पहले ठीक की हुई जमीनें जब उरांव लोगों ने हथियालीं तो वे बेचारे दूसरी फिक्र में लगे और उनने अपने लिये

पीछे जंगल काट के जो जमीनें तैयार कीं वह मुंडारी खुटकट्टी के नाम से विख्यात हुईं और उनकी पहली जमीनें भुंइहरी कही गईं। चाहे जो भी बात हो — या तो यहां मुंडा लोगों के साथ ही साथ रहने वाले उरांव लोगों ने जो जमीनें हथियाईं वहीं भुंइहरी हुईं और मुंडावाली मुंडारी खुटकट्टी या मुंडा लोगों से ही छिनी जमीनें भुंइहरी हुईं और उनने पीछे अपने लिये मुंडारी खुटकट्टी तैयार की — हर हालत में ये दो तरह की जमीनें पहले बनी थीं। यह ठीक है कि भुंइहरी जमीनें आमतौर से उरांव लोगों के पास ही हैं।

एक तीसरी जमीन भी है जिसे खुटकट्टी कहते हैं। वह मुंडारी खुटकट्टी से जुदी है। यहां के काश्तकारी कानून के अनुसार जिस किसी गांव के बसाने वालों ने खूंटी या जंगल काट के जमीनें शुरू में आबाद कीं वही तो खुटकट्टी के नाम से प्रसिद्ध हुईं। मगर चाहे गांव बसाने वाले रहे हों या न रहे हों, फिर भी मुंडा लोगों ने जंगलों को काट के जिन्हें बसाया वही मुंडारी खुटकट्टी कही गई। इस तरह खुटकट्टी जमीनें भी आमतौर से सिर्फ उरांव लोगों के ही हाथ में हैं। यहां भुंइहरी जमीन को भुंइहरी पत्थरगड़ी, खुटकट्टी को खुटकट्टी पत्थरगड़ी तथा मुंडारी को भी मुंडारी पत्थरगड़ी सिर्फ इसलिये कहते हैं कि जब पहले पहले १८६९ में या उसके आस पास यहां सर्वे हुआ तो इन जमीनों की चौहद्दी में पत्थर गाड़ के इन्हें जुदा जुदा कर दिया गया। नहीं तो पीछे चल के झमेला और गड़बड़ी हो सकती थी।

पहले जमाने में किसानों की जमीनें और भी दो प्रकार की थीं, जो मालूम होता है, पीछे छिन गईं। ये थीं मझिहस और बेठखेता। मझिहस का अर्थ है माझी का अंश, भाग या हिस्सा और माझी कहते हैं मुखिया को। इस तरह यह नाम बताता है कि जैसे आज प्रधान, मानकी या माझी वगैरह की खास जमीनें हैं तैसे बहुत पहले भी थीं। मगर जमींदारों ने पीछे छीन के उन्हें अपनी जिरात जमीन बना लीं। इसी तरह बेठखेता का अर्थ है बेगार के लिये दिया गया खेत। बेठ कहते हैं बेगार को। मालूम होता है, पहले जिन लोगों से खास तौर से जमींदार लोग बेगार करवाते थे, जैसा कि संथाल परगने के दामिन इलाके में अभीतक सड़क वगैरह बनाने में आमतौर से सभी ग्रामवासियों से बेगार कराई जाती है, उन्हें कुछ जमीनें इसीलिये देते थे। दामिन में रोडसेस के बदले यह बेगार करवाई जाती है जिसे जांच कमिटी ने बन्द करने को कहा है। वही जमीनें बेंठखेता कही जाती हैं। मगर अब ये दोनों ही — मझिहस और बेठखेता — जमींदार की खास या जिरात जमीन में गिनी जाती हैं। यह बात छोटानागपुर के काश्तकारी कानून की ११८(ब) धारा में लिखी है। उसी कानून की १२४वीं धारा

में यह भी लिखा है कि जिस मौजे में बेठखेता या मझिहस जमीन १८६९ के सर्वे में दर्ज है वहां उसके अलावे दूसरी जमीन जमींदार की खास, जिरात या कामत मानी नहीं जा सकती है। फलतः मझिहस और बेठखेता का ताल्लुक तो अब किसानों से रहा नहीं।

किसानों की और भी जमीनें हैं और वे हैं सबसे महत्वपूर्ण। मगर उनका विचार करने के पहले इन पूर्वोक्त तीन खास तरह की जमीनों की कुछ जरूरी खूबियों को भी जान लेना चाहिये। सबसे पहले भुंइहरी को लीजिये। यह ठीक है कि ये जमीनें पहले बनी थीं। अब तो वे घटती बढ़ती हैं नहीं। ज्यों की त्यों रहती हैं। इसीलिये भुंइहरी भी एक निश्चित परिमाण में ही है। उसका लगान भी बहुत कम होता है। हमें तो यह भी कहा गया है कि प्रायः चार आने बीघे से ज्यादा नहीं होता। लेकिन इस जमीन की जो सबसे बड़ी खूबी है वह यह है कि एक तो वह किसी भी हालत में किसी डिग्री में नीलाम नहीं हो सकती। दूसरे उस जमीन वाले किसान को किसी भी डिग्री में गिरफ्तार करके जेल में रखा नहीं जा सकता। तीसरे यदि वह भुंइहारी जमीन समूची या उसका एक भाग किसी को ठेके में दे दे तो ठेकेदार को उसमें कायमी (occupancy) हक हासिल हो नहीं सकता। चौथे जिस प्रकार पहली गिनाई हुई दोनों सूचियों वाली यहां की जातियों को यह हक नहीं है कि कोआपरेटिव सोसाइटी के हाथ में १५ साल से ज्यादा के लिये, सो भी सिवाय भोगबन्धक या भुगुतबन्ध (usufructary mortgage) के और किसी भी ढंग से, जमीन दे सकें, और न दूसरों के ही हाथ। इसी तरह सात साल से ज्यादे के लिये, या पांच साल से ज्यादे के लिये किसी भी हालत में ठेके पर किसी को नहीं दे सकते। ठीक यही हालत भुंइहारी जमीन की भी है। पांचवीं बात यह है कि जैसे पूर्वोक्त आदिवासी या पिछड़ी जाति वाले अपनी जमीन अपनी ही बिरादरी (दल) वालों के हाथ उसी थाने के अन्दर ही अदला बदली कर सकते या बेंच सकते हैं, या डिप्टी कमिश्नर की राय से अपने सगे सम्बन्धी को दे सकते हैं, ठीक वही बात भुंइहरी जमीन वाले किसानों की उन जमीनों पर लागू है जो भुईहरी वाले मौजे में भुइहरी के अलावे भी होती हैं। छठीं बात यह है कि भुइंहारी जमीन के खिलाफ न तो कोई डिग्री ही हो सकती है और न उसनें वह नीलाम हीं हो सकती है। सातवीं बात यह है कि यदि भुइहरी जमीन के लगान के बाकी होने पर उसकी डिग्री हो तो सिर्फ उस जमीन की पैदावार से ही वह सधाई जायगी, या उस किसान की किसी और भी चल सम्पत्ति से। छोटानागपुर के काश्तकारी कानून की ४७, ४८, ४८ (अ) तथा १८४ (अ) धाराओं में यह बातें लिखी हैं।

खुटकट्टी जमीन की खास बातें ये हैं कि एक बार उस जमीन का सर्वे हो जाने पर जितनी जमीन खुटकट्टी लिखी जा चुकी है, उससे अधिक वह कभी हो नहीं सकती। वह घटती बढ़ती नहीं है। यह पहली बात है। दूसरे यदि खुटकट्टी जमीन कायम होने के ही समय लगान बढ़ाने की कोई शर्त्त तय न पाई हो तो जितनी खुटकट्टी जमीनें १९०८ से पहले के बीस साल के भीतर न बनके उसके पहले बनी थीं उनका लगान कभी बढ़ नहीं सकता। तीसरे, अगर ऐसा न होने पर उस जमीन का लगान बढ़ाया भी जांय — क्योंकि १९०८ के पूर्व के बीस साल के भीतर ही वैसी जमीन कायम होने पर लगान बढ़ सकता है — तो हर हालत में उस जमीन का कुल लगान उस कायमी जमीन के लगान के आधे से ज्यादा हर्गिज नहीं हो सकता है जो उसी मौजे में उसी ढंग की हो और उसे उसी तरह की सभी सहूलियतें प्राप्त हों। उसी कानून की ३७ और १३४ धाराओं में यह बात लिखी है। आमतौर से जो बन्धन यहां के किसानों की जमीनों की खरीद बिक्री पर है वह तो खुदकट्टी के भी लिये हुई।

इसी प्रकार मुंडारी खुटकट्टी की भी कुछ विशेषतायें हैं। पहली यह है कि जो जमीन एक बार सर्वे में मुंडारी खुटकट्टी लिखी जा चुकी तो उसके अलावे और जमीन उसमें आ नहीं सकती। दूसरी यह कि उस जमीन का इजारा भुगुतबन्ध के सिवाय और तरह का हो नहीं सकता। सो भी किसी भी तरह सात साल से ज्यादा के लिये हर्गिज नहीं। तीसरे उस जमीन का ठेका किसी को दिया जा सकता नहीं, सिवा मुंडा रैयत को खेती के लिये गैर आबाद जमीन के ठेके के, या वैसे ही रैयत को गैर आवाद जमीन के मुकर्ररी ठेके के सिवा, जो इसलिये दिया जाय कि उसमें जितनी हो सके खेती के लिये आबाद करे। चौथे वह जमीन किसी डिग्री में बिक सकती नहीं। पांचवें विना डिप्टी कमिश्नर की आज्ञा के उस जमीन का लगान बढ़ाया जा सकता नहीं। उसमें भी यह बात सिद्ध करना होगा कि जब लगान बढ़ाने की दरखास्त पड़ी उससे पूर्व बीस साल के अन्दर ही वह जमीन मुंडारी खुटकट्टी बनी है। और अगर लगान बढ़ा भी तो ठीक वैसे ही बढ़ेगा जैसा कि खुटकट्टी के बारे में कहा गया है — यांनी वैसी ही जमीन के आधे से ज्यादा कुल मिलाके बढ़ा हुआ लगान नहीं हो सकता। छठें, उस जमीन का लगान सिर्फ सर्टिफिकेट या जब्तीकुर्की के द्वारा वसूल होता है। मगर यह बात वहीं होती है जहां उस जमीन का सर्वे हो चुका हो। लेकिन सर्वे न होने पर बकाये की नालिश होती है। फिर भी उसकी डिग्री की वसूली या तो उसकी चल सम्पत्ति से होती है, या यादि उसे किसी और से लगान या कर्ज वसूल होने को हो तो उसे ही जब्त करके। अगर यह कोई भी न हो सके

तो डिप्टी कमिश्नर उस जमीन को जब्त करके लगान वगैरह की वसूली का प्रबन्ध करता है। वसूली के बाद वह जमीन फिर वापस दे दी जाती है। यह बातें उस कानून की २४०, २४३, २४६, २४८ और २५६ आदि धाराओं में लिखी हैं।

इस प्रकार मुख्य मुख्य बातें इन तीनों जमीनों के सम्बन्ध की लिखो गई हैं। इनके अलावे और भी बातें हैं। मगर उन्हें जानने के लिये समूचा टेनेन्सी कानून ही पढ़ना उचित है।

अब जो सबसे महत्वपूर्ण बात झारखंडी किसानों की जमीन के बारे में है और जिस पर ही उनके आराम का दारमदार है उसका लिखा जाना ज़रूरी है। बात यह है कि इस पहाड़ी इलाके की यह हालत है कि जिस जमीन में खेती होती रहती है वह कुछी दिनों के बाद अकसर बेकार हो जाती है। या तो उसकी उत्पादन शक्ति ही नष्ट हो जाती है, या जंगली जानवरों का उत्पात बढ़ जाने से उसे छोड़ना हीं पड़ता है, या आसपास में जो झरना, नदी आदि सिंचाई का सामान था वही खत्म हो जाता है, या पहाड़ी पानी की कभी कभी बाढ़ आ जाने से वह जमीन बालू कंकड़ के नीचे दब जाती है। इसी प्रकार के अनेक कारणों से किसानों को जमीनें छोड़नी ही पड़ती हैं। यदि जमींदार या उसके अमलों का जुल्म बढ़ गया या जंगल से लकड़ी आदि मिलने का कष्ट हुआ तब भी छोड़ना हीं पड़ता है और वे दूसरी जगह जाके नई जमीन आबाद करते हैं। यों भी जमीन की कमी हो जाने पर या उपज की कमी होने पर यदि नई जमीन आबाद न की जाय तो गुजर कैसे हो? जंगल में फिजूल की पैदावार जमीनें तो पड़ी रहती हैं नहीं। इमेशा नई जमीनें ही खोदखाद और कोड़काड़ के आबाद की जाती हैं।

कभी कभी ऐसा होता है कि किसान की जमीन के तख्ते (holding) के अन्दर कुछ जमीन धनखर, धनखेत या धानी होती है, जिसे दोन भी कहते हैं और कुछ ऊंची, बारी या टांड़ होती है। फलतः मौका लगने पर ऊंची या टांड़ को ही खोदके और चारों ओर आर और बांध लगाके दोन या धनखेत तैयार करते हैं। टांड़ में तो चाहे कुछ रबी या मूंग वगैरह पैदा होती रहती है, या कुछ भी पैदा नहीं होता। हर हालत में उसे दोन बना लेते हैं। जो जमीन पहले खेती में थी, मगर पीछे गैर आवाद हो गई, उसे भी फिर से आर वार देके दोन बनाते हैं। आमतौर से ऐसी जमीन धान के ही लिये बनाई जाती हैं। इस तरह जो जमीन तैयार की जाती है उसे कोड़कर, अरियट, बाहुबला और जलसासन कहते हैं। इन शब्दों का अर्थ स्पष्ट है। कोड़ कर ही तो वह तैयार

की जाती है। विना कोड़े खोदे तो बन सकती नहीं। इसीलिये कोड़कर कही जाती है। उसकी चारों ओर आर या बांध देके पानी रोकने के कारण उसे अरियट कहते हैं। अपने बाहु के बल से ही वह तैयार की जाती है। इसीलिये उसे बाहुबला भी कहते हैं। जल के भीतर, जल के कब्जे में रहती है। पानी का उस पर बराबर शासन रहता है। धान की जमीन हीं तो ठहरी। इसीलिये उसका नाम जलशासन या जलसासन पड़ा होगा। उसे खंडवत भी कहते हैं। अकसर धान के खेतों में पानी जमा करते हैं और मौके से आर काट के बहा भी देते हैं। फिर भर भी लेते हैं। धान की खेती में ऐसा करना पड़ता है। बांध या आर को पानी बहाने के लिये जहां काट देते हैं उसे खांड़ कहते हैं। धानी जमीन इसीलिये खंडवत भी कही जाने लगी होगी।

<1.12.41> ऐसी जमीन को पलामू और रांची जिले में उटकर जमीन भी कहते हैं। आमतौर से कोड़कर और उटकर में कोई खास अन्तर नहीं है। लेकिन व्यवहार में साधारणतया यही माना जाता है कि जो जमीन दोन के साथ मिली होती है, या जो किसान के तख्ते के भीतर ही टांड़ जमीन होती है जब उसे कोड़ करके दोन बनाते हैं तो उसे कोड़कर नाम दिया जाता है। मगर जब उसके तख्ते से बाहर या दोन के पास न हो, किन्तु जमींदार की खास गैरमजरुआ जमीन को खोद कोड़ के आवाद करें और खेती के लायक बनायें तो उसे उटकर कहते हैं। इसीलिये उटकर का ज्यादा प्रचार पलामू जिले में ही है। उटकर में ज्यादातर गोंदली, सावां, मडुवा, कुर्थी, मकई आदि फसलें ही होती हैं। पलामू की तो अधिकांश जमीन ऐसी ही है। यदि कहीं दोन के पास मौके से जमीन मिल गई तब तो उसे कोड़कर बनायेंगे ही। मगर ऐसा मौका मिलता ही कहां है।

इसी प्रकार संथाल परगने में एक खास ढंग की जमीन खेती के लिये तैयार की जाती है। इसे दामिन इलाके के पहड़िया लोग तैयार करते हैं। पहड़िया लोग वहां के सबसे पुराने निवासी माने जाते हैं। संथाल लोग तो संथाल परगने में, कहा जाता है, १८१० में ही पहले पहल पहुंचे। पहड़िया लोग इतने लड़ाकू माने जाते थे कि किसी को घुसने नहीं देते थे। जो ऐसी कोशिश करता था उसे बड़ी बेरहमी से मारते काटते और भगा देते थे। वह निहायत ही भोली कौंम है। उन्हें खेतीबारी का कोई भी दूसरा तरीका नहीं मालूम है। वह हलबैलों वाली खेती जानते ही नहीं और न अबतक जीविका के लिये कोई दूसरा प्रचलित या सभ्य रास्ता उनने सीख पाया है। इसके लिये सरकार ने कोई खास उपाय किया भी नहीं है।

कहा जाता है कि सबसे पहले वार्न हेस्टिंग्स की नजर इन पहड़ियों की ओर गई और उसे उन्हें सर करने की सूझी। कैप्टेन ब्राउन की मातहती में उसने एक फौजी टुकड़ी, वहां पहले पहल भेजी। फिर कुछ दिन बाद मिस्टर जेम्स और क्लीवलैंड नामक दो अंग्रेज भेजे गये कि उनकी हालत जानी जाय। क्योंकि फौज से उनका सर होना य सभ्य बनाया जाना कुछ कठिन जान पड़ा। क्लीवलैंड ने कहा जाता है, तेरह सौ सरदारों को चुनके उनके भीतर काम करने और उन्हें सभ्य बनाने को भेजा जिन्हें मासिक दस रुपये दिये जाते थे। आज भी ये सीरदार या सरदार उन आदिवासियो के इलाके में पाये जाते हैं। क्लीवलैंड ने उनके सुधारने के कुछ रास्ते और भी सुझाये। मगर उन पर सरकार ने अमल किया ही नहीं।

पहड़िया लोगों की हालत यह है जंगलों में पहाड़ों पर ही ज्यादातर रहते हैं। इसीलिये पहड़िया बोले भी जाते हैं। जंगली फलों, मूलों और पत्तों के सिवाय वे एक तरह की खेती पुराने जमाने से करते आते हैं। यही दशा सभी मुल्कों में पहले, ऐतिहासिक युग के पूर्व, पाई जाती थी जब हल वगैरह का आविष्कार नहीं हुआ था। खेती के बाद जब कुछी दिनों में जमीनें उपजाऊ नहीं रह जाती थीं तो नये स्थान में जंगल वगैरह काट के नये खेत बनाये जाते थे। उनके पुराने पड़ जाने पर फिर दूसरी जमीन तैयार की जाती थी। जमीन में नोकीली लकड़ी से और पीछे औजार बनने पर उसीसे छोटे-छोटे — नन्हें नन्हें — गढ़े, छिद्र या कुंड बना के उन्हीं में बीज डालते थे। आज भी दियारे की जमीनों या बालू वालियों पर खरबूज, तरबूज, ककड़ी, करैले आदि खेती ऐसी ही ढंग से की जाती है। वही बीज मिट्टी के नीचे पड़े-पड़े उगते और फलते फूलते हैं।

पहड़िया लोग भी अब तक यही करते चले आ रहे हैं। उसी ढंग के छिद्र, सूराख या कुंड बना के उसमें मकई, ज्वार, अरहर और घघरा आदि अन्नों के बीज डाल देते हैं। जमीन के उन छिद्रों को संस्कृत के पुराने ग्रन्थों में कुंड भी कहते हैं। उनमें खेती करने के कारण हीं उसे कुंडचास या कुरांवचास कहने लगे। चास तो बंगला में खेती को कहते ही हैं और चासी कहते हैं किसान को। ''कुंड'' का ही कुंड़वा या कुडांव होके कुरांव हो गया और कुरांव चास कहने लग गये। संथाल परगने की जांच कमिटी की रिपोर्ट में भी उसे कुरवा या कुंडवा (kurwa) लिखा है। उसे ही झूमचास भी कहते हैं। बंगाल के जंगली इलाकों में झूम जमीन या झूमलैंड (Jhumland) के बारे में हमने पढ़ा है। जंगलों और झाड़ियों को काट या जला के साफ करते हैं। असल में जलाते ही हैं ज्यादातर।

बिना जलाये झाड़ियों का साफ होना कठिन होता है। जलाने से जो जमीन पर राख पैदा होती है उससे खाद का काम हो जाता है। इसी तरह की तैयार जमीन को झूमचास या झूमलैंड कहते हैं। पहड़िया लोग भी पहाड़ों पर और उनकी ढाबू जमीनों पर इसी तरह जमीनें तैयार करके खेती करते आ रहे हैं।

अब इधर पांच सात साल से उसमें बाधा दी जाने लगी है। बात असल यह है कि आज से प्रायः चालीस साल पहले उन सभी जंगलों को संरक्षित घोषित किया गया था। मगर संरक्षित (reserved) होने पर भी जानें किस खयाल से या डर से सरकार ने पहड़िया लोगों को छेड़ा नहीं। अब इधर कुछी साल से उस पर अमल होने लगा है। जमींदार या सरकार ने उन गरीबों के इस सनातन अधिकार पर प्रहार करना बड़ी बेमुरव्वती और बेरहमी से शुरू कर दिया है। जंगलों को रिजर्व कर लेना तो सरकार के हाथ की बात है। उसमें कोई फौजी लड़ाई या लाठी चलाने का सवाल तो है नहीं। मगर आखिर उन गरीब किसानों की जीवन यात्रा भी तो होना जरूरी है। जंगल रिजर्व (संरक्षित) किये जाते हैं लोगों की ही भलाई के नाम पर। मगर लोग ही मर जांय तो भलाई कैसी? तब जंगल से फायदा किसका होगा? क्या उसकी लकड़ी से उन अन्न बिना मरे हुए पहड़िया लोगों का शव दहन होगा? यह तो बंगाल के हिन्दुओं वाला ''हरिबोल'' वाला ही किस्सा हुआ कि मरणासन्न मनुष्य को पहले ही हरि बोलने को विवश करते थे और उसकी जबान से ज्योंही ''हरि'' निकला कि उसे गंगा या नदी में डाल दिया! समझते थे कि उसका उपकार हो गया और वैकुण्ठ चला गया! भूखों मार के रिजर्व फारेस्ट खड़ा करना तो कुछ अजीब चीज है। वे जिन्दा कैसे रहेंगे? इस तरह बलात् सभ्य बनाना तो अजीब बात है! और जब उनके बच्चों में एक को भी सरकार ने अब तक पढ़ाया तक नहीं, तो फिर वे सभ्य कैसे बनाये जायंगे? जंगलों को काटने से उन्हें रोकना घोर अन्याय और बेदर्दी है।

यह तो बेचारे मूक पहड़िया लोगों की बात हुई जिनमें एक भी पढ़ा लिखा है नहीं। मगर मुंडा, उरांव, संथाल आदि तो पढ़ने लिखने लगे हैं। उन्हें सभ्य बनाया जा भी रहा है। कम से कम मिशन वाले तो यह काम युगों से कर रहे हैं। मगर उनकी कोड़कर और उटकर जमीनों की भी कम फजीती नहीं है। यह हक उनसे प्रायः छीना जा चुका और बचा बचाया कानूनी दाव पेंच के जरिये बड़ी, निर्दयता से छीना जा रहा है। कोड़कर वगैरह का जो वर्णन पहले किया गया है वह यहां के काश्तकारी कानून की ३(१३) धारा में लिखा गया है। लेकिन उसकी ६४, ६५, ६६, ६७ और ६७ (अ) धाराओं में जो विशेष

बातें और शर्त्तें लिखी गई हैं उनमें एक प्रकार से घुमा फिरा के किसानों के कोड़कर और उटकर के हकों को, जो सनातन काल से चले आ रहे थे और जमींदारों तथा जमींदारी के जन्म से पहले से ही जिन्हें उनने प्राप्त किया था, छीन लिया है। कम से कन छीनने की कोशिश तो भरपूर की है और उसमें सफलता भी मिली है। कानूनी दाव पेंच ही तो ठहरा। असल में कोड़कर या उटकर के बारे में जमींदार की मंजूरी की जो शर्त्त ६४वीं धारा में लगा दी है उसी ने तो गजब कर दिया है।

यों कहने को तो उसमें कहा गया है कि (१) जो ऊंची या टांड़ जमीन किसान की कायमी जमीन की रैयती जमीन में शामिल हो, या (२) जहां जिस गांव में पुराने रिवाज के अनुसार जमींदार की मंजूरी जरूरी नहीं हो उन जमीनों को कोड़कर बनाने में किसान स्वतंत्र हैं और जमींदार की आज्ञा की उन्हें जरूरत नहीं। यह भी कहा गया है जिस मौजे में बेठखेता और मझिहस के सिवाय दूसरी जमीन १८६७ वाले सर्वे के कागज में दर्ज है – यानी भुंइहरी जमीन है – वहां भुंइहरी वालों किसानों को, तथा जहां मुंडारी खुटकट्टी जमीन लिखी गई हो वहां यदि मुंडा लोग जमीन जोतते हों, तो उन्हें भी, जमींदार से बिना पूछे ही कोड़कर बनाने की स्वतंत्रता है। (३) उस धारा में तीसरी बात यह भी लिखी गई है कि जहां जमींदार का हुक्म जरूरी भी हो वहां भी यदि किसान ने उटकर या कोड़कर बनाना शुरू कर दिया और उसके दो साल के भीतर उस जमीन से उसे बेदखल करने के लिये कलक्टर (डिप्टी कमिश्नर – क्योंकि झारखंड में कलक्टर को ही डिप्टी कमिश्नर कहते हैं) के पास जमींदार ने दरखास्त न दी तो माना जायगा कि किसान को जमींदार से हुक्म मिल चुका था। फलतः वह पीछे उस जमीन से बेदखल नहीं किया जा सकता। क्योंकि जो किसी मौजे का रहने वाला (देही) किसान उसी मौजे में कोड़कर बनाये तो बिना डिप्टी कमिश्नर की आज्ञा के वह उस जमीन से बेदखल हो सकता नहीं और डिप्टी कमिश्नर तो बेदखली की आज्ञा दे सकता नहीं।

इसके बाद ६५ और ६६ धाराओं में लिखा गया है कि जब बेदखली की दरखास्त डिप्टी कमिश्नर के पास दी जायगी तो वह जांच करने के बाद यदि ठीक समझेगा तो बेदखली का हुक्म दे देगा। किसान से जमींदार को हर्जाना भी दिला सकता है। इस तरह वह न सिर्फ जमीन से ही हाथ धोयेगा। बल्कि घर का आटा भी उसे गीला करना होगा। हां, यदि उसने बेदखली की आज्ञा न दी तब तो बात ही दूसरी है। मगर क्या यह मुमकिन है? यह भी लिखा है कि दूसरे की जोत जमीन, घर (वसौढ़ी) की जमीन या बाग बगीचे की जमीन को

कोड़कर बनाया जा सकता नहीं। भला यह कैसे होगा कि दूसरे के जोत पर कोई धावा बोल दे, या उसके बाग को काटके या मकान को गिरा के या जबर्दस्ती करके कोड़कर बना ले? मगर यह गोलमोल बातें इसीलिये की गई हैं कि इन्हीं के बहाने पर किसान को कोड़कर से बेदखल किया जा सके। जमींदार को झूठी गवाही तो आसानी से मिल सकती है। यहां के किसान अदालत में लड़ना क्या जानें?

अब जरा इन तीन धाराओं में लिखी शर्त्तों पर विचार तो करें। आखिरी (६७) वाली का तो विचार कर भी चुके कि उसकी शब्दावली बड़ी ही गोलमोल और पेचीदा है जिससे किसान धोके में पड़ सकता है। मगर शेष दो की भी शर्त्तें कम खतरनाक नहीं हैं। असल में जमींदार से पूछने का सवाल ही गलत है। इसी में धोका और चालबाजी है। यह कहना, कि जहां रस्मरिवाज हो वहां पूछने की जरूरत तो हई नहीं, भी गलत और धोखे का है। कोड़कर तो बनता है तब से जब यहां जमींदार थे भी नहीं और जब मुंडा, उरांव वगैरह यहां पहले पहल आये थे — जब से यहां आदमी बसे थे। फिर रिवाज की बात ही क्या है? वह तो समूचे झारखंड के लिये एक सा है। जब जमींदार थेई नहीं तो पूछने की बात ही कहां उठ सकती थी? फलतः सर्वत्र रिवाज ही था। ऐसी हालत में रिवाज की बात उठाना खामखा जमींदार को लाठी और रुपये के बल से ''दालभात में मूसरचंद'' बनने का मौका देना है। वह तो सभी जगह कह बैठेगा कि रिवाज नहीं है और बिना जमींदार के पूछे कोड़कर बनता नहीं। हां, केवल भुंइहरी और मुंडारी खुटकट्टी वाले गांवों में ही भुंइहर और मुंडारी खुटकट्टीदार के लिये साफ कहा गया है कि जमींदार से पूछना जरूरी नहीं है। सो भी तभी जब मुंडारी के पास कोई दूसरी जमीन हो। न होने पर उसे भी पूछना हीं होगा। ऐसे गांवों में भुंइहर और मुंडारी लोगों के बारे में जमींदार को ही सिद्ध करना होगा कि उससे हुक्म लेना जरूरी है। खूबी तो यह है कि, यदि जमींदार से आज्ञा लेना जरूरी भी हो तो यह बात जमींदार को ही सर्वत्र सिद्ध करनी होगी, ऐसी भी शर्त्त नहीं दी गई है। क्योंकि इससे किसानों को आसानी और जमींदार को दिक्कत होती। यहां तो ऐसी बेहूदा शर्त्त है जिससे यह बात सिद्ध होती है कि सर्वत्र जमींदार से पूछना ही होगा, और अगर कहीं न पूछना हो तो यह चीज किसान को ही साबित करनी होगी। इससे सारा भार किसान पर आ गया और यही इन शर्त्तों का असली जहर है।

यही बात जांच पड़ताल में भी है। क्योंकि डिप्टी कमिश्नर की जांच के समय कचहरी की चालबाजियों और खर्चों में गरीब किसान क्या पार पा सकता

है? उसे तो कानूनी पेचीदगी मालूम नहीं। इधर सारा मामला चौपट हो जाता है और वह न सिर्फ जमीन से हाथ धोता है — उस जमीन से जिसे बाहुबला कहते हैं और जिसे बनाने में उसने अपने खून को पानी कर दिया — किन्तु हर्जाना भी देने की नौबत आती है! हर्जाने की बात तो किसान को धमकाने के लिये है। ताकि इसी डर से पहले हो जमींदार का पांव पूजे और उसकी मुट्ठी गर्म करे। जमींदार की रजामंदी का तो यही अर्थ ही है। वह तो हर्जाने की बात सुनते ही कांप उठेगा। नहीं तो यह बात रखी ही क्यों गई? जो जमीन बेकार थी, जिसे कुत्ता भी पूछता न था उसे ही किसान ने अपने परिवार का खून पसीना बना के खेती के योग्य कर दी! उसके बेदखल होने पर जमींदार को क्या यही कम फायदा हुआ? अब तो इसी जमीन पर किसी से भी नजराना और लगान पा सकता है, जहां पहले कोई पूछता न था।

जो लोग कानूनी ज्ञान की बदहजमी मिटाते और नाहक वकालत करते फिरते हैं उन्हें पता नहीं कि ६४वीं धारा में यह लिखने पर भी, कि कायमी किसान की रैयती जमीन के भीतर वाली टांड़ जमीन को उटकर या कोड़कर बनाने में जमींदार की मंजूरी का सवाल उठता ही नहीं, ज्यों ही किसान ने ऐसा किया कि उस कोड़कर पर अलग लगान लाद दिया जाता है। काश्तकार की रैयती जमीन को तो छोड़िये। ऐसो जमीन तो कई होल्डिंगों में हो सकती है। मगर जिस होल्डिंग का एक भाग दोन तथा दूसरा टांड़ है उसके उसी टांड़ को दोन बनाने पर भी जमींदार लोग जबर्दस्ती लगान बांध देते हैं और रैयत को देना हीं पड़ता है। नहीं देने पर हजार ढंग से उसे तंग किया जाता है। आखिर ''जबर्दस्त की लाठी सर पर'' का भी तो कुछ मतलब होता ही है और वह लाठी जितनी झारखंड में चलती है उतनी शायद ही कहीं। यहां के किसान निरे अनजान जो ठहरे। अतएव कोड़कर के बारे में लगाई गईं सभी शर्त्तें जब तक हटा ली न जाय किसानों की खैरियत नहीं।

अब जरा उनके परीशान किये जाने की संक्षिप्त कहानी सुनिये। सबसे पहले तो जमींदार इसी बात पर जोर देता है कि कोड़कर बनाने के पहले ही उससे आज्ञा मानी जाय। और अगर किसान ऐसा करे तो मनमानी सलामी, मनचाहा नजराना उससे तलब किया जाता है — इतना ज्यादा कि सुनके तबीअत घबरा जाय। जितना बाहरी लोग सोच भी नहीं सकते उतना नजराना जमींदार मांग बैठता है।

यदि इस डर से किसान ने उससे पूछा नहीं, तो जमींदार के यमदूत ये अमले ढूंढ़ढांढ़ के पता लगा ही लेते हैं। उनका तो यही काम ही ठहरा। फिर

तो पहले वे खुद सौदा करते हैं और कहते हैं कि हमारी पूजा ठीक ठीक करो, नहीं तो न सिर्फ जमींदार को खबर देंगे, बल्कि तुम्हें यहीं दुरुस्त भी करेंगे। ऐसा प्रायः होता है कि कुछ या काफी घूस न पाने पर अमले मारपीट बहुत करते और बांध बूंध कर या घसीट के जमींदार की कचहरी में किसान को ले जाते हैं। फिर तो वहां उसे सब कुछ भुगतना पड़ता है। हां, यदि अमलों की पूजा हो गई तो मारपीट से जान बचती है। मगर जमींदार तो काफी नजराना लेता ही है और लगान भी मनचाहे ढंग पर बांध देता है। की कराई मिहनत बेकार न जाय इसी खयाल से किसान जमींदार को जैसे हो खुश करता ही है। नहीं तो जमीन से ही हाथ धोना पड़ जाय। हां, यदि अमलों को खूब पैसे दिये तो कह सुन के रिआयत करा देते हैं। मगर थोड़ी ही बहुत।

यदि किसान ने शायद हिम्मत से काम लिया और कह दिया कि कानून के अनुसार जमींदार को सचमुच ही बोलने का हक नहीं है, तो उसके लिये बला समझिये। कानून वानून क्या करेगा? यहां तो जमींदार की मर्जी ही कानून है। जबर्दस्ती लाठी के बल कोड़कर या उटकर से बेदखल कर दिया जायगा। यदि वह डंटा, तो सैंकड़ों ढंग के जालफरेब और मुकदमे में फंसाके तंग तबाह कर दिया जाता है। इसलिये हर हालत में बिना जमींदार की शरण गये और उसे खुश किये किसान को पनाह नहीं — उसकी खैरियत नहीं।

कानून यह भी कहता है, जैसा कि ६७वीं धारा से स्पष्ट है कि कोड़कर या उटकर जमीन ज्यों ही तैयार हुई उस पर किसान का कायमी हक हो जाता है। आमतौर से बारह साल लगातार जोतने की जरूरत जो और जमीनों पर कायमी हक होने के लिये होती है वह कोड़कर के लिये नहीं है। साथ ही, सेट्ल रैयत होने की भी शर्त्त इसमें नहीं है और न १८वीं धारा के अनुसार, जिसमें कि भुंइहर और मुंडारी खुटकट्टीदार को भुइहर, मुंडारी खुटकट्टी या जमींदार की जिरात के अलावे उस गांव की बाकी जमीनों के जोतते ही सेट्ल रैयत का हक मिल जाता है, कोड़कर वाले किसान को भुंइहर वगैरह होने की ही जरूरत है। यह इस जमीन की खूबी है। मगर क्या भरसक जमींदार ऐसा होने देते हैं। रैयत कुछ जानता नहीं और उसकी नादानी से अनुचित लाभ उठाते हैं जमींदार और उसके पापी अमले!

६७(अ) धारा में कोड़कर या उटकर के लगान का नियम है। वहां लिखा है कि उस जमीन में पहली फसल कट जाने के बाद चार साल तक — यानी पूरे पांच वर्ष तक फसल काटने के बाद ही कोड़कर जमीन पर लगान लग सकता है। उसके पहले हर्गिज नहीं। मगर जिस कानून से किसान को फायदा हो

उसे कौन माने? जमींदार की बला उसे मानने जाये। वह क्यों उसकी पर्वा करने लगा? वह तो जमीन तैयार होने के पहले से ही किसान का खून चूसने लगता है। तब उसी से पूरे पांच वर्ष तक खामोशी की उम्मीद?

उसी धारा में यह भी लिखा है कि पांच साल के बाद जब जमींदार उस जमीन पर लगान लगाये तो, आमतौर से उस गांव में जो धान की तीसरे दर्जे की — (यानी सबसे खराब) जमीन हो उसके लगान से ज्यादा लगान उस कोड़कर पर लगा नहीं सकता। मगर अगर मौजे का रिवाज ऐसा हो कि कोड़कर का लगान उतना भी न हो के उसका आधा ही होता हो, तो जमींदार को भी ऐसा ही करना होगा। इसके बाद इसका सारा ब्योरा डिप्टी कमिश्नर के पास वह जमींदार बाकायदा भेजेगा और डिप्टी कमिश्नर जांच पड़ताल करके और किसान से भी भरसक पूछताछ करके उस लगान पर मुहर देगा। तभी वह लगान वसूल किया जायगा। मगर यहां तो दूसरी ही गंगा बहती है। हमने तो जवाबदेह किसानों को रोते चिल्लाते पाया है कि जमींदार मनमाना लगान वसूल करता है। डिप्टी कमिश्नर को कौन पूछे? कानून फानून की धाराएं कौन देखे?

अब जरा उटकर की विशेष वार्त्ता सुनिये। कही चुके हैं कि कोड़कर ही का यह भी एक रूप है। मगर इसमें ज्यादातर ऊंची या बारी जमीन हीं होती है जिसमें मूंग वगैरः बोते हैं। ज्यादातर पलामू में और कहीं कहीं रांची में भी यह जमीन पाई जाती है। कुछ उटकर में तो हर साल खेती होती है। बाकियों में दो तीन साल का बीच देकर ही। मगर जमींदार शुरू से ही मनमाना लगान लेते हैं और रसीद देते ही नहीं। अगर देते हैं तो तभी जब और कायमी जमीन के साथ ही उटकर का लगान पाते हैं। मगर पूरा पूरा नहीं। फलतः उटकर की तो रसीद देते हैं और कायमी की नहीं देते। जिससे आगे चलके उसे नीलाम करवा लेते हैं। किसान को पहले क्या मालूम? वह रसीद पढ़ने थोड़े ही जाता है।

लगान भी नगदी और भावली दोनों ही होती है। अच्छी जमीन की भावली और खराब की नगदी! जमींदार तो गुरूघंटाल होते ही हैं। खूबी तो यह कि ऐसी जमीनों पर लगे पलास या महुवा के पेड़ों का अलग बन्दोबस्त करते और लगान लेते हैं। महुवा खाते हैं और पलास पर लाह जो होती है। कभी कभी अच्छी उटकर जमीनों से किसानों को इस्तीफा देने पर भी विवश किया जाता है। यह तो कही चुके हैं कि उटकर बनाने में शुरू में ही या बीच में भी सलामी मांगी जाती है। न देने पर मारपीट के सिवाय जबर्दस्ती जुर्माना वसूल किया जाता है और झूठा केस चलाने की धमकी भी दी जाती है। कभी कभी केस भी चल जाते हैं। लगान की दर तो गजब की होती है जिससे हार के किसान

जमीन छोड़ के भाग जाते हैं। भावली में जमींदार के हिस्से का गल्ला कभी कभी इतना ज्यादा ठहराया जाता है जितनी कि खेत की कुल पैदावार भी नहीं होती!

सबसे बड़ी दिक्कत ऐसी जमीनों को लेके यह होती है कि किसानों को कानून का पता तो रहता नहीं। एक बार हाल में ऐसा हुआ कि प्रायः पांच सौ किसानों ने पलामू में डिप्टी कमिश्नर के पास लगान ठीक करने की दरखास्त दी थी। मगर सब की सब रद्द कर दी गई। वे बेचारे मुंह ताकते रह गये।

(६)

जंगल की तकलीफें

यह ठीक है कि कुरांव, चास, कोड़कर और उटकर से ताल्लुक रखने वाली तकलीफें किसानों को सबसे ज्यादा अखरती हैं और असह्य हैं। इनसे तो मौत को ही वे ज्यादा पसन्द करते हैं। इसीलिये इन पर सबसे ज्यादा उनका ध्यान जाता है। मगर इनके अलावे उनकी और भी तकलीफें हैं जो कम अखरती नहीं हैं। कोड़कर आदि जमीनों की तकलीफों के ही मुकाबिले की दो तकलीफें उन पर और आ पड़ी हैं और इस तरह इन तीन विपदाओं की चट्टानें उन्हें पीस रही हैं। इन दो में एक तो है जंगल के फल, फूल, काठ, बांस, घास, पत्ते, मूल, जल आदि की। इन्हें पहले भी चाहे और तकलीफें हजार रही हों। लेकिन उन जंगली पदार्थों की तो कोई कमी न थी। जब चाहे जितना लाते और इस्तेमाल करते रहे। कपड़ा तो इनके पास पूरा होता ही नहीं। ज्यादातर तो लंगोटी ही रखते हैं। शेष शरीर नंग! औरतों की भी सारी देह तो कपड़े से ढंकती नहीं। इतने कपड़ें इन्हें मिले भी कहां से?

इसीलिये जाड़ों में आग जलाके और पुआल घास में घुसके गुजर करते थे। खेत की रखवाली के लिये कांटे और झाड़ियां काट लाते और किनारे किनारे गाड़ के घेरा तैयार कर देते थे। घर के चारों ओर न घेरें तो जंगली जानवरों से कभी न बच सकें। उन्हीं घेरों पर सेम वगैरः की लताएं भी फैलती और फूलती हैं। पानी खुद पीते, नहाते, पशुओं को पिलाते और खेत सींचने के काम में लाते थे। महुआ, गेंठी, केना वगैरः फल फूल खाते थे। इधर पलाश, कुसुम आदि पेड़ों पर लगी लाह बेंचके पैसे कुछ कमा लेते थे। गाड़ी, हल, घर की छाजन के लिए काफी काठ और बांस उन्हें मिलता था। पत्तों के पत्तल बना के बाजारों में बेच लाते, बरसात में पत्तों के सुन्दर छाते बना के भीगने से बचते और लकड़ियों बेंच के भी गुजर करते थे। मगर सब पर आफत आ गई! ये गरीब ताज्जुब में हैं कि यह क्या हो गया? वे समझी नहीं सकते कि यह हक क्यों छिन गया।

सर्वे में खतियान बनी और गुरूघंटाल जमींदारों और उनके अमलों ने घूस

दे के जंगलों पर अपना खास कब्जा लिखवा लिया! ऐसे ही जंगलों में नमूने के लिये पारसनाथ पहाड़ का भी जंगल है। सब कुछ जमींदार का ही लिखा है। सर्वे की खतियान दिखा के उसकी तराई के माझियों (संथालों) को लकड़ी, बांस, फल, फूल, पत्ते और झरने के पानी लेने तक से रोका जाता है! वे बेचारे खतियान क्या जानने गये? उन्हें क्या मालूम कि यह खतियान कौन सी बला है? वे तो सीधे और अपढ़ ठहरे। खतियान बनने के समय उन्हें पता भी न था कि क्या बन रहा या बिगड़ रहा है। उन्हें सपने में भी खयाल न था कि ये गौरवर्ण, अहिंसाव्रतधारी, जैनी मालदार दिल के ऐसे काले हैं कि उनके जंगली हक भी छीन लेंगे और उन्हें तथा उनके पशुओं को पानी तक पीने न देंगे। यदि ये जानते कि ये दोपाये खूंखार पशु भीतर के काले हैं और ऐसा करने आये हैं तो उसी समय निपट लेते। नतीजा चाहे जो होता। इस अत्याचार से उनके खून में आग लगी है। पीरटांड और डुमरी में जब मैं इनकी मीटिंग में गया तो इनमें इसी अत्याचार की चर्चा थी कि कैसे इसे खत्म करें। सुना कि उसके बाद पुलिस के लाख मना करने पर भी इनने जंगल पर धावा बोल ही तो दिया। उस कांग्रेसी मंत्रियों का आसन डिग गया। मगर उनसे इतना भी न हो सका कि इनके ये हक साफ साफ इन्हें दे डालें! यही तो उनकी जन-सेवा और किसान-प्रेम का नमूना है!

रिजर्व जंगलों के करते भी यही आफत आती है। इसका जिक्र पहले किया जा चुका है। सर्वे के बाद भी समय समय पर जंगल रिजर्व होते जाते हैं। इसीलिये पानी, फल, फूल वगैरः की तकलीफें इन किसानों की बढ़ती ही जाती हैं। उन्हें निश्चय ही नहीं कि कब कहां क्या बला आयेगी और उनके ये अधिकार छिन जायेंगे। कहने के लिये तो बताया जाता है कि घर गिरस्ती के काम के लिये सब चीजें जंगल से लेने का हक खतियान में है। मगर व्यवहार में क्या होता है हमें इसी से काम है। न कि लिखे हुए से। हम तो — ये किसान तो — लिखतं नहीं जानते। किन्तु करतं जानते हैं और उसी करतं में गड़बड़ी है। खतियान में लकड़ी के नाम और लम्बाई, चौड़ाई, मुटाई वगैरः की ऐसी बाल की खाल खिंची होती है कि ये बेचारे पार नहीं सकते। पहले ये लोग इन्जिनियरिंग पास करें और पास में स्कूल, परकाल वगैरः रखें। तब शायद काम चले तो चले। मगर ये तो ठहरे पूरे ''काले अक्षर भैंस बराबर'' और ''लिख लोढ़ा पढ़ पत्थर''। तब कैसे काम चलेगा?

और इतना हीं तो नहीं है। अभी तो बड़ा घनचक्कर बाकी ही है। यदि ये किसान और गरीब लकड़ी वगैरः ले के चले ही जायं और अपना काम चलाई

लें, तो जंगल विभाग के छोटे बड़े नौकर क्या मक्खी मारेंगे? उनका मजा तो किरकिरा होई जायगा। वे इन्हीं को सता के तो गुलछर्रे उड़ाते हैं। थोड़ी थोड़ी तनखाह वाले रेंजर, फारेस्टर, पेट्रोल, अर्दली और जानें कौन कौन से महारथी जंगलों में ताक लगायें खूंखार जानवरों की ही तरह शिकार की ताक में बैठे रहते हैं। यदि इनकी पूजा शुरू में ही, या बीच में ही सही, न कर दी जाय, तो हजार मीनमेख निकाल के गरीबों को तबाह कर छोड़ते हैं। मैंने यह तमाशा खुद देखा है। गावां थाना (हजारीबाग) के एक गांव में, जो गावां से हजारीबाग आने के समय सकरी नदी पार करने के बाद पड़ता है और जिसका नाम मैं भूलता हूँ, मुझे किसानों ने जो जो दर्दनाक दास्तानें सुनाईं उनसे मैं खून के आंसू रोया। ऐसी बातें जाने कितनी जगह हुई। मेरा तो खून खौल उठा। मगर लाचार था। जंगल विभाग और उसके नियम कायदे यहां के गरीबों को तिलतिल करके मारते हैं! दूसरों को क्या पता? जिनके सिर गुजरती है वही जानते हैं! मैं तो उनके दिलों में प्रवेश करने की भारी कोशिश करके ही थोड़ा समझ पाता हूं। बाबू लोग असेम्बलियों और सेक्रेटेरियट की कुर्सियां तोड़ते रहें। वे हजार जन्म में भी इन दुखिया लोगों की वेदना — आह — शायद ही समझ पायें। इसके लिये तो दिल चाहिये। सो भी दूसरे ही ढंग का।

<2.12.41> एक बात और भी है। दो तरह के जंगल होते हैं अलावे मामूली और उजड़े जंगलों के। एक तो सुरक्षित या प्रोटेक्टेड और दूसरे रक्षित या रिजर्व या यों कहिये कि जिनपर रोक लगी है। सुरक्षित (protected) जंगलों के भीतर तो कोई पांव दे नहीं सकता और न एक तृण छू सकता है। हां, रक्षित या रिजर्व (reserved) जंगलों में से ही समय समय पर घरेलू काम के लिये मामूली बल्ले वगैरः लिये जा सकते हैं जिनकी लम्बाई, चौड़ाई और मोटाई वगैरः निश्चित रहती है। साथ ही यह भी तय रहता है कि किन किन पेड़ों से ये लकड़ियां भी नहीं लो जा सकती हैं। यह तो एक तरह का जंगल-पुराण ही समझिये। पत्ते, घास वगैरः तो ले सकते ही नहीं। ये चीजें तो मामूली जंगलों से ही ली जा सकती हैं और रिजर्व से शायद ही बड़ी दिक्कत से। जंगल के हर गांव की खतियान में लिखा रहता है कि कहां तक जंगल में जा सकते हैं। ऐसा फासला चौहद्दी के साथ लिखा रहता है। तिस पर भी तुर्रा यह कि जमींदार लोग कर लेते हैं जिसे टंगकर या टांगीकर कहते हैं। पलामू के महुवाडांड थाने के सिवाय सभी जगह यह टंगकर है। इसके लिये बड़ा तूफान हुआ। महुंवाडांड़ वाले बहुत ही बागी बने थे। तब भी उनका पिंड छूटा नहीं। झमेला चलता ही रहता है। हरेक घरवाले को साल में चार आना देना ही पड़ता है

चाहे लकड़ी ले या न ले। मगर वे लोग कुछ लकड़ियां काट के बेंच भी सकते हैं। दूसरे थाने वाले तो घर गिरस्ती के ही लिये पा सकते हैं। बेंचने के लिये हर्गिज नहीं। बेंचने के लिये भी वही मामूली बल्ले, सो भी आदमी अपने सिर पर ही लाद के ला सकता है।

रांची वगैरहः में सभी जगह जमींदार का यह टंगकर या बनकर बड़ी सख्ती से वसूल होता है। इन जिलों में और मानभूम, हजारीबाग वगैरः में भी टंगकर, वनकर, पतकर, लहकर, चुल्हकर आदि नामों से ये टैक्स लिये जाते हैं। कांटने की टांगी के हिसाब से, जलाने की चूल्हे के हिसाब से या यों ही वसूल होता है। पत्ता लेने पर पतकर, लकड़ी के लिये वनकर। रांची जिले में तो पता चला कि पहले फी घर साल में सिर्फ एक आना देना होता था। सर्वे के समय चार आना हो गया। अब तो सवा रुपया वसूल होता है। इसके सिवाय रसीद देने में चपरासी और मुहर्रिर चार आने लेते हैं। जंगल में जो चपरासी या बरकन्दाज रहते हैं वह भी कुछ न कुछ लेते ही हैं। नहीं तो तरह तरह से परीशान करते हैं। और जगहों में भी व्यवहार में यह कर बढ़ गया है। चाहे कागज में कम हीं क्यों न लिखा हो। किसान देना नहीं चाहते। इसीलिये झमेले होते रहते हैं। पलामू के रांका जमींदारी में पहले चुलकर के नाम से यह कर वसूलते थे जबर्दस्ती। मगर जब सर्वे के समय यही चार आना लिखवाने की कोशिश जमींदार ने बहुत ही छल फरेब करके की। मगर सर्वे अफसर ने नहीं माना। महुवाडांड में तो जमींदारों ने धीरे से यह चार आना टंगकर सर्वे की खतियान में लिखवाई लिया। मगर बहुत दिनों तक चुप्पी साधे रहे, और एक पैसा नहीं वसूला। किसानों को पहले शक हुआ था कि कुछ न कुछ टंगकर लगा है। वे बौखलाये भी थे, जैसा कि कह चुके हैं। मगर जब वसूली नहीं हुई तो उनने समझ लिया कि खत्म हो गया और निश्चिन्त रहे। जब वहां की कई जमींदारियां कोर्ट आफ वार्डस् की मातहती में आ गईं तब फिर वसूली जारी हुई और किसानों की आंखें खुली। हलचल भी उनमें काफी हुई। बवंडर शुरू भी हुआ। मगर फिर कुछ कुछ ठंडे पड़े। आज भीतर ही भीतर असन्तोष की आग धक्धक् कर रही है। १९३९ के दिसम्बर में मैं जब वहां गया था तो यह बात साफ मालूम हुई।

मगर यह चार या आठ आने का कोई नियम एक तरह का नहीं है। मैंने तो हजारीबाग में और दूसरी जगह किसानों के पास रसीदें देखी हैं जिनसे पता चलता है कि हर तरह की लकड़ियों के लिये, जो सिर्फ घर गिरस्ती के ही काम आती हैं, जुदे जुदे कर निधार्रित हैं और बिना दिये बेचारों की गुजर नहीं है।

यह भी होता है कि रिजर्व जंगलों में कुछ खास खास जगहें होती हैं और वहीं से लकड़ी ले सकते हैं। जैसे मन्दिर का फाटक बन्द हो और खुले वैसे ही ये जगहें भी समय समय पर ही खुलती और बन्द होती हैं। खुलते ही दौड़ मचती है और पैसे देके लकड़ी काटना जरूरी होता है। फिर बन्द होने पर कुछ न हो सकेगा। एक बार खुलके तीन तीन साल के लिये ये बन्द हो जाते हैं। इसीलिये जल्दी जल्दी ईंधन, लकड़ी वगैरः लेना ही पड़ता है। नहीं तो तीन साल तक मरना ही पड़े। यह तो बर्फानी इलाकों और देशों की बात हुई कि अब सामान जमा कर लो, नहीं तो बर्फ के दिनों में मरना होगा। क्योंकि बाहर निकल नहीं सकते। कभी कभी तो गांवों से ये जगहें बहुत दूर होने के कारण किसानों को आपार कष्ट का सामना करना पड़ता है।

पलामू वगैरः में गाय भैंसों आदि के रखने वालों से खरचरी के नाम नाजायज कर लिया जाता था, जो पीछे बड़ी दिक्कत से बन्द हुआ था। रांका वगैरः के जमींदार खासतौर से कई ऐसे कर वसूलते थे। मुझे उस नोटिस की बात बखूबी याद है जो मिस्टर गोडबोले ने, जो आज बिहार सरकार के चीफ सेक्रेटरी हैं, और उस समय पलामू के डिप्टी कमिश्नर थे, उसी हैसियत से चारों ओर वंटवाई थी। उसमें जमींदारों को उनने धमकाया था कि खरचरी वगैरः नाजायज वसूलियां बन्द कर दो। नहीं तो सजा होगी। जहां जहां खरचरी वगैरः लेते थे तहां तहां मवेशियां बिना यह कर दिये जंगलों में जाने पाती न थीं। रिजर्व जंगलों में और प्रोटेक्टेड फारेस्ट में भी आज भी यही दशा है। वहां की घास सूख जाती है। मगर मजाल क्या कि कोई पशु पांव भी दे दे। ऐसा होने पर या तो फौरन हीं कानीहाउस (मवेशीखाना, अड़गड़ा, पौंड) में डाल दिये जाते हैं। नहीं तो जंगल के गार्ड (रक्षक) और चपरासी फारेस्टर कसके जुर्माने के नाम पैसे वसूल लेते हैं। जमींदारों की यह हालत है कि अपने जंगलों को आमतौर से ठेकेदारों को दे देते हैं। फिर तो किसान मजबूर होता है। जमींदार कहता है कि क्या करें, वह तो ठेके पर दे दिया है। किसान बेचारा ठेकेदार से सौदा करता और पैसे दे के लकड़ी वगैरः लेता है। यों सीधे पैसा नांगने और लेने में दिक्कतें होती हैं और गैर कानूनी बात भी हो जाने का डर है। क्योंकि खतियान में जहां ऐसा न हो वहां पैसे कैसे लेंगे। यही कारण है कि चालाकी से काम लिया जाता है।

जहां किसानों को लकड़ी वगैरः लेने का हक भी है वहां भी जमींदार लोग तरह तरह से उन पर दबाव डालते हैं कि बिना खबर दिये लकड़ी नहीं काट सकते और न जंगल में घुस सकते हो। बेचारे भोले भाले किसान क्या करें? वे

जब जमींदार के पास कहने जाते हैं तो बिना रुपया पैसा लिये हुक्म मिलता ही नहीं। यदि नहीं जायं तो जंगल के चपरासी वगैरः पकड़ के तरह तरह से सताते हैं। हमने जेल में ऐसे कैदी पाये हैं जो अपने हक के ही अनुसार जंगल से लकड़ी काटने गये थे, फिर भी रोके गये और न मानने पर मारपीट हो जाने से खून तक हो गया। वे बेचारे बेकार फंसाये गये। अदालत ने उनका हक तो कबूल कर लिया। इसीलिये उन्हें फांसी की सजा न हो सकी। मगर आत्मरक्षा (self defence) की मर्यादा से आगे बढ़ जाने के कारण उन्हें जेल की सजा हो गई और कई साल भुगतने पड़े! ऐसा क्यों हुआ? इसमें शैतानियत तो जमींदार के आदमियों की ही ठहरी। न वे रोकते, न मारपीट होती और न खून होता। फिर सीमा या मर्यादा लांघने की बात ही कैसे उठती?

जब कांग्रेसी मंत्रियों के जमाने में हजारीबाग के डुमरी और पीरटांड़ थानों के संथाल वगैरः किसानों ने पारसनाथ पहाड़ की तराई के जंगलों से जबर्दस्ती लकड़ी आदि काटना शुरू कर दिया था तो बड़ा तूफान मचा था। हथियारबन्द सिपाही वहां भेजे गये थे उन्हें रोकने, पकड़ने और सबक सिखाने के लिये। ऐसी सनसनी और हलचल थी कि कुछ कहिये मत। उसके पहले उन जगहों में किसानों की मीटिंगों में मैं गया था। मेरा दौरा जो हो रहा था। जब किसानों ने कुछ तो अपनी टूटीफूटी जंगली जबानों से और ज्यादातर भावभंगी से अपने अपार कष्टों का वर्णन किया तो मुझे बड़ा दर्द हुआ। मुझे कहा गया कि और जमींदारों की ही तरह, जिस जैनी सेठ ने उस पहाड़ को खरीदा है वह भी कहता है कि सर्वे में साफ लिखा है कि सोते (झरने) के पानी, जंगल के फल फूल और काठ बांस वगैरः पर किसानों का कोई हक नहीं है। फलतः बिना सेठ की मर्जी के और बिना हर चीज के लिये कर दिये वे लोग कोई चीज छू नहीं सकते! इस पर मैंने साफ सुना दिया कि सर्वे में अगर हवा और सूर्य की रोशनी पर भी जमींदार अपना कब्जा लिखा लें तो क्या गरीब लोग और किसान मर जायें और न सांस लें, न सूर्य की रोशनी शरीर पर लगने दें? किसानों को क्या पता कि खतियान में कब, किसने, क्या बला लिख लिखा दी? उन्हें किसने इस बात की नोटिस दी थी कि खतियान में ऐसा लिखा जा रहा है, तुम लोग चलके जो कुछ उज्र करना हो करो? उन्हें उस समय अगर ऐसा कहा गया होता उसी समय वे निपट लेते और चाहे जो भी होता, मगर खतियान को बदलवा के ही छोड़ते। मगर चोरी चोरी ऐसा लिखवा लेने के बाद अब इन्हें मारना यह शैतानियत है, निहायत वेजा बात है। शरीर और घर गिरस्ती के लिये काठ, बांस, फल, फूल, घासपात, जल वगैरः तो इन्हें चाहे

जैसे हो मिलना हीं चाहिये। यदि इन्हें यों ही घुल के मरना नहीं है तो ये चीजें ये लोग लेके ही रहेंगे।

इस पर बड़ी कानाफूंसी हुई थी कि मैंने भोले मांझियों को उसका दिया और वे कानून तोड़ने पर तैयार हो गये! अजीब बात है। वे जिन्दा रहना चाहते थे और चाहते हैं और इसीलिये पानी, काठ, वगैरः चाहते हैं। उन्हें ये चीजें देना नहीं और जबर्दस्ती घुल के मरने देना, फिर भी कहना कि उभाड़ा जाता है! चाहे जहां से जैसे हो जरूरी चीजें उन्हें दीजिये, दिलाइये। फिर देखिये कि कानून तोड़ने या उभाड़ने उभड़ने की बात कहां आती है। फिर भी जो लोग ऐसी बातें बोलते ही रहते हैं उन्हें संसार के एत्तसम्बन्धी इतिहास को पढ़के अपनी अक्ल की दवा कर लेना चाहिये। जंगल के इन्हीं हकों को लेके पहले के समय में संसार के किसानों ने क्या क्या नहीं कर डाला? इस बात की थोड़ी सी झांकी उन्हें कराने के लिये मैं श्री पाल लाफार्ग (Paul Lafargue) की किताब ''सम्पत्ति का विकास'' (Evolution of Property) से एक उद्धरण देना उचित समझता हूं। वह यों है :—

"The forests were grabbed up more brutally : eschewing all legal formalities, the landlords adjudged to themselves the ownership of the woods and underwood; they enclosed the forests and forbade hunting, and abolished the right of estovers; the right of taking wood for fuel and for the repairs of houses, fences, implements, etc. The encroachments of the nobles on the forest lands, which were the Common property of the village, gave rise to terrible revolts of the peasants. The Jacqueries, which broke out in the middle of the fourteenth century (1357-58) in the provinces of the north and the centre of France, were in fact, occasioned by the pretentions of the nobles to forbid hunting and to interfere with the right of common in the forests, and the enjoyment of the rivers. Similar conflicts arose in Germany, such as the famous revolt of the Saxons against the Emperor Henry II, and that of the Suabian peasants, who, in the time of Luther, took up arms against the lords, who debarred them from the enjoyment of the forests. These peasant insurections compelled the lords on several occasions to respect the ancient rights of Common, which consisted in the right — limited only by the peasents' wants — to take wood and brushwood for hedging, firing and repairing his implements (hedge-bote, fire-bote and plough-bote); and in the right of Common pasture, or the right to send his cows, horses, swine and in some cases his goats to graze on the commons throughout the year, the month of May alone excepted. So firmly were rooted these rights that Lapoix de Freminville declared, in 1760, that even in the event of their abuse by the peasants, they could not be taken away from them "for the right of usage is perpetual, and being so, it is accorded alike to the actual inhabitants and to those who may come after them; one cannot strip of an acquired right even those who are as yet unborn." But the revolutionary bourgoisie of 1789 felt none of the fedual legists' respect for the peasant's rights, and abolished them for the benefit of the landed proprietors."

''अधिक निर्दयता के साथ जंगलों को हथिया लिया गया। कानूनी बातों को ताक पर रखके जमींदारों ने जंगलों और झाड़ियों पर अपना अधिकार जमा लिया। उनने जंगलों को घेर दिया (रिजर्व और प्रोटेक्टेड बना लिया), उनमें औरों का शिकार खेलना रोक दिया और घर गिरस्ती के लिये काठबांस वगैरः लेना खत्म कर दिया, जिससे ईंधन तथा घर, घेरा, औजारों की मरम्मत वगैरः के लिये कुछ भी जंगल से लिया जा सकता न था। जो जंगल बराबर गांवों की सार्वजनिक सम्पत्ति थे उन्हें इस तरह जमींदारों के द्वारा हथियाये जाने का नतीजा यह हुआ कि किसानों के भयंकर विद्रोह होने लगे। फ्रांस के मध्य एवं उत्तरी हिस्सों में जो चौदहवीं सदी के मध्य में (१३५७-५८) जैकरी नाम के किसान-विद्रोह होते रहे वे दरअसल इसीलिये हुए कि जमींदारों ने जंगलों में आम लोगों के शिकारों और दूसरे हकों को छीनना शुरू कर दिया था और नाले नदियों के सम्बन्ध में भी यही किया था। जर्मनी में भी इस तरह के विद्रोह हुए, जैसा कि शाहंशाह द्वितीय हेनरी के विरुद्ध सैक्शनों (सैक्शनी प्रान्त के निवासियों) का विख्यात विद्रोह। स्वैव इलाके के किसानों ने भी लूथर के जमाने में इसी तरह उन जमींदारों के खिलाफ हथियार उठा लिया, जिनने उनके जंगल सम्बन्धी हकों को छीना था। किसानों की इन बगावतों और विद्रोहों का नतीजा यह हुआ कि जमींदार लोग बहुत मौकों पर आम लोगों के उन अधिकारों को कबूल करने के लिये मजबूर हुए जिनके फलस्वरूप लोग काठबांस और कांटेकुश घासपात वगैरः खेतों आदि के घेरने, जलाने और दूसरी जरूरतों के लिये, जैसा कि घेरने, आग जलाने और हल आदि के लिये, ले सकें। जमींदारों ने सार्वजनिक चरागाहों के हकों को भी माना जिससे किसान लोग अपनी गायें, घोड़े, सूअर और कभी कभी बकरियां भी चरागाहों में साल भर बराबर चरने को भेजा करें। जंगल के काठबांस वगैरः कितना लिया जाय इसमें किसान की जरूरत ही

निर्णायक थी। (न कि कोई शर्त्त थी कि इतना ही लिया जाय)। केवल मई मास में ही चराई पर रोक थी। ये अधिकार इतना ज्यादा सर्वजनप्रिय थे कि १७६० में फ्रांस में लापोआद फ्रेमिनविल नामक विद्वान ने घोषित किया था कि अगर किसान इन अधिकारों का दुरुपयोग भी करें, तो भी उनसे हक छीने जा सकते नहीं हैं। क्योंकि रस्म रिवाज के अनुसार जो हक हासिल होते हैं वे सनातन हैं। इसीलिये ये हक न सिर्फ उन्हें प्राप्त होते हैं जो मौजूद हों, किन्तु जो पीछे आयेंगे या पैदा होंगे उन्हें भी प्राप्त रहते हैं और जो लोग अभी पैदा हुए ही नहीं उनके हकों को कोई कैसे छीन सकता है? मगर १७८९ के क्रांतिकारी पूंजीवादियों के दिल में सामन्तयुग के कानूनी हकों के जानकारों की तरह इन हकों के लिये जरा भी खयाल न था। इसीलिये उनने जमीन के मालिकों के फायदे के लिये किसानों के इन हकों को मिटा दिया''।

इस उद्धरण पर टीका टिप्पणी बेकार है। यह इतना साफ है कि सारी बातें आईने की तरह झलक रही हैं। ऐसा मालूम होता है कि इसका लेखक झारखंड में बैठके सारी दास्तानें आंखों देखने के बाद ही ये पंक्तियां लिख रहा है! यहां की सारी बातें अक्षरशः इसमें चित्रित की गई हैं, सिवाय एक बात के। फ्रांस, जर्मनी आदि मुल्कों में किसानों ने लगातार विद्रोह करके और जमींदारों का सशस्त्र मुकाबिला करके ही उन्हें मजबूर किया था कि अपनी शैतानियत से बाज आयें और खुले आम किसानों के इन जंगल के हकों को कबूल करें। मगर यहां वह बात नहीं हुई। अगर कभी कभी किसानों ने कुछ किया भी तो शांति से थोड़ा आगे बढ़के खुद दब गये, दबा दिये गये। वे अपने बल से जमींदारों को विवश कर न सके, उनके मद को ध्वंस कर न सके। नदी नालों पर रोक की बात तो पारसनाथ पहाड़ के झरनों और सोतों पर जैनियों के द्वारा डाले गये प्रतिबन्ध को ही याद दिलाती है। रिजर्व जंगल में भी जो यह रोक लगी है वह भी एकाएक याद हो आती है। जिस प्रकार १७८९ में फ्रांस के धनियों ने किसानों के ये हक जबर्दस्ती छीन के बेरहमी से जमींदार को दे दिये ठीक वैसे ही यहां भी काम किया गया है। सनातन हक कलम की एक नोक से पूंजीपतियों की सरकार ने खत्म कर दिया और जमींदारों की पांचों घी में कर दी।

यहां एक कमी और भी है। फ्रांस में तो एक ऐसा विद्वान कानूनदां हो गया जो सामन्तयुग के कानूनी हकों को खूब जानता था। इसलिये उसने १७६० में ही यह घोषित कर दिया था कि ''चाहे किसान इन अधिकारों का दुरुपयोग भी करें। फिर भी उनके ये हक कथापि छिन नहीं सकते। ये हक इतने सर्वजन प्रिय माने जाते हैं और लोगों के दिलों में ये इतने जमें हैं कि जो आगे पैदा होंगे

उन्हें भी ये प्राप्त हैं। क्योंकि पुरानी रीति रिवाजों के ही अनुसार ये हासिल हुए हैं, न कि कानून के जरिये। इसीलिये सदा रहने वाले हैं और इसीलिये जो अभी तक जनमे ही नहीं या आये ही नहीं, किन्तु भविष्य में आने वाले हैं उनके ये हक कैसे छिन सकते हैं? यह बात हो नहीं सकती, आदि''। मगर यहां ऐसे कहने सुनने वाले विद्वान और ईमानदार लोगों का पता नहीं चलता। उनकी लिखी ऐसी बातें यहां पाई जाती हैं नहीं।

कितनी सुन्दर और स्वभाविक बात है कि जंगल के अधिकार कानून के जरिये न तो मिलते हैं और इसीलिये न छीने जा सकते हैं। ये तो परम्परा प्राप्त है। वंश परम्परा और रीति रिवाजों के अनुसार ही हासिल हैं। इसलिये कानून का सिर्फ एक काम है और वह यह कि इन पर अमिट मुहर लगा दे और ताम्रपत्र में लिखके घोषणा कर दे कि ये हक आदि औलाद के लिये हमेशा कायम रहेंगे। ये कभी छीने जा सकते नहीं। यदि इसका दुरुपयोग भी किसान करें तो भी उनसे इन्हें कोई छीनने की हिम्मत कभी न करे, खबरदार। आजकल के दिमागदार और देश सेवक कहे जाने वाले कहते हैं कि किसान लोग इन अधिकारों का दुरुपयोग करते हैं। इसलिये इनका छिना जाना या सीमित किया जाना जरूरी है। ऊपर के वाक्यों में आज से प्रायः दो साल पहले ही एक विद्वान ने इसका मुंहतोड़ उत्तर दे दिया है कि हर्गिज ऐसा नहीं हो सकता, नहीं होना चाहिये। यह तो सरासर जुल्म होगा। छीनना तो छीनना, वह तो कहता है कि इन्हें संकुचित भी नहीं कर सकते। किसान जितनी लकड़ी, जितनी घास, जितने बांस वगैरः चाहे खुशी से ले सकता है। जब सभ्यता का इतना विकास नहीं हुआ था तब यह बात कही गई ठेठ सामन्तयुग में। अब तो पूंजीवादी युग माना जाता है जहां सभ्यता अपनी टांगें तोड़के बैठी है और अधिकारों की बड़ी छानबीन होती देखी जाती है। मगर फिर भी यह अन्धेर! देखें, कब यहां के किसान अपने इस सनातन परम्परा प्राप्त अधिकारों को फिर पहले की ही तरह पूर्णरूप से प्राप्त करते हैं।

जंगल के अधिकारों के मुतल्लिक एक जरूरी बात कहके हम आगे बढ़ेंगे। जैसा पहले कहा गया है, लाह की बात लेके पलास वगैरः के पेड़ों पर किसानों का हक प्रायः छिन गया है। झारखंड के प्रायः सभी जिलों में कमबेश लाह पैदा होती है। पलास, कुसुम (वनवृक्ष) और बेर के ही पेड़ों में यह होती है। इन्हीं पर लाह के कीड़े लगते हैं, लगाये जाते हैं और उन्हीं से लाह पैदा होती है। हमने पलामू में यह चीज आंखों देखी है। किसानों के दुखड़े भी हमारे सामने वहां खासतौर से पेश हुए थे। रांका की जमींदारी की बात थी। हम सुन के

ताज्जुब में आ गये! मगर बात तो सही थी, सही है। जमींदारी के चलते जो न पाप हो जाय!

ऐसा होता है कि खेतों में पलास वगैरः के पेड़ लगे हैं और सर्वे की खतियान में वे खेत किसानों के कब्जे में ही उनके कायमी लिखे गये हैं। मगर ज्यादातर ऐसा किया गया है कि उन्हीं खेतों के भीतर के पलास वगैरहः के पेड़ों पर कब्जा लिखा गया है जमींदार का। यह गजब की बात है। चारों ओर किसानों के ही खेत हैं। जमींदार की खास कब्जे की, जिरात या गैर मजरूआ जमीन कहीं एक इंच भी नहीं है। किसान बेचारे बराबर ही उन खेतों में खेती करते और फसल उपजाते हैं, रखवाली करते, सोते बैठते और मरते मिटते हैं! जमींदार का या उसके यमदूतों का पांव भी वहां कभी नहीं पड़ता! फिर भी उन्हीं खेतों के बीच खड़े पलास के पेड़ों पर जमींदार का अधिकार और किसान का नहीं! यह तो महान अन्धेर है! यह भी नहीं कि उन पेड़ों को कभी जमींदारों ने ही लगाया लगवाया हो। वे तो जंगली हैं। यों ही पैदा हुए हैं। अब भी पैदा होते रहते हैं! फिर भी जमींदारों के! गजब है! एक बार सर्वे खतियान में किसी अक्ल के अन्धे ने लिख दिया! फिर तो जो नये भी पेड़ पैदा होंगे वह जमींदार के ही होंगे! यह तो गजब की अंधेरपुर नगरी है। कहते हैं, सर्वे के अफसर लोग बड़ी जांच पड़ताल करके असलियत का पता लगाते थे! तो क्या यही असलियत है? या कि उस समय संयोगवश शराब पीके वे मतवाले हो गये थे? या कि किसी और तरह की शराब के नशे ने अपना काम कर दिया?

यही हालत महुवा के पेड़ों की भी है। पलास वगैरः से तो लाह पैदा होती है और उससे मिलते हैं पैसे, काफी पैसे। मगर महुवा? उससे तो यह बात है नहीं। महुवा के फूल से तो शायद ही चार आठ आने कभी मिल सकें। हां, पहाड़ी इलाके के गरीबों का वह प्रधान खाद्य है। बेचारों को चीनी गुड़ तो पहले मिलते न थे और न दूसरा खाद्य ही। इसलिये मीठे मीठे महुवा के सूखे फूलों को जमा करके और सुखा के रखते थे, ताकि साल भर आवश्यकतानुसार काम चलाते रहें। वे मीठे बहुत होते हैं। गर्म भी इतने कि कुछ कहिये मत। मगर वे तो उन गरीबों के आधार ठहरे। हंड़िया नाम की उनकी अपनी शराब में भी शायद महुवों से मदद मिलती थी। चावल के भात से ही यह शराब पहाड़ी लोग तैयार करते और उसे ही पीते हैं। हमने कलेजे पर पत्थर रखके पहली बार एक किसान को देखा कि गमछे के किनारे एक मुट्ठी महुवा बांधे बहुत सबेरे जंगल की ओर टांगी लिये चला जा रहा है। रोक के पूछा कि कहां जा रहा है? उत्तर मिला कि लकड़ी काटने जंगल में। कब लौटेगा, यह पूछने पर उत्तर

मिला कि शाम के अन्धेरे तक। अगले दिन बाजार में बेंचने और उसी पैसे से गुजर करने की बात थी। पास में दिनभर का खाना? मैंने यह सवाल किया। उसने वही मुट्‌ठीभर महुवा दिखा दिया। चार पैसे भी थे। मैंने पूछा, ''और ये पैसे?'' उसने कहा कि यह तो घाट पर जमींदार के चौकीदार को देंगे! रोजरोज यही करते हैं। मुश्किल से दो आने की लकड़ी लाते हैं! उसमें एक आना तो जमींदार का ही हुआ। लकड़ी लाने और बेंचने में दो दिन लग जाते हैं। क्योंकि पहला दिन तो लाने में ही जाता है। बाजार दूर है। जाने आने में दूसरा दिन खत्म! एक आना रोज की कमाई! इतनी मिहनत! फिर भी खाने को सिर्फ मुट्‌ठी भर महुवा! एक आने में ही तो दो दिन गुजर करना था। फिर बच्चे और कपड़ा लत्ता चाहिये। ऐसी दशा में मुट्ठी भर महुवा से ज्यादा कैसे मिलता? हां, जमींदार को तो पूरे एक आने मुफ्त ही मिले! उसकी हड्‌डियां साफ दीखती थीं। गिन सकते थे कि कितनी हैं। मेरी हिम्मत टूट गई। बोल न सका! दिल में आया कि यदि अभी धरती फटे तो शर्म से समा जाऊं। नहीं तो जमींदारी को और वर्त्तमान समाज को मिटा के ही छोड़ूं!

यह है संक्षेप में महुवा की दर्दनाक दास्तान! खूबी तो यह है कि महुवा के पेड़ों पर भी जो खेतों में भी होते हैं और बाहर भी, जमींदार का ही कब्जा लिखा रहता है। मगर ये होते हैं काफी फैले। इसलिये एकाध कट्‌ठे में फसल होने ही नहीं देते। पलास तो ऐसे होते नहीं! मगर महुवा महाराज तो बड़े ही खतरनाक होते हैं। यह कोई नहीं पूछता कि यदि वे जमींदार के हैं तो खेत की फसल मारने का हर्जाना जमींदार क्यों नहीं देता? नहीं तो कम से कम उतनी जमीन का लगान तो छोड़ दे जितनी की फसल मारी जाती है। मगर यह पूछे कौन? यहां तो कूएं में ही भांग पड़ी है! म्याऊं का ठौर कौन पकड़े? सबके सब तो जमींदार के दोस्त दलाल ही ठहरे। और किसान सभा वालों की सुने कौन? वे तो सरकार तथा जमींदार दोनों के ही बागी ठहरे।

सबसे दर्द की बात तो यह है कि उन महुवा, पलास आदि पेड़ों का बन्दोबस्त उस किसान के साथ न करके हमेशा गैरों के साथ ही ये जमींदार भलेमानुस करते हैं? क्यों? इसीलिये कि अपने खेतों में दूसरों को जाने देना किसान चाहेगा नहीं। फलतः मजबूरन औरों से भी ज्यादा पैसे देके खुद बन्दोबस्त लेगा। इसे ही रक्त चूसना कहते हैं। जमींदार किसानों से खून निकालने की बेदर्द कोशिश उसी तरह करते हैं जिस तरह सूखी हड्‌डी से खून निकालने की कुत्ते करते हैं! किसान हजार चिल्लाये। मगर सुने कौन? सरकार बहरी, उसकी कचहरियां बहरी, हाकिम बहरे, पुलिस बहरी, नेता बहरे, साधु महात्मा बहरे, देवी देवता

बहरे और भगवान भी बहरा!

मेरे सामने जब यह दुखड़ा पेश हुआ तो मैंने मीटिंगों में साफ ही कह दिया कि "यदि ऐसी अन्धेर है और जमींदार नहीं मानते हैं तो उन्हें गैरों के साथ इन पेड़ों का बन्दोबस्त करने दो और चुपचाप रहो। मगर डंके की चोट सुना दो कि बन्दोबस्त लेने वालों को हमारे खेतों से कोई ताल्लुक नहीं। हमारे खेतों में पांव देने का उन्हें कोई कानूनी या नैतिक हक नहीं, जब तक हम आज्ञा न दें। और हम तो साफ कहते हैं कि किसी दूसरे का पांव खेतों में धरने हर्गिज न देंगे। पहले से ही सुना देते हैं। लोग सजग हो जायं, बन्दोबस्त और ठेका लेने वाले संभल जाएं। हवाई जहाजों से, जादू मंतर से या जैसे हो, ऊपर ही ऊपर उड़ के पेड़ों पर आयें और बिना जमीन छुए ही ऊपर से ही लाह या महुवे के फूल लेके चले जायें। तभी खैरियत है। तब हम कुछ न बोलेंगे। मगर अगर उनने हमारे खेतों में अपने पांव दिये तो जान लें कि हम उन पांवों को तोड़ देंगे और इसमें अपराधी वही होंगे। हमारा इसमें कुछ भी दोष न होगा। यह बात वे लोग कभी भूलें मत आदि आदि। बस, तुम्हारी जीत होके ही रहेगी। यही तो सीधी दवा है। मगर है यह अचूक। आज भी मैं यही उपाय उन किसानों को बता सकता हूं। दूसरा उपाय मेरे पास है नहीं। जालिम लोग आर्ज़ूमिन्त से या गिड़गिड़ाने से कभी नहीं मानते। बल्कि और ज्यादा हिम्मत से जुल्म करने लग जाते हैं। किसानों में स्वावलम्बन आये और वे अपने पांवों पर खड़े हों, तो उनका बेड़ा पार हो। वे हक के लिये मरना मिटना सीखें, निर्भय बनें और संगठित हों। क्योंकि एक दो चार के ऐसा कहने से भी जमींदार न मानेंगे जब तक सामूहिक रूप से उन्हें इन पेड़ों के बारे में डट के ललकारा न जाय। ज्योंही किसानों ने व्यापक और सामूहिक रूप से मीटिंगें करके और नोटिसें बांट के ऐसी ललकार शुरू की कि जमींदार और उनके ठेकेदार दोनों ही पस्त हो जायंगे।

<3.12.41> महुवा के सम्बन्ध से हमें एक महत्वपूर्ण घटना याद आ गई। जब पलामू के दौरे के सिलसिले में १९३९ के दिसम्बर में हम महुवाडांड़ गये थे तो वहां जो कुछ देखा कभी भूलने का नहीं। कई मील से ही वहां के आदिवासी किसानों ने बडे बड़ें झंडों के साथ गांव से जुलूस में निकल निकल के हमारा स्वागत किया। हमने तरह तरह के झंडे पहले पहले वहीं देखे। किसान स्त्री, पुरुष, बच्चे ऐसे सीधे और भोले कि कुछ पूछिये मत।

फिर जब हम मीटिंग में गये तो देखा कि डाकबंगले के लम्बे मैदान में ही सोलहों आने स्वदेशी ढग का मंच बना है। जंगली डाल पात से ही उसे

सजाया था। ऊंचा काफी था। चारों ओर दल के दल स्त्री पुरुष बैठे थे। बहुत बड़ी जमात थी। जाड़े के असली दिन और सबसे ठंडी वह जगह। नेतरहाट का पहाड़ जो सबसे ठंडा माना जाता है, महुवाडांड़ का पड़ोसी है। सभा से ही नजर आता था। फिर भी किसान स्त्री पुरुषों के पास कपड़े कहां? मामूली ही कपड़े थे। वे तो यों भी अधनंगे होते ही हैं। मगर हृष्टपुष्ट, काले काले और देखने में बड़े ही सुन्दर थे। मैं सदा इन लोगों की सुन्दरता और गठीले बदन को देख के मुग्ध हो जाता हूं। यदि इन्हें घी, दूध और सुन्दर खाना मिलता, तब ये कैसे होते, यही तो बात सोचने की है।

उस अपार भीड़ के बीच मंच पर जाते ही मैंने जंगली पत्तों की बड़ी बड़ी पुड़ियों में तीस पैंतीस ढंग के फलफूल वगैरः देखे। पूछने से पता लगा कि इन गरीबों की यही खुराक है। मगर जमींदारों के करते यह भी मिलने नहीं पाती! इस पर भी कर है! उफ! जंगली जड़ें, फूल, फल, पत्ते और उन पर भी आफत! कई तो चीजें इनमें ऐसी भी थीं जो बहुत कड़ुवी और एक तरह से जहरीली होती हैं। उन्हें बारबार उबालने और पानी में देर तक डुबों रखने पर ही गले के नीचे जैसे तैसे वे लोग भी उतार सकते हैं! आखिर भूख तो मानती नहीं। दृष्टान्त के लिये (१) गेंठी को लीजिये। यह एक जड़ है। इसे लगातार चार बार उबालने के बाद सारी रात पानी में डाल रखते हैं। तब कहीं खा सकते हैं। इसी तरह (२) सरई को लीजिये। यह बड़ी ही कड़ुवी होती है। यह है साखू के पेड़ों का फल। इसे छः बार पानी में उबालना जरूरी होता है। इन दो के सिवाय कुछ के नाम ये हैं, (३) तेंद, (४) डिंठोरा, (५) जंगली बेर, (६) गूलर, (७) पीपल, (८) बड़, (९) गूलर के फल, (१०) पाकड़ के फल, (११) महुवा, (१२) चकौंढ़ की पत्ती, (१३) क्योनार की पत्ती वगैरः। ये चीजें वे पैदा नहीं करते। पैदा की गई चीजें हैं (१४) गोंदली, (१५) सुरगुजा, (१६) कोदो, (१७) मड़ुवा, (१८) सावां, (१९) कुर्थी, (२०) बटरा, (२१) जटंगी (एक प्रकार का तेलहन), कहीं कहीं (२२) रहर, (२३) उड़द भी पैदा होती है। मगर बहुत ही कम। (२४) जंगली बेल तो उनकी खुराक ही है। इसी तरह की दस बारह चीजें और हैं। मैं उन्हें देख के ही मन में खूब रोया और सोचने लगा कि यदि संसार में कोई न्यायकारी सर्वशक्तिमान और दीनबन्धु भगवान होता उसका सिंहासन कभी हिलाया होता। इनसे बढ़के दीन और निर्दोष भक्त कौन हो सकता है?

सभा में तो मैंने अपना हृदय निकाल के ही रख दिया। वे लोग मंत्रमुग्ध की तरह सुनते रहे। मैं तो ऐसी सीधी भाषा बोलने का आदी हूं कि जंगल के

किसान भी उसे समझ सकते हैं। गुजरात वगैरः में भी मुझे जंगली लोगों से काम पड़ा है। बातें सुनके उनका चेहरा खिल उठा। जब मुझे पता सभा में ही चला कि पास के पुराने रोमन कैथलिक मिशन वालों ने जिन्हें ईसाई बनाया है वे सभा में नहीं आये हैं। वे रोके जाते हैं आदि आदि, तो मुझे बड़ा गुस्सा हुआ। मैंने साफ सुना दिया कि धर्म मजहब से मुझे कोई मतलब नहीं है। मैं तो आदमियों से मिलना और बातें करना चाहता हूं। मुझे तो उन्हें समझाना है। फिर चाहे वह किसी धर्म के हों। इसीलिये मुझे ईसाई धर्म से कोई भी लड़ाई नहीं। मगर जब उनकी यह हरकतें सुनता हूं तो गुस्सा आता है। क्या वे प्रभू ईसूमसीह की भेंडें तैयार करना चाहते हैं? यह तो गलत है।

मैं समझता था कि ईसाई लोग आदिवासियों को भले ही ईसाई बनाते होंगे। मगर उसी के साथ उन्हें हकों के लिये लड़ना सिखाते होंगे। ऐसा देखा भी गया था कि चमार वगैरः ईसाई होते ही हिन्दू जमींदारों से कहीं कहीं भिड़ गये थे। मैं यह भी सोचता था कि जब तक ये आदिवासी हिन्दू थे तब तक बेशक इनमें तीन गुण पाये जाते थे और वो थे सच बोलना, व्यभिचार से बचना और निर्भीकता। मगर उनका जीवन पशुवत् था। कम से कम हिन्दुओं ने उन्हें ऐसा ही बना दिया था। इसलिये ईसाई होते ही यद्यपि वे तीनों महान् गुण जाते रहे और यह पक्की बात है कि सभ्यता पिशाची जरूर ही उन तीनों को खा जाती है। उन्हीं की कब्र पर वह फलती फूलती है। तथापि वे पशु से आदमी जरूर बनते होंगे और मर्द की तरह हक के लिये लड़ते होंगे। मेरा यह भी खयाल था जिन यूरोपीय देशों से ये पादरी यहां आये हैं वहां के किसानों ने तो क्रांतियां की हैं और शाहंशाहों के तख्त उलट दिये हैं। जंगल के हकों के लिये तो जैसा कि पहले कहा है उनने क्या क्या नहीं कर डाला था। इसीलिये उन्हें यह शिक्षा भी दी जाती होगी।

मगर जब मैंने देखा और पास के गांवों में जाके पूछताछ करके पता भी लगाया कि ईसाइयों को वे लोग मसीह के मेमने के रूप में ही रखते हैं और बाकी किसानों से उनकी निराली ही दुनियां बना छोड़ते हैं तो मुझे बहुत दर्द हुआ। इस बात की आशा न थी। पास पड़ोस के ही अपने भाइयों से ही धर्म बदलते ही, वे लोग बिल्कुल ही नाता तोड़के गूलर के कीड़ों जैसी अपनी अलग दुनिया बना लें यह बात असह्य थी। तब तो मानना होगा कि ये मिशन भारी अनर्थ कर रहे हैं! केवल धर्म के नाम पर ही हिन्दुओं से लड़ा देना कोई अच्छी बात नहीं! यह तो संसार की पुरानी बीमारी है और हमारे अभागे देश में बुरी तरह फैली है। हम तो इससे बचना चाहते हैं और हमें आशा थी कि

पश्चिमी देशों वाले ये मिशन इस बात की रोशनी वहां से जरूर ही अपने साथ लेके ही पहुंचे होंगे। फलतः रोटी, जमीन और हक के लिए ही ईसाई किसान भी लड़ना सीख गये होंगे। मगर यह न पाके हमें बड़ी निराशा हुई। यह हमारे लिये पहला ही मौका था। और जब हम पास के गावों में पूछताछ करने गये और यह देखने कि किसानों की दशा कैसी है तो हमें एक दो अजीब बातें मालूम हुईं।

पहली तो यह कि रास्ते में शाम को तीन चार बच्चियां बच्चे मिशन की तरफ जाते मिले। हमने कौतूहल से जानना चाहा कि इस समय ये कहां जा रहे हैं। जब हमारे ''किसान'' जाति वाले एक साथी ने उनकी ही भाषा में उनसे पूछा तो उत्तर मिला कि ''पाप स्वीकार करने'' के लिये फादर (पादरी गुरू) के पास जा रहे हैं। एक बच्ची ने यह उत्तर दिया और हमने सुना। हम समझी न सके कि यह माजरा क्या है। मरने के समय तो ईसाई पादरी पाप स्वीकार (confession) करवाते हैं ऐसा जाना सुना था। यह क्या बात है? पीछे जांच से पता चला कि प्रतिदिन दो चार दिनों बाद फादर के पास जाके पाप स्वीकार करने का इनमें नियम है और जब घर वाले प्रायः काम के कारण छुट्टी नहीं पाते, तो बच्चे बच्चियों को ही सब की ओर से कनफेशन करने को भेज देते हैं! यह खूब रहा! प्रतिदिन सारे कुकर्मों के धोने का यह अच्छा साबुन मिला! जैसे हिन्दू संध्यागायत्री के जरिये और मुसलिम नमाज के जरिये रोज रोज पाप धोते हैं वैसे ही ईसाई कनफेशन के जरिये! इतिहास की ठीक ही पुनरावृत्ति हो रही है!

दूसरी बात यह मालूम हुई कि हिन्दु गुरुवों और मुसलिम पीरों की ही तरह पादरी गुरू साल में एक बार गांवों में चेलों के पास जरूर जाते और खा पी के तथा ''पूजा'' के रूप में रुपया, कपड़ा वगैरः लेके लौट आते हैं। हो सका तो कुछ नये चेले भी जरूर बना लेते हैं! यह भी वही गुरूवों की ''रामत'' हो गई! सिवाय धर्म के नाम पर पाखंड फैलाने के और कुछ भी सामयिक उपदेश गृहस्थों को वे भी नहीं देते! खुदा खैर करे!

अब महुवाडांड़ की सभा की एक ही बात रह जाती है और है वह दिलचस्प। सभा के बाद सभी किसान, जो दूर से चावल, लकड़ी और हांड़ी साथ लेते आये थे वहीं ठहर के जत्थे जत्थे खाना पकाने लगे। उनके खाने के पूर्व ही मैं सो गया। मगर अचानक आधी रात में नींद टूटी तो मृदंग वगैरः बाजे की ध्वनि के साथ गाने की मधुर तान सुनी। बाहर निकल के देखा तो जगह जगह स्त्री पुरुष गरोह के गरोह नाच गान कर रहे हैं! कितने ही गरोहों में एक

दल स्त्रियों का और दूसरा पुरूषों का आमने सामने खड़ा चक्कर देता और नाचता गाता है। ऐसी सुन्दर चीज कि क्या कहा जाय? नाच गाने के साथ व्यायाम और परिश्रम भी कितना सुन्दर! नजदीक से देखा! स्त्री पुरूषों की होड़ भी खूब थी! सारी रात यह बात चलती रही! जरा भी विराम नहीं! ठेठ सुबह उजाले में कहीं जाके खत्म हुई! किसी ने पलक भी न मारी! पहले सोचता था कि कपड़े बिना कड़ाके के जाड़े में यहां मैदान में इनकी रात कैसे कटेगी। मगर उत्तर मिल गया! व्यायाम भी हुआ, मनोरंजन भी, कला भी कायम रही और जाड़ा भी कट गया! बाहरे दिमाग जिसने एक ही साथ चार सुन्दर काम करने का रास्ता साफ किया! रात भर आग भी जगह जगह जलती जरूर रही। मगर उसके नजदीक ज्यादा देर तक तो कोई बैठ न सका! यह स्वर्गीय दृश्य मैं भूल नहीं सकता। गुजरात के जंगली प्रदेशों में भी मैंने ऐसा ही देखा है। दूसरी जगह भी ऐसा ही होता है!

अब जंगल के कष्टों से ही ताल्लुक रखने वाली खास बात एक ही रह जाती है और है वह बड़ी ही सख्त। मैंने उसके करते गरीब किसानों को छाती पीटते और हाय मारके रोते देखा है। उसके चलते वे लुट जाते हैं, तंग तबाह हो जाते हैं, सर्वस्व गंवा देते हैं। वे तो सचमुच लुट जाते हैं और उनकी कमर सीधी हो नहीं पाती। बात असल यह है कि कानी हाउस या अड़गड़े जंगली प्रदेशों में अकसर होते हैं जिनमें पशु घुसा दिये जाते हैं। यों तो अड़गड़े सर्वत्र ही कसाई खाने का काम करते हैं। उनमें जाने वाले पशु घास और पानी बिना मर जाते हैं। देखने के लिये शायद ही नाममात्र को जरा मरा चारा उनके सामने फेंक दिया जाता हो। मगर दरअसल पशुओं को वहां मार ही डालते हैं! मैंने इसका खूब अनुभव किया है। ये सभ्य कसाई खाने क्यों बने, यह समझने में मैं तो असमर्थ हूं।

मगर जंगलों के अड़बड़े तो गजब के होते हैं! जरा भी जंगल के चपरासी किसानों से रंज हुए या जमींदार के अमले रंज हुए कि ढूंढ ढांढ के उनके सभी पशुओं को जबर्दस्ती कानी हाउस में घुसा देते हैं! एक एक बार पचास पचास, सौ सौ या उनसे भी ज्यादा! और उन्हें वापस लाने में जुर्माना देना होता है उसके करते किसान का घर बार और जमीन बिक जाती है। कानून ऐसा है कि रोक सकते नहीं। नहीं तो फौजदारी में जा फंसे! दिन रात साबका पड़ने के कारण दूध, दही, घी, घूस वगैरः न देने पर अमले और चपरासी खामखा रंज होते ही हैं! किसानों ने हजारों बार खून के आंसू बहाके कहा है कि किसी प्रकार ये कानी हाउस तो यहां से मिटें! तब तो उन्हें सांस आ जायगी।

(७)

कमिया के कष्ट और सूदखोरी की लूट

झारखंड के खेतों के मजदूरों की, जिन्हें कमिया भी कहते हैं, भी बड़ी दुर्दशा है। पलामू जिले में इन्हें बहुत जगह सेवकिया कहते हैं। सेवकिया शब्द ''सेवक'' से बना है और सेवक का अर्थ है आमतौर से गुलाम। कमिया भी ''काम'' से बना है। काम के मानी हैं वही सेवा या सेवकाई। विहार में तो आमतौर से कमिया शब्द ही प्रचलित है। मानभूम और हजारीबाग में अकसर कमिया की जगह मूनिस और घरभतुआ भी कहा जाता है। मगर मूनिस और घरभतुआ में थोड़ा फर्क है। दोनों सोलह आना एक से नहीं हैं। जो लोग थोड़े ही समय के लिये (temporary) रखे जाते हैं उन्हें आमतौर से मूनिस कहते हैं। लेकिन जो ज्यादा दिनों के लिये रखे जाते हैं उन्हें आमतौर से घरभतुआ कहा जाता है। मूनिस शब्द कैसे बना पता नहीं चलता है। मगर घरभतुआ तो साफ है। उन्हें अपने यहां रखने वाले घर पर ही भात खिलाते होंगे। इसी से घरभतुआ कहाये। क्योंकि रात में चाहे सोने के समय घर भले ही चले जाते हों। मगर दिनभर तो मालिक के यहीं रहना जरूरी था। इसलिये वहीं भात खाते थे। अब चाहे यह बात न भी हो। मगर शुरू में यही रही होगी। दूसरे दूसरे नाम भी प्रचलित होंगे। सबों की जानकारी हमें है नहीं। उसकी जरूरत भी नहीं है। हमें तो नमूने के तौर पर कुछ नाम कह देने हैं। चीज तो सर्वत्र एक सी है। क्योंकि कमिया की प्रथा, जिसे कमिऔती कहते हैं, विहार में और दूसरे नामों से अन्य प्रान्तों में भी है। इसका ज्यादा विचार हमने ''खेत मजदूर'' में किया है।

अब जरा सेवकिया की बात पहले सुनिये। यह ठीक है कि झारखंड में जो जमींदार, बनिये या दूसरे सभ्य कहे जाने वाले बाहरी लोग हैं उन्हीं के यहां सेवकिया, कमिया, मूनिस, घरभतुआ वगैरः पाये जाते हैं। यहां के असली किसानों या आदिवासियों के यहां एक भी कमिया न मिलेगा। हां, जो अब सभ्य हो रहे हैं और जमींदार या भारी खेतिहार बने हों उनकी बात हम नहीं कहते। वे हैं तो कहीं कहीं एकाध ही। वे लोग ऐसा पाप कर सकते हैं। आखिर सभ्य जो हो गये हैं!

हालत यह है कि विवाह शादी या किसी भोज वगैरः के मौके पर किसी गरीब को जमीदार, बनिया या ऐसे ही लोगों ने कुछ थोड़े से रुपये कर्ज दिये जो भोजभात में खर्च हो गये! मगर उन्हीं रुपयों के लिये वे जन्मभर के लिये गुलाम बन गये। खाना कपड़ा पाते हैं और जीवन भर गुलामी करते हैं। कभी कभी तो ऐसा होता है कि बाप के मरने पर बेटा भी गुलाम बना लिया जाता है। जिन्दगी भर कमाते रहने पर भी यह दस बीस रुपये का मामूली कर्ज चुकता नहीं होता! यदि कहीं पचास साठ हुआ, तब तो आफत ही समझिये! यह तो खामखा बेटे पोते के सर पर भी चढ़ता ही है। हां, पांच, दस, बीस हो तो शायद जिन्दगी भर में ही फारखती हो जाय! सो भी कर्जदाता की नजरे इनायत पर ही यह बात निर्भर है। उसका सूद वह नहीं लेता यही गनीमत है! जिन्दगी भर में फारखती हो गई तो उसे धन्यवाद दीजिये! बड़ा ही उदार आदमी ठहरा! अगर न हुई तो मरिये! कमिया को रद्दी खाना कपड़ा ही देते हैं। यह ठीक है कि घोर देहातों में और जंगलों में ही सेवकिया या कमिया पाये जाते हैं। क्योंकि वहां आवाजाही का साधन न होने के कारण कोई छेड़छाड़ जो नहीं करेगा और सेवकिया पशु की तरह चुपचाप पड़ा रहेगा।

मूनिस तो मामूली मजदूर की तरह रहता है और काम न रहने पर चला जाता है — उसे टरका देते और जवाब दे देते हैं। उसकी मजदूरी क्या है एक सेर कच्चा चावल और तीन सेर धान या दूसरा अन्न! बस! बड़ी तकलीफ से उसका और बाल बच्चों का काम चलता है। चावल की जगह कभी चिउड़ा भी देते हैं। यह है तो नाश्ता के लिये और धान या दूसरा अन्न होता है भोजनार्थ। एक के ही भोजन से दूसरों की भी गुजर कैसे हो?

हां, घरभतुआ को रोज खाना कपड़ा के अलावे दस से चौदह मन तक धान भी साल में देते हैं। आषाढ़ से माघ तक ही ज्यादातर उसे रहना पड़ता है। बीच में जब कहीं कोई काम नहीं रहता तो उसे भी कभी कभी छुट्टी मिल जाती है। असल में ये घरभतुआ और मूनिस तो खेती के ही मजदूर और गुलाम हैं जिन्हें पहले सर्फ (serf) कहते थे। ये लोग तो मामूली गुलाम या विहार के खवास हैं नहीं। इसीलिये खेती का काम न रहने पर इन्हें छुट्टी मिल जाती है और शुरू होते ही घरभतुआ फिर आ जाता है। उसके साथ ऐसा ही तय रहता है। मगर मूनिस तो खामखा आयेगा नहीं। दिल चाहा तो आया और काम मिला तो रह भी गया। यदि और जगह मिला तो वहीं चला गया। जहां जरा भी ज्यादा आराम मिलता है वहीं चला जाता है। इसीलिये मूनिस और घरभतुवा को आमतौर से कोई कर्ज नहीं रहता है। मगर सेवकिया और कमिया तो कर्ज में

ही फंसा रहता है। वही तो पक्का गुलाम है। बेशक कमिया सर्फ है। मगर सेवकिया तो पक्का स्लेव (slave) है। इन सबों की भारी दुर्दशा है — इनका जीवन नारकीय है।

अब जरा सूदखोरी की बला तो देखिये। सीधे सादे किसानों से काइंया सूदखोर शुरू में ही पूछते हैं कि "कै सूद देवहीं?" कितने सूद साल में देगा? दो या तीन? वह कहता है कि "कतै लेबहू सरकार"! आप कितना लेंगे? यदि बड़ी दया हो गई तो दो, नहीं तो तीन तो खामखा और हो सका तो ज्यादा भी। हर तीसरे चौथे महीने सूद जोड़ के उसे मूल में मिला देना और इस मिले हुए पर सूद चालू करना यही दो सूद के मानी हैं। यदि तीन हुआ तो हर तीसरे चौथे महीने सूद को मूल में मिलाते जायंगे। जब तक साल के भीतर ही दो बार मिलाके उस पर तीसरी बार सूद चढ़ाने न लगें। चार होने पर साल के भीतर ही चौथी बार चढ़ने लगता है! यह है चक्रवृद्धि या सूद दर सूद का यह कितना भयंकर तरीका और प्रचार है! क्या ऐसी लूट झारखंड के सिवाय कहीं और भी आज संभव है? ऐसे भी नमूने देखने को पलामू वगैरः में मिले हैं, जहां नन्हें नन्हें बच्चे बाप के मरने पर कर्ज देने वाले के यहां दिन रात काम करने और डांटडपट सहने या मारपीट तक करवाने को मजबूर किये जाते हैं। एक वार तो ऐसा हुआ कि एक बिना जमीन वाले किसान को एक ने पांच पसेरी मकई और आठ पसेरी जटंगी दी। दोनों की कीमत कुल तीन रुपये होती थी। उसके लिये उसने लगातार तीन साल उस पापी सूदखोर के यहां काम किया। मगर कर्ज चुकता होने के बजाय बढ़के पूरा सोलह रुपया हो गया! जोड़ने वाले जोड़े कि साल में कितने सूद उसने लिये और दर क्या थी? शायद महीने महीने ही सूद जोड़ा गया और दर थी कई सौ फीसदी! तभी तो काम करवाने पर भी तीन के सोलह हो गये? उसने तो काबुली सूद की भी नाक काट ली! खैर, पता लगने पर हमारे साथी ने डांट डपट के उस पिशाच से किसान का पिंड किसी तरह छुड़वाया।

ये सूदखोर होते हैं यों तो गांवों और शहरों के बनिये। मगर शोषक गृहस्थ और टुटपुजिये जमींदार भी यही पेशा करते हैं। इनके अलावे काबुली, गोसाईं, मुसलमान, पंजाबी, कान्यकुब्ज, भूमिहार, मारवाड़ी और अग्रवाल बनिये भी यह काम झारखंड के विभिन्न जिलों में यही कारबार करते हैं। रांची जिले में तो बिहार से गोसाईं और ब्राह्मण भैंसा (काड़ा) बेचने आते हैं। क्योंकि भैंसे हल में जोते जाते हैं। वही लोग उन्हीं रुपयों को सूद पर लगा के चले जाते और फिर समय पर आके सूद दर सूद के साथ वसूलते हैं। ये लोग घर घर घूमके दो

चार रुपये ही कर्ज देते हैं। ज्यादा देने में वसूली में खतरा रहता है। सूद भी कस के नहीं मिल सकता। दो चार रुपयों का तो जितना भी सूद चाहें वसूल कर सकते हैं। आदिवासी किसान ज्यादा रुपये लेते भी नहीं। बीज आदि के लिये समय समय पर दोई चार से इनका काम निकलता है। गोसाईं और ब्राह्मण लोग उन्हीं के यहां खाते पीते भी हैं और रुपये लेके भिखमंगे के रूप में मांगते खाते वापस जाते हैं। धरना देके और डरवा धमका के भी जल्दी ही वसूल कर लेते हैं। भोलेभाले किसान इनसे डरते भी हैं। वे ईमानदार भी पूरे होते हैं और वचन के भी पक्के। इसलिये वसूली में देर तो यों भी नहीं होती।

हां, गोसाईं, काबुली और पंजाबी तो बड़ी सख्ती और बेमुरव्वती से वसूली करते हैं। ये पापी ताक में रहते हैं। ज्योंही मजदूरों को वेतन मिला, मजदूरी मिली, या किसान के गल्ले वगैरः बिके, कि इनने छापा मारा और बेरहमी से छीन ही के छोड़ा। छप्परों पर लाठियां पीटते भी हैं। मारपीट भी कर डालते हैं। इनकी वसूली तो निरी लाठियों के ही बल से होती है। पंजाबी कपड़े बेंचने आते और काबुली हींग वगैरः भी बेंचते हैं। उधार बेंच के एक के तीन कुछ्ही महीनों में बना लेते हैं! बेचारे किसान को क्या मालूम कि ऐसा होगा। इसीलिये जब वसूली में देर होती तो मारपीट, लट्ठबाजी, छप्पर पीटना जारी होता है!

सूद की दर आमतौर से महीने में एक से दो आना होती है। यह बात सभी जिलों में पाई जाती है। यों तो चार, छः और आठ आने तक भी हो जाया करता है। किसान की गरीबी और गर्ज के मुताबिक ही सूद की दर तय पाती है और वसूलने वालों की ताकत भी इस दर का फैसला करने में काफी मदद करती है। क्योंकि लिखा पढ़ी तो कुछ होती नहीं। जितना वसूल कर सके उतना ही समझिये। कानून और कचहरी की बात तो है नहीं । हां, रांची और पलामू में ज्यादातर गल्ले के बारे में और रुपये के बारे में भी बढ़ी या बाढ़ी और डेढ़ी का तरीका है। बढ़ी का अर्थ है मूल का दूना और डेढ़ी की मानी है उसका ड्योढ़ा। ज्यादे से ज्यादा छः महीने में, नहीं तो उससे कम - तीनी चार - में सूदखोर एक का डेढ़ जब वसूलते हैं तो उसे डेढ़ी कहते हैं। और अगर उनने एक का दो वसूल कर लिया तो बढ़ी या बाढ़ी समझिये। डेढ़ी मालूम होता है, आम चीज है। इसीलिये उससे बढ़ जाने के कारण ही दूने को बढ़ी या बाढ़ी कहते हैं।

हजारीबाग, मानभूम वगैरः में मारवाड़ी, दूकानदार, अग्रवाल बनिये और पंजाबी तीनों ही चीजें बेंचते और पैसे कर्ज पर लगाते हैं। सौ में पंजाबी - १०, अग्रवाल ६० और मारवाड़ी ३० हैं। पंजाबी, गोसाईं और काबुली का अनुपात

४०:४०:२० है। मारवाड़ी और अग्रवाल खेती भी करने लगे हैं। बाकी तीन खेती नहीं करते। यही आम बात है। मगर मारवाड़ी वगैरः छोटे छोटे खेतिहर। बड़े बड़े खेतिहर कान्यकुब्ज और भूमिहार हैं। ये दूकानदारी नहीं करते। गल्ला और रुपया सूद पर देते हैं। ज्यादातर गया जिले के मुसलमान सौदागर के नाम से प्रसिद्ध हैं। ये खेती तो शायद ही करते हैं। कपड़ा बेंचते और रुपया सूदपर देते हैं। कहीं कहीं यजुर्वेदी या और लोग भी यह काम करते हैं। यही हैं संक्षेप में यहां के सूदखोर। अब जरा इनकी करतूतों का संक्षिप्त ब्योरा सुनिये।

जो लोग कपड़े या अन्न आदि की दूकानें करते हैं उनके पास संथाल वगैरः खरीदने जाते हैं तो विना पैसा चीजें देते हैं और दो या तीन सूद की बात तय करके बही में असली दाम का ऽयोढ़ा लिख लेते हैं। मूल और सूद वसूली के लिये कहते हैं कि अन्न हीं देना। डेढ़ रुपये में आठ आने के तीन अन्न तय कर देते हैं कि जनेरा (मकई), मडुवा और कोदो बीस बीस सेर देना। यह बीस सेर मनमाना ही होता है, न कि कोई बाजार दर के अनुसार। संथाल बेचारा क्या समझे? आसाढ़ में यह बात तय पाई तो पहली वसूली अश्विन में, दूसरी पूस माघ में और तीसरे फागुन चैत में होती है। जिन वसूली के समय कुछ न मिला उसी में सूद और मूल को मिलाके मिले हुए पर आगे सूद चलेगा। अश्विन में न मिलने पर मूल डेढ़ और सूद डेढ़, कुल तीन रुपये हो गये। इसी तरह माघ में तीन के छः और चैत में बारह बने। सूद बढ़ाने के लिये ही किसान के देने पर भी नहीं लेते! फागुन चैत के बाद जो सूद लेते हैं उसे धुरिकारी कहते हैं। हां, जो लोग कर्ज पर रुपये देते हैं वे हर महीने मारपीट से, छप्पर पीटके या जैसे हो सूद वसूल करी लेते हैं। क्योंकि यह तो गैर कानूनी है। अदालतें तो ऐसा सूद दिलायेंगी नहीं।

कान्यकुब्ज और भूमिहार वगैरः की यह हालत होती है कि कर्ज देने के बाद दो चार साल चुप्प रहते हैं। छोड़ देते हैं। पीछे दस बीस गुना हो जाने पर सारी जमीन लिखवा के किसान को कमिया या मूनिस बना लेते हैं। एक ही जमा को बही पर भी सूदखोर लोग लिखते हैं और हैंडनोट भी बनवाते हैं। फलतः एक ही जमा दो हो जाती है। जिसका खेत नीलाम करवाया उसी के हल बैलों से उसी के हाथों जोतबाते बुनवाते हैं। अपने पास तो दोई चार हल रखते हैं। यदि बेगार में काम करवाते एक वक्त सिर्फ खाना दे देते हैं हल बैल सभी के बदले में, और अगर कमिया बना के करवाते तो कही चुके हैं कि एक सेर चावल और दो सेर धान बहुत है। कमिया को यदि बीच में एक मन धान फिर कर्ज दिया तो वही धान दस वर्ष में पचास साठ बन जाता है! यों भी मैंने

किसानों के मुंह से डुमरी (हजारीबाग) में सुना कि एक मन का पूरा अस्सी मन बन गया! यदि उसे थोडी सी बंटाई जमीन दी, तो जमीन वाले का आधे से लेकर दस आने तक उपज में हिस्सा हो गया और किसान का छः आना! यों भी जमींदार लोग धान की खेती जगह जगह खूब करते हैं। मौजों पर उनकी कचहरियां होती हैं जिन्हें भंडार कहते हैं। किसानों के हलबैलों से पहले जमींदार की खेती हो लेंती है। पीछे किसान की होती है या यों कहिये कि चौपट होती है। पटाने का जल भी पहले जमींदार ही लेते हैं। पीछे बचने पर ही किसान पाते हैं! दृष्टान्त के लिये कतरस के पास नवागढ़ के जमींदार राजा नीलकंठ नारायण सिंह का भंडार लालूडीह में है। वहां किसानों की खेती पहले हो पाती नहीं। ऐसी ही सर्वत्र होता है।

सूदखोर लोग किसानों को कैसे उजाड़ते हैं इसके दो चार प्रसिद्ध दृष्टान्त हजारीबाग और मानभूम के सरहदी इलाकों से दे के यह दुःख गाथा खत्म करेंगे। (१) पीरटांड (हजारीबाग) थाने के खुखरा मौजे के दुलारचन्द साहु ने उसी थाने के गम्हरा मौजे के खांड़ेमाझी को कुछी रुपये कर्ज दिये। पीछे गम्हरा और जितपुर गांवों की तीन सौ मन सालाना धान उपजाने वाली सारी जमीन साहु ने नीलाम करवा लीं। खांड़े के मरने पर उसकी स्त्री से झूठमूठ कहके जमीनें नीलाम कराईं। अब स्त्री और तीन बच्चे मारे मारे फिरते हैं।

(२) दुलार चंद ने ही गम्हरा के जीतू मांझी की ढाई सौ मन धान वाली जमीन भी नीलाम करवाली यों ही मामूली रुपयों के लिये। वह जीतू तीस साल का है। मारा फिरता है।

(३) दुलार चन्द ने ही गम्हरा के मंगर महतो से ६० रुपये लेके एक जमीन जोतने को दी। कुछ दिनों बाद जमीन ले ली और रुपये भी वापस नहीं देता । वहीं की दो मुसमातों के साथ भी उसने ऐसा ही किया है।

(४) मानभूम जिले के तोपचांची में कपड़े और चावल की दूकान करने वाले श्री त्रिलोक सिंह पंजाबी उसी तोपचांची थाने के गनेसपुर के मंगरमांझी की डेढ़ सौ मन धान की जमीन नीलाम करवाली। मांझी तो भाग के पीरटांड़ के केंहुवारी मौजे में ससुराल में चला गया। बूढ़ी मां मारी फिरती है।

(५) गनेसपुर के ही चूनूमांझी, झरीमांझी और दरबनमांझी की ८४ एकड़ लाखिराज जमीन थी। गोविंदपुर थाने के खरनी मौजे के बाबू मनभरन सिंह ने तीन चार साल हुए सभी जमीन केवल सौ रुपये मूल में ही नीलाम करवा ली। पहले तो इजारा लिखाया। पीछे नालिश और डिग्री कराके नीलाम करवा ली। सिर्फ डेढ़ रुपया सेस उस सारी जमीन का देना होता है। हजार कहने पर भी

किश्त करके लेने को राजी न हुए।

यह भी होता है कि यदि माझी किसी से मजदूरी करवाते हैं तो उसे कुछ जमीन भी दे देते हैं और वही एक सेर चावल तथा तीन सेर धान मजदूरी देते हैं। दूसरे लोग तो जमीन देते ही नहीं। सिर्फ दो सेर धान और एक वक्त का खाना देते हैं!

(८)

काश्तकारी कानून की दिक्कतें

संथाल परगने की तो बात ही निराली है। वहां तो कोई बाकायदा काश्तकारी कानून अभी तक हई नहीं। कुछ नियम कायदे और रेगुलेशन पुरानी या फर्मान हैं और उन्हीं के आधार पर जो बातें तय पाई हैं उन्हीं के अनुसार वहां की जमीनों का इन्तजाम होता है। यह कितनी अन्धेर है कि अब तक वहां कोई निश्चित काश्तकारी कानून बना ही नहीं। इस कमी को जांच कमिटी ने भी महसूस किया है और छोटानागपुर के ही ढंग का वहां के लिये भी काश्तकारी कानून बनाने की सिफारिश उसने की है।

रह गई छोटानागपुर काश्तकारी कानून की बात। उसकी एक ही चीज हमें पसन्द आई। जहां विहार के कानून में खड़ी फसल की जब्ती कुर्की की घृणित धारायें मौजूद ही नहीं हैं। किन्तु कांग्रेसी मंत्रियों ने उनकी धार ऐसी पैनी कर दी और उनका प्रयोग इतना आसान बना दिया कि जमींदार लोग किसानों का गला आसानी से साफ कर दें। तहां छोटानागपुर में उनने ऐसी दया नहीं की। पहले से भी ऐसी धारायें नहीं थीं और उनने भी नये सिरे न जोड़ीं। एतदर्थ उन्हें अनेक धन्यवाद!

मगर इसी के साथ यहां के कानून में जो सर्टिफिकेट या जब्ती कुर्की की खतरनाक धारायें पड़ी हैं वह नहीं निकाली गईं! विहार के कानून से तो वे धारायें मंत्रियों को मजबूरन निकाल फेंकनी पड़ीं। किसान सभा ने उनकी नाकों दम जो कर दी थी। पर हमें उस समय पता न था कि छोटानागपुर से वे निकाली ही नहीं गईं। असल में यहां के जो आदिवासी मेम्बर असेम्बली में हैं वे तो कुछ अजीब से हैं। वे कांग्रेसी होने के नाते चुप्पी मारे रहे। हमें भी नहीं बताया! या कि, वे यह बात समझी न सके कि यह सर्टिफिकेट कौन सी बला है? इसी घपले में यह जहर का प्याला रही गया! ये धारायें किसानों की छाती पर बैठी कोदों दल रही हैं। शायद खड़ी फसल की जब्ती कुर्की की ही जगह सर्टिफिकेट या जब्ती कुर्की को रख के प्रायश्चित किया गया है! जमींदारों को भी तो आखिर खुश करना था!

मगर इनसे भी बुरी जो चीज हमारी समझ में आई न सकी वह है उस कानून का एक लम्बा १३वां परिच्छेद ही, जिसे जमीन सम्बन्धी शर्त्तों का अध्याय कहते हैं और जिसमें कुल सत्रह धारायें हैं। इसे अंग्रेजी में चैप्टर औफ प्रीडियल कन्डीशन्स (Chapter of Praedial Conditions) कहते हैं। इस कानून में जगह जगह इन शर्त्तों का जो जिक्र है और इस लम्बे प्रकरण में जो उनका पूरा विवरण दिया और गोत्रोच्चार किया गया है उससे स्पष्ट है कि हरी, बेगारी वगैरः गैर कानूनी काम कह के जिन्हें और जगह पुकारा जाता है और जिनके मिटाने के लिये बड़ा तूफान मचाया गया है वही सब चीजें झारखंड में ''जमीन सम्बन्धी शर्त्तों'' या ''प्रीडियल कंडीशन्स'' के नाम से कानूनी करार दे दी गई हैं। अजीब बात है। जिन बातों को अब अववाब और गैर कानूनी काम कहके और जगह रोका गया है वही यहां कानूनी ठहराये गये हैं और उन पर कांग्रेसी मंत्रियों ने मुहर लगा दी है! जैसे भावली लगान को कानून के जरिये नगद बनाया जा सकता है। ठीक उसी तरह इन शर्त्तों के बदले जमींदार को नगद रुपये दे सकते हैं और ऐसा करने के लिये डिप्टी कमिश्नर के यहां भावली की ही तरह दरखास्त देनी पड़ती है। ये बातें उन्हीं धाराओं में लिखी हैं और नगद बनाने का लम्बा चौड़ा तरीका तथा अदालती कार्यवाही विस्तार से वहीं लिखी गई है!

जैसे संथाल परगने में अभी तक दामिन इलाके में रोड सेस के बदले सड़कों वगैरः की मरम्मत के लिये किसानों से बेगारी करवाने का तरीका था, मालूम होता है यहां भी जमींदार लोग पहले किसानों को कुछ खासतौर से ऐसी जमीनें दे देते थे जिनके बदले आहर, पैन, नहर आदि खोद खुदवाने का काम किसानों को ही करना पड़ता था। ताकि उनकी और जमींदारों की भी खेती के लिये पानी वगैरः का पूरा पूरा इन्तजाम हो सके। जैसा कि बेठखेता की बात पहले कही चुके हैं, उसी तरह और भी जमीनें किसानों को इसीलिये दी जाती होंगी कि जमींदार की खेती में वे लोग मदद कर दें। लगान के बदले उनसे इसी तरह का काम लिया जाता होगा। इसी तरह ये जमीऩ देने के लिये कुछ खास शर्त्तें तय होंगी, जिन्हें पूरा करने वाले जमीन पाते होंगे। धारा १०१ (अ) से भी ऐसा ही प्रतीत होता है। सभी जगह पहले ऐसा ही होता था। सामन्तयुग की तो यही रीति ही थी। मगर आज तो नगद या गल्ले का लगान ठीक करके इस तरह के काम खत्म कर दिये गये हैं। जहां जमींदार लोग फिर भी करवाते थे वहां कानून के जरिये ये रोक दिये गये हैं। मगर छोटानागपुर में लगान के अलावे ये अभी तक पड़े हैं। हां, यदि किसान चाहे तो इनकी जगह नगद रुपये

देने की बात तय करके इनसे पिंड छुड़ा ले! खूब है! छोटानागपुर में पुरानी सामन्तयुग वाली वेगार (feudal levies) अभी जारी है! यहां के एम.एल.ए. लोगों को क्या यह भी नहीं सूझा कि इसे तो खत्म करवा दें? याकि उन पर कोई दबाव था?

इसी सिलसिले में मुझे एक बात याद आ गई! इस बार जेल में दो झारखंडी एम.एल.ए. लोगों से मेरी बात होते होते प्रसंग छिड़ा कि वहां भावली में अठारह और बाईस के हिस्से की बात कैसी मानी गई! उनने उत्तर दिया — दोनों ने ही — कि इस बात का कानून विहार के ही लिये बना था। छोटानागपुर में तो बना नहीं! मैं भौचक में आ गया! पर विश्वास न कर सका और छोटानागपुर के काश्तकारी कानून के पन्ने उलटने लगा! बहुत हैरानी के बाद मेरी नजर ७९(अ) और ७९(ब) धाराओं पर पड़ी। उनमें तो साफ साफ वही बातें मिलीं जो बिहार के काश्तकारी कानून में हैं। मैंने उन्हें दिखाया और कहा कि कायमी जमीनों में दानाबंदी का हक अब जमींदार को है नहीं। वह तो पैदावार में से एक मन में १८ सेर से ज्यादा ले सकता नहीं! ऐसा करने पर उस पर केस चल सकता है! वे बेचारे ठक्क से रह गये और कुछ बोल न सके! बोलते भी क्या? जब उन्हीं को यह मालूम नहीं, तो फिर जमींदार क्यों इसके मुताबिक काम करने लगा? फलतः, जैसा कि मुझ से कहा गया, छोटानागपुर में कहीं भी जमींदारों ने १८ और २२ का हिस्सा नहीं लिया! उनकी तो "वही रफ्तार बेढ़ंगी, जो पहले थी सो अब भी है"। इसे ही कहते हैं अंग्रेजी कानून का इनसाफ और इसी का दमामा बजाया जाता है।

इससे किसानों की कितनी हकतलफी हुई इसका एक नमूना सुनिये। ताजे आंकड़े तो मेरे पास नहीं है। मगर मैं १९१७ वाला हजारीबाग का गजेटियर देखता था तो उसके १२७वें पृष्ठ में उस जिले की उन जमीनों का ब्योरा मिला जिनका लगान नकद नहीं वसूल होके गल्ले के रूप में मिलता है। वह ब्योरा एकड़ों में यों है :— (१) खुटकट्टीदार (धानी) २९.१५ और (भीठ या बारी) २५.८६, (२) सेट्लरैयत (धानी) ९३३१.९० और (बारी) ७९३४.३०, (३) कायमी ४५२.८९ और ६९४.९४, (४) गैरकायमी ८१५.९७ और १२७८.६०, (५) शिकमी २०८४.५१ और ३२३३.३७। इस तरह देखा कि धानी और बारी जमीनें कुल मिला के करीब वीस हजार एकड़ निकलीं जिनकी दानाबंदी बन्द हो जानी चाहिये। अब तो बहुत ज्यादा बढी होगी। सिर्फ सात ही हजार एकड़ के करीब गैरकायमी या शिकमी थीं जिन पर १८ और २२ लागू नहीं होता। हो सकता है, वह भी बढ़ी हों। इस तरह किसानों की

कितनी हानि और जमींदारों की धांधली होती है कानून की ठीक जानकारी नहीं होने के कारण!

जमींदार की जिरात या प्राइवेट जमीन के बारे में भी जो ११८ धारा है वह ठीक नहीं है। जिस तरह बिहार वाले कानून में यह धारा दी गई है उसी तरह की यहां भी क्यों नहीं दी गई? एक तो इस धारा की उपधारा १(ब) में जो मझिहस और बेठखेता को भी जिरात जमीन करार दिया है, वह ठीक नहीं है। वह तो ज्यादे से ज्यादा बकाश्त हो सकती थी। या नहीं तो किसान की रैयती। उसे जिरात करार देने का कोई उचित कारण नहीं दीखता। इस ढंग की जमीनें बिहार में भी ''जागीर'' वगैरः के रूप में मिल सकती हैं जैसा कि पहले कहा है। और अगर वहां इन्हें जिरात का कामत नहीं लिखा, तो यहां भी लिखा जाना उचित नहीं है।

दूसरी बात है उपधारा १(अ) की और यह तो खतरनाक है। उसमें भी पहले वही था जो विहार के कानून में है। मगर १९२० में जो सुधार किया गया वही खतरनाक है। विहार के कानून में लिखा है कि वह जमीन पट्टे पर चाहे एक या कई साल के लिये भी दी जाय, फिर भी जमींदार की जिरात ही रहेगी ज्योंही पट्टे की मीयाद पूरी हो जाय। और पट्टे के मानी ही हैं रजिस्टरी के जरिये लिखा गया पट्टा। जबानी या बिना रजिस्टरी किये कोई भी पट्टेदार कहा जा सकता नहीं। मगर इस कानून में जो १९२० में संशोधन किया गया है कि ''या जो लिखा या जबानी पट्टा एक साल से कम के लिये दिया जाय''। इसमें सबसे बड़ा धोका यही है कि जबानी या बिना रजिस्टरी के भी पट्टेदार हो सकते हैं और इससे सारा मामला खटाई में पड़ सकता है। उपधारा (2) में जो यह कहा गया है कि सरकार एक तारीख मुकर्रर कर देगी, जिसके बाद एक से ज्यादा साल का पट्टा जबानी नहीं हो सकता, उससे यह बात और पक्की हो जाती है कि जबानी भी पट्टा हो सकता है। इस तरह एक से ज्यादे साल तक जो लोग जमींदार की जिरात को बिना रजिस्टरी पट्टे के ही सिर्फ जबानी हीं लेके जोतते रहे हैं उन्हें उस जमीन में इसी कानून की १९वीं धारा के अनुसार कायमी हक नहीं मिल सकता, जबकि शुरू में बनी ११८वीं धारा के अनुसार मिल सकता था। दूसरी दिक्कत यह हो गई कि एक साल या कम के लिये जब जबानी या बिना रजिस्टरी का ही पट्टा हो सकता है तो जमींदार किसी को ज्यादे दिन के लिये क्यों रजिस्टरी से देने जाय? ज्यादे से ज्यादा एक एक साल के लिये देता जायगा और उसका जिराती हक बना रहेगा। जब रजिस्टरी की शर्त्त थी तब वह ऐसा कर नहीं सकता था। ऐसा करने

पर उसी १९वीं धारा के अनुसार किसान को कायमी हक जो मिल जाता। इससे साफ है कि जमींदारों के ही फायदे के लिये यह संशोधन किया गया है, जो अनुचित है और कम से कम कांग्रेसी युग में तो यह कलंक मिट जाना चाहता था।

यह बात जरा पेचोदा है। इसलिये इसका कुछ स्पष्टीकरण जरूरी है। विहार कानून की २०वीं और छोटानागपुर की १७वीं धारा के अनुसार मोटा मोटी यह बात मानी गई है कि किसी मौजे में जो किसान लगातार बारह साल तक खेती करता रहे वह उस मौजे का सेट्ल्ड रैयत या देही किसान माना जाता है। यह जरूरी नहीं है कि वह एक ही जमीन में बारह साल करता रहे, या कायमी में करे। किसी तरह बटाई वगैरः के जरिये भी किसान के परिवार में बारह साल तक लगातार खेती होती रहना जरूरी है। चाहे एक ही पीढ़ी ने १२ साल किया या दो तीन ने भी। इससे कोई फर्क नहीं होता। उस परिवार की खेती से ही मतलब है।

इसके बाद बिहार की २१वीं और यहां की १९वीं धारा के अनुसार उस देही रैयत के जोत में जोई जमीन आ जायगी, चाहे वह जिरात हो या बकाश्त, उस पर उसका कायमो हक हो जायगा और जमींदार अपनी मर्जी से उसे बेदखल नहीं कर सकता। केवल उचित लगान ले सकता है। जमींदार लोग इसी धारा से बचने के लिये हजार उपाय करते हैं और जाल फरेब, धोकाधड़ी सब कुछ कर डालते हैं। उससे बचने का कानूनी उपाय किसी हद तक जिरात जमीन में होता है और यही बात बिहार की १२०वीं तथा यहां के कानून की ११८ वीं धारा में की गई है।

यह भी जान लेना चाहिये कि जमींदार की जिरात जमीन तो तय है। वह बढ़ नहीं सकती। काश्तकारी कानून पहले पहल बनने के बाद जो पहला सर्वे हुआ था उसमें जांचने पर जब पता चला कि लगातार बारह साल से जमींदार अपने ही हल बैल से अपनी हीं जमीन में खेती करता आ रहा है तभी वह जमीन जिरात लिखी गई। मगर जिसमें जरा भी गड़बड़ी मालूम हुई वह बकाश्त या खुदकाश्त लिखी गई। उसके बाद जो भी जमीन किसी तरह जमींदार के कब्जे में आई है या आती है वह जिरात न हो के बकाश्त ही बनती है।

अब १९वीं धारा (विहार की २१वीं) के अनुसार बकाश्त जमीन पर तो देही किसान का हल गया और वह उसकी कायमी हुई। यह ठीक है कि चोरी या बिना पूछे जमीन पर हल नहीं जाना चाहिये और कोई किसान ऐसा करने की हिम्मत भी कैसे कर सकता है। जमींदार मजबूरी से या किसी और कारण

से जब किसान को या तो हुक्म देता है, या कम से कम इतना हीं करता है कि नीलाम करवाने पर भी किसान के ही कब्जे में छोड़ देता है तभी तो किसान जोतता है। इसलिये उसका कायमी हक हो जाता है।

लेकिन जिरात जमीन में जरा सी गड़बड़ी है। देही किसान उसे भी जोतते ही कायमी बना लेता है। मगर अगर जमींदार ने रजिस्टरी पट्‌टे के जरिये किसान के साथ जिरात का बन्दोबस्त कर दिया तो उस पर कायमी हक न होगा और पट्‌टे की मीयाद के पूरा होते ही जमींदार का उस पर फिर जिरात के रूप में ही कब्जा हो जायगा। और आमतौर से होता यही रहा है कि बिना रजिस्टरी के ही यों ही जमींदार ऐसी जमीन दे देते रहे हैं। पूछने कौन जाता था? मगर ऐसा करने पर तो खतरा यही है कि किसान की रैयती हो जायगी। इसी खतरे को बचाने के लिये छोटानागपुर के कानून में ऐसी तरमीम (संशोधन) कर दी गई कि बिना रजिस्टरी वाला या जबानी भी पट्‌टा माना जाय। नहीं तो कायदा यही है कि पट्‌टा उसे ही कहते हैं जिसकी रजिस्टरी की जाय। दूसरे ढंग की चीज को पट्‌टा कह नहीं सकते। हम चाहते हैं कि यह चीज न रहे और यहां के तथा विहार के कानून जिरात के बारे में समान हीं रहें।

हमें यह देखके ताज्जुब हुआ कि जहां विहार के कानून में किसानों को अपनी कायमी जमीन में पेड़, बांस वगैरः लगाने और इसे काटने का तथा मकान, ईंट, खपड़ा, कूआं, तालाब घरगिरस्ती के कामों के लिये बनाने का पूरा हक दिया गया है तहां यहां के कानून में यह बात है नहीं। और संथाल परगने में तो और भी गड़बड़ है। क्योंकि वहां तो कोई काश्तकारी कानून है नहीं। यही कारण है कि बाग वगैरः के लगाने पर जमींदार यहां के किसानों को बहुत परीशान करते हैं और न सिर्फ जमीन छीन लेते हैं, किन्तु हर्जाना भी वसूलना चाहते हैं। संथाल परगने के गोड्डा इलाके में तो कांग्रेसी मंत्रियों के समय में भी ऐसी दिक्कत हुई थी और आखिर पीछे लड़ते लड़ते हाइकोर्ट से किसान हार भी गये।

इन चीजों के हकों के लिये विहार में हमें बड़ी लड़ाइयां लड़नी पड़ी हैं। यह तो बहुत ही प्रसिद्ध बात है। तब कहीं जाके यह हक हासिल हो सका है। विहार प्रान्तीय किसान सभा का जन्म ही इसी बात को लेकर हुआ था। मगर अफसोस कि सूबे के एक हिस्से के किसानों को जहां यह हक मिला है तहां उसके दूसरे पूरे आधे हिस्से को अबतक इस हक से महरूम रखा गया है। यह तो निहायत ही अनुचित है। हमने इस कानून को अच्छी तरह पढ़ा न था। इसीसे हमें इसका पता ही न था। यह नहीं कि छोटानागपुर वालों को या संथाल परगने

को इसकी जरूरत ही नहीं है। जरूरत तो ऐसी है कि कुछ पूछिये मत।

मनीऔर्डर से लगान भेजने की बात में भी यहां दिक्कत है। विहार के और यहां के भी कानून में पहले भी यह बात मानी गई थी कि किसान मनीऔर्डर से भी जमींदार के पास लगान भेज सकता है। कभी कभी जमींदार लगान लेते ही नहीं और किसान को दिक करना या चुपके से बाकी लगान की नालिश और डिग्री कराके जमीन ही छीनना चाहते हैं। लेते भी तो रसीद नहीं देते। इसीलिये मनीऔर्डर से भेजने का हक किसान को दिया गया था।

मगर फिर गड़बड़ी चली। ऐसा होता कि वे मनीऔर्डर लौटा देते और नालिश ठोक देते। यदि किसान मनीऔर्डर का कूपन पेश करता तो उसे जाली ठहराते। फलतः डाकिये या पोस्टमैन की गवाही की जरूरत होती और यह काम किसान के लिये असंभव सा हो जाता। पोस्टमैन कौन है, कहां है, आये न आये, उस पर जमींदार दबाव डाले, कहीं दूर बदल के चला गया, वगैरः दिक्कतें थीं। इसीलिये आन्दोलन हुआ। जिसके फलस्वरूप विहारी कानून में तो ५४ वीं धारा में उपधारा (३) जोड़ दी गई। मगर यहां की ५३ वीं धारा में, जिसमें मनीऔर्डर की बात है, कुछ नहीं जोड़ा गया! यह अजीब बात है! उसके जोड़ने से यह हो गया कि कूपन पेश करने से ही काम चल जाता है! पोस्टमैन की गवाही साखी की जरूरत नहीं होती।

बकाया लगान की तमादी के लिये जो २३१वीं धारा में एक साल की ही मीयाद रखी गई है वह तो अच्छी है। विहार में भी भावली के लिये ऐसा ही है। मगर नगदी के लिये जो वहां तीन साल की मीयाद है वह ठीक नहीं है। संथाल परगने की जांच कमिटी ने जो दलीलें, वहां के प्रधानों और उन्हीं के द्वारा किसानों की तबाही बचाने के लिये, एक ही साल के बाद तमादी होने के बारे में ५६वें पृष्ठ के १५०वें लम्बे पैराग्राफ में दी हैं वही सर्वत्र लागू हैं और हम सरकार तथा जमींदारों से कहेंगे कि फिर से सोचें और हमारी बातें ठीक गुजरेंगी। इसलिये इस मामले में यहां का कानून अच्छा है। मगर अफसोस यह कि कुछ दूर बाद २३४वीं धारा में मुंडारी खुटकट्टीदार के लिये न जानें क्यों तीन साल की मुद्दत कर दी गई है। हमारे जानते यह बात गलत है और मिट जानी चाहिये।

यहां के कानून की ६०वीं धारा में लिखा गया है कि किसान के खेत की पैदावार में सबसे पहले (first charge) लगान हीं का हक होता है। यही बात बिहार के कानून की ६४वीं धारा में भी है। मगर इससे क्या? हम इस चीज के सख्त दुश्मन हैं। यह तो सिद्धान्त ही गलत है। मुनासिब तो यह है कि

पैदावार में सबसे पहले खर्च कटे और उसके बाद किसान परिवार के खाने पीने वगैरः की बात आये। लगान का सवाल तो उसके बाद ही उठना चाहिये। कोई भूखे नंगे रहके लगान चुकायेगा नहीं और न सरकार या जमींदार ही यह बात साफ साफ स्वीकार करने की हिम्मत कर सकते हैं। मगर खेती का खर्च तो उससे भी पहले आता है। वह तो अनिवार्य है। वह तो पैदावार के पहले से ही शुरू हो जाता है। ऐसी दशा में जो वस्तुस्थिति है उसी को कानून में भी कबूल क्यों नहीं किया जाता? और अगर नहीं, तो साफ साफ वहीं लिख क्यों नहीं दिया जाता कि भूखे, नंगे और दवा के विना मरके भी लगान चुकाना हीं होगा? बात बोलना दूसरी। मगर मतलब उसका यही हो। यह बात — यह तरीका — धोके का है। इसीसे छोड़ना पड़ेगा।

यह ठीक है कि झारखंड के असली किसानों आदिवासियों तथा पिछड़े लोगों के बारे में काश्तकारी कानून में शर्त्तें दी गई हैं जिनके करते दूसरे लोग आमतौर से इनकी जमीनें खरीद नहीं सकते और न इजारा या रेहन वगैरः में ही ले सकते हैं। इनकी अपनी विरादरी और दल के ही लोग, सो भी उसी थाने के ही ले सकते हैं और वह भी पांच, सात या ऐसे ही सीमित समय के ही लिये। उसके बाद ज्यादातर जमीनें पुनरपि किसानों के पास लौट जाने का भी नियम है। यह बात तो ठीक ही है। मगर क्या इन शर्त्तों का जो लक्ष्य है वह पूरा होता है? उद्देश्य तो यही है कि जमीनें किसानों के हाथ से बनियों या धनियों के पास या बाहरियों के पास जाने न पायें। मगर क्या ऐसा होता है? इस समय मेरे कागजात नहीं हैं कि आंकड़े पेश करके बताऊं कि यह लक्ष्य पूरा नहीं हुआ है, नहीं हो रहा है।

बीसवीं सदी के शुरू में ही इसी खयाल से पंजाब में किसानों की जमीनें बेंचनें का कानून (Land Alienation Act) बना। उसमें भी कुछ ऐसी ही शर्त्तें लगाई गईं ताकि किसानों की जमीनें गैर किसान खरीद न सकें। मगर नतीजा क्या हुआ? क्या मकसद पूरा हुआ? हर्गिज नहीं। जाल फरेब और बेनामी तरीकों से एक तो गैर किसानों ने फिर भी जमीनें हड़प ली हीं। दूसरे किसान हीं दूसरों की जमीनें खरीद खरीद करके बनिये महाजनों से भी खतरनाक बन गये। आखिर बनिये महाजनों के सींग पूछें तो होती नहीं। वे भी तो यही करते हैं और ऐसा करते ही करते पीछे चलके खतरनाक बने, बनिये महाजन बने। शुरू में तो कोई भी बनिया महाजन था नहीं। फिर किसान भी क्यों न वैसे ही बन जाय? इसीलिये तो अब इधर फिर चार चार कानून पंजाब में हाल में बनाये गये हैं जिससे जाल फरेब रुके। मगर उनसे भी कुछ होगा क्या?

असल में जड़ को तो पकड़ा जाता नहीं। किसान जमीनें बेंचता है क्या शौक से? जो ऐसा समझते हैं वह भूलते हैं? जिन जमीनों पर उसकी पुश्तें मरखप गईं, जिनके खून को उनने पानी बना डाला, क्या उनसे ही उन्हें मुहब्बत नहीं होती? होती तो है ऐसी कि एक इंच के जाने पर उनका कलेजा कट जाता है। मगर करें क्या? मजबूरी जो ठहरी। माली हालत उन्हें मजबूर करती है। आखिर पेट और तकलीफ से मजबूर हो के कलेजे के टुकड़े निजी बच्चों को भी तो लोग बेचते ही या मार डालते ही हैं। बस यही बात यहां भी समझिये। उनकी माली हालत सुधार दीजिये, उसे सुधारने की मुनासिब तरकीब कर दीजिये। फिर देखिये कि जमीनें बिकती हैं या रुकती हैं। उसके बाद जरूरत देख के बेंचने वगैरः पर पख लगाइये तो ठीक होगा। इसे ही जड़ को पकड़ना कहते हैं।

लेकिन इधर तो फिक्र है कि जमींदार को खामखा लगान मिले चाहे फसल मारा ही क्यों न पड़े, किसान परिवार भूखा नंगा ही क्यों न मरे (लगान तो फर्स्ट चार्ज होगा)। तब तो हजार करने पर भी जमीनें चली ही जांयगी। जब जमींदार को फिक्र होगी कि पैदावार बढ़े तभी लगान पायेगा तो वह खुद अच्छे बीज, सुन्दर खाद और काफी पानी वगैरः का प्रबन्ध करेगा। उसे और सर को भी तभी चिन्ता होगी कि किसान के लिये खेती के सिवाय दूसरी आय का भी प्रबन्ध हो, ताकि उसकी माली हालत सुधरे और लगान चुकता करे। यही है जड़ को पकड़ना। क्या सरकार ने, जमींदारों ने या नेताओं ने ईमानदारी से यह बात कभी सोची है? क्या उनने इसकी कोशिश तहे दिल से की है? जमीन तो नीलाम न हो। मगर सारी की सारी खड़ी फसल जब्त हो जाय, नीलाम हो जाय यह तो और भी बुरा है। इसीलिये न तो पंजाब में सफलता मिली और न दूसरी जगह। फसल का खाने पीने भर का हिस्सा तो कभी नीलाम या जब्त होना ही नही चाहिये। इस ओर थोड़ा सा ध्यान यू.पी. में गया है और जब्ती के कानून कुछ ऐसी पख लगी है। मगर वह भी अधूरी है। देखते हैं झारखंड में भी पैदावार से ही लगान चुकता करने की बात बार बार कही गई है। यह नहीं सोचा गया है कि किसान परिवार खायेगा क्या? असल में जिन चीजों से परिवार की गुजर हो उन्हें तो खुदा भी ले नहीं सकता, यही नियम कानून बने तभी काम चल सकता है। दूसरा उपाय है नहीं।

यहां के कानून की ५८वीं धारा में एक सुन्दर बात है। मगर उसमें जो थोड़ी सी कमी है वह यदि पूरी कर दी जाय तो वह बहुत ही अच्छी चीज हो जाय। उसमें लिखा है कि यों तो बकाया लगान पर आमतौर से रुपये में एक

आना सूद साल में देना होता है। मगर अगर साल खत्म होने के पहले ही किसान लगान चुका दे तो किस्त बीतने के बाद जो सूद उससे लिया जायगा वह रुपये में दोई पैसा सालाना की दर से होगा। विहारी कानून में यह दो पैसे वाली बात नहीं है। इसीसे यह उससे अच्छा है। मगर असल में होना यह चाहिये कि साल के भीतर चुका देने पर सूद एक पैसा भी नहीं लगेगा। सूद लगेगा साल के बाद ही। हमारा मतलब साफ है। साल भर तक किसान को मौका दिया जाना चाहिये कि लगान चुकता कर दे। उसके बाद केस से या जैसे हो वसूली का यत्न होना चाहिये। कम में तो करना ही नहीं चाहिये। देर भी नहीं होने दी जाय। क्योंकि दो तीन साल के बकाया में वह तबाह हो जाता है। क्योंकि रकम बहुत बड़ी हो जाती है जिसे वह आसानी से चुकता कर नहीं सकता।

हमने जो कुछ छोटानागपुर के काश्तकारी कानून के बारे में या यों कहिये कि समूचे झारखंड के ही कानून के सम्बन्ध में लिखा है वह खास खास बातों को ही लेकर है। ये बातें ज्यादा मोटी हैं और आमतौर से सबों को खटकती हैं। यों तो बहुत सी बातें हैं जिन पर लिखने और जिन्हें सुधारने की जरूरत है। मगर हमारा काम उस कानून की पूर्ण समालोचना नहीं है।

(९)

किसानों की दूसरी तकलीफें

जितनी दिक्कतें और तकलीफें अब तक दिखाई गई हैं उन्हीं से इस दुःखगाथा की समाप्ति हो नहीं जाती। किन्तु बहुत सी और भी दिक्कतें और मुसीबतें हैं जिन पर ध्यान देना जरूरी है। उनसे किसानों की परीशानी और तबाही भी काफी होती है और सबों का सम्मिलित परिणाम उसके लिये बड़ा ही भयंकर होता है, हो रहा है। इसलिये यदि सबों का नहीं तो उनमें कुछ अहम मसलों और चुनी चुनाई विपदाओं की जानकारी जरूरी है।

जब इस दृष्टि से हम देखते हैं तो सबसे पहले जो मसला हमारे सामने आता है वह है सिंचाई या आबपाशी का। पहाड़ों और पहाड़ी नदी नालों की तो कमी यहां है नहीं। यों भी वर्षा में पहाड़ का पानी बह के नीचे जाता ही है। इसलिये जगह जगह बड़े बड़े आहर होने उनमें बरसात में इतना पानी जमा हो सकता है कि धान और रबी — दोनों ही — फसलों के लिये काफी हो। यदि आहरों की संख्या काफी हो और मुनासिब स्थान देख देख के ही वे बनाये जांय तो यह मतलब जरूर पूरा हो सकता है। मगर नये तो क्या बनेंगे। पहले के भी बने बनाये खत्म हो गये और हो रहे हैं। न सरकार को इसकी पर्वा है और न जमींदारों को। क्योंकि इनके बिना भी तो लगान वसूल होई जाता है।

जहां आहर न हों या उनसे काम चलने वाला न हो वहां नदी नालों और झरनों को बांध के और उनसे नाली या पैन निकाल के सिंचाई का काम बखूबी हो सकता है। हमने कई जगह ऐसा खुद देखा है। मगर इसमें भी दिक्कत है पैसे और खर्च की। किसान तो तबाह है। वह कहां से खर्च लाये? और जमींदार को गर्ज ही नहीं है! अमतौर से झारखंड की जमीन पैदावार नहीं है। सिर्फ पहाड़ों की तली की जमीनें ही ऐसी हैं जिनकी पैदावार अच्छी होती है। मगर ये जमीनें ज्यादा हैं नहीं ज्यादातर जमीनें मामूली दर्जे की है और जब तक सिंचाई का इन्तजाम पूरा न हो पैदावार अच्छी हो नहीं सकती। हजारीबाग के उक्त गजेटियर के ७२-७३ पृष्ठों में इस सम्बन्ध में ऐसा लिखा गया है, "It is, however, certain that the soil is for the most part inherently unfertile.

Extensive irrigation works of a character beyond the means and equipment of local agriculturists might render some of the waste land cultivable. But the poverty of the soil and the irregularity of the surface make the chances of profit very doubtful."

''यह बात पक्की है कि यहां की ज्यादातर जमीन स्वभावतः ही उपजाऊ नहीं है। हां, बहुत विस्तृत रूप में सिंचाई का इन्तजाम हो तो मुमकिन है कि कुछ उजड़ जमीनें आबाद हो जांय। मगर यह बात तो किसानों की ताकत के बाहर की चीज है। लेकिन जमीनों की अनुर्वरता और बेढंगी ऊंचाई निचाई के करते खेती से नफा करने का शायद ही अवसर हो।''

इसमें कई बातें महत्त्वपूर्ण हैं। एक तो अधिकांश जमीन अनुर्वर और रद्दी मानी गई है, ऊसर जैसी है। तिस पर तुर्रा यह कि समतल नहीं है। हां, सिंचाई का खूब अच्छा इन्तजाम हो तो कुछ ज्यादा जमीनों में खेती हो सकती है। लेकिन किसान के बूते से बाहर की यह चीज है। इसीलिये यहां की खेती में उसका खर्च ही सध जाय तो गनीमत! फिर भी जमींदारों के मुनाफे की बात पहले ही कही जा चुकी है। तब उन्हें गर्ज क्यों हो कि आहर और नहर बनायें? यह काम है तो यहां के किसानों की भूख मिटाने के लिये निहायत जरूरी — सबसे जरूरी। गर्मियों और जाड़ों में उनके मवेशियों के लिये पीने का पानी भी तभी रह सकता है — मिल सकता है और किसानों को मिल सकता है। क्योंकि वे खुद कूंए बना सकते हैं नहीं।

पानी के ही सिलसिले में एक दूसरी बात आ जाती है। हर हालत में जगह जगह कूंए काफी संख्या में बनाये जांय यदि इनकी प्यास बुझानी हों और इन्हें बीमारी से बचाना हो। हमने देखा है कि पहाड़ी जमीन के खेतों में जो पसेई होती है, पसीज के पानी थोड़ा थोड़ा निकलता है बहुतेरे किसान मजबूरन उसे ही पीते हैं। उसे रांची में पझरा भी बोलते हैं और वहां तथा और जगह दूसरे दूसरे नाम भी उसके हैं। कहीं कहीं दोन का पानी भी कहते हैं, जो ज्यादातर बरसात में ही निकलता है। मगर उसमें बीमारी का खतरा तो हजार रहता है। लेकिन किसान गरीब क्या करें? पहाड़ों में कूआं तो हजारों रुपये लगने पर ही बन सकता है। पत्थर काटे बिना कैसे बनेगा? इसीलिये कहीं कहीं खेतों में कच्चा कूआं और बालुकामय भूमि में बालू हटा के भी पानी निकालते और प्यास बुझाते हैं।

तीसरी भारी दिक्कत है कानूनी मदद की। हमें जेलों में हजारों ऐसे झारखंडी कैदी मिले हैं जिन्हें ठीक ठीक कानूनी मदद मिलने पर वे जेल नहीं आते और उनकी जमीन जायदाद बच जाती। हमें वकील मुखतारों को अपमानित नहीं

करना है और न उस पेशे को खामखा गाली देना हमारा मतलब है। मगर जो अनुभव हमें हुआ है उसके बल पर हम यह कह सकते हैं कि बहुत अंशों में वकीलों की गड़बड़ी से ही यह काम बिगड़ता है। धीरे धीरे यह पेशा ऐसा होता जा रहा है कि लोग इसमें भरते जा रहे हैं। मगर सबों का काम तो चलना हीं चाहिये। इसलिये तरह तरह के तरीके निकलते हैं, निकाले जाते हैं। बेईमानी शैतानी और जालसाजी भी होती है। दलाल भी रखे जाते हैं जो चालाकी से सीधे सादे मुवक्किलों को फंसाते हैं। कई केस हमें ऐसे भी मिले हैं जिनके देखने से पता चला है कि वकील ने ही गरीब किसान को धोखा दिया। कठिनाई यह होती है कि यहां के किसान वकीलों की भाषा ठीक समझ पाते नहीं और न वकील ही इनकी समझते हैं। इसलिये भी धोका होता है। कभी तो ऐसा हुआ कि मुवक्किल का सबूत लेके भी वकील ने पेरा ही न किया। इसी तरह की और भी बातें हुई हैं। संथाल परगने की जांच कमिटी ने यह बातें कबूल की हैं और रिपोर्ट के ५५वें पैराग्राफ में लिखा गया है कि "Unrestricted recruitment would probably lead to touting, the fostering of litigation and other malpractices." ''वकील मुखतारें की संख्या पर रोक न होने पर संभवतः दलाली, मुकदमेबाजी बढ़ाना और दूसरी बुरी बातें पैदा होंगी''।

और जिलों में भी ऐसी बातें कभी कभी हो जाती हैं। मगर यहां के किसान तो निरे सीधे हैं। वे कुछ समझते ही नहीं। सबों पर विश्वास करते हैं। शिक्षा का विस्तार यहां है नहीं। इसीलिये यहां वे बुराइयां बहुत ज्यादा पाई जाती हैं। मेरे जानते तो बहुत बड़ी देश की सेवा इस एक बात से हो जाय, अगर सभी कचहरियों के स्थानों पर एक एक, दो दो भी ऐसे वकील मुखतार रखे जांय जो खासकर यही काम करें। उन्हें फीस की उतनी फिक्र न हो, दरअसल भीतर से त्यागी हों, केवल गुजर कर लें और गरीबों की सहायता करें। बेशक, यहां के किसानों में बहुतेरे फीस न दे सकने के कारण भी हारते और कष्ट भोगते हैं।

चौथी बात है देशी या पहाड़ी शराब की जिसे हंड़िया कहते हैं। यहां के लोगों का परम्परागत स्वभाव है हंड़िया तैयार करना और पीना। यह चीज इनके जीवन का एक अभिन्न अंग हो गई है और इसके बिना ये लोग अपनी मौत समझते हैं। मगर एक तो कानूनी अड़ंगे के चलते उस पर बाधा खड़ी हुई है। दूसरे देहात देहात में सरकारी शराब की दूकानें खुल जाने से उसी का प्रचार बहुत ज्यादा होता है। जैसे सस्ती और अपने हाथों बन सकने वाली भी खादी मिल के कपड़ों के सामने खत्म हो गई थी और आज भी हजार यत्न करने पर भी उसका संभलना असंभव है। ठीक यही बात हंड़िया के बारे में भी है। देशी

शराब या सरकारी शराब ने भी उस पर हमला किया है। फलतः वह खत्म होने चली है। जब तक उस पर आजादी नहीं हो जाती और शराब की सरकारी दूकानें देहातों से हटा दी नहीं जाती हैं तब तक इनका यह दुःख दूर नहीं होगा। केवल शहरों में भी अंग्रेजी शराब और शराब की सरकारी दूकानें रहें तो रहें। मगर जहां भी रहें, पीने वालों की गणना (census) करके उन्हीं को सर्टीफिकेट रहे। तभी खरीद सकें। दूसरे खरीदने न पायें। आदिवासियों और पिछड़े लोगों को इसकी सर्टीफिकेट हर्गिज न दी जाय। तभी काम चलेगा।

इससे हमारा मतलब यह नहीं है शराबबन्दी का प्रचार न हो। हो और जरूर हो। मगर गला दबा के नहीं जैसा कि सरकार कहती है कि वह शराब रोकना चाहती है। शराब की रोक रुपया पैदा करने का साधन न बने। रोक के बहाने रुपया न कमाया जाय। दूसरी बात यह है कि पहले उन्हें इसका निर्वाध अधिकार हो जिनके जीवन का यह अभिन्न अंग है। यह से हमारा मतलब है हंड़िया जैसी ही चीजों से। जो आसानी से चावल वगैरः से बनती हैं या तैयार हो जाती हैं। हंड़िया या ताड़ी का हक उन्हें दीजिये और समझा बुझाके रोकिये। लाठी के बल से या तलवार के बल से हर्गिज नहीं। तभी तो चोरी से और हजार कुकर्म से भी लोग पीते ही हैं। नैतिक बल और समझाने बुझाने की बात दूसरी है। दृष्टान्त के लिये टाना आन्दोलन को लीजिये। यह इसी झारखंड का है। मगर धार्मिक ढंग से या प्रचार से ही होने के कारण टाना लोग शराब, मांस आदि सभी चीजों से अलग हो गये और इनकी संख्या यहां काफी है। मांस भी यहां के लोगों का प्रधान खाद्य है। मगर टाना लोगों ने कतई छोड़ दिया। कानून के जरिये ऐसा कभी नहीं हो सकता था। इसलिये इस बारे में हम कानून बनाने के विरोधी हैं।

जो भी कानून किसानों के फायदे के बनते हैं उनका प्रचार व्यापक रूप से नहीं होता। केवल रस्म अदाई कर दी जाती है। एक ओर तो सरकार झारखंड को पिछड़ा हुआ प्रदेश मानती है। दूसरी ओर इस बात की भरपूर कोशिश नहीं करती कि गांव गांव, घर घर में उन कानूनी बातों का प्रचार हो जाय जिनसे किसानों का लाभ हो। दृष्टान्त के लिये पहले बताया गया १८ और २२ वाले कानून को ही लीजिये। इसका कहां प्रचार हुआ? जब एम.एल.ए. तक नहीं जानते कि कानून बना है तो औरों का क्या कहना?

(१०)

सहयोग समितियों का रवैया

झारखंड में सहयोग समितियों (Cooperative credit societies) के वारे में भी कुछ कहे बिना काम नहीं चलता। हमने देखा है कि यहां के काश्तकारी कानून में उन समितियों के लिये खास रिआयतें रखी गई हैं। दृष्टांत के लिये हमें पहले बतायी गयी काश्तकारी कानून की ४६(२अ) धारा को ही लेंगे। जहां औरों के साथ सिर्फ सात ही साल के भुगुतबन्ध लिखने का हक आदिवासी किसानों को हैं तहां इन समितियों के लिये वे पन्द्रह साल तक के लिये लिख सकते हैं। इसी तरह के और भी अनेक दृष्टान्त दिये जा सकते हैं, जिनसे सिद्ध हो जाता है कि सरकार और कानून बनाने वालों की नजर में ये समितियां बहुत ज्यादा महत्त्व रखती हैं। सो भी न केवल सिद्धान्त की दृष्टि से। किन्तु व्यावहारिक और अमली दृष्टि से। क्योंकि सहयोग समितियों का सिद्धान्त तो बहुत ही उत्तम और ऊंचा है। मगर मतभेद है केवल इस बात में व्यवहार में वे आया किसानों को लाभ पहुंचाती हैं या नहीं।

हमें तो विहार खंड के दरभंगा, मुंगेर, पटना आदि जिलों का कड़ुवा अनुभव इनके वारे में है। ये जिले तो झारखंड की तरह पिछड़े नहीं हैं। मगर वहां के किसानों पर इन समितियों और सोसाइटियों के करते जो गुजरी है उसे याद करके भी रोंगटे खड़े हो जाते हैं। विहार प्रान्तीय किसान सभा ने अपने अनुभव के ही आधार इन समितियों की कड़ी समालोचना भी कई बार की है, जिसके चलते इस सोसाइटियों के कर्णधार न सिर्फ रंज हुए हैं। वल्कि प्रतिवाद भी किया है कि इल्जाम सरासर गलत हैं। मगर हम तो कच्चे धाग ठहरे नहीं कि टूट जाते, या उनकी बन्दर घुड़की से दबक जाते। इसलिये अपनी जगह हमारी सभा डंटी रही।

हमारे साथियों को इन समितियों के अत्याचारों से जमुई वगैरः में बचाने में जो करारे अनुभव हुए हैं और जिस धांधली का पता वकील वगैरः की हैसियत से उन्हें हुआ है उसका हृदय विद्रावक वर्णन उनने किया है। यही बात पटना तथा दूसरे जिलों के सम्बन्ध में भी समय समय पर हमें मालूम होती रही है।

दरभंगे की आपबीती सुनाता हूं। गिरिजा स्थान - धनुषा - की मीटिंग करके हम लौट रहे थे। जहां तक याद है, कुछ किसान हीं हमें एक गांव में, जो मोटर के रास्ते पर ही सड़क पर है और जिसका नाम भूलता हूं, हमें अपने घर लिवा ले गये। और बातों के सिवाय उनने एक मुश्चंड आदमी को दिखाया जो डंडा लिये खड़ा था। मालूम हुआ, यह सोसाइटी का आदमी है और बकाया वसूलने आया है। जब तक वसूल न होगा रोज आयेगा और खायेगा! सिर्फ एक रुपये के बकाये में यह बात थी। ज्यादा रुपये के बकाये में, पता लगा, पांच आदमी आते हैं और छः आने के हिसाब से उनकी खुराक चार्ज होती है! यह तो कानूनी चीज कही जाती है। मगर वे मुश्चंड जबर्दस्ती कुछ खा पी भी लेते हैं। किसान गरीब क्या करे? यह गजब का छः आना तलबाना की तरह उनकी छाती पर चढ़ता जाता था!

चौपट भी आखिर ये समितियां क्यों हुईं? कुछ यार और पढ़े लिखे वकील या दूसरे घुस आये और उनका अपना काम चल गया, उनका पेशा जम गया! एक एक आदमी आठ आठ समितियों तक का ग्रूप सेक्रेटरी बना दिया गया! किसानों और जनता को तो पता ही न चला कि यह कोआपरेटिव सोसाइटी (देहात में तो सुसाइटी कहते हैं) क्या बला है। उनने समझा कि कर्ज देने वाले नये महाजन या एक नई संस्था खुली! बस! और इसीसे वे लुट गये। सोसाइटियां भी चौपट हुईं! जनता को इनका महत्त्व बताया न गया, समझाया ही नहीं गया। यह बात समझाने की दरअसल कोशिश हुई नहीं। रस्मअदाई को कोशिश नहीं कहते। अपढ़ देहाती जनता को समझाने के लिये आकाश पाताल एक करना होता है। यही नहीं किया गया! गर्ज किसे थी? देहातों की आर्थिक दशा सुधारने की खूब व्यवस्था हो रही है ऐसी लम्बी लम्बी रिपोर्टें निकाल के दुनियां को धोखे में रखा गया! यारों ने समझा, चलो अच्छा मौका है। कुछ बन जाओ। और नहीं तो चुनाव में वोट ही मिलेगा! फिर तो दिवाला जरूरी था!

जब प्रगतिशील लोगों में ऐसा हुआ तो झारखंड के पिछड़े और असभ्य कहे जाने वाले प्रदेश में क्या हुआ होगा यह बात आसानी से समझी जा सकती है। यहां तो "अन्धे की गैया, राम रखवैया" वाली बात ठहरी। फलतः जो न हुआ हो उसी में आश्चर्य है। यहां जब किसानों के लिये दी गई कानूनी सुविधाएं तक हजम हो जाती हैं और पता ही नहीं चलता, तो फिर दूसरी बातों का क्या कहना? और तो और खुद सरकारी जांच कमिटी ने हीं इस ओर काफी इशारा किया है। संथाल परगने की जांच कमिटी ने इसके बारे में जो कुछ लिखा है वह सारे झारखंड के लिये ही है।

<5.12.41> उस कमिटी की रिपोर्ट के ३६-३७ पृष्ठों में (९३ पैराग्राफ में) यह बात यों लिखी गई है, "Cooperative societies do not exist in many parts of the district, and even where they do, they do not seem to have helped very much. We were struck by the amount of criticism of the cooperative societies that we received. It was not possible for us to investigate the working of these societies and the evidence that we have heard came mainly from those who have complaints to make, but many people feel that the rates of interest are too high and that they are nearly as oppressive in realising their debts as the mahajans themselves. This is largely inevitable, since land is inalienable and the only method of recovering debts is by attachment of crops. The Santal law does not allow attachment of standing crops for mahajan's debts. Even in the case of rent decrees attachment of standing crops is restricted to the amount sufficient to cover one year's rent, but under section 35 of the Cooperative Societies Act there is no limit to the extent to which standing crops can be attached to recover a society's debts. Since the cooperative societies must recover their loans if they are to function at all, and since they have had to resort increasingly to this procedure, borrowers feel that they are being as harshly treated by the cooperative societies as they would have been by the mahajans. There is also much complaint that in the Rajmahal subdivision where the right of transfer exists too little care and discrimination is used when putting property to sale for the recovery of cooperative dues, and that excessive areas are sold. The movement is distrusted. If it is to make further progress in the district, it will require remodelling. At present it is identified with all the oppressions of the mahajan and there is no constructive side to its work. If it is to succeed it will be necessary to reduce the rates of interest, to insure that much more care is taken in the granting of loans and to develop the constructive side of cooperation."

'जिले के बहुत हिस्सों में तो सहयोग समितियां हुई नहीं। जहां है भी वहां भी उनने कुछ ज्यादा मदद नहीं की है ऐसा मालूम होता है। इन समितियों के सम्बन्ध में हमें इतनी ज्यादा शिकायतें मिलीं कि आवाक् हो जाना पड़ा! इनके कामों की जांच करने की बात मुमकिन न हो सकी और हमें जो गवाही (सबूत) मिले हैं वह प्रधानतः उन्हीं से जिन्हें इन समितियों के खिलाफ शिकायतें थी।

लेकिन बहुत लोग ऐसा मानते हैं कि इनकी सूद की दर बहुत ही ज्यादा है और कर्ज की वसूली ये समितियां प्रायः वैसा ही जुल्म करती हैं जैसा कि खुद महाजन करते हैं। अधिकांश में ऐसा होना अनिवार्य है। क्योंकि जमीन तो बिक सकती नहीं। इसलिये कर्ज की वसूली का सिर्फ एक ही तरीका है कि फसलें जब्त की जायं। संथाली कानून के अनुसार महाजनों के कर्ज में खड़ी फसल भी जब्त की जा सकती नहीं। बाकी लगान की डिग्री में भी सिर्फ एक ही साल के लगान की वसूली भर खड़ी फसल जब्त हो सकती है। लेकिन सहयोग समितियों के कानून की ३५वीं धारा के मुताबिक तो किसी भी सहयोग समिति के कर्ज की वसूली के लिये चाहे जितनी भी खड़ी फसल जब्त कर ली जा सकती है! यदि इन समितियों को कायम रहना है तो इन्हें अपनी देन (कर्ज) को वसूल करना हीं होगा। इसीलिये तो ज्यादातर फसल जब्ती पर ही अधिकाधिक ये जोर देती हैं। यही कारण है कि कर्ज लेने वाले महसूस करते हैं कि हम लोगों के साथ तो उतनी ही बेरहमी से सहयोग समितियां भी पेश आती हैं जितनी महाजन कर सकते थे। यह शिकायत भी बहुत ज्यादा है कि राजमहाल सबडिविजन में जमीन बेंचने का हक होने पर भी जब सोसाइटी के कर्ज में किसी जायदाद को नीलाम करवाने का मौका आता है तो जरा भी पर्वाह और विचार से काम नहीं लिया जाता और बहुत ज्यादा जमीनें नीलाम करवा ली जाती हैं! सहयोग आन्दोलन पर ही अविश्वास हो गया है। यदि इसे इस जिले में कुछ भी तरक्की करनी है तो इसे नये सिरे से ढालना होगा। फिल तो महाजनों के सभी जुल्मों के साथ इसका नाता जुट गया है और इसका कोई रचनात्मक काम हई नहीं। यदि इसे सफल बनाना है तो सूद की दर घटाना जरूरी है। पक्का इन्तजाम करना होगा कि कर्ज देने के समय खूब देखभाल के दिया जाय और रचनात्मक कामों को भी प्रगति देनी होगी।''

हमें इस पर कुछ भी टीका टिप्पणी करना है नहीं। जितनी जानकारी हमारी किसान सभा को थी और जिसका जिक्र हमने शुरू में ही इशारे से किया है वह सब की सब इसमें आ गई है। आखिर बात दूसरी हो तब न न आये? सर्वत्र तो एक ही बेढ़ंगी रफ्तार है — एक सा जुल्म है। मामूली सी रकमों के लिये इतनी ज्यादा जमीनें बेदर्दी से नीलाम करवा ली गई हैं कि किसानों का कलेजा फट गया है! तब उनकी आंखें खुली हैं कि यह कौन सी बला है। रचनात्मक काम तो है इन समितियों की असलियत और इनके असली कामों की जानकारी लोगों में कराना और बताना कि ये कैसे चलाई जांय तभी सफलता होगी और तभी चल सकती हैं। नहीं तो बर्बादी अनिवार्य है। मगर ऐसा करने

की गर्ज किसे थी? प्रत्युत यारों की तो इसमें हानि थी। कर्ज देने में भी आंखमूंद के काम होता था। मगर जवाबदेही समूह की थी जिसे अंग्रेजी में क्लेक्टिव लायबिलिटी (collective liability) कहते हैं। नतीजा यह हुआ कि काइयां लोगों ने कर्ज लिया और बिक गये सीधे लोग। यह भी नहीं कि ज्यादे से ज्यादा सूद की दर रखने और सख्ती से अन्धाधुन्ध वसूली और नीलामी के करते ये समितियां बच सकीं। अन्त में तो इनका दिवाला निकली गया और यह बात सर्वजन प्रसिद्ध है।

यह भी याद रखना चाहिये कि संथाल परगना जांच कमिटी को जो सबूत और गवाहियां मिलीं उनमें एक भी किसान सभा की न थी। उसने लिखा ही है कि २३० लिखित उत्तर और १११ गवाहों में सभी सरकारी अफसर, वकील, जमींदार, घटवाल, इनकी सभायें, एम.एल.ए., प्रधान, सिरदार, परगनैत आदि ही थे।

(११)

झारखंड की अनुकरणीय बातें

यहां पर झारखंड की दो चार ऐसी बातें भी लिखनी हैं जो दरअसल अनुकरणीय हैं। सब से सुन्दर बात तो यह है कि संथाल परगने में गांव की जमीन किसी एक की या व्यक्तियों की जुदा जुदा नहीं मानी जाती है। वह तो गांव के समूचे समाज की सम्पत्ति समझी जाती है। यही बात पहले बाकी जिलों में भी होगी। मगर शेष पांच में लापता हो रही है और केवल एक ही जिले में है। इसीलिये जो आदमी लावारिस मरता या कहीं चला जाता है उसकी जमीन समूचे गांव के समाज की हो जाती है और जिसके पास जमीन न हो या कम हो उसके ही साथ उसका बन्दोबस्त होता है। बन्दोबस्त होने और लावारिस पड़ जाने के बीच में उस गांव के मुखिया को ही, जिसे प्रधान कहते हैं, उस पर अधिकार मिलता है। तब तक वही उसे जोतता बोता है।

सहयोग समितियों के सिलसिले में अभी अभी कहा गया है कि वहां जमीन बेंचने का हक नहीं है। फलतः यदि किसी ने चुपके अपनी जमीन किसी महाजन के हाथ बेंची, तो पता लगते ही कानूनन महाजन तो बेदखल होता ही है। साथ ही बेंचने वाला भी बेदखल हो जाता है और वह जमीन भी सारे समाज की हो जाती है। इसी तरह गांव के किसी किसान का लगान बाकी पड़ने पर सिर्फ उसी पर नालिश नहीं होती, किन्तु सभी किसानों पर और सभी के ऊपर जवाबदेही आती है। यों तो लगान का जवाबदेह होता है सिर्फ प्रधान और जमींदार उसी पर नालिश करता है। मगर प्रधान सब किसानों पर ही नालिश करता है। इस प्रकार देखते हैं कि संसारव्यापी पुरानी पंचायतों या कम्यूनों (communes) की प्रथा यहां अब भी है। हां, धीरे धीरे दूषित हो रही है।

दूसरी चीज है यहां की प्रधानी प्रथा। प्रधान के तीन काम माने गये हैं। जांच कमिटी के ही शब्दों में उसके तीन कर्त्तव्य हैं। एक तो वह स्वायत्तशासन प्राप्त गांव के समाज का मुखिया या प्रधान माना जाता है। गो कि वह पुरानी स्वतंत्रता प्रायः खत्म हो चुकी है। वही पंचायत का सभापति होने के नाते सामाजिक और धार्मिक कामों को पूरा करता है और छोटे मोटे झगड़ों को निपटाता है। दूसरी

बात यह है कि समूचे गांव की ओर से केवल प्रधान हीं जमींदार के साथ व्यवहार करता है, लगान देता है। जनींदारों का कोई ताल्लुक किसानों से सीधे न होने के नाते उसका न तो उन पर रोबदाब होता है और न वे या उनके अमले ही हरी, बेगारी, अबवाब वगैरः का नाम ले सकते हैं। अमले तो होते ही नहीं। गैरमजरुवा या लवारिस वगैरः जमीनों पर उसी का कब्जा रहता है और एस.डी.ओ. की देखरेख में वही उन्हें पीछे बन्दोबस्त करता है। प्रधान का तीसरा काम है मजिस्ट्रेट के साथ गांव की बातों के बारे में सरोकार रखना। सेस, चौकीदारी आदि वही वसूल करता है। मारपीट या चोरी आदि की खबर देना और फरारों को पकड़वाना उसी का काम है। गांव के जंगल वगैरः की देखरेख वही करता है और सबके हकों की निगरानी करता है। सड़क, नहर आदि की देखभाल भी वहो करता और मरम्मत करवाता है।

इसके लिये उसे एक तो लगान की वसूली में उसे एक आना फी रुपया जमींदार देता है और एक ही आना किसान। वसूल न होने पर यह कमिशन कट जाता है। साथ ही उसके पास दो तरह के जोत होते हैं। एक तो प्रधान की हैसियत से खास जोत की जमीन होती है जिस पर लगान नहीं देना पड़ता है। वह इसीलिये होती है कि यदि किसान बाकी रखें तो उसी की पैदावार से चुकता करके पीछे वसूल करे। कमिटी ने गांव के कुल लगान के बारहवें हिस्से के लिये जितनी जमीन जरूरी हो उतनी हीं यह खास जमीन प्रधान को दी जाने की सिफारिश की है। क्योंकि कम हो गई है। और जब तक उतनी पूरी न हो जाय तब तक उसी हिसाब से उसके किसानी जोत में लगान की माफी हो। किसान जोत पर उसे औरों की तरह ही लगान देना होता है। किसानी जोत तो उसका अपना है। मगर अगर वह प्रधानी से किसी कारण से हट जाय, हटाया जाय तो प्रधानी जोत चला जायगा और जोई प्रधान होगा वही उसे पायेगा। यह प्रधानी प्रथा संथालों और दूसरे मूलवासियों में ही है। अब इसकी वह बात नहीं रही।

प्रधानों के सिवाय संथालों के मुखिया एक प्रकार के और हैं जो केवल दामिन इलाके में ही हैं। इन्हें परगनैत कहते हैं, मालूम होता है कि गाव के लिये प्रधान और परगने के लिये पहले परगनैत थे। अब भी वे लोग वहां हैं। दामिन के प्रबन्ध के लिये वह अनेक टुकड़ों में बांटा गया है, जैसे तहसीलदारी या थाने होते हैं। एक इलाके में एक सरकारी आफिस या वंगला (bungalow) होता है और वंगले के ही इलाके का एक परगनैत होता है। वह भी माल की वसूली के सिवाय पुलिस के कामों में भी मदद करता है। माली और फौजी

मुकदमों का भी फैसला वही करता था। अब मजिस्ट्रेट और पुलिस का सिर्फ मददगार है। मजिस्ट्रेट को हाकिम कहते हैं। उसके साथ ही उसका नाता रहता है। उसी के द्वारा गांवों में सरकारी खबरें पहुंचती हैं। ये परगनैत जमींदारियों में नहीं होते हैं। प्रधान और परगनैत खान्दानी होते हैं। मगर यह जरूरी नहीं है और बदले भी जा सकते हैं यदि योग्य आदमी न मिलें। असल में खांदानी होने से ही इनका पतन हो गया है। प्रधानों की तरह परगनैतों को सरकार माल की वसूली पर पहले दो रुपया सैकड़ा देती थी। मगर पीछे कुछ बढ़ा है और कम या वेश वसूली पर उसकी दर घटती बढ़ती है। इसके सिवाय हर गांव से साल में उसे एक रुपया दस आना मिलता है। प्रधान की तरह उसे परगनैती जमीन नहीं होती। पुलिस के दारोगा की ही जगह वहां परगनैत समझे जाते हैं। वहां बाकायदा पुलिस के थाने वगैरः नहीं हैं।

दुमका और जामतारा में तथा गोड्डा में भी सीरदार पाये जाते हैं। यह भी पुलिस का ही काम करते हैं। गोड्डा में तो चौकीदारी सरपंच का भी काम यही करते हैं। महीने में बारह रुपया वेतन इन्हें दिया जाता है। ये भी आदिवासियों के ही लिये होते हैं। अब तो बात बदल रही है। फिर भी आदिवासियों और संथाल वगैरः के साथ जब काम पड़ता है तो सिरदारों के बिना नहीं चलता। पहड़िया लोगों में भी सिरदार होते हैं। असल में पहले तो परगनैत, प्रधान और सिरदार उन्हीं में से चुने जाते थे। मगर अब तो दूसरे लोगों में से भी सिरदार चुने जाते हैं। हालांकि परगनैत अभी वही हैं। प्रधान भी वही हैं। असल में दूसरे लोगों की आवादी बढ़ने और मेलहेल या मिश्रित जनसंख्या हो जाने से ही यह बात होती है। संथाल वगैरः आदिवासियों के सिवाय जो प्रगतिशील या सभ्य लोग वहां है उन्हें संथाली भाषा में दिक्कू कहते हैं। यदि प्रधान वगैरः की प्रथा का ठीक ठीक उपयोग और प्रबन्ध हो तो यह बड़े काम की चीज हो जाय।

यों तो प्रधान, मानकी वगैरः शेष पांच जिलों में भी है। मगर वे लोग विहार के जेठरैयत या चौकीदारी सरपंच से ज्यादा महत्व अब नहीं रखते। अब तो चौकीदारी पंच चुने भी जाते हैं। इसी प्रकार छोटानागपुर में जो पाहन और देवकली होते हैं उनका भी कोई आधुनिक उपयोग नहीं है। पाहन तो पुरोहित की तरह के होते हैं जो मंतत्र तंतर भी जानते हैं और भूत प्रेत भी झाड़ते हैं। मगर देवकली तो ओझा को ही कहते हैं। वह तो खास खास भूत प्रेतों को ही हटाता और बुलाता है। इनके लिये गांव वाले ही खान पान वगैरः का प्रबन्ध करते हैं। हां, प्रधानों के कुछ खास कानूनी हक जमीन वगैरः के हैं।

प्रधान युग के लिहाज से यहां की नई और सब से काम की परिस्थिति यह

है कि प्रायः सभी जिलों में लोहे, अब्रक, कोयले आदि की खाने और कारखाने हैं और सीमेन्ट वगैरः की भी फैक्टरियां हैं। पलामू में तो जपला की सीमेन्ट फैक्टरी प्रसिद्ध ही है। फलतः लाखों मजदूर काम करते हैं। सो भी गरोह के गरोह। उनका ताल्लुक यहां के गांवों से काफी रहता है। गांव वाले भी बहुत से काम करते हैं। ऐसी दशा में यहीं पर तो किसानों और मजदूरों के संगठन एक दूसरे के साथ पूरा पूरा सहयोग कर सकते हैं और एक दूसरे की लड़ाई में काफी मदद पहुंचा सकते हैं। दोनों का पूर्ण सहयोग, जिसकी नितान्त आवश्यकता आज के युग को है और जो इस युग की खास चीज है, यहीं तो संभव है और वह हो सकता है न केवल कागजी, किन्तु क्रियात्मक। जहां खाने हैं वहां भी ऊपर की जमीन में किसानों को कष्ट है। दूसरी जगह तो हई। मजदूरों के कष्ट तो सभी को विदित हईं।

(१२)

ताता और होमी

झारखंड की बात अधूरी ही रह जायगी यदि ताता का विशेष वर्णन न किया जाय। पारसनाथ पहाड़ के सिलसिले में जैनी सेठों की करतूतों का जिक्र तो होई चुका है। मगर ताता का महत्त्व उनसे कहीं ज्यादा है। ताता का यहां जमींदार और पूंजीपति दोनों ही हैसियत से प्रभाव है। लाखों मजदूरों पर उसकी हुकूमत चलती है। जानें कितने नेताओं और कार्यकर्त्ताओं को ताता ने अपने पाकेट में रख लिया है। ऐसा जादू चलता है कि सबों की बोलती ही बन्द हो जाती है और छोटे बड़े सभी नेता वहीं — जमशेदपुर में ही — हजम हो जाते हैं। ताता की ही कृपा का फल है कि अब तक जाने कितने नेता जमशेदपुर के मजदूरों का संगठन करने गये और नाकामयाब रहे। नेताओं के प्रति जितना अविश्वास वहां के मजदूरों में है उतना और कहीं शायद ही है। फलतः वहां जोई जाता है उसी पर अविश्वास किया जाता है। "धरी न काबू धीर सब के मन मन सिज हरे" वहीं चरितार्थ होता है। यह ताता की चातुरी और व्यवहार कुशलता का ज्वलन्त प्रमाण है।

मगर मुझे तो किसान सभा के कार्यकर्त्ता की हैसियत से सिर्फ ताता की वही बातें लिखनी है जिसका ताल्लुक किसानों और सर्व साधारण से है। कारखाने और मजदूरों की दशा के बारे में लिखना इस पुस्तक का लक्ष्य भी नहीं है जैसा कि इसके नाम से ही स्पष्ट है। मैं उस विषय की विशेष जानकारी भी नहीं रखता। कांग्रेस की स्वराज्य पार्टी जब केन्द्रीय असेम्बली में थी तो ताता को सरकारी सहायता देने का प्रश्न उठा था। उसने इसका समर्थन किया। जब वहां के मजदूरों के हक में यह शर्त्त पेश की गई कि ताता कम्पनी उन्हें आराम पहुंचाने की गारन्टी करे तभी सहायता दी जाय, तो इसका विरोध स्वराज्य पार्टी ने किया था और बिना शर्त्त ही सहायता का समर्थन किया। जब मजदूरों के सम्बन्ध में बड़े बड़ों और ऐसी संस्थाओं की कार्यवाहियां पहेली की तरह खड़ी हो जाती हैं तो हमारे जैसा आदमी घबराता है और उस झमेले से अलग रहके

किसानों का ही सवाल हल करने की कोशिश करता है। इसीलिये यहां भी वही सवाल है। जमशेदपुर के पुराने मजदूर लीडर कहे जाने वाले मिस्टर होमी को भी हम किसानों के ही सिलसिले में याद रखना चाहते हैं। इसीलिये उनका भी थोड़ा उल्लेख होगा। मगर इस सम्बन्ध में सिंहभूम जिला किसान कान्फ्रेंस, घाटशिला में ३, ४ जुलाई १९३९ को हमने जो भाषण दिया था उसे ही यहां उद्धृत करके सन्तोष कर लेना चाहते हैं। ज्यादा कहने की जरूरत नहीं प्रतीत होती है। वह इस तरह है :—

''बाहरी दुनिया की नजरों में तो आमतौर से ताता का काम है जमशेदपुर में केवल इस्पात वगैरः तैयार करना और इस तरह ताता कम्पनी सबसे बड़ी पूंजीवादी है। ताता से ताल्लुक रखने वाले और किसानों के लिये दिल रखने दूसरे लोगों में भी चन्द लोग ही ऐसे हैं जो यह जानते हैं कि ताता कम्पनी जमींदार भी है और प्रायः बीस छोटे बड़े गांवों से, जो जमशेदपुर मे और इर्द गिर्द शामिल हैं, बीस पच्चीस लाख लगान वसूलती है। इन गावों के नाम हैं उलियान, भाटिया, गोभरोगोड़ा, सोनाड़ी, खुटाड़ी, बेलड़ी, जोजाबेरा, साकची, बारा, बारीडीह, महरड़ा, मुड़कटी, निलदी, कालीमाटी, सुसनिगड़िया, गोलमुड़ी, सिद्धगोड़ा वगैरः। इनके कष्ट वर्णनातीत हैं। ताता के लिये सरकार ने इन मौजों को १९१९-२० में ले लिया। आगे इन गांवों के कुछ भयंकर कष्टों का वर्णन वहीं के लोगों के शब्दों में किया जाता है। उनने मेरी जमशेदपुर की अप्रैल वाली उसी साल की यात्रा के समय मुझे जो कुछ लिख के दिया था वही यहां लिख दिया जाता है। उनका कहना है कि ''जमशेदपुर और आसपास के जो गांव पहले दलभूम के राजा के मातहत थे हम उन्हीं के शुरू के ही वाशिन्दे हैं। कम्पनी के लिये सरकार ने इन्हें तथा और गावों को १९१९-२० में ही राजा से हासिल किया था। कम्पनी ने हमें कहा कि आप लोग पूर्ववत् पड़े रहें। क्योंकि हमें अपने ही लिये आपकी सेवाओं की मजदूर, गाड़ीवान, साग तरकारी उपजाने वाले आदि के रूप में जरूरत है। इसलिये गांवों का राजा से लिया जाना तो केवल कागजी लिखा पढ़ी है। स्थिति में अन्तर न होगा।

''१९०६-०९ के सर्वे में जो लगान ठीक था उसे इस कम्पनी ने इन गांवों को बकायदा दखल करने के बाद, धीरे धीरे बढ़ाना और हमारी जमीनों से भारी लगान वसूलना शुरू कर दिया। उस समय तो हमने यह चीज किसी तरह बर्दाश्त की। क्योंकि उस समय चावल, साग तरकारी वगैरः की कीमत काफी ऊंची थी।

''चन्द साल के बाद, जब कि बिना हमारी मदद के भी कम्पनी का कारबार

चलने लगा, उसने हमें अपने झोंपड़ों और घरों वगैरः से निकाल के अपने काम के लिये सब कुछ कबजाना चाहा। फलतः तरह तरह से हमें परीशान किया जाने लगा। १९३२ में लगान न देने के बहाने हमारी बेदखली के केस किये गये। मगर हम लोग सभी केस जीत गये। तब बल प्रयोग शुरू हुआ और इसके चलते कम्पनी का जो प्रधान रूप से इस शहर का प्रबन्धक है। वही नोटिफाइड एरिया कमिटी का चेयरमैन भी है। वह कुछ औरों के साथ नाजायज दूसरे के घर आदि में घुसने के लिये फौजदारी में भी फंसा था और हाईकोर्ट तक सजा बहाल रही। उसके बाद हम लोगों के विरुद्ध १४५ धारा के अनुसार फौजदारी के बहुत ज्यादा मुकदमे चलवाये गये। मगर उनमें भी हम जीते।

''अब जमशेदपुर एरिया कमिटी की ही मदद से हमें तंग करने लगे हैं। कहा जाता है कि इस कमिटी के इलाके के भीतर हैं। मगर इस म्युनिसिपेलिटी का कोई भी फायदा तो पहुंचता नहीं। हां, इससे हमारी दिक्कतें जरूर बढ़ गई हैं''।

''अपने छप्परों को फिर से छाने में भी हमें प्लान बनवाने और कमिटी से मंजूरी लेने को कहा जा रहा है। हमें साफ पीने का पानी तो मिलता नहीं। गन्दा पानी हममें बीमारियां फैला रहा है। मगर कूआं खोदने की हमें इजाजत नहीं! हमारे न तो सड़कें हैं, न रोशनी और न मेहतरों का प्रबन्ध। हमारे गांवों में पढ़ाने के प्रबन्ध की तो बातें ही मत पूछें।

''हमारे यहां जो पड़ती जमीनें चरागाह के काम आती थीं। वे गत साल से जोत जात के ईंटों के बनाने के लिये कम्पनी के द्वारा ठीके पर दी जाने लगी हैं। इसका तो सीधा अर्थ है कि हम खेती के जानवरों को खत्म कर दें। क्योंकि अड़गड़े में डाले जाने के डर से उन्हें बाहर तो निकाल सकते नहीं। कम्पनी की इस करतूत ने हमें सबसे ज्यादा परीशान किया है। क्योंकि पशुओं के बिना तो खेती हो नहीं सकती। फलतः हमें गांव छोड़ के भागना पड़ेगा। इन कारणों से और लगान की कड़ाई के करते भी हम उसे चुकता कर पाते नहीं। फलतः हमारी बहुत सी जमीन नीलाम हो रही हैं। आ जो लगान है वह दलभूम के मौजूदा लगान से चौगुना और सर्वे के लगान से पूरा दस गुना है। यह बात नीचे की तालिका से साफ हो जाती है। धानी (धान की जमीनों) और बारी या भीठे (गोड़ा) जमीनों के लगान की दर अलग अलग दी गई है।

दलभूम का लगान फीबीघा	कम्पनी का लगान फी बीघा
धानी अब्बल नम्बर एक रुपया	चार रुपया, तीन रुपबा, दो रुपया और
धानी दोयम नम्बर आठ आना	तीन रुपया क्रमशः इन्हीं चारों जमीनों का।
धानी सोयम नम्बर छः आना	साग तरकारी वाली का तो आठ रुपया है।
गोड़ा जमीन दो आना	सभी गांवों में कम्पनी की दर एक सी नहीं है।

"साकची तो जमशेदपुर शहर का ही हिस्सा है। इसीलिये वहां के लोगों को बाजार, आबपाशी और सड़क वगैरः की आसानी भी है जो अन्य गावों को नहीं है। मगर वहां का लगान कम है और कम्पनी के हो एक अफसर कबूल किया है कि दूसरे गांवों के किसानों को सभी दिक्कतें बढ़ी चढ़ी है। देखिये न :—

साकची की धानी अब्बल का लगान तीन रुपया	उल्यान, मांटिया, गोभागोड़ा का चार रुपया।
साकची की धानी दोयम का लगान करीब सवा दो।	उल्यान, मांटिया, गोभागोड़ा का तीन रुपया
साकची की धानी सोयम	उल्यान, मांटिया, गोभागोड़ा का दो रुपया
साकची गोड़ा अव्वल डेढ़ रुपया	इन तीन गावों की सभी तरह की गोड़ा
साकची गोड़ा दोयम सात आना	जमीनों का लगान तीन रुपया फी बीघा।
साकची गोड़ा सोयम सवा दो आना	साग तरकारी का आठ रुपया फी बीघा

"ताता कम्पनी के मिल का निकला हुआ पानी नदी को गन्दा करता है। मगर क्या मजाल कि किसान उससे अपना खेत पटा लें? गाड़ी पर टैक्स है और जानवरों के मरने पर उन्हें हटाने के लिये जो पांच रुपया टैक्स है वह तो हमें तबाह कर रहा है।

"सिंचाई की सुविधा पहले थी। मगर अब नहीं रही। लगान की बकायदा रसीद नहीं मिलती। छः मास हुए हम विहार के अर्थमंत्री से और बाद में प्रधानमंत्री के पास भी लिखित प्रार्थना ले के पहुंचे थे। मगर नतीजा अब तक कुछ मालूम नहीं हुआ!" इस लम्बी दास्तान पर टीका टिप्पणी बेकार है।

अब जरा मिस्टर होमी की बात सुनिये। अब तक तो यही सुना जाता था कि मिस्टर होमी यहां के मजदूरों की लीडरी का दावा करते हैं और दूसरे लोग

इसका विरोध करते हैं। यह तो उन्हीं का काम है जो मजदूर हैं कि फैसला करें कि किसे वे अपना लीडर मानते हैं। हमें तो उनके बारे में पड़ोस के ही मानभूम जिले के पोटम्बा थाने के गांव मांगों के जमींदार या मुकर्ररीदार के रूप में ही यहां सामने लाना और कुछ सुनाना है। मांगों गांव सुवर्ण रेखा नदी के उस पार ही यहीं है। पिछली बार जो मैं वहां गया था और पता लगाया तो मालूम पड़ा कि उस गांव पर जो उनने मुकर्ररीदार का दावा ठोंक दिया है उसके चलते वहां के किसानों और कमिया लोगों को बड़ा कष्ट है। श्री मानिक होमी के भाड़े वाले आदमी किस तरह वहां के लोगों को सताते और जलील करते हैं इसकी दर्दनाक कहानी वहां के स्त्री पुरुषों और श्री क्रिस्टो गौड़ प्रधान ने रो रो के कह सुनाई। उस जुल्म के बारे में अपनी ओर से कुछ न कहके न्यायालय के दो फैसलों के कुछ अंश उद्धृत कर देता हूँ और मामला साफ हो जायगा। यह गांव मानभूम जिले के किनारे पर थाने से सोलह मील पर पड़ता है। इसलिये चालाक और चलते पुर्जे यार लोग यहां के हो और भूमिज आदि निवासियों को खूब ही सताते हैं। पहला फैसला — पुरुलिया के एस.डी.ओ. मिस्टर एस.के.अहसान का लिखा हुआ अंग्रेजी में है। दूसरा फैसला मिस्टर बी. के गोखले, डिस्ट्रिक्ट मजिस्ट्रेट मानभूम का ५.९.२७ का है। दोनों का हिन्दी अनुवाद ही दिया जाता है। पहला यों है :—

"पुलिस की रिपोर्ट में होमी और उसके आदमियों के विरुद्ध यह शिकायत थी कि होमी, उसके आदमी और उसी के साथी कुछ और लोग भी किसानों को अनेक ढंग से सताते हैं और धमका के, मारपीट के और जबर्दस्ती रुपया वसूल के दिक करते हैं।

"अपनी पार्टी की तरफ से उसने साफ साफ यह शर्त्त कबूल की है कि बिना अदालती कार्यवाही के दूसरे ढंग से हमलोग अपना अधिकार जबर्दस्ती न चलायेंगे और न किसी को सतायेंगे ही, जैसा कि इलजाम है। इसलिये इस समय तो मैं उनके खिलाफ कोई कार्यवाही न करता। मगर इसी के साथ मिस्टर होमी और उनके आदमियों को साफ साफ चेतावनी देता हूं कि किसानों को, फिर चाहे वह कोई भी हों, वे लोग किसी भी तरह दिक या परीशान हर्गिज न करें। इस हुक्म की एक नकल पोटम्बा के थानेदार के पास भेजी जाय। ताकि यदि वे लोग अपना वादा तोड़ें तो वह उनके खिलाफ रिपोर्ट करे"।

दूसरा केस का, जो १९३६ के स्फुट केसों में ३०९ का है, फैसला यों है :—

"जो कुछ सबूत है उससे मुझे पता चलता है कि मिस्टर होमी जंगल और

पेड़ों को अपनी निजी जायदाद मानता है जिन्हें जब जैसे चाहे काट सकता है और गांव वालों के जो परम्परा प्राप्त अधिकार जंगल पेड़ों में हैं उन्हें उनका उपभोग रोकना चाहता है। इसी तरह गैर आबाद जमीन के बारे में भी वह किसानों को रोकना चाहता है कि आबद न करें। हालांकि प्रधानी प्रथा के अनुसार उन्हें यह अधिकार है कि आबाद करें और उसके लिये उचित लगान दें। मिस्टर होमी का अपना बयान है कि मुझे पता नहीं कि किसान लोग आबाद की गई जमीनों का मुनासिब लगान देना चाहते हैं''। इससे पता चलता है कि पुश्त दर पुश्त से वहां रहने वाले किसानों से कोई वास्ता न रख के वह अपने मन के ही लोगों को वहां बसाना चाहता है। इसलिये समस्त ग्रामवासी इसे खामखा नापसन्द करते हैं। पुलिस सुपरिन्टेन्डेन्ट को जो पत्र मिस्टर होमी ने २६.१.२७ को लिखा था उसके पांचवें पैराग्राफ में लिखा है कि ''हमने जो पहले पहल दो हजार एकड़ जमीन हास्लि की थी उस समूची को एक आदर्श फार्न बनाके उसे नये ढंग से चलाने का हमारा पक्का इरादा है''। मुझे अफसोस है कि यहां की हालातों के सम्बन्ध की अपनी नादानी के करते उसने नया ढंग के आदर्श फार्म के लिये एक प्रधानी (प्रधानवाला) गांव चुन लिया, जिसमें कि गांव के समूचे वाशिन्दों के अपने खास हक होते हैं और वे बखूबी माने जाते हैं।

''पुश्त दर पुश्त से गांवों में प्रचलित रीति रिवाजों के विरुद्ध काम करने के अपने इस विचार को मिस्टर होमी जितनी जल्दी छोड़ दें उतना हीं खुद उनके लिये अच्छा है और नैं वहां जिस अमन और शान्ति के लिये फिक्रमन्द हूं उसके लिये भी उतना ही अच्छा है''।

इस पर भी और कुछ लिखना वेकार है। इसने मिस्टर मानिक होमी की जन सेवा का सुन्दर चित्र खींचा है। मजदूरों का नेता तो बना जाता है उन जैसों की सेवा के ही लिये। मगर उनका अमली तरीका तो बड़ा ही खतरनाक है। उसी मांगों गांव में उनने अपने कहने के लिये एक वंगला अलग बनवाया है। गांव वालों ने पहले समझा होगा कि ये गरीबों के सेवक आ रहे हैं। इनसे हमारा कल्याण होगा। मगर पीछे उन्हें पता चला कि ''मुनि न होय यह निशिचर घोरा''। मगर अब तो देर हो गई और उनका पांव वहां जम चुका है। अब तो रह रह के उन गरीबों को अनेक ढंग से उनके फौलादी पंजे का मजा चखना ही होगा जब तक कि गरीबों में अपने हकों के रक्षा करने की पूरी ताकत आ नहीं जाती। वह ताकत तो आयेगी जरूर। सवाल यही है कि जल्द आये।

(१३)

किसानों की मुख्य मांगें

हमें जो कुछ कहना था कह चुके। अब कोई भी नई बात कहनी है नहीं। जो बातें पहले विस्तार के साथ कही गई हैं और उनके ही सिलसिले में झारखंड के किसानों के अभाव अभियोग भी आ गये हैं उन्हीं में से कुछ प्रमुख बातों को, या यों कहिये कि किसानों की खास खास और चुनी चुनाई मांगों को, मुतालबों को यहां अन्त में हम इसीलिये लिख देना चाहते हैं कि जिन्हें उनमें काम करना हो वह आसानी से उनकी जरूरतों को संक्षेप में समझ जांय। यों तो पूर्व लिखी सारी बातें पढ़े और जाने विना हम यहां की दशा समझ सकते नहीं। इसलिये सभी को पढ़ना और मनन करना निहायत जरूरी है। सबको पढ़ने और गांवों में घूम के पता लगाने पर और भी कितनी ही जरूरी बातें मालूम हो सकती हैं जिनका जिक्र हम कर न सके हैं। मगर जो हैं वह हैं बहुत ही अहम्। इसलिये भी सबका अध्ययन जरूरी है। ताकि पूरी जानकारी हो सके और कमी की पूर्ति की जा सके। हर हालत में कुछ सवाल तो ऐसे रहतेई हैं जो सबसे आगे आते हैं और सब से ज्यादा चुभते हैं। उन्हीं को लेके आगे बढ़ने में आसानी भी होती है। शुरू में ही कम चुभने वाले प्रश्नों को उठाना ठीक नहीं होता है। इसीलिये चुनी चुनाई मांगें यहां लिख दी जाती हैं।

(१) झारखंडी किसानों के लिये सबसे पहली और जरूरी बात यह है कि कोड़कर और उटकर आदि नामों से जो भी जमीनें आवाद की जाती हैं, की जा सकती हैं उनके बारे में जमींदार की हर तरह की रोक सख्ती के साथ कानून और इन्तजाम के जरिये अविलम्ब बन्द कर दी जाय। जिससे स्वच्छन्दता के साथ किसान ये जमीनें तैयार करें। अब तक जो भी कानूनी अड़चनें हैं वह फौरन हटा ली जांय। ऐसी जमीनों का लगान उनके तैयार हो जाने और फसल उपजाना शुरू करने के कम से कम पांच साल बाद ही तय किया जाय। मगर जहां ऐसी जमीनें बनें वहां की सबसे कमजोर और खराब जोत जमीनों के लगान से ज्यादा तो वह हर हालत में न हो। आमतौर से उसका आधा ही हो।

(२) घर गिरस्ती के कामों और जीविका चलाने के लिये जंगल से पत्थर,

बालू, काठ, बांस, घास, पात, कांट, कुश, फल, फूल, मूल, शहद वगैरः लेने में कोई रुकावट या बन्धन न रहे। महुवा के फूल चुनने का उन्हें पूरा हक हो और उस पर कोई कर न लगे, चाहे महुवा के पेड़ खेतों में हों या जंगल में। किसानों के खेतों में लगे पलास, कुसुम और बेर के पेड़ों पर लाह लगाने और लगी हुई को उतारने, बेंचने आदि का उन्हें पूरा हक हो और कोई भी कर देना न पड़े। अब तक जो भी बन्धन या रोक हो वह कानून या और इन्तजाम के जरिये फौरन सख्ती से हटा दिया जाय। टंगकर, पतकर, वनकर, चुल्हकर या खरचरी आदि के नामों से प्रसिद्ध कर गैर कानूनी करार दिये जांय।

(३) किसानों और उनके पशुओं के पीने वगैरह के लिये शुद्ध जल का जरूरत के मुताबिक फौरन इन्तजाम किया जाय और जगह जगह कुएं वगैरः तैयार कराये जांय। जहां कहीं भी सोते, झरने आदि हों वहां उन्हें और उनके पशुओं के जाने आने पर कोई रोक रहने न पाये। यदि ऐसे झरने आदि रिजर्व या प्रोटेक्टेड फारेस्ट में हो तो वहां तक जाने का रास्ता बना दिया जाय और रास्ते के दोनों तरफ और झरनों के भी इर्द गिर्द ऐसा जबर्दस्त ऊँचा और मजबूत घेरा बना दिया जाय कि कोई भी उसे आसानी से पार न कर सके और मवेशी उसे फांद न सकें।

(४) झारखंड से एक एक करके सभी कानीहौस, अड़गड़े या कैटल पाउंड फौरन हटा लिये, और तोड़ दिये जांय।

(५) यहां का लगान सरकारी माल की अपेक्षा बहुत ही ज्यादा और प्रायः तीस चालीस गुना होने के कारण वर्दाश्त के बाहर है। इसलिये वह इतना हीं कर दिया जाय कि सरकारी माल और वसूली का खर्च बाद देने पर जमींदारों के पास ज्यादे से ज्यादा माल के बराबर ही बचे।

(६) दामिन इलाके के पहड़िया लोगों की कुरांव या झूमचास को आजादी पूरी तरह कायम रखी जांय और उसमें जो भी रुकावटें हों वह फौरन हटा ली जांय।

(७) झारखंड के जो आदिवासी या पिछड़े हुए किसान और दल हैं उनके पढ़ने के लिये उन्हीं की भाषा में जल्द से जल्द प्रबन्ध किया जाय और उनकी अपनी हीं भाषा में प्रारम्भिक पढ़ाई अनिवार्य कर दी जाय। साथ ही उन्हें हर तरह की ऊंची से ऊंची शिक्षा मुफ्त ही देने का पर्याप्त प्रबन्ध शीघ्र से शीघ्र किया जाय।

(८) आबपाशी का पूरा पूरा प्रबन्ध किया जांय और इस ओर मुस्तैदी के साथ फौरन काम शुरू किया जाय। हर तरह की आबपाशी के लिये पूरा प्रबन्ध

करने की सोलह आना जिम्मेदारी जमींदारों पर ही हो और जब तक वे ऐसा नहीं करते, उन्हें एक पैसा भी लगान लेने का हक न हो। सरकार का फर्ज है कि उनके इस काम की जांच और देख रेख सख्ती के साथ बराबर की और उनके चूकने पर लगान रोक के खुद आबपाशी का प्रबन्ध करे और लगान वसूले। यदि उन्हें फिर वसूली का हक मिले तो दंड के साथ। यह दंड बढ़ता जाय, यदि वे बार बार चूकते रहें।

(९) किसान परिवार के साल भर के गुजर के लिये खड़ी फसल या गल्ला वगैरः छोड़ के ही बाकी लगान में बचा बचाया ही जब्त हो या बिके या नीलाम हो।

(१०) बकाया लगान की नालिश न तो एक साल से कम की हो और न ज्यादे की। यदि किसान साल खत्म होने के पहले लगान चुकता कर दे तो उसे सूद एक पाई न लगे।

(११) झारखंड के सभी जिलों के लिये एक ही तरह का काश्तकारी कानून बने और वह हो विहार के काश्तकारी कानून जैसा ही। फलतः समूचे सूबे के लिये एक ही कानून हो। बेशक आदिवासियों या पिछड़े किसानों के फायदे की धारायें जरूर रहें, खड़ी फसल की जब्ती कुर्की या सर्टिफिकेट का अधिकार जमींदार को कहीं न रहे और जमीन सम्बन्धी शर्त्ते (Predial Conditions) कतई खत्म कर दिये जांय।

(१२) सरकार की ओर से अधिक से अधिक तीन रुपया सैकड़ा सालाना सूद की दर पर किसानों को कर्ज देने का इन्तजाम किया जाय, सूद दर सूद किसी भी सूरत में जायज न हो। इससे ज्यादा सूद की दर गैरकानूनी हो और किसी भी हालत में मूलधन से दूने की डिक्री न हो ऐसा कानून हो। सूदखोरी पर सख्त से सख्त कानूनी और इन्तजामी नियंत्रण किया जाय।

(१३) सेवकाई, कमिऔती आदि किसी भी नाम से प्रचलित गुलामी और कमिया प्रथा गैर कानूनी करार दी जाय और सख्ती के साथ ऐसा इन्तजाम किया जाय कि इस चीज का नामोनिशान रहने न पाये।

(१४) इस बात का मुस्तैदी के साथ इन्तजाम किया जाय कि आदिवासी और पिछड़े किसानों की भाषाओं और रस्म रिवाजों को बखूबी जानने समझने वाले ही हाकिम इनके मुकदमों पर विचार करें। एतदर्थ ऐसे लोग जल्द से जल्द तैयार किये जांय। यदि इन्हें ये मिल सकें तो और भी अच्छा।

(१५) इनके केसों में जो वकील, मुखतार आदि कानूनी सलाहकार और मददगार हों उनके लिये खासतौर के कुछ नियम बनाये जांय जिससे इन लोगों

को धोका और परीशानी न रहे। इसीलिये ऐसे कानूनदां लोगों पर नियंत्रण और निगरानी रहे।

(१६) जो भी कानून बने, कानूनी या इन्तजामी व्यवस्था हो या कोई ऐसी नई बात हो जिससे किसानों का ताल्लुक हो, तो उसके घर घर और गांव गांव में पूर्ण प्रचार का पक्का इन्तजाम सख्ती के साथ किया जाय।

(१७) अबरक को जहां तहां से चुन और निकाल के जो किसान या गरीब गुजर करते हैं चोरी के बहाने उन्हें सताने का जो कानून है वह रद्द हो और कोयले की खानों की ऊपरी जमीन पर किसानों की खेती बारी वगैरह में जो बाधा पड़ती है वह हटा दी जाय।

(१८) एक ही जुडिंशल कमिश्नर के कई जिलों के लिये होने के कारण सेसन्स के केसों में बहुत ज्यादा समय लग जाता है। तब कहीं फैसला होता है। यह बात दूर हो जानी चाहिये।

Glossary

Apart from the factual definitions they provide, the great value of glossaries is the access they give us to the social, cultural, and political world they describe. They are thus more than dictionaries explaining the specialized meanings of technical terms in a given field, though this purpose should not be undervalued. It is precisely these kinds of specialized explanations which the Indian and British revenue settlement officers of the late nineteenth and early twentieth centuries gave us, and in an even broader and less formally legal sense, so also the authors of the district gazetteers during the same period. But their purpose was ultimately an official one and in those almost exclusive cases where their authors were Englishmen, the settlement reports and gazetteers, however valuable, were filtered through the mind's eye of a representative of the Raj, that is, the colonial state. That makes them no less valuable as historical documents but rather states their limitations, a fact which most scholarship has long since recognized.

In the present instance, however, we are more concerned with the social and cultural meanings Sahajanand's language conveys as it describes the condition of the peasants of Jharkhand in 1941, now more than half a century in India's past. The year was a critical moment in the nation's history and in the life of Sahajanand as he wrestled with his own perceptions of the world of peasant experience whether in the districts of Gangetic Bihar in the north or in the fields and forests of Jharkhand in the Chotanagpur plateau, what is in 1994 referred to as South Bihar. The richness of this glossary is in a very real sense doubled inasmuch as it emerges from the local Hindi vernacular which Sahajanand employs in this tract, thereby opening a window to those cultural sensitivities in the rural countryside which can only be revealed by the people themselves, in their language. I comment briefly in my introductory remarks to the Hindi text of *Jharkhand ke Kisan* in Part II of this volume on the issue of

Sahajanand's use of the spoken, colloquial Hindi of the peasants in what he writes and how he writes it, that is, *bol chal ki bhasha*. What Sahajanand wrote is exactly what he intended and what has been reproduced in this text; these are not misprints or spelling errors. As example zamindar becomes *jamidar*, or also commonly *kuch* meaning some, becomes *kuchee* in Sahajanand's use. There are literally hundreds of other examples which could be cited, but these will suffice briefly to explain these local Hindi usages in this tract.

The obvious caveat at this point is that Sahajanand was not Adivasi and was presumably not using a tribal language in his Jharkhand encounters with the peasants (though virtually all sources comment on the importance of Hindi/Hindustani in public and inter group communication). I discuss the issue of language, communication, and mobilization at some length in Editor's Endnote 18 of Chapter VI. It is also true, as Sahajanand says often in this tract, that he had not devoted much of his career of peasant activism in the 1930s to the Jharkhand districts of Chotanagpur. Remarkably, that very fact is Sahajanand's point of departure in this tract, and he sets about the task of providing a corrective to his own activist deficiencies, so to speak, by putting on the record a cogent, indeed vivid account of the condition of the kisans of Jharkhand. Anyone who reads this tract will know that apart from his brief visits to Singhbhum, Palamau, Hazaribagh and other districts of the region, Sahajanand made a powerful effort to inform himself about Jharkhand peasant life, and from a background as India's most active and intimately involved peasant leader, he reveals in this tract a sense of Jharkhand peasant life which tells us much about the region and its people in 1941, and in many respects the issues they confront in 1994. The 1941 story, as the glossary which follows reveals, is one of exploitation in many complex and elaborate ways. Of the more than 350 terms which are included here, nearly 150 refer directly or indirectly to forms of peasant exploitation. The edited translation in Part I of this book, the original unedited Devanagri text in Part II, and the glossary which follows define that story not as something new and unfamiliar but as a painfully familiar history, as socially and politically significant in 1994 as it was in 1941.

I must make clear that this is a glossary emerging specifically from Sahajanand's unpublished tract, *Jharkhand ke Kisan*, as it appears in Part II of this small volume. While it has benefitted from the work of specialist scholars and activists whose work is cited in the endnotes to each chapter, this is neither a full glossary of agrarian and revenue terms nor of the history of the Jharkhand movement. It tells us what Sahajanand saw in the 1930s and reflected on in the Hazaribagh Central Jail in 1941. That is its intent and its value. I have attempted to define terms in the context in which they are used in the text itself. Where Roman numerals appear following definitions, these refer to the chapters in which the word and its meanings are first or most forcefully used. These chapter references, however, are not meant to serve as an index to terms, most of which are used frequently throughout the text. In many cases, references to related terms follow the definitions given. It is also the case that many terms are specifically defined in the text itself. Where Sahajanand has provided such definitions or English equivalents, they appear in the edited translation precisely as Sahajanand gave them in the original Hindi text, either in parentheses or in inverted commas. When terms are added for editorial clarification, they appear in brackets. These details are obvious when comparing the edited translation of Part I with the original Hindi text of Part II.

One final word of explanation on transliteration and word form in this glossary. The effort in what follows is not to meet particular standards of orthography or linguistic correctness but rather to follow generally accepted practice in attempting to convey the meanings Sahajanand intended when he wrote in 1941. The use of double vowels in the English transliteration will imply the long sound, single vowels the short vowel sound as in the case aa and a. But if meanings are not changed with such usages, the most common form, or the one I am most comfortable with in the given context will be used. So too with the oo and u, and ee and i usages. Using the Devanagri in the glossary would have avoided this problem, but transliteration was thought to make these definitions more widely accessible, and those who read the Hindi text will benefit from Sahajanand's detailed and sometimes repetitive explanation of terms and meanings. Persons familiar with Hindi will of course have no problem with pronunciations, or they will be appropriately critical of this amateur effort at transliteration, which, as most such efforts is almost inevitably flawed. To repeat, the attempt here is to convey something of what Sahajanand was thinking and writing and what Adivasi kisans were experiencing at the time. The intention is obviously not to be exhaustive and there will certainly be many, more intimately familiar with Jharkhand than I, who will find omissions or who will wish to propose more sensitive definitions than I have given. The effort to access the world of tribal peasants is clearly a continuing process.

Any glossary which purports to provide access to the social and cultural world of rural Chotanagpur cannot fail to mention the monumental work of Father John B. Hoffmann, S.J. and his successors, that is the *Encyclopaedia Mundarica*, issued in multi-volumes from 1930 to 1979, successively by the Bihar and Orissa, and then the Bihar Government Press and happily now available in a sixteen volume reprint (New Delhi: Gian Publishing House, 1990.) I have commented briefly on this important reference work and its publication history in my Editor's Endnote 6 of Chapter III. George A. Grierson, *Bihar Peasant Life*, published initially in 1885 is also now available in a 1975 reprint (Delhi: Cosmo Publications), as is H.H. Wilson's *Glossary of Judicial and Revenue Terms* first issued in 1855 and reprinted in 1968 in Delhi by Munshiram Manoharlal. Both are important reference tools.

[*Please note that no diacritical marks are used either in this glossary or in the text itself. Ed.*]

Aabpashi: Irrigation. See also Sinchai. IX

Aabroo: Honour, dignity of the tribals which is demeaned by the extractions of the moneylenders. IV

Aafat: The calamity suffered by the Adivasis at being deprived of access to the jungle and its products. VI

Aage barhi jatiyon: Non-tribal, exploiting castes. That is, forward castes but not simply in the late twentieth century sense of upper castes relative to Other Backward Classes and Scheduled Castes. Sahajanand is referring to Brahmans, Kshatriyas, Bania-Mahajans, Kayasths, and also to Bengalis. II

Aah: The sigh of pain, agony, and sorrow at the oppressions imposed on the kisans of Jharkhand by the zamindars, their amlas, and the forest contractors. VI

Aawaz: Voice, as to raise one's voice in protest. The tribal people are backward and are not yet in a position to raise their voices on their own as the Biharis and Bengalis have done. II

Abbal, Doyam, Soyam: Successively less fertile paddy land. XII

Abrak: Mica, found in Jharkhand, especially in Hazaribagh and the Giridih subdivision as one of the world's major sources of this mineral. I

Adhikaron: Rights, which the law defines and which critics claim the kisans misuse and which the kisans assert are never fully implemented, if not denied. Also used in the sense of Adivasi rights to the resources of Jharkhand. II, VI

Adivasi, adi janata, moolvasi: Original inhabitants, aboriginals, tribals. See also Mool nivasiyon.

Adivasi andolan: An Adivasi movement, said to be in the hands of Adivasis, but in Sahajanand's critical opening reactions to Jharkhand politics of the 30s and early 40s, the movement is in fact a "middle class affair." Intro.

Adhivasiyon: See Adivasi, Moolvasi. Aboriginal, primeval, domiciled, those who live in this particular place and cultural space II

Aksharon: Script, as the Kaithi script, which is commonly used in the revenue survey *khatian* or register, and which is of course both unfamiliar to the Adivasis and thus places them outside any sensibility of this official documentation. They must depend for access to this record on yet other outsiders, mukhtars, vakils, etc. II

Amla: The agent of the zamindar, landcontroller, landlord. V

Andhe ki gaiya, Ram rakhvaiya: One of the many colloquial usages in this tract which Sahajanand employs often to reinforce a point. In this case, literally, if a blind man has a cow, then only Ram [i.e., God] can take care of that cow. So too with the cooperatives, only Ram can protect the Adivasi peasants against the manipulations of the cooperative managers. X

Andher: Injustice, grave irregularity as in the case of using an official non-tribal script in the revenue records, which inevitably places the tribals at an explicit disadvantage. Sahajanand considers this an absolute travesty. He also uses the term referring to the general quality of lawlessness to which the Adivasi kisans are subject and which must be ended and their just rights restored. II, VI.

Andhkar: Darkness, as the social and political climate in which the tribals live in their world of exploitation. II

Andolan: Movement, as in the political agitation and activism of the Adivasi kisans and the potential of their mobilizing a full fledged kisan andolan or peasant movement. IV

Anjan: Unaware, the peasants in the ultimate analysis are victim to their failure to understand the rules and regulations which govern their rights in the land. V

Anuchit: Unjust, the injustice of tailoring tenancy legislation to meet specific zamindar interests. See also Kalank. VIII

Anyay: Injustice, in Sahajanand's use, *Bhari anyay*, that is great injustice, in this context referring to the fact that even occupancy raiyats in Jharkhand do not have rights over the trees on their own land. V

Apne pawon par khare hon: Self-dependent, self-reliant, only in those circumstances will the kisans be able to win their rights over the zamindars. VI

Apurva shakti: Great strength, the powerful force which an organized tribal movement could bring to bear in assuring Adivasi rights. II

Ardh asabhya: Semi-civilized, used by Sahajanand in describing the populations of the border districts of Chotanagpur. I

Argara: Animal pound, also Maveshikhana, Kanihaus. VI

Asabhya: Literally, uncivilized, as the tribals of Jharkhand are perceived by the "civilized" outsiders, who oblige the Jharkhandis to learn their languages, whether Bengali, Hindi, English, or the Kaithi of the land revenue records. In another context, Sahajanand is concerned with the damage the cooperative societies might do among the relatively less educated Adivasi kisans of Jharkhand. III, X

Asli kisan: True kisan, a real peasant, those kisans and Adivasis who are the object of Sahajanand's concern, not those non-tribal outsiders who have come to Chotanagpur and Jharkhand only to loot the real kisans, the people of that place. II

Asli nivasi: Original, real inhabitants, also Adivasi, i.e., primeval, ancient people, aboriginal, also tribal. Intro.

Asli nivasi kisanon: The original kisan inhabitants of Jharkhand, for whom there is no provision for education in their own languages, thus perpetrating the fraud of forcing other languages into their minds and cultures. III

Asliyat: Actual, as in the actual conditions in Jharkhand.

Astitva: An independent, historical identity and existence, as is the case with tribal cultures and languages of the Santals, Munda, Oraon, and Ho, among others. These cultures are not in any sense inferior because they happen to be unfamiliar to Hindi and Bengali speakers, or to other outsiders. II

Atmaraksha: Literally, self defence, as in the resistance by the Adivasi kisans to the taxes, cesses, and other extortions placed on them for their legitimate use of the forest. VI

Atyachar: Tyranny, exploitation. (See also zulumon.) IV

Avnati: Downfall, the bottom, the place from which the kisans of Jharkhand have not yet risen, as opposed to the kisans of the rest of Bihar who have begun to demand their rights and develop a leadership in the process. II

Avsarvadi: Opportunists. Sahajanand's description of those leaders of Adivasi and Kisan Sabha movements in Jharkhand who are in fact middle class opportunists. Intro.

Azadi: Freedom, independence, of which the tribals have only recently been deprived, and which they are now in a position to regain through the strength which is a fundamental part of their being. II

Babela: Furor. With reference to the fact that Bengalis and Hindi speakers in Jharkhand raise a great hue and cry to establish vernacular schools in their respective languages, while almost totally ignoring the educational needs of the Jharkhandis to be educated in their tribal languages. III

Badha: Obstructions placed in the way of Paharia cultivation, especially by declaring the forests reserved. V

Bagavaton: Uprisings, revolts as the tribal insurrections of 1820, 1831-32, 1855, 1889-90, 1895, and 1914. IV

Bagh: Orchard, referring here to the fact that zamindars literally control the rights to trees on the land of the kisans. VIII

Bagi: Rebel. Sahajanand's description of the Adivasi kisans of Mahuadand thana in Hazaribagh and their reactions to the tax imposed by the zamindars for gaining access to the jungle. It had in fact become a rebel area, the Swami reports. VI

Bahi: Registers maintained by shopkeepers to record purchase amounts and the loans covering those purchases, most often in amounts exceeding the actual price of the purchase by fifty percent. VII

Bakasht: Literally self-cultivated land of the zamindar or landlord, which is most often let out for cultivation on various tenancy arrangements. See also Zirat. VIII

Bakaya, Bakaye: Arrears as in *bakaya lagan*, rent arrears, hence, unpaid balance, namely the unpaid balance of the zamindar's rent demand. V, VIII

Bal: Force, in this context the use of force by the peasants of Europe and by example, Sahajanand would hope, so too by the Adivasi kisans in achieving their just demands and relief from the exploitations which are imposed on them in the fields and forests of Jharkhand. VI, XII

Bandar ghurki: Literally, chattering monkies. Sahajanand's reference to the idle and ineffective reactions of the cooperative societies to the attacks levelled against them by the Kisan Sabha in Gangetic Bihar. X

Bandh boondh: Literally to tie up and bind the kisan in the coercive application of force. V

Bandobast: Land settlement agreement, terms of that settlement defining the time limit of the agreement and its terms of rent. V

Bandobasti vyavastha: Land tenure, land settlement system IV

Bare bahadur: The bravery of the kisans of Jharkhand. IV

Bare bare khetihar: Big landholders. See also Chote chote khetihar. VII

Barhi, Derhi: Realization of grain loans or money debt at double the principal amount or one and one half times the money advanced. VII

Barhi jatiyon: The "progressive" castes, those non-tribal castes of the region who benefit most from the educational, material, and administrative resources which they dominate. The term pragatisheel is also used in this context. III

Bari berahmi se marte katate: The beatings and brutal assaults administered by the Paharias of the Damin area in Santal Parganas to anyone who intruded into their space. V

Bari laraiyan: Major confrontations and struggles which the peasants of Gangetic Bihar waged through the Bihar Provincial Kisan Sabha to win the rights which have not yet been achieved in Jharkhand. VIII

Batai: A share of the crop defined as such for purposes of making a rent payment in kind. Hence also *bataidar*, or sharecropper. II, VII

Bechaini aur uttejna: Restlessness, turmoil, and uprising as a historically significant feature in the lives of the Adivasi kisans of Jharkhand. IV, V

Bedakhal: Dispossession, to which the kisan is victim when he is unsuccessful in countering the zamindar's rent suits and other efforts to evict him. V

Begane: Others, outsiders. That is, in Jharkhand the tribals are effectively viewed as outsiders precisely by those persons who are in fact real outsiders. Sahajanand compares this situation with the republics of Soviet Central Asia which, he explains, are governed by the people themselves and in their local languages. III

Begar: Unpaid, forced labour. V, VII

Bekar kharch: Wastage, Sahajanand's candid and accurate description of the loss of physical and mental capital incurred by forcing Adivasis to learn in new and alien languages, which effectively imposes on them double demands and double standards. III

Bhagwan ko thagnewale: Those pilgrims to places like Deoghar who are prepared to cheat the Adivasis and by exploiting them to serve their personal religious ends, thereby in fact cheating the gods. I

Bhandar: Shops, stores, or storehouses of the zamindars, maintained at various locations throughout their extended landholdings and utilized as one of the many instruments of selling, moneylending, and control in this or any other agrarian environment. VII

Bhaoli: Rent payment in kind and involving the determination of that rent by a share [*batai*] of the crop. See also Krishani. II

Bhari anyay: The very great injustice, perpetrated on the Adivasi kisans by virtue of the fact that they do not have rights to the trees and their products on the very lands which they themselves hold. V

Bhayankar kashton: Dreadful suffering, here in an extreme sense. See also Kasht. XII

Bhojan: Food given as part payment to some labourers attached to the malik. VII

Bhole bhale logon: As in the Adivasis are simple, innocent people. Intro. and II

Bhookhon mar ke: Hunger, starvation, to which the Paharias and other tribals are subject without normally accepted access to the jungle. V

Bhoot pret: Evil spirits and ghosts, which are driven out by the pahans. XI

Bhugutbandh ya bhogbandhak: Usufructuary mortgage. See also Ijara. V

Bhuinhar kisan, Khutkattidar kisan, and Mundari Khutkattidar kisan: Peasants holding Bhuinhari, Khutkatti, and Mundari Khutkatti tenures, particular types of fixed rent tenancies in Jharkhand. Each of these tenancies is also described as Bhuinhari Patthargari, etc., for the stone pillars or markers [*patthar*] which are used to demarcate these different kinds of holdings. V

Biradari: Brotherhood, within which particular rights of mortgage are permitted. V

Bol nahin sakte: Unable to speak, speechless. See also Mook. Sahajanand refers again and again to the fact that the Adivasis have not had the advantage of education and the consequent ability to represent and mobilize their interests politically. They are unable to raise their voices against the domination of outsiders, a domination which most often happens in a language they do not understand, whether Hindi, Bengali, Kaithi, or English. "Who cares for them," Sahajanand asks rhetorically. II

Boli aur bhasha: The local languages of the Jharkhand region, among others Santali, Mundari, Oraon, and Ho, as apart from the Hindi, Bengali, Magahi, Bhojpuri, and English of the outsiders and the Kaithi in which the record of land rights is written. II

Bolna aur toofan machana: To raise one's voice, to raise a storm against the use of non-tribal languages in official discourse. II

Buraiyan: The evils which an absence of education among the tribals permits in Jharkhand. IX

Chakravridhi ya sood dar sood: Compound interest, whose variations, complexities, and elaborations are almost beyond imagination, but always to the disadvantage of the Adivasi kisan. VII

Chalbajiyon: The fraud with which the kisan must contend in responding to pressures of the zamindar and the official regulations when he is taken to court. V

Chappar pitna: To intimidate, specifically here by the beating of the thatched roof of the kisan's hutment by the moneylender or more often his agent, in demanding loan and heavy interest payments. VII

Chaukidar: In this context the subordinate official assisting the Ghatwar in the execution of his duties. V

Chaupat: Failed, as in explaining why the cooperative societies have inevitably failed. X

Chawal: Husked, uncooked rice. Unhusked it is dhan or paddy, boiled plain it is bhat.

Chidra: A hole made in the soil by the Paharias for planting various grain crops. See also Soorakh. V

Chote chote khetihar: Petty landholder, as in the case of some outside moneylenders, specifically Marwaris and Agarwals in this context, and as opposed to Kanyakubjas and Bhumihars referred to as *bare bare khetihar* , i.e., big landholders.

Daba: To crush. When the tribals recognize their strength and mobilize it, no one will be able to crush them. II

Dakhal karne ke bad: On assuming control of the villages which would subsequently form the core site of the Jamshedpur steel facility, the allegation is that the Tatas systematically increased the rent. XII

Dal: Group, or party.

Dalal: Zamindar's agent, broker, tout. V

Damin, Damin-i-Koh: Literally at the foot of or in the lap of the mountains, that area of Santal Parganas home to the Paharias. II

Danabandi: A system of produce rent wherein the assessment is based on an estimate of the standing crop, rather than an exact division of the cut crop. VIII

Dand: Punishment, in effect a consequence of the zamindars not providing necessary irrigation facilities on lands for which they realize rent. XIII

Danke ki chot: Literally to beat the drum, here used to define the challenge which must be raised against the zamindars who control not only the land, but the trees on the land of the peasants. VI

Darkhast: Petition or application, in this case to the Deputy Commissioner of Palamau for revising the rent assessment, a petition which was denied. V

Darwa dhamka: To create fear, to intimidate, as in the threats made by the moneylender in demanding repayment of the loan he has earlier extended to the Adivasi kisan. VII

Dehi kisan: Settled kisan, literally meaning a peasant resident in a particular village, especially here with reference to Korkar land. V, VIII

Desh sevak: Servants of the nation, patriots. A term Sahajanand uses sarcastcally here in criticizing those, sometimes in the Indian National Congress who would not only avoid protecting peasant rights but urge that they be limited. VI

Dhaboo zaminon: Hills, terraces, sloping fields. V

Dhamka: Threats against the villagers. XII

Dhamkane: To intimidate, to threaten in an effort to force the kisan to come to terms demanded by the zamindar, in this case especially on *bahubala* land, specifically brought under cultivation by the physical efforts of the kisan. V

Dhandhli: Fraud, corruption, manipulation, practised by the cooperative societies. X

Dhankhar, Dhankhet, Dhani and Don: Different jungle holdings prepared for the cultivation of paddy. V

Dharna: One of the devices of the petty moneylender, sitting at the doorstep of the kisan, demanding repayment of the loan amount while also taking meals at the household of the Adivasi kisan, thereby imposing a double burden on that kisan and his family.

Dhokhebaji: Fraud, cheating, as in the fraud of consciously undervaluing or ignoring a people's culture on the one hand and forcing another language and culture on them as somehow richer or superior. Also the fraud and deception practised by many legal advisers against the Adivasi kisans and which must be stopped. III, XIII

Dhurikari: Interest realized after Phagun Chait [February/March/April] at the time most advantageous to the moneylender. VII

Diku, dikku, dikkuon: In this tract referring to outsiders, non-Adivasis in an exploiting, pejorative sense, as apart from *sadans*, non-Adivasis who are integrated as full participants in the life of Jharkhand. III

Dil ke aise kale: A sarcastic reference to the black deeds and black hearts of the non-violent, wealthy Jains, who exploit the local Adivasi residents of the Parasnath Hills of Hazaribagh in creating there a sacred site of Jainism. VI

Dohan: Exploitation of the kisans of Jharkhand by outsiders. IV

Don: Upland which is converted to paddy cultivation, hence terraced paddy land. See also Unchi. V

Doosre: Others, outsiders, which is how the people of Jharkhand are viewed by the government and those non-tribals who are in fact real outsiders. See also Begane. III

Doosri hi Ganga bahti hai: Literally, here a different Ganga flows, meaning that in Jharkhand different rules apply, whatever the regulations or their attempted implementation by the Deputy Commissioner. It is ultimately the zamindar who makes the rules and defines their implementation. V

Dukh dard: Sorrow, pain to which the tribals are victim and which they cannot express because of their separation from the language and law which controls them, although on occasion of course, they explode in dramatic and collective upheaval. II

Dukh gatha: The sorrowful, painful stories of exploitation of the Adivasi kisans by the shopkeepers and moneylenders of Jharkhand. VII

Dukhiya: Depressed, harassed, pained, by the exploitations of the system, and in this case especially by the forest staff of the Jharkhand. Without experiencing this exploitation or entering the hearts of the Adivasi kisans one cannot fully understand their pain and sorrow. It is this kind of understanding Sahajanand seeks in this tract. VI

Durdasha: Adversity, misery, plight, sad condition of the people of Jharkhand. I

Dushpravesh aur agam: A self-defined, inaccessible, geographical space as in the jungle homeland of the Adivasi kisans. I

Gair aabad zamin: Uncultivated land. V

Gair Kaimi Kisan: Non-occupancy raiyat. V

Gair sarkari: Non-government, as in non-government zamindars. IV

Gala daba ke: Literally, strangulation, in explaining that prohibition cannot be imposed by force but only by moral persuasion. See also Talwar. IX

Gandhi bhakti: Devotion to Gandhi by followers of the Mahatma, a comment Sahajanand makes sarcastically in Chapter III, referring to those who showed their devotion by turning the spinning wheel rather than concerning themselves with the educational needs of the common people of Champaran, the North Bihar district of Gandhi's first public activism.

Ganthjora: Joint, adjacent, as those areas of U.P., Madhya Pradesh, and Orissa which resemble in geographic and cultural terms the tribal regions of Jharkhand I

Garbari: Disturbances of the kind which happened throughout the history of tribal agitation in Jharkhand. IV

Gazab: Outrageous, exhorbitant as in the case of *bhaoli* rent or rent in kind, which sometimes exceeds the entire land produce of the tenant. V

Ghat, Ghati: Passes and valleys in the mountain terrain of Jharkhand and which are under the control of Ghatwals. V

Ghatwal, Ghatwar: The holders of a specific type of service tenure zamindari which Sahajanand defines at great length in Chapter V. Literally, protector of the passes. IV, V

Ghoos: Bribe, a common demand made by the amla against the Adivasi kisan in order to soften the pressures of intimidation posed by the zamindar. V

Gondli, Sama, Marua, Kurthi, and Makai: Coarse grains generally grown on Utkar land, and especially common in Palamau District. V

Goonge: Simple, uneducated, transparently honest and accepting, most often describing the Adivasi kisans. See also Mook . II

Gufa, andheri gufa Cave, an unknown, unfamiliar place, as in Sahajanand's description of Jharkhand, a "no man's land." Intro.

Gujashtedar kisan: Fixed rate tenants, also *istamrari* kisans.

Gulam: Slave. Sahajanand also uses the English term serf in this connection. IV, VII

Gwala, kurmi: Among those non-Adivasi castes which have historically come to Jharkhand as an integrated population of the agrarian economy of the region. See also Sadan, Diku.

Hak: Rights of the peasants of Jharkhand *vis-a-vis* the zamindars, rights which Sahajanand had hoped the Christian missions would assist the kisans in achieving. VI

Hakim: Official, government officer. I

Hakon ke liye larna: To fight for their rights. Sahajanand had thought that the Christian priests, coming from European lands where peasants had revolted and brought down kings, might represent peasant interests in the same manner in Jharkhand. VI

Hakon ke raksha: The people must learn to defend their rights in dealing with Mr. Homi, the early representative of the Tatas in Singhbhum. XII

Hal bailon: Plough and oxen, a form of cultivation not utilized by the Paharias, although it is of course, used by other Adivasi cultivators. V

Hanriya: Local alcohol made from boiled rice, an inseparable part of the lives of the Adivasi kisans of Jharkhand by Sahajanand's definition. See also Mahua. IX

Hathiyarband : Armed, as in armed police were often called in to prevent the Adivasi kisans from cutting wood in the jungle. VI

Ijara: Mortgage, lease, as in those sections of the Chotanagpur Tenancy Act introduced to prevent mortgaging and other kinds of land alienation. Hence also Ijaradar, holder of a lease. II, V

Isai dharma: Christianity, which in Chotanagpur had made significant contributions in the area of education, but had also maintained a degree of separateness from the non-Christian Adivasi population as it struggled to define and achieve its rights. This and the role of the priests in confessions was less than acceptable to Sahajanand, who was also critical of the lamb-like actions of the followers of Jesus Christ, Isu Maseeh, in not condemning zamindar exploitation. VI

Isai kisan: A Christian Adivasi kisan. VI

Istamrari: Fixed rate tenancy. V

Isu Maseeh: Jesus Christ. VI

Jaban: Referring to the fact that even in Khas Mahal government estates, there too the kisans have no voice. IV

Jabani: Oral, verbal agreement or *patta* in defining the relationships between the tenant and the zamindar, which almost by definition is to the advantage of the zamindar. VIII

Jabti kurkee: Seizure and attachment, as of standing crops and movable property of the kisans in settlement of unpaid debts, rent arrears, etc. VIII

Jagir: That grant, most often revenue-free, made in a service tenure zamindari appointment. Hence *jagirdar*, a holder of a jagir. See also Ghatwal. V

Jagriti: Awakening, consciousness, as in the fact that the remoteness of the region has not permitted the kind of political awakening and mobilization in Jharkhand which has taken place in other parts of Bihar. Sahajanand assumes some responsibility here, first for not having been sufficiently aware of the painfully exploitive conditions of Jharkhand and then for not having acted accordingly. At the same time, there is an awareness among the Advisai kisans to their conditions of exploitation, which in turn accounts for their history of insurgent activism. See also Bagavaten. I, II

Jal fareb, also dhokadhari: Forgery, fraud, and deception utilized by the zamindar to realize a rent beyond that which has been agreed. See also Dhokebaji. VIII

Jalil: The humiliations forced on the villagers, either to drive them out of the village or to oblige them to meet the demands of the Tatas. XII

Jawabdeh: Responsible, as in responsible kisans, who despite their efforts to meet the regulations, are nevertheless exploited, moving Sahajanand to ask rhetorically at the end of Chapter V, who among the exploiters cares for the rulings of the Deputy Commissioner, or for the many sections and subsections of the Tenancy Act. It is the writ of the zamindar which effectively functions as law in Jharkhand. V

Jeevdaya: Kindness to living beings, a central belief of the Jains, used here by Sahajanand as a sarcastic description of their exploitation of the Adivasis in creating a religious site in Jharkhand at the Parasnath Hills. I

Jeth raiyat, Mukhiya, Pradhan, Manjhi, Manki, Ijaradar, Thikedar: Various kinds of special tenancies found in the different districts of Jharkhand and more specifically the holders of these tenures. V

Jhandon: Banners, flags, which greeted Sahajanand on a visit to Mahuadand in Palamau in December 1939. VI

Jhar: Trees, scrub, underbrush, forest undergrowth, hence Jharkhand, the place of this forest and jungle environment. I

Jharkhand vasiyon: People of Jharkhand, inhabitants of the Jharkhand region. I

Jharna: A small stream to which the Adivasi kisans and their cattle must have regular access for water but which is often denied them. XIII

Jhoomchas: See Kundchas. V

Juloos: The procession of Adivasi kisans, men, women, and children which greeted Sahajanand at Mahuadand in Palamau in December 1939. VI

Kabuli sood: Afghan moneylenders, who commonly also traded in *hing*, or asafoetida. VII

Kachhari: Court or headquarters of a government office or a zamindari. Intro., VII

Kaimi, kayami, kayamee kisan: Occupancy raiyat. V

Kalank: The stigma of retaining elements of the Chotanagpur Tenancy Act which are clearly meant to benefit the zamindars, a fact Sahajanand considers to be grossly unjust. See also Anuchit. VIII

Kamat: As in *zirat ka kamat*, that is kamat of zirat, which refers to the zamindar's zirat or personal holding but which is remote from his village or main holdings. VIII

Kamiya, sevakiya, moonis, gharbhatua: Different forms of agricultural labour found in Jharkhand. Elements of bonded labour are included in these definitions which Sahajanand does not pursue at length here. He does so in his tract *Khet Mazdoor*. VII, XIII

Kamiauti, kamiya pratha: System of bonded labour in Bihar, which must be declared illegal, Sahjananand argues. VII, XIII

Kanihaus: Animal pound. See Maveshikhana, Argara. VI

Kanooni gyan: Knowledge of the law as used and employed by its local practitioners, the vakils, mukhtars, and advocates, most frequently to the disadvantage of the Adivasi kisans. V

Karbandi: Non-payment of tax. IV

Kari samalochna: The damning criticisms of the cooperative societies made by the Bihar Provincial Kisan Sabha in the Gangetic districts of Bihar. X

Karyakartaon: Workers, activists in an organizational sense, and who are controlled by the Tatas in the industrial experience Sahajanand describes briefly in this tract. XII

Karz: A loan, but in this context, the loan extended by the malik to his labourer which then becomes the basis of his long term indebtedness and bonding. VII

Karzdata: The loan giver, whether the zamindar, malik, sahukar, or bania, in a sense a moneylender although moneylending is not inevitably his primary or sole preoccupation. VII

Kasht: The suffering of the villagers of which the Tatas are the zamindars. See also Bhayankar kashton, that is the great sufferings of these people. XII

Kashtkari kanoon: Tenancy Act, here the Chotanagpur Tenancy Act. IV

Kathor aur apriya satya: The plain and unvarnished truth that Adivasis are painfully less educated and dramatically undereducated in comparison with the non-tribal population of Bihar. It is a condition Sahajanand finds grossly unacceptable. III

Khabren: News, as the official news and information conveyed by the parganait. See also Rasma adai. XI

Khad: Manure and natural fertilizer as used by the Paharias in their form of slash and burn agriculture. V

Khadya: Food, as in the case of the dried flower from the Mahua tree, the main staple of many poor Adivasi kisans. VI

Khandan-mandan: Uninvolved analysis, not concerned with representing one position or another, as in Sahajanand's independent approach to achieving a thorough and detailed understanding of conditions in Jharkhand. Intro.

Khandani: Hereditary. The offices of pradhan and parganait are hereditary. XI

Khanr: A breach in the bandh surrounding a paddy field, hence these fields are referred to as Khanrwat. V

Kharchari: Grazing tax for the right of allowing cattle into the jungle areas. See also Maveshiyan and Tangkar. VI

Khas: Special, as in the treatment and concessions which are demanded by those middle caste groups which are neither high nor low but seek special considerations. In a revenue sense, that land for the personal use of the zamindar. See also Riayaten II

Khasmahal: Government zamindari, government estate. III

Khatian: The register maintaining the record of rights of all landholding in a district. I

Khawas: Personal attendant, ploughman, field labourer, i.e., *khet mazdoor*, etc. VII

Khazana: Treasure, as in the "black gold," and other minerals and wealth of this richest place in Bihar, yet not a single Adivasi has been made a minister in the first Congress Ministry of 1937. II

Khetihar: Landholder, either large, *bare bare*, or small, *chote chote*. VII

Khetibari: Agriculture, cultivation. V

Kheti se garhi kamai: The hard-earned returns of agriculture which are then seized by the zamindars and moneylenders. IV

Khoob hai: Remarkable, astonishing, as in the lump sum payment the kisan may make to extricate himself from the responsibility of cultivating the zamindar's land in lieu of rent or lagan. See also Samantyug wali begar. VIII

Khoobi: The peculiarity of the zamindar's maintaining a separate settlement and thus collecting a separate rent on the Palas and Mahua trees on a tenant's land. V

Khoon choosne: Blood sucking, Sahajanand's graphic description of the zamindars' unremitting demands on the kisans, no matter the provisions of existing rules and regulations. See also Rakt choosna. V

Khoontee: The underbrush, scrub, stubble, and roots which were cleared by the Mundas thus creating Mundari Khutkatti holdings. V, VIII

Khortha boli: the language spoken in the border regions between Bengal and Chotanagpur. I

Khud utha nahin sakte: The inability to raise one's voice, a function of the failure of the Adivasi kisans to benefit from normal facilities of education. See also Aawaz. II

Kisan: Peasant. Used throughout this manuscript.

Kisano ne to krantiyan ki hain: Sahajanand's reference to the European uprisings and revolts achieved by the kisans of those places and which he felt were not only possible but necessary in Jharkhand and in India. VI

Kol: The Munda and Oraon are both referred to as Kol. II

Korkar, Ariyat, Bahubala, Jalsasan, Khanrwat, Utkar: Varying definitions for upland holdings in different parts of Jharkhand depending on their means of preparation and the manner of their use. V

Krishani: Both a jati or tribal group in Santal Parganas and a form of share cropping rent payment in kind. II

Kuchle: Oppressed, depressed, suppressed. Sahajanand makes the distinction in the conclusion of his second chapter that the Adivasis are a vital and active people, not so depressed and downtrodden as the Untouchables and *khet mazdoors* of Gangetic Bihar. If they are organized on the basis of their class interest they can in fact, become a powerful force. II

Kund: A hole made in the earth by the Paharias for planting a variety of grain crops. V

Kul lagan: Total rent or full rent. V

Kundchas, Kunrawchas, Jhoomchas: A particular kind of cultivation among the Paharias wherein sowing is done by placing seeds in a *kund* or hole made in the ground. In Bengal jungle tracts the terms Jhoomchas or Jhoomland also refer to slash and burn agriculture. V

Lac, lah: One of the primary products of the jungle, a resinous substance produced from the Palas [Butea Frondosa, Butea Monos Perma], Kusum [Schleichera Trijuga, Schleichera Olcosa], and Ber [Zizyphus Jujuba] trees, found especially in the districts of Manbhum, Palamau, Ranchi, and the Santal Parganas. The Palas is also referred to as the Flame of the Forest and in Hindi it is Dhak, Chalcha, and Kankrei. For references to other important trees of Jharkhand see also Mahua and Sal. I

Lagan: Rent paid by the peasant tenant to the zamindar, as distinct from *malguzari*, or revenue paid by the zamindar to the government.

Lagan ka niyam: The rules or system pertaining to rent payment. In this context explaining that rent cannot be collected by the zamindar on Korkar and Utkar land within four years of the first harvest. V

Laganbandi: Non-payment of rent. IV

Lakhiraj: A rent free landholding. VII

Lalkar: Challenge. Only with an organized challenge to their unjust exploitations will the zamindars and their contractors lose heart. VI

Langoti: The loin cloth worn by the Adivasi men of Jharkhand. VI

Larte larte: Continued conflict or litigation, here used with reference to the final loss of a case by the kisans in the High Court. VIII

Latthabaji: The use of the lathi in forcing payment of loans both by pounding the roof of the kisan's house and in beating the kisan himself. VII

Lavaris: Heirless. In Santal Parganas if someone dies without an heir, the property of that person reverts to the village as a whole. XI

Lootmar: Looting, beating. See also Lootpat. IV

Lootpat: Looting, beating, exploiting, ripping off. I

Mahajan: Moneylender. See also Sahukar, Soodkhor. I, VII

Mahasamar: World War I, 1914-1918. IV

Mahua: One of the many trees of Jharkhand, known especially for its sweet flowers which are a critical source of food and are eaten raw, cooked, and preserved dry for later use. They are also used in the production of a local alcohol. The seed of the Mahua fruit is a rich source of oil. [Bassia Latifolia, Madhuka Latifolia.] For references to other trees of Jharkhand see also Sal and Lac. V

Majhihas, Bethkheta: Early kinds of tenancies in Chotanagpur, defined as the landlord's privileged land and in the second case, land on which peasant tenants render only labour services. See also Zirat. V, VIII

Makai: Maize, corn, one of the many food grains grown in Jharkhand and which figure in many of Sahajanand's descriptions of agriculture in the region. VI, VII

Mal ya malguzari: Cess, revenue, land revenue paid to government, as distinct from lagan or rent paid by the peasant tenant to the zamindar or other superior tenure holder. IV

Maldaron: Wealthy, as those outsiders like the Jain millionaires who have come to take control of the Parasnath Hills as a Jain religious site, depriving the Adivasis of their local survival base in the forest. I

Malik: Owner, master of the Kamiyas, etc. IV, VII

Manki: A headman of a village or group of villages, especially among the Mundas and Hos. See also Mukhiya and Pradhan. V

Marmitne ka madda: The courage and determination of the tribals to fight and die for their rights. IV

Marpeet: Physical assault, violence, beating of the Adivasi kisan by the moneylender or his agent, for realization of and outstanding loan amount. V, VII

Marua, kodo: Millet. Among the many coarse food grains produced by the kisans of Jharkhand. VI, VII

Masala: Issues, namely those issues of creating a separate state of Jharkhand or removing parts of Chotanagpur and including them in Bengal. How, why, and from where did these sharp, specific issues emerge, Sahajanand asks rhetorically. II

Maseeh ke memne: Literally lambs of Christ, Sahajanand's reference to the separation of Christian tribals from other Adivasis, which he viewed as nothing less than communalism. VI

Mat, Doras, Bhith, Tal, Tand, Bari, Diara: Various soil types and agricultural settings in Bihar and Jharkhand described at length by Sahajanand in Chapter II of this tract. II, VIII

Mathat thikedar: Subordinate thikedar, that is an under tenure holder. Hence also mathat raiyat, or under raiyat. V

Maveshikhana: Cattle pound, also Kanihaus, Argara. VI

Maveshiyan: Cows, water buffalo and other cattle, discussed here in terms of their use of the forests and the Adivasi kisans having to pay a grazing tax for that right. VI

Mook: Simple, uneducated, used by Sahajanand throughout this tract to describe the simple, unassuming tribal people of Jharkhand, who at the same time are victim to their lack of education and understanding of the system. See also Goonge. Intro. and II

Mool nivasiyon, moolvasiyon: Original inhabitants. See also Asli nivasi, Adivasi, etc. I, XI

Muhabbat: Love, in this case referring to the Adivasi kisan's love of his land. See also Pusht dar pusht. VIII

Mukadma: Court cases. XI

Mukarrari thike: Land given in contract to a Munda kisan under condition that he bring it under cultivation. Also Mukarrari and Mukarraridar, a permanent tenancy right, a zamindar. V, XII

Mukhiya: Headman, chief of the village. See also Sirdar and Sardar. IV, V

Mukhtar: Local practitioner functioning as an advocate or lawyer in the lower courts. Term no longer used in recent post-Independence years.

Muni na hoy yah nishichar ghora: Literally, a horse of the night cannot become a muni, or saint by morning, describing the role of Mr. Manik Homi of Tata as a wolf in sheep's clothing. XII

Mushchand: The heavy-set enforcer, sent by the cooperative societies to collect their dues from the kisans. X

Nabalig: Minor, as in minor estates. IV

Nadi nale: River, riverlet found in the mountainous regions of Jharkhand. I, IX

Nali ya pain: Minor irrigation canals. IX

Najayaz: Unjust, improper, illegal. VI

Narkiya: Hellish, describing the life of the slave, serf, and the various forms of bonded service described in Chapter VII.

Nazrana: One of the infinite number of perquisite cesses, taxes, and other demands made on zamindars, their agents, and others is positions of authority on the Adivasi kisans. See also Salami. IV, V

Neech manovriti: Meanness, a mean, low mentality which has no respect for the culture and languages of the tribals, but presumes they can only be "civilized" by learning in and about a culture and language other than their own. III

Nihayat hi anuchit: The deep injustice of the fact that rights achieved by kisans in one part of the province do not apply in the province as a whole, in this case in Chotanagpur. VIII

Nilam: Auction, as in auctioning the land of the kisan for non-payment of rent. IV

Nirale: Different, strange, as the Adivasi are perceived by outsiders, or in the sense of the uniqueness of each of the major tribal groups, one from the other. Intro., II

Nirbhayta: Fearlessness, which the Adivasis might and must express to claim their just rights. II

Nirbheekta: Fearlessness, a concept Sahajanand hoped the Adivasi kisans would retain in their new-found Christianity, in opposition the exploitations of their lives by the zamindars and forest contractors. VI

Nire seedhe: Simple people, in describing the Adivasi kisans. IX

Nistar: Total, dramatic change, as that change which could be achieved in Jharkhand were the full power of the kisans unleashed by representing their real class interests. Intro.

Nivasiyon: Inhabitants, hence Mool nivasiyon, the original inhabitants of Jharkhand. . XII

Oobkar: The end of endurance, fed up, no longer capable of absorbing the exploitations of moneylenders. IV

Pahan, Deokali: Priests, purohits, and ojhas whose function it is to drive out evil spirits. XI

Pakhand: Hypocrisy, which draws Christian priests to the villages more in their interest and in the name of religion rather than responding to the more urgent conditions of daily life. In this they differ not at all from Hindu priests or Muslim Pirs. VI

Pakke kisan: True kisan, real kisan. See also Asli kisan. Sahajanand uses the term here to include those groups who have come into the area like Kurmis and Gwalas but who have adapted totally to the people and the environment. They have not come as exploiters but as citizens of the land. These are the Sadans, as opposed to the Dikus. II

Pap: Sin. Here the sin of not permitting the kisans to take the lac from the trees which lie on their own property but which remarkably have been let in separate settlements to the zamindars. VI

Papi: Sinful, as the practices of the many different external moneylenders who extort rupees from the Adivasi kisans in multiple guises of service. V, VII

Parha likha nahin: The inability of the Paharias to read and write, and the exploitations they and other tribals suffer as a consequence of misunderstanding or not understanding the new forest and land regulations. V

Parhne likhne, Parhe likhon: To read and write, literate, educated. It is these few educated outsiders whose role is central to the governance and control of life in Jharkhand. Intro., II

Parishram: Physical labour, physical activity, achieved in the all-night performance of music and dance noted in Sahajanand's Mahuadand experience. See also Vyayam. VI

Pasei, Pajhra: Minor water arteries, springs, from which water seeps onto the fields in the hilly tracts of Jharkhand. The fact that this water, impure as it is, is used by the Adivasi kisans for drinking, is a matter of concern to Sahajanand in describing some of the specific problems faced by the people of Jharkhand. IX

Paseri: Five seers are the equivalent of one paseri. VII

Pashu: Cattle and other animals of the kisans, who are literally prevented from feeding and drinking in the forests. IV

Patta: The registered settlement agreement defining the nature of a given tenure in the official record of rights or Khatian. V

Pichri dasha: Backward condition of the place and the people, here with specific reference to those southern, hilly tracts of Monghyr, Gaya, Bhagalpur, and Patna districts, which are relatively inaccessible and which Sahajanand has not been able to organize to the same degree in which Kisan Sabha activism was possible in other parts of the province north and south of the Ganges. In these circumstances it was even less likely that such mobilization could be carried out in the more remote and backward districts of Jharkhand and Chotanagpur, a fact which Sahajanand reflects on with much regret and concern in this tract. I, II

Pichri jatiyon: Backward castes, but in this 1941 tract Sahajanand uses the term to describe Untouchable castes. II

Pir, Guru, Padri: The Muslim Pir, Hindu Guru, and Christian Priest.

whom Sahajanand sees as sharing common practices and procedures in taking advantage of the Adivasi kisans. VI

Piriton: Oppressed, as is so dramatically the case with the Adivasis of Jharkhand. II

Pis rahi hain: Being crushed, ground down, as between the wheels of a millstone, in the various forms of tenancy specific to Jharkhand. In colloquial American usage, being caught between a rock and a hard place. VI

Prabhavshali: Effective, impressive, forcefully as in the ways the demands of the Adivasi kisans might have been made and must be made. II

Pradarshan: Demonstration, as required by the tribals to achieve their objectives, but which because of their remoteness and unfamiliarity with modern techniques of mobilization they do not fully understand.

Pradhan: Headman, especially in Santal Parganas. See also Mukhiya, Manki, Sirdar. Hence, a Pradhan zamindar is essentially a main landlord or zamindar. IV, V

Pragatisheel jatiyon: Progressive castes, most often outsiders who have benefitted from the availability of education, whereas the cause of the Adivasis in this respect has been neglected if not ignored. Not limited to particular castes as such, or groups. See also Barhi jatiyon. II

Prayashchit: Atonement, propitiation, in the sense of making concessions to the zamindars in the Chotanagpur Tenancy Act, "to keep them happy," Sahajanand suggests sarcastically. VIII

Pual: Paddy straw, for which there are many uses, but in this context for sleeping and to achieve warmth in the cold winter months.

Pusht dar pusht: From generation to generation, from an official judgement referring to the commitment of the villagers to their land and the efforts of Tata representatives to intrude into that commitment. See also Muhabbat. XII

Raiyat: Peasant, kisan, specifically a tenant most often holding tenancy rights of varying degrees under a superordinate landholder, zamindar, or tenure holder. V, VIII

Rakshit: Reserved, the reserved jungles of Jharkhand. See also Surakshit. VI

Rakt choosna: Blood suckers, as in the blood suckers and exploiters of the Adivasi kisans. See also Khoon choosna. IV, VI

Raseed: Receipt, a document which is seldom issued by the zamindar or his agent at the time of the tenant's payment of rent. V

Rasma adai: The legalisms and formality of legislation is not sufficient to the needs of the Adivasi environment in Jharkhand. Rather clear explanations and effective publicity are required to enable the kisans of Jharkhand to respond fully and effectively to the official provisions of government and the law which confront them. See also Khabren. IX

Rehan: Mortgage. See also Ijara. VIII

Riayaten: Concessions, reservations, as those castes like Kurmi, Gwala [Yadav], and Koeri who in matters of Assembly seats and other positions want special concessions, but do not wish to be included among the backward castes of Jharkhand, by which Sahajanand in 1941 means Untouchbles, those now referred to as Scheduled Castes. See also Khas. II

Rongte khare ho jate hain: Sahajanand's reference to the bitter experiences he had with cooperative societies in the non-tribal districts of North and South Bihar and he shudders to think what damage they might do in Jharkhand. X

Sabak sikhane: To teach a lesson, to the kisans, most often by calling in armed police or otherwise intimidating and harassing the Adivasi kisans by the use of force. VI

Sabha: In this context specifically used to refer to a meeting of Adivasi kisans in Palamau district. But also used in a broader context to mean an organization or association, as in the Bihar Provincial Kisan Sabha. VI

Sabhya: Civilized, literate, as in those "civilized," castes who have come from the outside to take advantage of the less-educated, less-worldly-wise, local tribal peoples. II

Sabhyata pishachi: The demon of civilization which subjected the Adivasi kisans to demeaning cultural and economic exploitation, no matter its religious source. VI

Sabse pahle: The first charge against the kisan's production is his payment of land rent, even before any costs of agricultural production itself are covered. Sahajanand considers this a crudely unjust position both in the Bihar and Chotanagpur Tenancy Acts. VIII

Sachmuch hi janata ki: Truly a government of the people, Sahajanand argues, which existed in the Soviet republics of Central Asia who instituted educational changes in the local languages, unlike what was done in Jharkhand. III

Sadan: The term used to describe the non-Adivasi outsiders who have historically come into Jharkhand not as exploiters but to become an integral part of the agrarian economy of the region. These include Gwalas, Kurmis, Koeris, and others. See also Diku, describing outsiders who have come to exploit to local population. Sadan is not a term Sahajanand uses specifically in this tract, except by inference, definition, and comparison.

Sadharan vidhanon se bahar: Outside the purview of general rules, as in the case of Santal Parganas, a non-regulation area. IV

Sage sambandhi: Kith and kin, close relatives with whom particular tenancy exchanges may be implemented. V

Sahukar: Moneylender. See also Soodkhor, Mahajan. VII

Sajhe ka khet: Literally, jointly owned fields, which Sahajanand uses as a metaphor for the Bengal Bihar border dispute and the uncertainties it generated and the consequent failure for any party to own responsibility for the development of the immediate area itself. I

Sakht andolan: A strong movement, of the kind which the middle classes of Jharkhand have initiated for a separate state. II

Sal, Sakhoo, Sakhua: One of the primary trees of the Jharkhand jungle [Shorea Robusta], a primary source of timber, firewood, and seed oil. See also Mahua and Lac for references to other important trees of Jharkhand. I

Salami, nazrana, abwab, sood, tawan: Various forms of perquisite demands by the zamindar on the tenant, some customary, many illegal, which Sahajanand defines unambiguously in his Chapter V, as loot. IV, V

Samantyug wali begari: Involuntary labour, or the cash payment demanded in its place which Sajahanand likens to a feudal levy still prevalent in Chotnagpur and in the 20th century an entirely remarkable and unacceptable phenomenon. VIII

Samayik: Contemporary issues of daily life, which Sahajanand felt were rather more central to the needs of the people than the ritual actions of religion, any religion, he mentions in the conclusion of Chapter. VI.

Sampraday, sampradaya: Religious sect, community. Intro.

Samrajyavad: Imperialism. Though Christian missionaries did good works, especially in the area of education Sahajanand argues, their ultimate purpose was to enhance the position of capitalism and hence imperialism in India. III

Samtal zamin: Level land, in a geographic environment which is comprised mostly of hills, mountains, and valleys. I

Sanatan hak: Eternal, ancient rights, which by definition must be restored to the Adivasi kisans of Jharkhand. VI

Sangathan: Organization. IV

Sanstha: Institution, organization, of Adivasis and kisans. Intro.

Santali, Mundari, Oraon, Ho: The languages of the four major Adivasi tribal groups of the Jharkhand. II

Sarkari mehekme: Government officials. Intro.

Sarvasadharan: The people in general with whose welfare Sahajanand is concerned in this tract. XII

Sashatra mukabila: Armed rebellion of the kind pursued by the peasants of France and Germany. See also Vidroh. VI

Satate, satayenge: The oppressions and harassments applied to the people of Mango village by the agents of Shri Manik Homi in the early beginnings of the Tata enterprise. XII

Seedhe: The transparently simple kisans of Jharkhand who know little of the revenue registers, the khatians and other official mechanisms of government and the restrictions they place on their life style in the jungle. VI

Seedhe aur bhole: Simple and innocent, Sahajanand's description of the Adivasi kisans of Jharkhand generally and in this context Palamau specifically. VI

Shaitaniyat: The misguided acts and exploitations against which the peasants of Europe rebelled and by which they were able to achieve some measure of relief. It is this kind of action and change Sahajanand seeks for Jharkhand. VI

Shaskon: Rulers, as in rulers, rajas, and maharajas who were a part of the structure of rulership and protection in the mountains and valleys of Jharkhand. IV

Shikmee: Under-raiyat. V

Shiksha ki kami: Lack of education, which prevents the Adivasis from achieving their goals. IV

Shoshak: Exploiter, used in this tract in many complex ways to define those persons and groups of Jharkhand and especially those outsiders who manipulate the place and the people to their personal advantage. I

Shoshan: Exploitation, as in the exploitation of the remarkable natural wealth of the Jharkhand region by outsiders. I

Shoshit: Exploited, as the tribals are systematically exploited by outsiders. II

Sinchai: Irrigation. See also Abpashi. IX

Sirdar, Sardar, and Mukhiya: Headman, chief of the village.

See also Pradhan and Manki.IV, V

Soodkhor: Moneylender. See also Mahajan, Sahukar. Intro., VII

Soojhta: To come to mind, to occur. With reference to Gandhi's followers in Champaran, it didn't occur to them to educate the less fortunate, but rather to engage in symbolic spinning. III

Soorakh: Holes made in the ground by the Paharias and used for sowing *makai* [maize], *jowar* [oats] and *arhar* [a kind of pulse]. Same as *chidra* and *kund.* V

Sote: Spring, that is a water source to which the kisans and their cattle must have access but which is often denied them. XIII

Surakshit jangal: The protected forests, to which access for the Adivasi kisans and hence to the use of its products is severely limited. See also Rakshit. VI

Susaiti: The village term for society, that is the cooperative society. X

Swavalamban: The self-reliance which the kisans must achieve in order to succeed in the face of zamindar oppression.VI

Tabah: Harassed, ruined, destroyed. IV

Tajjub: Astonished, stunned, amazed. The Adivasi kisans are stunned by the calamaity which deprives them of their rights in the jungle and its products. VI

Tali ki zamin: Limited but fertile tracts at the foot of the hills. IX

Talwar: The force of the sword is not the way to introduce prohibition. Rather it must be done by moral suasion if it is to be done. See Gala daba ke. IX

Tang: Harass, the kinds of harassments which are a constant threat and pressure in the lives of the Adivasi kisans of Jharkhand at the hands of the zamindars. V

Tangkar, Vankar, Patkar, Lahkar, Chulhakar, Kharchari: Various levies and taxes demanded of the Adivasi kisans for use of the jungle and access to its products, many of which Sahajanand describes in Chapter VI.

Tyag aur validan: Sufferings and sacrifices of the peasants of Santal Parganas which resulted in special rules being implemented in the district in the latter half of the 19th century. IV

Uchit lagan: A just and appropriate rent, which the zamindars will persistently seek to override to their advantage. VIII

Un garibon ki loot: Looting, exploiting of the poor kisans of Jharkhand. IV

Unchi, Bari, Tanr: Upland, tableland, terraces which are less fertile and left fallow or sown with rabi crops and also converted to Don for paddy cultivation by constructing bandhs and embankments to retain the necessary water. Defined in some sources as village waste land. See also Don. V

Unchi kahi janewali jatiyan: Again, the castes which are called high caste as in *Aage barhi jatiyon* above. Those who came not to settle and live with the people, as many others have, but those outsiders, who like the British, came rather to exploit the place and the people. II

Unhin ki bhasha: Literally, their own language. Sahajanand makes the obvious appeal that provision should be made for teaching the Adivasis in their own languages. XIII

Vakil: Advocate, legal practitioner, lawyer. Intro., I

Vananchal: The place of the forest, the term used in the 1990s by the Bharatiya Janata Party as their designation for the proposed Jharkhand State. II

Vanchit: Deprived. The tribals are deprived of wood, leaves, flowers, water and other forest products, by the incursions of government and non-tribal outsiders. I

Vankhand, vanshand: A jungle and mountainous tract as mentioned in classical Sanskrit texts. I

Varg chetna: Class consciousness. If the tribals possessed a degree of awareness of themselves, a class consciousness, they could have made their demands more forcefully, Sahajanand maintains. II

Varghit: Potential class interest of the Adivasi kisans. II

Varg svarthon: Class interest, as in the real class interests of the kisans. Intro.

Varnanatit: Beyond description, as in the manner in which the local tribal populations are exploited by wealthy outsiders. I

Vartaman samaj: Modern, present, existing society, which in fact denies the basic necessities of life to the people. Such a society or the zamindari system which accepts such injustices must be ended. VI

Vasaurhi: Homestead land, which according to the Chotanagpur Tenancy Act cannot be converted to Korkar. V

Vecharon: Helpless, poor kisans, who are driven to survive on the dried sweet Mahua flower in the absence of sugar, gur, or other foods adequate to a normal diet. VI

Vedana: Pain, sorrow, agony as experienced by the Adivasi kisans. VI

Vidroh: Revolt, rebellion, insurrection as those which occurred among the peasants of Europe in circumstances not dissimilar from those existing in Jharkhand at the time Sahajanand was writing. It is similar reactions Sahajanand seeks to right the injustices perpetrated on the Adivasi kisans of Jharkhand. See also Sashatra mukabila, Bagavaten. VI

Vishwas: The transparent faith, trust, and confidence the Adivasi kisans have in everyone with whom they deal. IX

Vyayam: Physical exercise, achieved in the rhythmic, all night dancing and singing Sahajanand observed at Mahuadand in Palamau as he had also on other occasions in Gujarat. VI

Yaar: A clever and cunning person concerned with his self interest alone and who in this context pursued that interest in the cooperative societies to the disadvantage of the kisans of Jharkhand. It is a term of derision. X

Zabardast ki lathi sar par: Literally, the force of the lathi on your head, figuratively the concept that "might is right." V

Zabardast larai: The great struggle against the injustices of the British at the time of the Rowlatt agitations. IV

Zabardasti: Forcefully extracting money from the villagers. With reference to the early days of the Tata enterprise. XII

Zahar ka pyala: Literally, the cup of poison of certificate and attachment powers retained in the Chotanagpur Tenancy Act, and of which Sahajanand concedes he was not aware. VII

Zamidar, jamidar: The colloquial usage for Zamindar, as spoken in the villages and as used most frequently by Sahajanand throughout this tract, with dozens of other local, rural usages, which I have discussed in the introduction to this glossary and to Part II of this volume.

Zamin ke bandobast: Land tenure. IV

Zamin ke sachche premi: True lovers of the land. See also Muhabbat. IV

Zamin sambandhi sharton: That section of the Chotanagpur Tenancy Act concerned with land related conditions, referred to here specifically as praedial conditions. VIII

Zamindar: A superior tenure holder with permanent rights to many categories of the land in his control. A landlord. See also Mukarraridar.

Zirat, kamat, bakasht: Zamindari tenures defining land in the personal possession or under the personal cultivation of the zamindar. Whether or the degree to which tenancy rights may accrue on these tenures varies from region to region. V

Zulumon: Injustices, tyrannies, exploitations. See also Atyachar. IV

Index

As with all other parts of Sahajanand's text, this index is designed to facilitate access both to the document itself and to the social, cultural, and political meanings its author intended. Accordingly, I have included all proper names, references to most legislation, and many other subject headings, but in the interest of space and logic I have not included many of the most common and often repeated terms. For example, Sahajanand, Jharkhand, Chotanagpur, Bihar, the names of the Bihar districts, and terms like tribal, Adivasi, peasant, kisan, landlord, zamindar, and jungle, which appear on virtually every page of this manuscript or in the Editor's Endnotes are not included here. By the same token, I have not listed all of the many terms of exploitation which appear in this text, and which comprise nearly one half the definitions given in the Editor's Glossary. So too with the many terms for struggle, insurgency, and violence, though in both cases I have provided sample listings which will be immediately recognizable. The reader familiar with Jharkhand will note that both in the text and the glossary Sahajanand does not use local terms for the historic uprisings of the region. But his rich vocabulary and the text itself leave little doubt about his understanding of that history. Explicit definitions emerging from the manuscript will, of course, be found in the Glossary, which is roughly coded and may accordingly serve as a supplement to this index. The inevitable overlap which occurs in this index as in any other, can only serve to reinforce Sahajanand's argument and the point of this book. Ed.

5